1994

REDISCOVERING
FORGOTTEN
RADICALS

EDITED BY ANGELA INGRAM & DAPHNE PATAI

REDISCOVERING FORGOTTEN RADICALS

BRITISH WOMEN WRITERS, 1889-1939

The University of North Carolina Press

Chapel Hill and London

© 1993 The University of North Carolina Press
All rights reserved
Manufactured in the United States of America

Library of Congress Cataloging-in-Publication Data
Rediscovering forgotten radicals : British women
writers, 1889–1939 / edited by Angela Ingram and
Daphne Patai.
p. cm.
Includes bibliographical references and index.
ISBN 0-8078-2087-3 (cloth: alk. paper). —
ISBN 0-8078-4414-4 (pbk. : alk. paper)
1. English literature—Women authors—History and
criticism. 2. Radicalism—Great Britain—History—
20th century. 3. English literature—20th century—
History and criticism. 4. English literature—19th
century—History and criticism. 5. Radicalism—Great
Britain—History—19th century. 6. Feminism and
literature—Great Britain—History. 7. Literature and
society—Great Britain—History. 8. Women and
literature—Great Britain—History. 9. Social problems
in literature. 10. Radicalism in literature.
I. Ingram, Angela, J. C., 1944– .
II. Patai, Daphne, 1943– .
PR478.R33R44 1993
820.9'9287'0904—dc20   92-46074
CIP

The paper in this book meets the guidelines for
permanence and durability of the Committee on
Production Guidelines for Book Longevity of the
Council on Library Resources.

97 96 95 94 93   5 4 3 2 1

CONTENTS

Contents

ANGELA INGRAM & DAPHNE PATAI

Introduction: "An Intelligent

Discontent with . . . Conditions"

Two historical events define the temporal borders of this book: London's East End dock strike in 1889 and the start of World War II in 1939. The fifty years between these events have hardly gone unstudied, whether in terms of their politics or their culture. Yet little is known of the many British women during this period to whom writing was a form of decisive political action. These are the forgotten radicals of our title: writers in the shadows, who used fiction to give voice to their desire to see sweeping changes in their society.

The idea for this book grew out of our own work on several fascinating authors the mere mention of whom typically evoked blank looks from even our feminist colleagues. How should one explain these writers' virtual disappearance from literary history? How did writers whose texts, and often whose very lives, were so passionately engaged in the major political issues of their times—the suffrage movement, feminism, antivivisection, reproductive rights, trade unionism, pacifism, socialism, antifascism—fade so completely from both the historical and the literary record? All the writers discussed in these pages brought strong political convictions to their work. All expressed those convictions forcefully, anticipating in their readers what one of the earliest of them, Isabella Ford, called "an intelligent discontent with . . . conditions," and wishing to develop this reasoned dissatisfaction into a posture of opposition. Some wrote under pseudonyms; many found their concerns scorned as trivial or irrelevant; others were judged peripheral writers by the critical standards of their time, which presupposed a disjunction between art and politics and consigned to oblivion those who ignored or challenged this division. Some enjoyed considerable popularity in their own time but not the establishment of reputations that would have carried them into ours. The thirteen essays in our volume reintroduce nearly twenty writers, show how they responded to the political questions of their day, and analyze the interrelations between their literary and political commitments. These essays are offered as correctives not only to the neglect of the particular writers to whom this book is devoted but also to the marginalization of women from British political life and literary history, even socialist literary history.

The recuperation of these unremembered figures alters our sense of the literary scene in England between 1889 and 1939. Although the essays do not principally address the vagaries of these writers' literary fates, it seems a reasonable inference that their obscurity resulted in good measure from the serious challenges they posed to the status quo in their society. Given the generally conservative criteria for inclusion in the modernist canon, it is not surprising that many disturbing authors were excluded. As we, who live in an age in which the process of reputation building has begun to come under systematic critical scrutiny, now know, the appraisal and the survival of a literary text are not matters of objective or absolute aesthetic criteria.[1] Most important in understanding the cultural mechanics that drive the making of a reputation is the recognition that a writer's inclusion in literary histories and her or his achievement of canonical status there do not result from the ascription of literary value to that writer's work but are themselves constituent factors in the very procedures by which such value is bestowed. In the case of our forgotten radicals, in their day there was apparently no critical standard capable of allowing their writing to be incorporated. Even Virginia Woolf's most strongly feminist texts disappeared from view for many years, and, though her fiction was celebrated, her feminism was not mentioned when her work was taught (as those of us who did our undergraduate work in the early 1960s clearly recall).

But new critical perspectives bring into focus themes and patterns within literary works that the dominant aesthetic of earlier times ignored and devalued. It is thus left to our criticism and analysis to establish—by the age-old strategies of publicity and argumentation—the value of neglected literary works. This is the spirit in which the essays in this volume have been composed and assembled. A kindred spirit is our recognition that many of the lessons taught by these writers have been lost not once but at least twice: first in the 1950s and again in the 1980s. We are now living through a time of trivialization and opposition similar to that which effaced our writers. And many of the social ills that, through their writing, they attempted to understand and combat still confront us today. It should not surprise us that the passions and terrors of the periods preceding and following World War I still weigh upon our lives. The promise of socialism, marred in the nineteenth century by its failure to take the concerns of women seriously, is in the late twentieth century fractured by the insistent claims of nationalism, by ethnic animosities, by the demise of communism, and by a seeming inability to resist the lures of competitive consumerism. The apparent solutions to questions of women's reproductive rights in European and North American countries can now be seen as perhaps no more than that—apparent. And in another round of what is being called the "war against women," many women and their children find themselves without even roofs over their heads, let alone the "little house" that, seventy years ago, Leonora Eyles deplored for the isolation, degradation, and spiritual impoverishment it forced on women. The daughters of the women who wrote the story of the Nazis now have to write the story of the militarization of life in general—though the object has shifted from opposition to a monolithic enemy to the pursuit of power in economically exploited regions of what some still call the Third World. In German cities, neo-Nazi skinheads attack foreigners; in French and British cities, immigrants are ghettoized and persecuted; in cities in the United States, hundreds of thousands still gather in celebration of high-tech weaponry while television depictions of sociopathic violence and aggression multiply. And so the radicals of 1889–1939, often trivialized in their own time and virtually written out of history thereafter, speak in their different ways to the "intelligent discontent" of many people in our time. Our recuperation of them not only alters our appraisal of their literary period but also makes them and, we hope, this collection part of the struggles taking place today.

Our sense of the importance and value of these writers would, we suspect, be both gladly welcomed and, in rather conflicting ways, resisted by their contemporary Virginia Woolf, who at different times in her life shared many of their concerns. In *A Room of One's Own,* Virginia Woolf deliberately rejects discussing "canonized" writers—Fanny Burney, Jane Austen, the Brontës, Miss Mitford, George Eliot, Mrs. Gaskell—in order to suggest, often not very subtly, that her readers search out unknown writers (in all genres), to revivify the isolated canon-dwellers. We cannot tell, of course, how familiar Woolf's audience was with Lady Murasaki, the Duchess of Newcastle, or Eliza Carter. Whatever the readers' knowledge of these historical figures, Virginia Woolf found it necessary (as well as fun) to invent Judith Shakespeare, Mary Carmichael, and, less specifically, "Anon." to enrich the tradition of women's writing. Obviously, she had numerous other, extremely subversive, intentions too. Focusing on writers working at the same time as

Virginia Woolf, however, we cannot avoid noting that no contributor to this volume has needed to invent anyone at all. Thus, one aim of this collection is not unlike Woolf's: she asked her audience to write more books and to find more "Anons"; we hope our readers will read more books and help introduce even more writers into our collective (literary) history.

There is considerable irony in the fact that Virginia Woolf, herself such an iconoclastic thinker and writer, should come to be seen by later critics as a veritable exemplar of modernism. If Woolf's prose in significant measure set the terms for literary modernism, those terms were of little or no consequence to many other writers during her time. Thus, the literary contexts for the subjects of these essays are as varied and rich as the concerns of the writers themselves—who, as Virginia Woolf said, wrote books "for [their] good and for the good of the world at large."[2] It is, perhaps, the second part of that sentence, hinting at didacticism as an element in fiction, that, in many ways, explains the neglect of the writers studied in this volume.

Between early 1933 and early 1935, Virginia Woolf herself struggled with the issue of didacticism in literature as she composed her "novel of fact" (then called "The Pargiters," eventually published as *The Years*). In 1933 she wrote in her diary that she was "leaving out the interchapters." Later, she noted that the book would end with "the press of daily normal life continuing." She added: "And there are to be millions of ideas but no preaching—history, politics, feminism, art, literature—in short a summing up of all I know, feel, laugh at, despise, like, admire, hate & so on."[3] Two years later, having recorded that W. B. Yeats and Aldous Huxley had agreed that their aim was to avoid the "literary," she commented about Huxley's *Point Counter Point*: "Not a good novel. all raw, uncooked, protesting . . . interest in ideas; makes people into ideas." And shortly afterward, still trying to get a recalcitrant but "essential" *Pargiters* character "into the mainstream," she acknowledged "the burden of something I wont call propaganda. I have a horror of the Aldous novel: that must be avoided. But ideas are sticky things: wont coalesce; hold up the creative, subconscious faculty: thats it I suppose [*sic*]."[4]

Virginia Woolf managed to put in writing much of what she wanted to say in the twenties and thirties by publishing not only novels but also reviews and essays, including, of course, *A Room of One's Own* and *Three Guineas*. Novels explore and enact the "creative, subconscious" qualities that accord in so many ways with high modernism and with feminist revisions of that much-prized classification. Reviews and essays facilitate Woolf's inclination to separate didacticism—"preaching"—from the "good novel," in a maneuver that allows her to keep intact the "literary" as a category distinct from the "polemical." As Bradford Mudge has persuasively shown, Virginia Woolf's "world of imagination" was always shaped by this dichotomy:

> However feminist its orientation, however much its dependence on and allegiance to the world of "sober fact," it remained structured by gradations of taste, standards of judgement which at a moment's notice could separate the "genuine" from the "inferior," the "major" from the "minor." Regardless of her political commitments, her hatred for patriarchy, and her disgust at the hegemony of the literary canon (not to mention history in general), Woolf could not renounce her belief in the liberating world of art. She could not abandon the security of "Literature" as a category objectively verifiable and ideologically unfettered. To do so would be to relinquish "art" for "propaganda" and "disinterestedness" for "unreal loyalties."[5]

And, Mudge suggests, even though recent revisionist critics have worked hard to reevaluate "minor" writers or to include them in a revised system of evaluation, so that "the 'minor' writer is shown to be as complex, subtle, engaging, or powerful as the 'major' writer but on significantly different terms," still, he contends, in a way that is certainly relevant to our project here, "such a move challenges the values of the literary without questioning the framework."[6]

Although it would certainly be wrong to accuse Woolf of what might be laid at the door of many high modernists, namely a tendency to deny the social responsibility of art, it is pertinent to note that her most obviously political novel, *The Years*, continues to be relatively neglected in favor of those more evident records of "the creative, subconscious faculty": *To the Lighthouse*, *The Waves*, *Mrs. Dalloway*, even *Between the Acts*. This is despite the work of scholars who, in 1977 and subsequently, have shown the extent to which *The Years* should be read as one of Woolf's most important novels. Ironically, this very neglect is in part a result of Woolf's own failure of nerve,[7] her inability, ultimately, to overturn a system in which some literature was judged "art" (valuable) and some was "other" (interesting but of dubious relevance to art).

Few of the writers discussed in this volume placed themselves in specific literary contexts. Nonetheless, it is useful to suggest what those contexts were. Some of these writers certainly experimented with the "New Woman" novel, and some used a rather loosely defined "romance" as a vehicle for their political concerns. But the "new" forms that developed to express apparently new forms of consciousness (or at least a different attitude to "art"), which traditionally characterize "modernism," did not much interest these radicals.

More flexible notions of "modernisms" suggested, for example, in Celeste Schenck's recent essays on poets of roughly this period—essays that urge us to take notice of "conventional" forms with radical content[8]—are perhaps more appropriate, but poetry itself remains a more convention-bound genre (as Virginia Woolf recognizes in *A Room of One's Own*) than could or would have served these writers. Like Schenck, however, we are not concerned with arguing that to be "nonexperimental" was to be "more radical." Rather, we propose to make use of a wry suggestion, made by Sylvia Townsend Warner in a 1959 lecture, about women writers: "I have sometimes wondered if women are literary at all. It is not a thing which is strenuously required of them, and perhaps, finding something not required of them, they thank God and do no more about it. They write. They dive into writing like ducks into water. One would almost think it came naturally to them—at any rate as naturally as plain sewing." Then, after giving some examples of women's writing from the fifteenth, seventeenth, and nineteenth centuries, Warner assured her audience that she had not "cheated" in choosing such examples: "I . . . went to their writings to see what I would find. I found them alike in making themselves clear."[9]

Making themselves clear is one thing the writers introduced here have in common. Although they wrote during that troubled period—troubling to later critics but so much more troubling for those who lived it—called (exclusively or expansively and possibly differently next year) "modernist," their concern was not to find new ways to express new forms of consciousness but rather to expose the resilience of *old* forms of consciousness that prevailed then and that still prevail now. Today we have a virtual litany to define those old forms of consciousness; we call them sexist, ethnocentric, racist, and elitist, and some of us consider them variations on domination and institutionalized violence in all their guises. They were all components of the literary productions of the "remembered" writers of this period. Virginia Woolf's 1924 essay "Mr. Bennett and Mrs. Brown" is identified by Suzette Henke as a "passionate call to aesthetic arms, a rhetorical plea for a modernist revolution." Concluding her essay by quoting Woolf's reason for such a call— "For . . . we are trembling on the verge of one of the great ages of English literature"—Henke says, "And so, indeed, we were."[10]

But at roughly the midpoint of the period covered by this collection, "human character" had *not* changed, as Virginia Woolf, in "Mr. Bennett and Mrs. Brown," famously claimed it had "on or about December, 1910." She asserted then: "All human relations have shifted—those between masters and servants, husbands and wives, parents and children. And when human relations change there is at the same time a change in religion, conduct, politics, and literature."[11] The writers discussed here perceived, with fairly good reason, that we might well have been "trembling on the verge" of the end of the world as it then was. And in the last decade of the twentieth century, no matter what our aesthetics or our characters seem to be, we know that we have gone a long way toward achieving that "end."

Because we recognize this, and because the "paradigm shift" (in terms of aesthetics, character, or human relations) was in so many ways superficial and allowed for the continued neglect of major social issues, the contributors to this volume do not take any agreed-upon ideology or critical stance as their point of departure. Certainly, in terms of the modernism(s) used to identify the period under discussion, many of the writers introduced here are caught between nineteenth-century realism—including that represented by definitely ended plots in whose narratives, as Rachel Blau DuPlessis so engagingly puts it, "ideology is coiled"[12]—and the literary (often political) expectations of those who valued "making it new." However, the urgency of their ideas, and their notions of how those ideas might work on the world, frequently led them to employ some of the most popular literary forms available in order to reach the widest possible audience. Jane Marcus, discussing another relatively forgotten writer, Elizabeth Robins, observed, "It was too late [for Robins] in 1924 . . . to develop the narcissism necessary to write a great novel [because] she had seen writing as a way to earn her living; social ideas and moral power animate her prose but art for art's sake or even the artist's sake were notions utterly foreign to her."[13]

The writers we are concerned with here may or may not have developed the narcissism of which Marcus speaks (though, judging by the evidence, Ethel Mannin and Marie Stopes, for example, most certainly did). In many cases they earned a living by writing—or attempted to do so—even as they insisted on their political and moral views, often exploring in literary genres that cannot be contained by the most analyzed movement of their time. In a recent essay Carolyn Burke quotes Mina Loy's response to an interviewer: "Some people think that women are the cause of modernism, whatever that is."[14] We would venture to say that all the forgotten radicals here might have responded in a similar way to questions about literary movements. Their concern was to say plainly what they felt was important: that injustice and violence should be *eradicated* (however much this might strike someone like Virginia Woolf as "preaching"). In romance, in children's stories, in New Woman novels whose time in the sun was brief, from points of view they might not have defined as feminist, materialist-feminist, or even anything but politically urgent, they said their say.

We note with interest that when another writer of their time, George Orwell, adopted a "plain style," announced that all art was propaganda,[15] and addressed a variety of contemporary social issues (with the significant exclusion of feminism), he was celebrated for this stance, both then and subsequently. The point seems to be that Orwell's carefully crafted self-image as a tough-minded socialist—not to be confused with those crankish teetotaling, antivivisection, vegetarian, feminist, sandal-wearing, birth-control fanatics he so despised[16]—was a position congenial and acceptable to those around him who were able to create and bequeath literary fame and repute.

Orwell was very careful to stay away from not only feminist but "feminine" concerns. By contrast, the writers reintroduced in this volume, however varied their points of view, included in their radical visions virtually every item Orwell ridiculed and also, significantly, concerns both feminine and feminist. What to an earlier age may have seemed like weaknesses in these texts—their particularism, their location within specific social and historical moments and struggles—to us appear as their strengths. Avoiding claims of universality, these writers located their arguments and concerns with an unrelenting specificity—and this specificity, we readily realize, is likely to have provided the very grounds for their rejection by conventional reviewers and, we imagine, by critics whose tastes were rooted in a Great Tradition that saw such clear expressions of marginalized political commitments as the telltale signs of inferior art. Caught between the Scylla of art and the Charybdis of (acceptable) politics, these writers, though often enjoying a wide readership in their day, could ultimately please neither the kinds of critics who sustained Virginia Woolf's reputation as a priestess of high modernism nor those who celebrated Orwell as the bad boy of British socialism.

"Is a work closer to being great literature when it masks or somehow sublimates its rhetorical, propagandistic designs upon its readers, or when it puts them up front?" asks Patrick Brantlinger.[17] In the past, the answer to this question has been clear—above all for women writers, as we see in the contrasting publishing histories and reputations of Orwell and Woolf. But as we strive to recuperate undervalued and little-known writers, we come up with quite a different answer, one that sees this very

dichotomy as itself a political move, designed to irretrievably, and suspiciously, separate art from life. The writers studied in this book do not
participate in any such separation. Had they done so, they would surely
never have taken the trouble to lift pen to paper. For us, in other words,
to subject such writers to the niceties of either modernist definitions or
postmodernist paradoxes is to do violence to their own commitments
and to their historical moments.

In this book we quite self-consciously attempt to situate these writers
in a pre-postmodern framework. They are not "politically ambivalent,"
to use Linda Hutcheon's characterization of the postmodern as a posture that, through its double encoding, allows itself to be read as both
complicity and critique.[18] They are not ambivalent, nor unable or unwilling to take positions because no positions are left unscathed. They
are committed writers; they are *engagées*—often in a quite old-fashioned
sense. It seems obvious that, in trying to understand their political commitments, we must reject the entire deconstruction/postmodern turn
that treats referents with suspicion and sees subjects (whether as themes
or as authors) as caught in an endless process of dissolution. Let us not
rush to challenge the existence of the subjectivities that these writers
struggled to enact in their work and their lives.

Moreover, we cannot avoid expressing some suspicion at the tim-
ing of the emergence of postmodern sophisms. Is it a coincidence that
only recently, as women and other people labeled "minorities" have approached the literary banquet table, the status of *all* diners at the table
has been thrown into doubt? And is it a coincidence that just as women's
version of their social reality, and their ability to narrate it, has gained
more notice (to the point where there is a market for a book such as
ours), everyone's textual production, except perhaps that of the critics themselves, has been threatened with effacement, its social messages
self-destructing, its critique of the real world evaporating into mere
polysemous language?

The issues of literary reputation and evaluation, as noted earlier, go
beyond the concerns of the present volume, though these issues are certainly implied here. The process by which literary history is established
and literary reputation secured is clearly one of constant renegotiation
from generation to generation. But the process must start somewhere.
In this volume, we suggest that it start with acquaintance. We seek to
reintroduce these forgotten writers to a contemporary readership likely
to appreciate the depths of their concerns and share their belief that
literature was an appropriate medium for the expression of those concerns. This is not the only possible reading of their work, as we of course

recognize; but a reading such as ours represents an indispensable stage in the process of recuperation of forgotten figures. Writers need first to be known, literally, if work on them is to be generated, including the labor-intensive kind of work that traces the vicissitudes of their literary and historical fates.

That we find ourselves still tussling today with the issues raised between 1889 and 1939 suggests that more is required than a constant revision of the canon, "whatever that is." To obtain a truer picture of our literary/intellectual history, we would do well to pay attention also to writers for whom clearly expressed ideas, though perhaps "sticky things," were the radically necessary components of art for life's sake and for "the good of the world at large."

In 1889 the East End Dockers won "the first and biggest victory of their history . . . [and] victories for a great many other workers besides themselves."[19] In the same year that Labour was transformed, the women's movement saw two small but very significant developments: the Women's Protective Provident League, often rebuffed by union men, was "officially adopted," changing its name to the Women's Trade Union League, and henceforth women's concerns were increasingly taken into account in union negotiations.[20] Middle-class women moved in slightly different directions. In January 1889, two women were elected to the newly formed London County Council. At the national level, as a result of the refusal of both existing suffrage societies to work seriously to remove the "disabilities" of married women, the Women's Franchise League was formed by a small group of people who had gathered, rather fittingly, in Mrs. Pankhurst's bedroom to congratulate her on the birth of a son.[21]

Represented in these events are concerns addressed by many of the political novelists discussed in this volume: the rights of workers, the strengthening of socialism, the needs of working women in their daily lives, the claims of sexuality, the demands of middle-class women for meaningful participation in the country's political life, and the struggle of women for a voice as much as for a vote. A voice for women might have been expected within the labor movement and socialism in general; but the difficulty of making it heard is reflected as strongly in the work of the novelists discussed in the first part of this book—and in the reception of that work—as it was in the actual world. Although we are now familiar with the enormous endeavors of working-class women in the suffrage struggle, it is perhaps significant that the title by which we know Jill Liddington and Jill Norris's chronicle of the radical suffragist, northern working women's movement is *One Hand Tied behind Us: The Rise of the Women's Suffrage Movement.*[22] This does not tell us who it was that tied the hand. But we find out from the complete title, as printed on the cover of the original Virago edition: *"No cause can be won between dinner and tea, and most of us who were married had to work with one hand tied behind us": The Rise of the Women's Suffrage Movement.* Liddington and Norris's book was first published in 1978, when middle-class suffragette history had again become eminently marketable. We might say that the hands of working-class women were tied by the Liberal establishment to which, despite some very tense relations in and after 1906, the suffrage movement "of record" was intimately linked. But most notably, they were tied by those people who demanded their dinner and their tea—the husband and, secondarily, the children who defined the workplace home of working women, whether or not those women also worked for wages.

Writing, sometimes in circuitous ways, about this dilemma, socialist women, both middle-class and working-class, faced enormous obstacles. Dominated by men, the labor movement naturally focused its attention on the production site, identifying that site as the workplace where men labored for wages. Defining the struggle in terms of class, socialist leaders distrusted any analysis lacking that focus—an analysis in terms of gender, for example—as divisive and ultimately disloyal to the cause. One contributory factor in such distrust was that the women's suffrage movement, in its most visible manifestation, did indeed appear dominated by middle-class women. Another was that feminism, perceived by socialist men as a "middle-class" issue, seemed to cater to a dangerous individualism capable of weakening the class struggle and, by criticizing conventional gender relations, threatened to direct attention to the private sphere and away from the shop floors, the mines, the docks.

The first six novelists discussed here incorporated these concerns in their fiction, attempting—in the words of Isabella Ford (quoted by Chris Waters)—to promote "an intelligent discontent with . . . conditions" in women "enslaved" by Victorian notions not only of class but also of gender roles. As writers, these novelists were themselves, if not enslaved, at least seriously hampered by Victorian notions of genre. Chris Waters's essay describes the attempts of Isabella Ford and Katharine Bruce Glasier, both lifelong activists, to voice their politics by producing fiction for a rapidly growing readership of working-class and middle-class women (and men), so as to create a truly socialist-feminist literature. They accomplished this by adapting for their purposes one of the 1890s' major genres—the New Woman novel.

The difficulty here, as Chris Waters shows, was that most New Woman fiction concerned itself with middle-class women's aspirations to independence; both novelists sought not only to address those concerns but also to demonstrate that socialism was as good for women as women were good for socialism. If their first novels failed in this enterprise, each writer's second novel dramatized the power of women to transform their own lives (the New Woman model) even as they work effectively toward changing both society and socialism itself. *On the Threshold* (1895) and *Aimée Furniss, Scholar* (1896) are strong novels, able to encourage "intelligent discontent." Still, Ford and Glasier continued to be neglected as novelists for the very reasons, it would seem, that socialist men attacked them in the 1890s: the former writer was seen to be appealing to a middle-class audience, the latter to be purveying sentimental "propaganda" (a notion she defended) and catering to "debased" tastes. Attempting, perhaps, to meet such criticism, Ford and Glasier— for whom finding the time to write fiction was in itself an extraordinary accomplishment—turned in the early 1900s to more conventionally focused novels. In this effort, as Chris Waters suggests, they lost the edge of effectiveness that had distinguished the two mid-nineties novels with their "heroic attempt to carve out a new literary space in which a genuinely transformative socialist-feminist politics could be explored."

Chris Waters's essay sketches a context for the three that follow. These expand our understanding in two directions: the continuing difficulties faced by women who put their fiction at the service of socialist politics and feminism, and the relations between the content of that fiction and the political world. As is suggested by the title of one novel discussed by Ann Ardis, *Gloriana; or, The Revolution of 1900*, the 1890s were, in some ways, a time of optimism concerning the potentially revolutionary marriage of feminism and socialism. Writing in 1890, Lady Florence Dixie offered a utopian vision of a social (and socialist) transformation whose basis is a revolution in women's political and economic empowerment, which, inter alia, raises urban poverty and squalor to what we would today label a state of ecological health. Like Isabella Ford, whose socialism reinforced her feminism and her pacifism, Dixie, in *Gloriana* at least, refuses to consider these causes as unrelated and of unequal significance, and this cohesive vision produces a revolutionary utopia.

Published in the very year of Gloriana's intended revolution, Gertrude Dix's *The Image-Breakers* presents a far more skeptical view of socialist politics and its relation to women. Indeed, one of Dix's heroines has to distance herself from "women's issues" so as to be taken at all seriously and, in the end, withdraws from political activism when confronted by the sexism of socialist men. The book's other heroine espouses a very cautious gradualism. Although pessimism is perhaps too strong a word to describe Dix's turn-of-the-century view of feminist-socialist politics, the skepticism of her novel reflects developments in the actual political world during a period that Ray Strachey labeled "a phase of temporary discouragement."[23]

As suffragists, justifiably, lost faith in the Labour Party by 1900, so writers in the early decades of the new century had to contend with what Pamela Fox in her essay calls the "overall masculinization of the Left." That masculinization coincided with the increasing parliamentary power of Labour and the institutionalization of socialism, which failed for decades to seriously address the concerns of women. In such a climate, Pamela Fox shows, it was "trangressive" even to suggest, as Ethel Carnie Holdsworth did, that working-class women desired a "romance script." In *Miss Nobody* (1913) and *This Slavery* (1925), Holdsworth questions the (male) working-class/proletarian tradition's insistence on the triviality of both romance and individual subjectivity (especially female). Employing the romance to analyze both middle- and working-class gender relations, Holdsworth, like Katharine Bruce Glasier before her, hoped to appeal to working-class women's "comprehension of a kind of mutual grammar of sentimentality" (a phrase Chris Waters borrows from Carolyn Steedman). A working-class activist who realized that the quest for romance was, in a working-class context, a "quest of trouble," Holdsworth nevertheless, in maintaining that love was as central to life as bread, helped to redefine the scope of "political" narrative in working-class writing.

The criticism leveled at these writers by socialist men seems clearly to carry over into the neglect they have suffered in recent socialist literary criticism, a neglect Maroula Joannou succinctly outlines in the introduction to her discussion of Leonora Eyles. Like the other writers, Eyles tried to interweave critiques of the class structure and the "masculinist" traditions of socialism, though she approached the task from her own cross-class perspective. Concerned about birth control, the destruction wrought by industrialism, and the "spiritual impoverishment" of women confined to the "little house," Eyles presents provocatively conflicting views of "the woman question" and the status accorded the "private" sphere as these issues were being debated and lived in the postwar period.

Eyles's solution seems, ultimately, to be an escape from, rather than a dismantling of, patriarchy, and it is significant that *Margaret Protests* (1919) remained a popular book into the 1960s. A work that enlarges on the slum novel to give it specifically feminist concerns and that ends in a sort of pastoral paradise raises questions that have not yet been answered. The union of feminism and socialism remains a troubled one, and given this situation, it is not surprising, though it is deplorable, that the women whose writing analyzed the fragility of that union are, by and large, dismissed from the official record.

The sometimes insurmountable obstacles to a happy marriage between feminism and socialism in the abstract, and the frequent betrayal of women's concerns by the Labour Party (Keir Hardie always excepted), made the militant suffrage movement increasingly attractive to great numbers of women. It is this movement, Shirley Peterson argues in her essay, that provided the historical context for Gertrude Colmore's work, particularly her novel *Suffragette Sally* (1911). The novel brings together women from the working, the middle, and the upper classes in a campaign that can be seen as the political manifestation of feminism coming of age. Equally important, *Suffragette Sally*, with its complex display of the contradictions and tensions stemming from the suffrage movement's competing political ideologies and its unabashed polemical style, dares to challenge the contention that "propaganda" cannot be "art" (and vice versa). In this fashion, Colmore's novel also participates in the debate about aesthetic standards and about the relationship between life and art—a debate that had marginalized New Woman novels in the 1890s, that would fuel the engine of the "new criticism" in England and America in the middle decades of the twentieth century, and that plagues politically challenging fiction to this day. Peterson's essay demonstrates how a "materialist-feminist" approach to literature (a term she borrows from Judith Newton and Deborah Rosenfelt's book *Feminist Criticism and Social Change*) undermines the never stable distinction between propaganda and art by documenting women's intervention in processes that are cultural, ideological, historical, *and* literary—the very processes that shape identity and out of which fiction itself springs.

In a way, the suffrage campaign and Colmore's novel are pivotal in this fifty-year period in terms of both politics and fiction: at the height of suffrage militancy, many suffrage leaders took up the jingoism that drove World War I. Whereas the campaign, like Colmore's novel, had brought together women from different classes, the war divided women according to their responses to it and to the wartime establishment's priorities. Thus, attitudes toward pacifism and toward motherhood, for example, became significant factors in women's evaluation of their place in public and private life. In addition, the failure of international socialism to prevent war—comrades did march off to kill other comrades—meant, for many socialist and liberal women, a reassessment of internationalism as a basis for social and political institutions in which women and other people excluded from power could live safe, useful, and creative lives.

The war indeed brought into focus issues both broader and deeper than those previously defined as feminist and socialist. Certainly present during the 1890s and before, such issues include what we would now call "reproductive rights," complicated by demands for married women's sexual fulfillment. Lesley Hall's essay on Marie Stopes's narratives of marriage restores a dimension missing from conventional accounts of this indefatigable propagandist for birth control and female sexual satisfaction: Stopes's aspirations as a creative writer. These aspirations are best represented by her 1928 novel *Love's Creation*. Even before Stopes's marriage manual, *Married Love* (1918), became a best-seller, she was writing fiction, poetry, and drama. But *Love's Creation*, as Hall's essay demonstrates, conflicts in important respects with Stopes's nonfictional work on marriage. The case of Marie Stopes, furthermore, raises intriguing questions about genre and neglect, for though widely credited for her achievements in rendering contraception acceptable, Stopes is rarely remembered today as what she in fact was: one of the most widely read and important writers of her day and a forerunner of contemporary debates on women's reproductive choice and sexual pleasure.

World War I also made motherhood an increasingly contested issue. It was lauded not only by a militarist establishment with its collective eye on "the next war" but also by feminists such as Charlotte Haldane who, paradoxically, saw the suffrage movement as one of the enemies of motherhood. Like other postwar writers awash in eugenicist ideas and aware of the potential of science, Haldane saw more hope, but also more danger, in the application of scientific ideas to human life. Susan Squier's essay on Haldane's novel *Man's World* (1926) explores the conflicts and contradictions in Haldane's response to the discourse of modern science. Scientific advances in reproduction, after all, held the key to major social shifts in family life, gender roles, and national and international politics—but that key could as easily close doors as open them. In particular, eugenics and the possibility of prenatal sex selection threatened (as they still do) to facilitate social and political domination by disguising them in the garb of scientific neutrality. Squier's essay displaces arguments about whether *Man's World* is to be read as a utopia (a good place) or a dystopia (a bad place) and focuses instead on the novel as a work "poised between celebration and critique of the scientific control project" that begins with control of reproduction and ends with control of women.

The representation of science as seductive and also corrupt extends, in this period, to writing about nonhuman animals as well, as demonstrated by Shoshana Knapp's essay on "Victoria Cross" (pseudonym of Vivian Cory). A prolific writer, well known in her own time chiefly for her portrayal of untrammeled sexual passion, Cross carried on the antivivisectionist argument earlier taken to the streets by riotous activists. She viewed cruelty to animals as an index of attitudes toward humans and toward life itself—which should be experienced freely and passionately by *all* animals. To mistreat nonhuman animals, she argued, is to train oneself in cruelty; to do so in the name of science is particularly corrupt. Knapp's essay explores Cross's interweaving of a call for "real passion" with an attack on vivisection in a society practiced in cruelty.

Moving beyond the realm of reproduction and the treatment of animals, the potential of science for massive destruction in war, already emphasized by international peace groups in the late nineteenth century, was also a major focus for pacifist writers such as Theodora Wilson Wilson (and, later, for anti-Fascist writers as well). The war seems to have led some writers, true socialists all, to recognize that in a world in which cruelty to children and to animals was ever present, the development of an international and pacifist code of ethics was a matter of the greatest urgency. Angela Ingram's essay on the radical pacifist Theodora Wilson Wilson, a Quaker who personally embraced the fearless and active pacifism of which she so prolifically wrote, explores Wilson's most passionately pacifist works. These include *The Last Weapon: A Vision*, a novel whose political relevance was so transparent that it was pulped by the censor in 1918. This and other works combine sentimental realism with religious allegory to document the opposition of government, church, and armaments manufacturers to peace work in the early years of the 1914–18 war. Theodora Wilson Wilson's pacifist message, the essay shows, was as uncompromising as it was compassionate and encompassed gender and class concerns in writing that crossed generational no less than national boundaries.

Even already established writers could be compromised by their political activism. Ethel Mannin, immensely popular in the 1920s for her romantic novels, joined the Independent Labour Party in 1933 and became known as a political speaker and journalist. As Andy Croft demonstrates, Mannin's new political commitments—to socialism, internationalism, and pacifism—brought her into open conflict with the ideological basis of much romantic writing of the type for which she herself was so well known. Although she came to view such writing as part of the political exploitation of women, Mannin, rather than abandon the genre and her huge readership, set out on a unique project: to adapt romantic fiction as an effective vehicle for her political concerns. This led her first to interrogate the genre and then to subvert it altogether. Croft explores several of Mannin's novels of this period in which she urged on her readers nothing less than the reeducation of desire.

By the thirties, of course, socialism—especially when it had "National" in front of it—was rather different from what it had been in the hopeful days of the 1890s. The issues addressed by earlier writers retained their importance: the trivialization of women's concerns within the socialist movement; the ugly turn (or return) to glorifying women only insofar as they were mothers—"womanly women" with a vengeance—which we note uncomfortably in Stopes and Haldane, for example; a disregard for or actual cruelty toward "Others" such as children and animals, together with a manipulation of scientific knowledge and experimentation against which some writers had warned. All these highly charged political concerns, reflecting deep moral commitments, are among those that come together in the novels of Katharine Burdekin ("Murray Constantine"), who in the 1930s wrote the danger signals of patriarchy's blind adherence to the compartmentalization of gender, ethnicity, and nationality—a compartmentalization that encouraged the totalizing impulses called, in shorthand, fascism. Daphne Patai's essay focuses on the ways in which Burdekin experimented with diverse narrative stances that would allow her to illuminate the political reality of the 1930s, particularly the cult of masculinity expressed in the rise of fascism. In a number of utopian and dystopian novels that disregarded conventional notions of how novels should function, Burdekin highlighted the centrality of gender as a political category that effaces the distinction between public and private. By practicing a kind of "anthropology at home," Burdekin was able to perceive everyday inequalities and to develop, through her fiction, a political critique of our cultural adherence to the discourse and practice of domination.

Yet the officially recognized British chroniclers of life in Fascist Europe (or its analogue) have been men. The politics of reputation is such that it is George Orwell's vision, not Burdekin's, that is conventionally credited. The thirties writers are "the Auden generation," and we know not only the writers themselves but also their schoolboy friends. By contrast, we hardly know the work—let alone the friendships and personal histories—of such anti-Fascist women writers as Katharine

Burdekin, Phyllis Bottome, Sally Carson, and Sarah Campion. Unlike earlier writers, these women did not have much trouble finding a voice— though they evidently did have trouble making that voice heard loudly enough to ensure them of a place in literary history. The explicitly political nature of their writing was perhaps sufficient to render them (like those labeled pacifist "propagandists") forgettable—which is to say, excluded by a literary establishment that considered atrocities committed against Jews, Communists, homosexuals, and women in general as appropriate subjects for male writers. Like Hedda Gabler, women who write politically committed works are not supposed to "*do* such things." If they do, they had better be in a position such as that enjoyed by Virginia Woolf, who, on finishing *Three Guineas* (1938), wrote in her diary: "Have committed myself. am [*sic*] afraid of nothing. Can do anything I like." And, of course, owning the Hogarth Press, she could.

Virginia Woolf locates the germ of fascism in the patriarchal family. She is far from being the only—or the first—writer of the time to have articulated this connection. Katharine Burdekin preceded her. So did some other now little-known writers. As Barbara Brothers demonstrates in her essay on British women writing the story of the Nazis, Phyllis Bottome, Sarah Campion, and Sally Carson (among others) displayed, in their fiction, a detailed understanding of Germany in the 1930s, including the appeal of Hitler to "unliberated" women and to both idealistic and opportunistic young men. Chronicling daily family life, with its divided and divisive loyalties, their analyses persistently give a perspective that, ironically, we call gendered because it includes women, children, and the family. These novelists see public events through the private lives of individuals living in Germany and England. Their depictions of both Christian and Jewish experience are compelling and often troubling, and Carson at least lays some emphasis on the propaganda that kept Germans knowing less than people outside the country. In the third book of her trilogy, Carson explores the responsibility of those outside, especially the English. Barbara Brothers argues that reactions to these writers in the 1930s were consonant with the British anti-Semitism that existed alongside newspaper reports detailing attacks on Jews, women, Communists, and other "enemies" of the state. The silence of literary history about these writers, the essay suggests, reflects the disturbing tendency of such history to claim aesthetic-critical disinterestedness and to insist, by omission, that women and politics, like art and politics, don't mix. Indeed, the fact that these novelists examined political conflict through a domestic lens caused their wholly undeserved relegation to infrequent footnotes in the histories of the "Auden generation."

The last essay in this volume focuses on "Irene Clyde," whose identity has until now been obscured behind the pseudonym. In the 1909 novel *Beatrice the Sixteenth* and in subsequent writing, as Daphne Patai and Angela Ingram demonstrate, Irene Clyde began to dissect the ideology of gender, exposing its will to violence, its mindless restrictiveness, and its denial of complete humanity to anyone—including those men who benefit from this ideology and those women who collude in it. These connections were further elaborated in Irene Clyde's 1934 book of essays, *Eve's Sour Apples*. The search for the identity of this intriguing figure led to the obscure feminist journal *Urania*. Published between 1916 and 1940, with Irene Clyde as its principal contributor, this journal explicitly aimed at nothing less than the elimination of gender duality. As Patai and Ingram argue, early in this century Irene Clyde, a precursor of what today is called "radical feminism," understood that not only gender but sexuality itself is a political issue.

In their different ways, over an extraordinary period of "fifty years of Europe," the writers discussed here acted and wrote against restrictiveness, against denial, against violence. The recovery of their work alters and enriches our sense of women's participation in the cultural and political life of the time between the great Labourite rebirth of 1889 and the onset of World War II in 1939.

Notes

1. To fully trace the vagaries of these writers' reputations is beyond the scope of the present volume. That would require, first of all, the same type of study for their period as was done for the 1980s in *Reviewing Reviews: A Woman's Place on the Book Page*, written and edited by Women in Publishing (Margaret Cooter et al.) (London: Journeyman Press, 1987). A very rich source of information on the relative treatment that British newspapers and magazines gave to women's books as opposed to men's books, this study monitored twenty-eight British publications for the year 1985, looking at such issues as how much space was devoted to women's books compared to men's, where reviews of women's books were placed in the journal and on the page, the space allotted to fiction as opposed to nonfiction work by men and women, the kinds of books reviewed by women reviewers, the number of women reviewers, and whether reviews influenced book buyers and librarians and helped sell books. The authors also attempted to analyze what went on behind the scenes. Using statistical analysis, they concluded that the twenty-eight diverse publications clearly revealed overall patterns of sex bias (38). The authors further observed that this bias operated in favor of women only in those magazines specifically designated as "women's magazines." The remaining publications, biased toward men, are considered of

"general interest." The study's most surprising results relate to national newspapers, which "reviewed fewer women's books than the percentage published, gave them less prominence and shorter reviews," and yet had readerships that averaged 55 percent male and 45 percent female. The bias, the study showed, was most prevalent in the most influential publications. "Despite their blatant discrimination against women, most of the editorial staff we talked to were supremely complacent, shrugging off our questions and claiming that there was no bias in their choice of books for review or of the reviewer" (89). By contrast, editorial staff of specialist publications appeared to be aware of imbalance on their book page and tried to justify it in terms of a smaller number of female academics and specialists. The study also noted that most publications seemed uncomfortable with women's books; books on feminism, for instance, tended to be labeled "women's interest" rather than "politics," whereas male-oriented political books were judged to be of "general interest" (89–90). Another finding of the study was that male reviewers made remarks about women's appearance and sexual attractiveness, which never occurred in a review of a man's book (90). Women's writing, furthermore, was ghettoized, relegated to composite reviews at the bottom of the page under the heading "Women Writers" or, worse, moved to the women's page. Since women's magazines are more likely to review books by women, publishers target review copies there and less to general publications; the result, once again, is that "books by women authors are categorized as 'women's interest'. This definition is arbitrary—it is certainly not that of the author or of the reader" (90). A further problem is that women's magazines, even if they cover women's books well, are not regarded seriously by either the book trade or the literary world. (Our thanks to Professor Charlotte Templin for bringing this book to our attention.)

A similar study needs to be undertaken for earlier periods in order for us to begin to appraise how and why certain writers were celebrated and passed on to the next generation of readers while others were not. Such a study would also need to consider the work of Joanna Russ, in *How to Suppress Women's Writing* (Austin: University of Texas Press, 1983), which provides interesting hints (and details) of the ways in which certain books are dismissed or undermined, at times based on nothing more than suppositions about gender. A number of other important studies of the process by which books become "successful" have appeared in the past ten years. See, for example, Richard Ohmann, "The Shaping of a Canon: U.S. Fiction, 1960–1975," *Critical Inquiry* 10 (September 1983): 199–223. In this essay, Ohmann identified a small number of publications in which a book needed to be reviewed if it was to become a commercial and intellectual success. He also explored the relationship between the books selected for review and the publishers who advertised in these publications. This troubling relationship was also noted by George Orwell in several essays on book reviewing. See his "In Defence of the Novel" (1936), in *The Collected Essays, Journalism, and Letters of George Orwell*, edited by Sonia Orwell and Ian Angus, 4 vols. (New York: Harcourt Brace Jovanovich, 1968), 1:249–55, and the somewhat recycled version of this essay published in 1946 as "Confessions of a Book Reviewer," also in *Collected Essays* 4:181–84. In a 1938 letter to Jack Common, Orwell speaks more bluntly on the subject: "The number & favourableness of the reviews you get is directly dependent on the amount your publisher spends on advertising. I think if I was a publisher I wouldn't even do it in such a roundabout way as that, but simply pay the leading hack-reviewers a monthly retaining fee to keep my books to the fore" (ibid. 1:330).

On the subject of canon formation, see also Paul Lauter, "Race and Gender in the Shaping of the American Literary Canon: A Case Study from the Twenties," *Feminist Studies* 9 (Fall 1983): 435–63. For a compelling critique of the notion of objective value in art, see Barbara Herrnstein Smith, *Contingencies of Value: Alternative Perspectives for Critical Theory* (Cambridge: Harvard University Press, 1988).

2. Virginia Woolf, *A Room of One's Own* (1929; reprint, New York: Harcourt Brace Jovanovich, 1957), 113.

3. *The Diary of Virginia Woolf*, vol. 4, *1931–1935*, edited by Anne Olivier Bell, assisted by Andrew McNeillie (New York: Harcourt Brace Jovanovich, 1982), 152.

4. *Diary of Virginia Woolf* 4:268. We were reminded of this development, which Woolf records in her thinking, by a note in Rachel Blau DuPlessis's *Writing beyond the Ending: Narrative Strategies of Twentieth-Century Women Writers* (Bloomington: Indiana University Press, 1985), 242 n. 28.

5. Bradford K. Mudge, "Exiled as Exiler: Sara Coleridge, Virginia Woolf, and the Politics of Literary Revision," in *Women's Writing in Exile*, edited by Mary Lynn Broe and Angela Ingram (Chapel Hill: University of North Carolina Press, 1989), 205.

6. Ibid., 216. See also his introduction to *Sara Coleridge, A Victorian Daughter: Her Life and Essays* (New Haven: Yale University Press, 1989).

7. See *Bulletin of the New York Public Library*, Virginia Woolf issue (Winter 1977). Of early drafts and revisions, Grace Radin says: "It is important to know that as the novel changed it moved away from its original frank indictment of the sexual biases of British society. In the process of compressing and organizing this long discursive work, Virginia Woolf deleted or obscured much of its political and social content. Eventually many of these ideas found their way into *Three Guineas*, which was published in 1938 as a complement to *The Years*" ("'Two Enormous Chunks': Episodes Excluded during the Final Revisions of *The Years*," *Bulletin of the New York Public Library*, 221). And see Radin, *Virginia Woolf's The Years: The Evolution of a Novel* (Knoxville: University of Tennessee Press, 1981).

8. Celeste Schenck, "Exiled by Genre: Modernism, Canonicity, and the Politics of Exclusion," in *Women's Writing in Exile*, 225–50. See also "Charlotte Mew (1870–1928)" and "Anna Wickham" in *The Gender of Modernism: A Critical Anthology*, edited by Bonnie Kime Scott (Bloomington: Indiana University Press, 1990).

9. The lecture is reprinted in "Sylvia Townsend Warner (1893–1978)" in *The Gender of Modernism* and is introduced by Jane Marcus, who has some illuminating things to say about it. A nice little historical point is that after delivering her lecture, Sylvia Townsend Warner wrote to Leonard Woolf: "It was very kind of you to preside over me yesterday. It made me feel proud and enabled me to feel confident. I wanted to say at the beginning of the lecture that all women writers owe you a debt of gratitude for what you did for one particular woman writer.

But I don't think these things should be said in public; so let me say it now. I have long wanted to" (Sylvia Townsend Warner, *Letters*, edited by William Maxwell [New York: Viking Press, 1982], 172).

10. Suzette Henke, "Virginia Woolf: The Modern Tradition," in *The Gender of Modernism*, 627.

11. Virginia Woolf, *The Captain's Death Bed and Other Essays* (New York: Harcourt Brace Jovanovich, 1950), 96–97.

12. DuPlessis, *Writing beyond the Ending*, 5.

13. Jane Marcus, "Art and Anger," *Feminist Studies* 4 (February 1978): 74.

14. Carolyn Burke, "Mina Loy (1882–1966)," in *The Gender of Modernism*, 230.

15. "Few people have the guts to say outright that art and propaganda are the same thing," Orwell wrote in 1936 (exhibiting the characteristically belligerent tone that greatly contributed to his reputation for plain speaking), in a review in which he took to task the hypocrisy of ideologically committed critics who pretend to judge a work on aesthetic grounds. See Orwell, *Collected Essays* 1:257. Over the years he modified this judgment somewhat. "All art is to some extent propaganda," he wrote in a 1942 review of T. S. Eliot (ibid. 2:239–40). And in 1943 he noted, "A writer's political and religious beliefs are not excrescences to be laughed away, but something that will leave their mark even on the smallest detail of his work" (ibid. 2:276).

16. On Orwell's ambivalence toward socialism because of his fear that it would deprive men of masculinity, see Daphne Patai, *The Orwell Mystique: A Study in Male Ideology* (Amherst: University of Massachusetts Press, 1984), especially the discussion (69–94) of *The Road to Wigan Pier*.

17. Patrick Brantlinger, *Crusoe's Footprints: Cultural Studies in Britain and America* (New York: Routledge, 1990), 155.

18. Linda Hutcheon, *The Politics of Postmodernism* (London: Routledge, 1989), 168. Hutcheon adds, "Feminisms [*sic*] will continue to resist incorporation into postmodernism, largely because of their revolutionary force as political movements working for real social change."

19. G.D.H. Cole and R. Postgate, *The Common People: 1746–1946* (1938; reprint, London: Methuen, 1964), 430.

20. Ibid., 432.

21. Sylvia Pankhurst, *The Suffragette Movement* (1931; reprint, London: Virago, 1984), 92–95.

22. Jill Liddington and Jill Norris, *One Hand Tied behind Us: The Rise of the Women's Suffrage Movement* (1978; reprint, London: Virago, 1985).

23. Ray Strachey, *"The Cause": A Short History of the Women's Movement in Great Britain* (London: G. Bell, 1928), 284.

PART ONE

The Troubled Union

of Feminism and

Socialism

CHRIS WATERS

New Women

and Socialist-Feminist Fiction:

The Novels of Isabella Ford

and Katharine Bruce Glasier

If the 1890s in Britain was the decade of the "New Woman," it was also a time when socialist organizations proliferated and when many activists believed that profound changes in society were not only desirable but possible. Individuals seized by a vision of justice and equality devoted their energies to campaigning on behalf of that vision and convincing others of its importance. On the political platform, in polemical tracts, in the pages of the socialist and feminist periodical press—and through their fiction—they worked tirelessly to convey their aspirations to as large an audience as possible. As the pioneer feminist and socialist Isabella Ford put it, "We must fill the minds of those we wish to emancipate with an intelligent discontent with the conditions enslaving them."[1] For women like Ford, committed both to socialism and to the transformation of Victorian gender roles, arousing that discontent—thereby intensifying the desire for change—was the central task of the novels they wrote. Although such women often worked with dominant literary conventions, they also attempted to transform these conventions, carving out a literary space for a new kind of socialist-feminist fiction. In so doing, they developed new literary vehicles for their politics, a politics

150,809

that sought radically to undermine deeply entrenched beliefs that held the "political" to be distinct from the "personal" and that marginalized the latter.

This essay is concerned with the novels written by two women, Isabella Ford (1855–1924) and Katharine Bruce Glasier (1867–1950), who both sought to voice their aspirations through the New Woman fiction they wrote in the 1890s. An "explicitly didactic and feminist" literary project,[2] such fiction, as Ann Ardis has suggested, engaged in a "massive reconceptualization of the relations between public and private spheres [and between] erotic and political ambitions."[3] Today the novels of Ford and Glasier are virtually forgotten, their fate sealed by men like Glasier's biographer, who wrote, "She was not destined to take a position in the literature of her country."[4] But the best of Glasier's fiction, like Ford's, does not deserve to be forgotten, for it still offers compelling insights into women's struggles to chart their own destiny and to link it with that of the socialist movement. Here were two women who worked to transform New Woman fiction and insert a socialist vision into its midst—sometimes with little success, other times to great effect, but always conscious of the need to develop an adequate means through which to convey the full complexity of their multifarious political concerns. Like other women who were committed to socialism and who attempted to convey the excitement of that commitment in their fiction, however, Ford and Glasier confronted numerous obstacles in giving literary shape to their politics. It is to these obstacles that we must first turn.

Most of all, women committed to socialist politics found themselves part of a largely male-dominated movement that often considered feminism to be a bourgeois deviation from the more important class struggle. In some parts of the country, men and women did work together, developing a "new life politics" that focused equally on issues of class and gender. Nevertheless, in a period when "class" as a category of analysis had come to dominate political thinking, women's issues seemed irrelevant to many men. John Bruce Glasier, for example, a member of the Independent Labour Party (ILP) and the second editor of the *Labour Leader*—and Katharine's husband—wrote, "The women's movement is not Socialist, but individualist in feeling."[5] His attitude was widely shared. This deprecation of women's concerns was evident in the socialist fiction written by men; hence Robert Blatchford's popular utopian novel *The Sorcery Shop* (1907) was attacked by one woman who criticized its author's inability to envisage any change in women's roles in his imagined community.[6] Women socialists thus confronted a movement that too often demonstrated a blatant disregard for the politics of gender, along with a literature that ignored feminist aspirations. Moreover, as Maroula Joannou suggests in this volume, much of the writing produced by women in the socialist movement is only beginning to be recovered, largely because it is often still viewed as marginal to "mainstream" socialist ideology.

Struggling against men who cherished their own vision of the socialist millennium, women also, like their male comrades, faced the problem of translating their political aspirations into fiction. Martha Vicinus has argued that Chartist writers faced a similar dilemma earlier in the century: having selected the popular novel as a form, they soon found themselves enmeshed in its conventions, unable to make use of those conventions for their own didactic purposes.[7] Moreover, didacticism was itself scorned by the literary establishment. As Angela Ingram and Daphne Patai suggest in their Introduction, in a period when the categories of the "literary" and the "polemical" were supposed to remain distinct, the writing of a polemical novel was an act of transgression, destined to be attacked—as were the novels of Ford and Glasier—by critics who sought to maintain the purity of "art" from the corruption of politics.

Women socialists also confronted a third dilemma, that of being accused of pandering to what were often perceived as women's "debased" literary tastes. The expansion of the commercial press led to the rapid growth of popular fiction for women readers, much of which was condemned as a "desert of triviality and frivolity."[8] In the 1860s, popular magazines targeted at women began to appear, and by the 1890s, most newspapers carried special women's columns. With their domestic hints, fashion news, and romantic stories, these columns found little favor with many socialists—nor, in fact, with an emerging generation of politically active women. As early as the 1790s, Mary Wollstonecraft had argued that sentimental fiction encouraged romantic escapism,[9] a belief held by many activists a century later. Nevertheless, some women in the late Victorian and Edwardian socialist movement realized they could appeal to other women by including fiction in the movement's periodicals. One woman in the Social Democratic Federation suggested that the organization's weekly, *Justice*, could do with "a good socialist story" once in a while to secure women readers.[10] Most socialist periodicals did publish fiction, although socialists continued to worry about whether or not they were pandering to "debased" tastes. Women socialists were thus confronted by a form of literature that was often deemed objectionable yet was widely read. To reject it altogether would mean closing themselves off from a vast reading public. But to attempt to utilize its conventions might result in being accused of writing pulp fiction for the masses.

These, then, were three of the difficulties faced by women committed both to socialist and to feminist politics, women eager to communicate their ideas through imaginative literature: being part of a movement that often failed to take their concerns seriously; finding adequate literary conventions through which to convey their political aspirations; and writing for other women in a period when many women's reading preferences were viewed with suspicion. Attempting to negotiate this treacherous terrain, Isabella Ford and Katharine Bruce Glasier chose to adopt one of the dominant literary genres of the era: New Woman fiction. But this too was not without its difficulties.

New Woman fiction flourished in the 1890s, the decade in which Ford and Glasier began their literary careers. Sarah Grand's *The Heavenly Twins* was published in 1893; "George Egerton" [Mary Chavelita Dunne] published *Keynotes* in 1893 and *Discords* in 1894; and Emma Brooke's *A Superfluous Woman*, Mona Caird's *The Daughters of Danaus*, and Grant Allen's *The Woman Who Did* all appeared in 1894.[11] Authors of New Woman fiction focused on women's thwarted desires for independence in late Victorian Britain, although some also attempted to imagine a different kind of existence for women in a transformed society. Nevertheless, New Woman fiction dealt primarily with the aspirations of middle-class women. As Gail Cunningham has suggested, "The New Woman was . . . essentially middle class. Working-class women . . . still led lives so totally remote from the cosy domesticity and shining feminine ideal against which the New Woman was reacting that this kind of revolt could do nothing for them."[12] Thus it was not uncommon for socialist men to attack New Woman writers as bourgeois and individualistic. Moreover, many women active in the movement also viewed middle-class feminism and New Woman fiction with suspicion: Ethel Snowden believed there was a vast difference between middle-class and working-class feminism, admonishing socialists to encourage the latter; and although the women's columnist in the *Labour Leader* praised Sarah Grand's discussion of the "many and mighty sex barriers" that hindered women's progress, she also claimed that Grand would never reach a working-class audience.[13]

Despite the fact that many socialists approached New Woman fiction with a degree of caution, if not outright hostility, its conventions were nevertheless deployed by Ford and Glasier in their attempts to give literary shape to their political beliefs. Most of all, it was through New Woman fiction that they could explore how middle-class women, like themselves, could escape the roles expected of them in Victorian society by finding communion with others in the socialist movement. Not only did Ford and Glasier struggle to turn the New Woman novel into a forum for their politics, but they also, in so doing, sought to demonstrate to their women readers that a commitment to socialism was a viable alternative to a life of frustration. Thus, by attempting to write themselves into the socialist movement—and by making that movement central in the fiction they wrote—they hoped both to expand the possible meanings of socialism and to open up new opportunities for those middle-class women who longed for a different kind of existence.

That these possibilities were indeed inherent in the New Woman novel can be seen in *Margaret Dunmore; or, A Socialist Home*, written by Jane Hume Clapperton in 1888. Born in 1832, Clapperton was already a well-known feminist by the time New Woman fiction made its mark. A staunch advocate of marriage reform, birth control, and women's suffrage, Clapperton was also an active socialist. *Margaret Dunmore* is her story of a wealthy young woman who suffers the "misery of idleness" and seeks redemption in the "Socialism of the new era." Realizing that many of her friends also feel trapped, she invites them to join her in establishing a "Unitary Home," run on socialist and cooperative principles. In the commune's early days, its members debate the question of whether there was "any work proper to men that women may not . . . share." [14] Despite some tensions, the residents largely succeed in putting their convictions into practice. For our purposes, the novel is interesting because it deals with a number of issues with which the next generation of women writers in the socialist movement experienced initial difficulty. Unlike the first novels of Ford and Glasier, for example, *Margaret Dunmore* breaks with those New Woman novels that did little more than evoke compassion for the suffering of their own heroines. *Margaret Dunmore* not only considers the limitations of Victorian gender roles but also conceives of alternatives to those roles, alternatives that entail a number of wide-ranging individual and social changes. As Ann Ardis has argued, the novel "symbolizes Margaret's personal success in creating a life for herself other than that assigned to her in the traditional Victorian scheme of things." [15]

Margaret Dunmore asserts that socialism could assist women in negotiating the dilemmas they faced in late Victorian Britain. It also suggests that women could play a role in educating socialists about the politics of gender, expanding the boundaries of socialist discourse in the process. The novel thus demonstrates the capacity of New Woman fiction to become a forum for the exploration of socialist and feminist ideas.

But New Woman fiction was a double-edged sword, as much concerned with depicting the plight of middle-class women as it was with elaborating solutions to that plight. The way in which Isabella Ford and Katharine Bruce Glasier, like Clapperton, struggled to offer a political resolution to their respective heroines' crises can be seen if we turn to a chronological consideration of the four novels they wrote between 1890 and 1896: Ford's *Miss Blake of Monkshalton* (1890); Glasier's *Husband and Brother* (1894); Ford's *On the Threshold* (1895); and Glasier's *Aimée Furniss, Scholar* (1896).[16]

Born in 1855, the youngest of eight children, Isabella Ford grew up in a wealthy Quaker family in Leeds. Her father, a solicitor, championed various progressive causes while her mother, also an activist, joined Josephine Butler's campaign against the Contagious Diseases Acts. Serving her political apprenticeship in her parents' household, Isabella Ford became an acknowledged advocate of working women's rights in the 1880s, organizing women textile workers in the West Riding of Yorkshire. She joined the Independent Labour Party in 1893, convinced that it was the only party to promise full equality to women. Between 1893 and 1907 she served on the ILP's National Administrative Council, tirelessly working to create an atmosphere conducive to the struggle for women's rights in the party. Ford's belief that there could be no economic freedom for women without political freedom also led her to embrace the cause of women's suffrage. Before World War I, she worked extensively for the National Union of Women's Suffrage Societies and was the vice president of the Leeds Women's Suffrage Society. Whereas labor historians have concentrated on her trade-union activity, suffrage historians have focused primarily on her work for the vote. But as her biographer has asserted, this merely "serves to compartmentalize activities which she saw 'as branches of the same great tree.'"[17] Attempting to develop a politics that linked issues of class and gender, Ford argued, "Unless the relation of the Labour movement . . . to the Women's movement be clearly recognised, the real inner meaning of Socialism itself cannot be understood, for the two movements have the same common origins and the same aims."[18]

Her first novel, *Miss Blake of Monkshalton*, was written when Ford was involved in the great Manningham Mills strike over a threatened reduction in wages in Bradford. Despite the importance that Ford attached to women's trade unionism and socialism, *Miss Blake* never touches on these issues. It is concerned instead with the plight of largely middle-class women, confined at home and unable to escape, trapped—as the novel's heroine, Anne Blake, sees it—in a "dusty uninteresting world, full of sordid people and unsatisfied desires" (2). Few other New Woman novels capture with such intensity the "stifling monotony" (110) of women's domestic confinement as does *Miss Blake*. Indeed, it offers a vitriolic indictment of the expectations that thwarted women's ambitions, in a way that anticipates Radclyffe Hall's novel *The Unlit Lamp* (1924). In Ford's novel, Jane Blake tyrannically controls the purse strings in the family home—and also the lives of her younger sister, Emma, and her niece, Anne. Although Anne seeks to rebel against what she perceives to be the outdated conventions of female propriety and to establish a career for herself in London, she does so at the cost of shattering domestic tranquility at Monkshalton, exacerbating her aunts' illnesses in the process. The price of Anne's freedom is thus the guilt of being responsible for defying the conventions that brought stability, if not happiness, to life at Monkshalton.

The reviews of *Miss Blake* were not favorable. Echoing a widely shared sentiment, one paper claimed that the novel was "too sombre to be attractive."[19] Ford did portray life at Monkshalton in somber tones, but only in order to emphasize her belief that such an existence was anything but attractive. Nevertheless, rather than encourage Ford's indictment of the gendered expectations that led to such despair, papers like the conservative *St. James' Gazette* (4 December 1890) merely berated Anne in the novel for ignoring her duty to her aunts. By dwelling on the "defects" of Anne's character, the paper attempted—as did many critics of New Woman fiction—to defend the very forms of domestic life against which New Women sought to rebel. Other critics also complained that the novel was too depressing and suggested that Ford should have added more romance and a happy ending to her story to make it more "attractive."[20] Such criticism implicitly attempted to subvert the political project of New Woman fiction in general and of Ford's novel in particular. But Ford ignored the conventions of popular romance and adamantly refused to capitulate to those who accepted Victorian gender roles as right and proper. *Miss Blake* is a powerful novel precisely because of its bleak vision, because of its intense portrayal of the psychological damage experienced by women forced to live up to the social expectations of others.

Not only does *Miss Blake* compel the reader to empathize with Anne's rebellion, but it also focuses dramatically on the injustice of a gender-role system that for Ford was as odious as the exploitation associated with late Victorian capitalism. Nevertheless, in her first literary venture, Ford worked within the conventions of New Woman fiction, failing to open them up to encompass her interests as a socialist and trade-union organizer. Unlike Clapperton's *Margaret Dunmore*, Ford's novel made no attempt to link the promise of socialism with the transformation of those roles that rendered her characters so tragic. By 1890 Ford had committed herself to a cause that she profoundly believed could change the lives of "redundant" women, such as Anne Blake, by giving them an ideal to believe in and work toward. But this cause is conspicuously absent in *Miss Blake*, as it is in Katharine Bruce Glasier's first novel, *Husband and Brother*.

Glasier, born in 1867, was twelve years younger than Ford. Like Ford, she came from a politically active and religious middle-class family. After reading classics at Newnham College, Cambridge, she secured a teaching position at the Redland School for Girls in Bristol, later drawing on this experience in her second novel. In Bristol she became involved in socialist politics and abandoned her job to lecture for the Fabian Society and to write for the *Workman's Times* and Manchester's radical *Sunday Chronicle*. As a popular speaker on the socialist circuit, she met Isabella Ford, and the two established a lifelong friendship. In 1893, the year she married John Bruce Glasier, she was elected to the National Administrative Council of the Independent Labour Party. Determined not to let her marriage interfere with her propaganda and literary work, she once wrote to her husband that their mutual efforts on behalf of the socialist cause must be seen "as the *reason* and *justification* of our marriage."[21] For the next twenty years, Glasier spoke at socialist gatherings and continued to write, becoming the editor of the women's column in the *Labour Leader* between 1906 and 1909. Unlike Ford, the Glasiers were constantly short of money and relied heavily on Katharine's income from writing. For her, writing was less a luxury than a necessity; deftly attuned to market demand, she wrote many popular stories that dealt neither with the New Woman nor with socialism. Although the publisher George Allen once declined to publish a novel she offered him, and although the Clarion Press paid her only five pounds for *Aimée Furniss*, Glasier also wrote a number of romances for the popular weekly *Family Herald*, earning twelve pounds for a novelette and thirty pounds for a serial.[22]

Glasier once claimed that her Newnham education had made her a feminist and that her experience as a Fabian lecturer had led her to repudiate her "narrow 'feminist' attitude" in favor of socialism.[23] Along with her husband, she remained suspicious of women who devoted all their energies to the suffrage movement; she believed that the campaign for the vote drew women away from the more important struggle for socialism. Nevertheless, she also recognized the plight of many middle-class women, a theme she explored in her first novel, *Husband and Brother*. The novel dissects the relationship of John Gilfillan, a successful essayist, and his wife, Levitia Veron, a French-Canadian writer. Together they enjoy a "new" marriage, each financially and professionally independent of the other. But with them lives Barbara, John's younger sister, who resents her enforced dependence. "While you . . . are working," she asks, "what do I do? Wander about the woods, read, think, till I nearly go mad" (30). When Barbara announces her desire to become a Board School teacher, her brother ridicules the idea. Nonetheless, Levitia offers Barbara her support: "As a woman myself I acknowledge her right, and will defend it" (52). Barbara moves to London, where she is visited by Levitia and told that women should stick together because men won't help them. But the two don't stick together: Barbara ends up a lonely nurse after rejecting a teaching career and being abandoned by a married doctor with whom she had an affair; Levitia returns to John, realizing that her own marriage was more problematic than she had once believed.

As in *Miss Blake*, the conclusion of *Husband and Brother* is not a happy one. Liverpool's *Labour Chronicle* suggested that the novel raised the important question of a woman's right to regulate her own life: "It tells of comradeship . . . between women. . . . It is . . . the city of the dear love of comrades, where 'the women also hold one another's hands.' "[24] Perhaps the *Chronicle*'s enthusiastic claims were exaggerated, for although the novel depicts the potential for women to help one another achieve economic freedom outside of marriage, and although it also offers a vision of a harmonious "new" marriage, it ends on a pessimistic note. Moreover, like Ford's first novel, *Husband and Brother* is entirely silent about how socialism might influence the lives of its protagonists. Neither author, at this point in her literary career, moved beyond the traditional concerns of the New Woman novel.

In the late 1880s and early 1890s, when Ford and Glasier wrote their first novels, both women were fresh converts to the cause of socialism. They were, however, already keenly aware of the problems confronting women who desired an independent existence, each having only recently—and after much soul-searching and struggle—established a role for herself that defied traditional Victorian gender expectations. The New Woman novel offered a means of exploring the difficulties faced by women who wished to follow a similar path. But it was only later in the decade, after Ford and Glasier became more fully immersed in the work of the socialist movement, that they began to conceive of ways to combine discussions of both their earlier struggles and their present convictions. It was in their second novels that they opened up the possibilities offered by New Woman fiction, exploring the ways in which various kinds of activism could help women find a "new life" and overcome the experience of frustration that was portrayed so dramatically in the authors' first literary ventures.

In 1894, Isabella Ford claimed that in attacking the New Woman, male socialists ignored the fact that such "intelligent" and "questioning" women were the kind most needed by the movement.[25] The following year, in *On the Threshold*, Ford set out to demonstrate both how socialism could benefit women and how women could transform socialism, charting a journey that Anne Blake might have made but did not. The novel recounts the story of Kitty and Lucretia, two middle-class friends bound by conventions and social expectations from which they desire to escape. They move to London, Kitty to study art and Lucretia to study music. In London their socialist convictions are deepened through their encounter with Mr. Estcourt, a socialist poet, who invites them to discuss the establishment of a socialist home. From the women's point of view, the men at the meeting are not very enlightened: one of them asserts, "Woman is naturally conservative" (36). Kitty believes that the awakening of women is central to socialism, although Estcourt prefers to place his faith in the wage earners of the nation, prompting one woman to lament that socialism "takes no more heed of women . . . than does any other creed" (31). Despite their initial hostility to male socialists, Kitty and Lucretia are introduced to London's East End slum life by their maid, an experience that proves to be a major awakening for them. "I suddenly realised," says Lucretia, "that I had stepped into a new world, where nothing in my past life could . . . guide me" (65).

Unlike *Miss Blake*, *On the Threshold* is set largely in London, vividly capturing the excitement generated by contemporary debates on social problems and the "woman question," debates that were central to Bloomsbury intellectual life in the 1890s. That excitement is conveyed by Lucretia, who relates the story of the two friends' lives in London. *On the Threshold* is Ford's only novel narrated in the first person, a device that allows Ford, through the musings of Lucretia, to detail the hopes and fears of women as they set out on an uncharted voyage. In particular, it is Lucretia, as the novel's narrator, who explores the special character and intense nature of women's friendships in late Victorian Britain. Kitty's growing attachment to Estcourt forces Lucretia to contemplate the strength and guidance she had gained from her friendship with Kitty. Although Kitty, in announcing her engagement to Estcourt, claims that marriage could be a "great and noble companionship" (124),

Ford's insight into the threat that marriage posed to women's friend-ships (Ford herself never married) is eloquently conveyed by Lucretia, who notes, "Women's lives are so cut up when they marry" (201).

One reviewer recognized that *On the Threshold* not only dealt with the individual demands of the New Woman but also sought to illumi-nate the emergence of a growing social conscience among such women: although the novel's plot unfolded "through the medium of subjective individuality," its heroines developed a "deep compassion for the sor-rows of humanity."[26] Two years before she published the novel, Ford had argued that middle-class women ought to arouse feelings of dis-content among their working-class sisters, as indeed Ford herself had done.[27] Kitty and Lucretia begin to contemplate this, discovering a meaningful identity in the process. *On the Threshold* is thus a New Woman novel, skillfully charting the obstacles faced by women in their struggle for independence, but it is also a socialist novel, a polemi-cal work aimed at informing its women readers that a commitment to socialism could assist them in their own quest for personal liberation. But if the novel claimed that socialism could help emancipate women, it also strongly argued that women might emancipate socialism from its own chauvinistic tendencies. By pondering the advantages of women's presumed spirituality, the novel suggested that women could carve out an important space in which to be active, both in the socialist movement and in society at large.[28]

It was thus in *On the Threshold* that Ford managed to integrate a dis-cussion of the would-be New Woman with a plea for socialism. But what of the complaints, made by socialist men, that a focus on the New Woman detracted from the "more important" work of organizing work-ing women? Ford, as we have seen, was committed to the women's trade-union movement while she wrote fiction about middle-class women. Many men in the socialist movement praised the former and virtually ignored the latter, resulting in the marginalization of Ford's fictional writing. Nevertheless, it is possible to see these two tasks as homolo-gous. Ford believed that women's trade unionism fostered a sense of women's collective identity; moreover, by encouraging women to work together, trade union activity was part of a broader "moral revolu-tion."[29] Likewise, in *On the Threshold* Ford argued that middle-class women could also work together, mutually charting their own destiny, to some extent by developing important forms of comradeship that tran-scended class barriers. Because she believed that the women's movement and the labor movement stemmed from "the common evil of economic dependence,"[30] she saw no discrepancy in appealing both to working-class and to middle-class women. What differed was simply the way she reached out to them, speaking to the former on the platform and the latter through her novels.

Katharine Bruce Glasier's second novel, *Aimée Furniss*, like *On the Threshold*, is a bold attempt to rewrite the New Woman novel as an explicitly socialist-feminist enterprise. Just as Glasier went to Newnham and then taught at a girls' school before being "converted" to socialism, so her protagonist, Aimée Furniss, follows a similar path in the novel. Although she secures a teaching position in a northern industrial town, Aimée remains unhappy. She befriends Edgar Howardon, a Catholic priest and a socialist who is involved in social-rescue work. By assisting him in his working-boys' club, she awakens "to a new sense of gladness in life" (86). Socialism soon gives Aimée direction, just as it had Glasier herself. "If it weren't for the hope of a realised 'oneness' in Socialism," Glasier wrote, "I don't know what I should do sometimes."[31] Glasier had also come to appreciate the importance of Walt Whitman's vision of democratic comradeship through her friendship with Edward Carpenter, a socialist and pioneer of homosexual rights, and an emphasis on comradeship thus occupies a prominent place in her second novel. After embracing the cause of socialism, Aimée meets Annie Deardon, a shopgirl who has lost her job and for whom she develops an intense fondness. Together they move to a village in the South where they read Whitman, Percy Bysshe Shelley, Giuseppe Mazzini, and William Morris and work as intimate comrades to spread the socialist gospel: "Slowly a new hunger grew up with them and a new hope" (124).

Whereas *Husband and Brother* chronicles the bitter struggle of a woman to secure her independence, *Aimée Furniss* suggests that independence can be realized by embracing a social cause. Aimée's union with Annie is thus depicted not only as an answer to her own loneliness but also as a prologue to the emergence of their mutual commitment to social activism. Moreover, their union cements the cross-class alliance that both Ford and Glasier called for, an alliance that, in *Aimée Furniss*, subverts the heterosexual imperative of much New Woman fiction and opens up a space for women to support each other's ambitions. This demonstrates the importance of Carroll Smith-Rosenberg's claim (as applicable to Glasier as it is to the Americans she discusses): "The more politically radical of the New Women used the loving world of female bonding . . . to forge a network of women reformers . . . into a singularly effective political machine."[32] In 1894 Glasier declared that she wished to see a "race of men and women who work together for the need of each, and who strive in every way that the powers of every man, woman, and child may be called forth to the utmost."[33] Two years later, *Aimée Furniss* brought the New Woman firmly into the world of socialist politics, cementing a homosocial bond between women from different classes who work together for the liberation of men and women of all classes and who, to borrow from Ann Ardis's assessment of similar characters in New Woman fiction, come to understand "the public and private worlds not as mutually exclusive territories . . . but as a singular cultural space that is theirs for the claiming."[34]

Aimée Furniss was attacked in the *Labour Leader*. Glasier responded by claiming that the novel was a work of propaganda, aimed at awakening the desire to alleviate the "sufferings of humanity."[35] New Woman novels seldom appealed to working-class readers, and Ford's novels were priced beyond their means.[36] But *Aimée Furniss* was published by a socialist press and cost a mere sixpence. Moreover, although the *Leader* disliked the novel's sentimentality, that very quality might have made it appealing to working-class women who, familiar with popular romance (and perhaps with Glasier's own nonsocialist stories), would have found little to identify with in *Husband and Brother* or *Miss Blake*. Perhaps, like her friend and co-worker Margaret McMillan, Glasier hoped to reach working-class women by tapping into what Carolyn Steedman has termed their "comprehension of a kind of mutual grammar of sentimentality."[37] Although men often viewed popular romances as odious forms of escapism, Cicely Hamilton, the journalist, novelist, and militant suffragist, viewed them not as "frivolous fantasies, but [as] accounts of female survival."[38] In her article in this volume, Pamela Fox discusses the potential for radical writers like Ethel Carnie Holdsworth to subvert the traditional romance plot. Like Carnie Holdsworth, Glasier expressed her political convictions through the conventions of popular romance, charting a relationship that transcended the barriers of heterosexuality and class, a union in which the well-being of its participants grew from their mutual commitment to radical social change. In short, *Aimée Furniss* was, as Glasier proudly claimed, a work of propaganda, one that showed its working-class readers a utopian space where it was possible to imagine a world in which women no longer experienced restrictions on their activity.

If the New Woman novel was traditionally concerned with the restricted nature of women's lives, along with women's attempts to overcome those restrictions, Glasier, in *Aimée Furniss*, and Ford, in *On The Threshold*, pushed the narrative conventions of New Woman fiction further, suggesting that in refashioning their own lives women could also substantively influence men, socialist politics, and society. And yet by

1900, New Woman fiction was in decline. Moreover, the ethical impulses central to "new life" socialism in the 1890s had also faded. Hence
Ford and Glasier attempted a different kind of fictional writing in the
new century, Ford in *Mr. Elliott* and Glasier in *Marget*.[39] A brief examination of these less focused, and ultimately less successful, novels can
help illuminate how, in the hands of Ford and Glasier in the mid-1890s,
the New Woman novel had become a forum both for a discussion of
the complex relationship between public and private spheres and for a
politics that held the transformation of each to be intimately bound up
with the transformation of the other.

Sam Elliott, in Ford's novel that bears his name, was once a foreman
in the cotton mill he now owns. An arrogant, self-made man, he alien-
ates those around him, especially his wife, Tilly, who is as isolated in
her home as was Anne Blake at Monkshalton. His behavior ultimately
leads both to Tilly's death and to his son's repudiation of the father's
success. It also prompts a woman trade unionist to declare, despite the
failure of the union's strike, "We shall win in the long run" (314). Perhaps because Ford chose to focus on industrial life, men in the labor
movement praised the book for offering a strong "indictment of our
entire industrial system."[40] In many respects *Mr. Elliott* shares more
with the "Industrial Novel" of the mid-nineteenth century than it does
with Ford's earlier work. Reviewers noted the similarities, comparing
Mr. Elliott to Charles Dickens's Gradgrind.[41] And yet, as in Dickens's
Hard Times, the only answer that Ford offers is the need for "sympathy,"
for a change of heart. Although *Mr. Elliott* affords the reader a vivid
portrait of working conditions and a superb analysis of the complexities
of social life in a small manufacturing town in Yorkshire, the novel's cast
of characters is large, and the work often loses its focus as it moves back
and forth between distinct social worlds. In short, the novel lacks the
cohesiveness that made Ford's earlier works so appealing. By concentrating more than she previously had on the complex dynamics of an
entire society, Ford lost her ability to chart the ways in which specific
individuals in that society both suffered exploitation and imaginatively
sought to transcend it.

A similar problem pervades Glasier's *Marget*, the story of Margaret
Ayrton, daughter of the gardener at Guildesmere, and of Harry Burne,
owner of the Guildesmere estate. Harry studies in Germany, becoming
a socialist, and Margaret attends Newnham on a scholarship. Whereas
her education at first distances Margaret from her working-class background, Harry's radical education prepares him to work for the working
class, and he soon becomes a Labour Party M.P. for a Welsh mining

constituency. He also marries Margaret, who begins to organize women workers. Like Aimée Furniss and Annie Deardon, Harry and Margaret develop a cross-class relationship and work to spread the socialist gospel. Yet despite its elaborate discussion of the complexities of gender roles and class relations, *Marget*, like *Mr. Elliott*, lapses into the sentimental rhetoric of social reconciliation that had characterized the Industrial Novel. As Harry notes: "The two nations . . . have drifted so far apart that they cannot even understand each other's language. The crying need of the day is for interpreters."[42] Bridging the chasm that separated the classes in Britain was a central aspect of Glasier's politics. Nevertheless, whereas the conventions of New Woman fiction had once allowed her to address that issue through her discussion of women's struggles for independence, *Marget* breaks with those conventions, losing its focus in the process. Like Ford's *Mr. Elliott*, Glasier's *Marget* lacks the powerful narrative structure that made *Husband and Brother* and *Aimée Furniss* so engaging and so successful as polemical novels.

Mr. Elliott was the last novel that Isabella Ford published, although she continued to write short stories, mostly concerned with the lives of working women, for the socialist press. But as World War I approached, Ford directed all her energies to the peace movement. Along with Glasier, she was active in the British branch of the Women's International League (WIL), an organization dedicated to a negotiated end to the war. She died in 1924. Katharine Bruce Glasier also remained politically active in the new century. She led the campaign for pithead baths for miners, edited the *Labour Leader* between 1916 and 1921, contributed regularly to *Labour's Northern Voice* between the wars, and spoke at Labour Party rallies as late as 1944. In addition, she continued to write short stories, always more interested than Ford in communicating with a large, working-class audience. Although these stories provided her readers with light entertainment, they no longer dealt with the issues of gender, class, and politics that had inspired her literary talents in the 1890s.

In 1906 one critic suggested, "The ardent novelist full of a social cause or a political ideal can by his art give them a personal and imaginative setting, and arouse in their supporters the emotions of his readers."[43] This is what Ford and Glasier tried to do in much of their fiction. But their first novels failed to address the concerns of the working-class movement to which they were both dedicated and also failed to convey their beliefs that middle-class women's commitment to socialism not only could offer a solution to many of the dilemmas these women experienced but also could transform socialist ideology itself. Nevertheless, by writing New Woman fiction, Ford and Glasier were able to explore in detail the psychology of individuals struggling for new meaning in their lives. Indeed, the conventions of New Woman fiction allowed them to focus their narratives and express their politics clearly, in a manner that was subsequently lost in *Mr. Elliott* and *Marget*.

Lucy Bland has suggested that in the 1890s, it was arguably "only in an ideal fictitious world that the woman writer could explore some of the different visions of what transformed sexual relations might mean—a utopian world in which women no longer face restrictions on their freedom of action and choice."[44] Ford and Glasier were at their literary best when they sought to introduce their socialist convictions into the midst of the New Woman novel and when they sought, through the novel, to imagine another reality in which women, freed from the expectations of others, might work with each other and with men toward the new society promised by socialism. That is why *On the Threshold* and *Aimée Furniss*, though forgotten today, are still so important. Both novels prefigure the attempts made by women of a later generation to reintroduce and redefine notions of subjectivity in leftist politics. Although the Left has often sought to define economic issues as political, relegating all else to the "lesser" sphere of the private and personal, these two novels steadfastly refuse to accept such thinking. They both represent a heroic attempt to carve out a new literary space in which a genuinely transformative socialist-feminist politics could be explored.

Notes

For helpful comments on earlier drafts of this essay, I want to thank Polly Beals, Seth Koven, Regina Kunzel, Anita Levy, Sally Mitchell, Carolyn Steedman, and the editors of this volume.

1. Isabella O. Ford, *Industrial Women and How to Help Them* (London: Humanitarian League, 1900), 2.

2. Lucy Bland, "The Married Woman, the 'New Woman,' and the Feminist: Sexual Politics of the 1890s," in *Equal or Different: Women's Politics 1800–1914*, edited by Jane Rendall (Oxford: Basil Blackwell, 1987), 143.

3. Ann L. Ardis, *New Women, New Novels: Feminism and Early Modernism* (New Brunswick: Rutgers University Press, 1990), 122.

4. Laurence Thompson, *The Enthusiasts: A Biography of John and Katharine Bruce Glasier* (London: Victor Gollancz Ltd., 1971), 68.

5. Quoted in ibid., 136. For an elaboration of these themes, see Christine Collette, "Socialism and Scandal: The Sexual Politics of the Early Labour Movement," *History Workshop Journal* 23 (Spring 1987): 102–11; Chris Waters, *British*

Socialists and the Politics of Popular Culture, 1884–1914 (Stanford: Stanford University Press; Manchester: Manchester University Press, 1990), 165–70.

6. Carra Lyle in *Woman Worker*, 25 September 1908, 431.

7. Martha Vicinus, "Chartist Fiction and the Development of a Class-Based Literature," in *The Socialist Novel in Britain: Towards the Recovery of a Tradition*, edited by H. Gustav Klaus (New York: St. Martin's Press; Brighton: Harvester Press, 1982), 12.

8. 'X,' "Woman's Progress and the Woman's Press," *Albany Review* 3 (May 1908): 198.

9. See Cora Kaplan, "Pandora's Box: Subjectivity, Class, and Sexuality in Socialist Feminist Criticism," in *Making a Difference: Feminist Literary Criticism*, edited by Gayle Greene and Coppélia Kahn (London: Methuen, 1985), 158–59.

10. *Justice*, 21 October 1893, 3; see also *Justice*, 18 August 1894, 6.

11. See Ardis, *New Women*; Gail Cunningham, *The New Woman and the Victorian Novel* (London: Macmillan, 1978); David Rubinstein, *Before the Suffragettes: Women's Emancipation in the 1890s* (Brighton: Harvester Press, 1986), chap. 3; Elaine Showalter, *A Literature of Their Own: British Women Novelists from Brontë to Lessing* (London: Virago, 1982), chaps. 7–9; Patricia Stubbs, *Women and Fiction: Feminism and the Novel, 1880–1920* (London: Methuen, 1979).

12. Cunningham, *New Woman*, 10.

13. Ethel Snowden, *The Feminist Movement* (London: Collins, 1911), 40; "Matrons and Maidens," *Labour Leader*, 27 November 1897.

14. Jane Hume Clapperton, *Margaret Dunmore; or, A Socialist Home* (London: Swan Sonnenschein, Lowrey and Co., 1888), 21, 60, 92.

15. Ardis, *New Women*, 119. For similar themes, see Brunhild de la Motte, "Radicalism—Feminism—Socialism: The Case of the Women Novelists," in *The Rise of Socialist Fiction, 1880–1914*, edited by H. Gustav Klaus (New York: St. Martin's Press; Brighton: Harvester Press, 1987), 28–48.

16. Isabella Ford, *Miss Blake of Monkshalton* (London: John Murray, 1890; first serialized in *Murray's Magazine* in 1890); Katharine Bruce Glasier, *Husband and Brother: A Few Chapters in a Woman's Life To-Day* (Bristol: J. W. Arrowsmith, 1894); Isabella Ford, *On the Threshold* (London: Edward Arnold, 1895); Katharine Bruce Glasier, *Aimée Furniss, Scholar* (London: Clarion Office, 1896).

17. June Hannam, *Isabella Ford* (Oxford: Basil Blackwell, 1989), 4.

18. I. O. Ford, *Women and Socialism* (London: Independent Labour Party, 1904), 2.

19. *Liverpool Mercury*, 19 November 1890. All reviews of Ford's *Miss Blake* and *Mr. Elliott* referred to are in "Scrapbook of I.O. Ford's Book Reviews and Some Correspondence," Acc. No. 2727, West Yorkshire Archive Service, Leeds (hereafter cited as "Scrapbook").

20. See *Manchester Guardian*, 4 November 1890, in "Scrapbook."

21. Quoted in Thompson, *Enthusiasts*, 83.

22. Ibid., 112, 135.

23. Katharine Bruce Glasier, "The Part Women Played in Founding the ILP," *Labour Leader*, 9 April 1914, 6–7.

24. Liverpool *Labour Chronicle*, 1 February 1895, 3.

25. I. O. Ford, "Women in the Labour Movement," *Labour Prophet*, December 1894, 161–62.

26. *Athenaeum* 3554 (7 December 1895): 788.

27. Isabella O. Ford, *Women's Wages, and the Conditions under Which They Are Earned* (London: William Reeves, 1893).

28. See Carolyn Steedman, *Childhood, Culture, and Class in Britain: Margaret McMillan, 1860–1931* (New Brunswick: Rutgers University Press, 1990), 100, 125–26, 131.

29. Hannam, *Ford*, 52.

30. Ford, *Women and Socialism*, 3.

31. Quoted in Thompson, *Enthusiasts*, 72.

32. Carroll Smith-Rosenberg, "The New Woman as Androgyne: Social Disorder and Gender Crisis, 1870–1936," *Disorderly Conduct: Visions of Gender in Victorian America* (New York: Alfred A. Knopf, 1985), 255.

33. Katharine St. John Conway and J. Bruce Glasier, *The Religion of Socialism* (Manchester: Labour Press Society, 1894), 5.

34. Ardis, *New Women*, 138.

35. A. R. Orage in *Labour Leader*, 6 March 1897, 74; Glasier to James Keir Hardie, 16 March 1897, I.1, 1897/15, Glasier Papers, University of Liverpool Library.

36. *On the Threshold* cost three shillings and six pence; *Mr. Elliott* cost six shillings.

37. Steedman, *Childhood, Culture, and Class*, 142.

38. Quoted in Showalter, *A Literature of Their Own*, 225.

39. Isabella Ford, *Mr. Elliott* (London: Edward Arnold, 1901); Katharine Bruce Glasier, *Marget*, serialized in *Weekly Times and Echo*, September 1902 to March 1903.

40. *Labour Leader*, 19 November 1901, in "Scrapbook."

41. *Illustrated London News*, 23 November 1901, in "Scrapbook."

42. Glasier, *Marget*, in *Weekly Times and Echo*, 11 January 1903, 10.

43. Norman Bentwich, "The Novel as a Political Force," *Nineteenth Century* 60 (November 1906): 786.

44. Bland, "The Married Woman," 155.

ANN ARDIS

"The Journey from Fantasy to Politics":

The Representation of Socialism and Feminism

in *Gloriana* and *The Image-Breakers*

In *British Socialists: The Journey from Fantasy to Politics*, Stanley Pier-son describes the transformation of British socialism between 1880 and 1910 as a journey from the glorious utopian fantasies of New Life pro-moted by William Morris, Edward Carpenter, and Havelock Ellis to the realpolitik of early-twentieth-century Independent Labour Party (ILP) activists and Fabian socialists. The loss of a certain quality of "vision and commitment," Pierson argues, attended British socialists' acquisition of parliamentary power, and his study traces the internal disagreements, defections, and schisms within the major socialist organizations of the period as they set out to realize abstract socialist principles.[1]

Pierson's characterization of British socialism's transformation at the turn of the century is apt, but at least one reason for the appropriate-ness of his central metaphor remains beyond the scope of his research. Although Pierson does not neglect to mention women's participation in socialist organizations at the turn of the century, he does tend to mini-mize the importance of the way in which "the Woman Question . . . moved in and out of socialist politics" during this period. Thus, as is true of so many historians of socialism, he persists in deeming women's efforts to integrate socialist and feminist politics as "tangential to [the history] of mainstream socialism."[2]

While retaining Pierson's metaphor, I want to redress his notion of
the relationship between socialist and feminist agendas at the turn of
the century through a discussion of two novels by Lady Florence Dixie
and Gertrude Dix. This essay seeks to account for two things: first,
the differences between traditional labor historians' characterizations of
turn-of-the-century British socialism and those of Dixie and Dix; and
second, the equally notable differences between Dixie's and Dix's views.
The journey to be traced here takes us from Dixie's feminist-socialist
utopia in *Gloriana; or, The Revolution of 1900* (1890) to the decidedly non-
utopian world of Dix's *The Image-Breakers* (1900). And the question that
powers the journey is this: why wasn't Dix, writing in 1900, the year of
Dixie's imagined revolution, able to sustain Dixie's political optimism?
Why, to frame the issue more broadly, wasn't late-nineteenth-century
feminist-socialist utopianism more helpful to women writers in modeling Britain's future after the turn of the century?

Imagining a Feminist-Socialist Collective

The main character of Dixie's novel, Gloriana DeLara, is the illegiti-
mate daughter of a woman who, forced to marry a rich man, eloped
with her lover and then witnessed his murder by her husband. Whereas
many heroines in turn-of-the-century New Woman novels are radical-
ized through their own experiences of gender-based oppression, Gloriana's knowledge of "all the wrongs that girls and women have to suffer" under Victorian patriarchy is her mother's legacy to her;[3] however,
whereas her mother has given up all hope of doing anything but raising
her daughter, Gloriana is determined to change the world. Already
touched by the "glowing sign of genius" at age twelve, she tells her
mother in the novel's opening scene that she wants the women of the
world to "rise as one" (1:6).

To lead this revolution, Gloriana notes, she must first go to Eton,
which she does by assuming a male identity. Known subsequently as
"Hector D'Estrange," Gloriana achieves notoriety at Oxford for her/his
writings on women's rights. She trains a legion of Amazonian "White
Guards"; she helps finance and build a Hall of Liberty; and later still,
as a member of Parliament, "Hector" introduces a women's suffrage
bill that earns the ire of her conservative colleagues. Cross-dressing for
years, she reveals her female identity only after these disgruntled members of Parliament, anxious that their political base will be altered by the
success of the suffrage bill, plot to have "Hector" arrested after a pub-

lic meeting. Rather than allow herself to be captured, "Hector" ends her speech by revealing herself as Gloriana and asking the working-class crowd to protect her from the soldiers skirting the demonstration.

The willingness of these working-class men and women to do so marks the turning point in the political tide of Gloriana's long-dreamed-of revolution. With the full support of the working classes now behind her, and with more and more middle-class ladies joining the cause as well, Gloriana's supporters in Parliament finally succeed in passing a bill for universal suffrage, and Gloriana is offered the prime ministership. The institutions of government remain the same after this, Britain's second and truly glorious revolution. But as is suggested by the glowing description of London with which the novel ends, both the British population and the landscape of London will be utterly transformed under Gloriana's leadership: the city that the narrator views from a hot-air balloon in 1999 is full of green parks, and we are told that no one goes hungry or without work in this new world.

To read this novel in the early 1990s is to be struck by the vast discrepancies between Dixie's utopian vision of life at the end of the twentieth century and the world we know today. But perhaps these same discrepancies can also help us identify the distinctive features of Dixie's socialist-feminist agenda for political and social reform.

First, and most important, Dixie and her protagonist are committed to the idea that women's political and economic entitlement functions as the first step toward universal entitlement. Unlike so many of her female contemporaries who became active in class politics, Dixie refuses to postpone or subordinate a revolution in gender roles to a strictly class-based agenda of social(ist) reform. In 1892 Eleanor Marx, for example, publicly argued, "We will organize—not as 'women' but as *proletarians* . . . for us there is nothing but the working-class movement." Similarly, Clara Zetkin claimed in 1896, "It is not women's petty interests of the moment that we should put in the foreground . . . our task must be to enroll the modern proletarian woman in the class struggle."[4] By contrast, Dixie refuses to define oppression as something that can be analyzed using a hierarchically organized set of nonoverlapping categories (e.g., class first, then gender). Moreover, she does not conceive of feminism and socialism as political movements in competition with each other for supporters. Although *Gloriana* initially highlights the "evils" of "sex-parasitism,"[5] Dixie's program of social change quickly moves beyond issues of gender to include reference to Irish Home Rule, Britain's treatment of its colonial subjects, and animal rights, as well as the condition of labor in England itself.

The inclusiveness of this political vision suggests that Dixie is recuperating some of the ideals of early-nineteenth-century British Owenite socialism. As Barbara Taylor has shown in *Eve and the New Jerusalem*, the Owenites viewed female freedom as a useful index of the wider struggle for human liberation. Notwithstanding the Owenites' importance in the late 1820s and 1830s, however, their "'stupendously grand' vision of a communist-feminist society" was dismissed by British socialists in the 1880s. Arguing that the "'fantastic' dreams of the early socialists were 'foredoomed' to failure . . . because they were based merely on an optimism of the will rather than a 'scientific' assessment of the historical balance of class forces," Marx and Engels introduced a "new set of conceptual tools" into socialist theory in the 1890s, tools that evacuated sexism from the socialist agenda by reducing it to a problem of bourgeois property relations.[6]

Dixie, however, refuses to follow Marx and Engels's lead in this regard. Instead, she proposes an agenda for British socialism in the 1890s that restores part of what was lost when the Owenites were dismissed as crude idealists: in *Gloriana*, feminism once again plays a key role in a radical agenda for political, economic, and social reform. Women's entitlement, in Dixie's view, is the crucial opening gambit in a long series of reforms that will ultimately result in "the comfort . . . and happiness of the toiling millions" (1:182). In other words, feminism isn't about the "petty interests" (Clara Zetkin's phrasing) of middle-class individualists; instead, Gloriana's life story shows how "self is buried" in the work of the collective (3:291).

Thus, not only are women's rights featured in *Gloriana* as the first step toward the economic and political entitlement of all, but middle-class women serve as catalysts in the revolution, role models for the shift from individualism to collectivism. The scene midway through the novel in which "Hector" reveals herself as Gloriana is crucial in this context because Gloriana's sense of her identification with the people's cause (in spite of her middle-class background) is substantiated here by the crowd's willingness to protect her from her enemies.[7] As she watches these working-class men and women gather around her, Gloriana finds inspiration in the fact that these men—unlike her middle-class colleagues in Parliament—do not "deprecate her deeds . . . [or] belittle her acts, because she is a woman. Their reason tells them that she understands their wants . . . [and] that her great heart is in sympathy with their needs" (2:182). To her surprise and great pleasure, neither sexism nor cross-class antagonism will disrupt and fracture this newly politicized collectivity.

The loss of individual identity and absorption into the life of the collective that is so powerfully visualized in this scene exemplifies the kind of political conversion experience[8] that Dixie's introduction models for her middle-class readers as well. Dedicating her work "to all . . . [who] will bravely assert and uphold the Laws of Justice, of Nature, and of Right" (1:vii), Dixie concludes her introduction in the following manner: "If, therefore, the following story should help one [person] to be generous and just, should awaken the sluggards among women to a sense of their Position, and should thus lead to a rapid Revolution[,] it will not have been written in vain" (1:ix–x). The New Woman novel has often been dismissed—by recent critics as well as by turn-of-the-century reviewers—for its exclusive focus on middle-class women.[9] But Chris Waters's observation in this volume about the fiction of Isabella Ford and Katharine Bruce Glasier can be extended to Florence Dixie's *Gloriana* as well: like Ford and Glasier, Dixie expands the boundaries of socialist discourse as she seeks to convince her middle-class readers that a commitment to socialism is a viable alternative to the life of a domestic angel. By attempting to write herself into the socialist movement, by presuming to envision a socialist revolution led by a New Woman, Dixie seeks to transform the very meaning of socialism itself as she encourages middle-class women to become active in collectivist politics.

The metaphor of an awakening and the reference to the "Laws of Justice, of Nature, and of Right" in the passages cited above from Dixie's introduction exemplify the third distinctive feature of her feminist-socialist agenda: her social Darwinism, her absolute faith in the amelioration of the human condition and nature's progress through history. Nan Bowman Albinski has argued that late-nineteenth-century British women utopia writers refused to identify themselves with nature. Emphasizing the human capacity for reason "in order to dissociate themselves from the interior status of [women's] 'natural' roles," they produced utopias that are "national in scope, highly urbanized and politicized, and generally limited to the public ('male') sphere."[10] This seems only partially accurate as a characterization of *Gloriana*. Although Dixie's novel does indeed make little reference to the domestic world and is national in scope, it nonetheless culminates with a vision of London as an urban environment that accommodates both humankind *and* nature. In other words, instead of dissociating women from nature in her utopia, Dixie seeks ultimately to restore a vital connection between the two; additionally, she views urbanization not as a process that entails the destruction of nature but as one that engineers the most ecologically sound and economically productive "fit" between human beings and the environment. Turn-of-the-century male utopia writers' visions of the future often retreat into the past, into feudal rather than futuristic characterizations of the city;[11] in contrast, and more in keeping with the Kyrle Society and the Commons Preservation Society's "back-to-nature" social improvement plans, Dixie imagines the London of the future as a city where parks have replaced the infamous ghettos of the East End and where increasingly unified, committed, and purposive collective work is possible.[12]

The World As It Is

Gertrude Dix challenges all three distinguishing features of Dixie's utopian vision: her happy marriage of feminism and socialism, her confidence in the middle-class woman's effectiveness as an agent of the revolution, and her social Darwinism. Rejecting Dixie's optimism about Victorian England's willingness to accept both the leadership of a New Woman and the goals of revolution, Dix, in The Image-Breakers, raises questions that Dixie does not address—perhaps even prefers to ignore. For example, how does a middle-class woman committed to socialism handle her male comrades' sexism as well as the class-based suspicions of her working-class constituents? What forces beyond her control limit her effectiveness as an activist? Should the acquisition of parliamentary power be a goal, or does the institutionalization of socialism, together with the establishment of alliances with other political parties and organizations, contribute to the effective containment of socialism in general as well as of a socialist-feminist women's rights platform more specifically?

If more were known about both women's lives, it might be possible to reflect on the personal experiences that might have fueled the differences between their answers to these questions. What we know about Florence Dixie's career as a travel writer, a war correspondent, a public lecturer, a novelist, and a political activist has been well summarized recently by Catherine Barnes Stevenson.[13] Except for one undocumented reference to Dix's involvement in the socialist movement in Bristol in a recent essay,[14] however, I have not been able to learn anything about Gertrude Dix. Little remains to document her life, it seems, aside from the novels The Girl from the Farm and The Image-Breakers, published in 1895 and 1900 respectively. This lack of basic information makes me reluctant to speculate about the relationship between these women's "real" lives and their fictional representations of women's involvement in socialist organizations at the turn of the century (or the influence of one on the other). What I will do here instead, before looking closely at *The Image-Breakers*, is offer a brief historical overview of new developments in British labor politics at the turn of the century, developments that would not have been a concern for Dixie when she wrote *Gloriana* in 1890.

In 1890, Britain was still reeling from the success of the London dock strike of 1889. Trade-union membership would continue to expand "massively" through 1892.[15] Workingmen's clubs and socialist fellowships of various persuasions were thriving. Robert Blatchford's establishment of the *Clarion* in 1891, together with the subsequent organization of the socialist Sunday schools, the Clarion Cycling Club, and the famous propaganda vans, offered new opportunities for the production of socialist (popular) culture.[16] On the one hand, the organization of the ILP in 1893 in the context of a defeated strike at Bradford represented a setback: the ILP's commitment to achieving "labour representation in Parliament reflected [socialists'] awareness that the groups of workers they were organizing were too weak to win their trade union battles without positive support from the state."[17] But on the other hand, the ILP itself functioned as an important new forum for policy debates between political gradualists and old-guard defenders of utopian idealism, as well as between women's rights supporters and their antagonists.

That Dix does not share Dixie's confidence in the eminent achievement of a socialist revolution is suggested early in *The Image-Breakers* through her characterization of the male socialist leaders' attitude toward the female factory workers whose strike they are organizing, their disdain for the domestic social reforms proposed by female party members, and their treatment of the upper-middle-class lady who has broken social caste to join the cause. In chapter 2, for example, a debate among the strike leaders, many of whom are what Raymond Williams would term "negatively identified" middle-class radicals,[18] reveals their condescension toward "the girls" they are championing. Both this debate and a subsequent discussion of a proposal to collectivize domestic labor by setting up cooperative kitchens and affordable day care for working women's children—an idea dismissed by the men as a threat to their advocacy of the "family wage"[19] for male workers—suggest the extent to which Dix views British socialism at the turn of the century as a middle-class movement dominated by men. The revolution of 1900 will not be achieved, for any number of reasons. Class distinctions continue to divide "the comrades" from the workers they champion and from each other. The political effectiveness of any middle-class woman who aspires to be a "Gloriana" is thwarted by these men's refusal to take her seriously; additionally, these men, refusing to entertain alternatives to the sexual division of labor, sustain an exclusive focus on the public sector of the economy. And the "natural" hierarchy of the sexes is endorsed even by those who attack the institution of marriage as a function of bourgeois property relations.

Elsewhere I have discussed how these policy debates affect Rosalind Dangerfield, one of Dix's two protagonists.[20] I want to focus here on Leslie Ardent, the second of Dix's female characters, a lower-middle-class woman who withdraws from any kind of political activism quite early in the novel. Having been initially instrumental in the political radicalization of her friend Rosalind, Leslie enrolls in a teacher-training course, then searches for work as an artist, instead of accepting Rosalind's invitation to join a back-to-the-land settlement that seeks to provide "self-supporting employment for [London's] surplus working-class population."[21] Notably, Leslie does not challenge or criticize the new colony's goals; she simply suggests that she wishes "to go [her] own way—fight [her] own battle" (102).

This decision to strike out on her own, to claim the right to be an individual, takes her to London, where she soon becomes involved with a man named John Redgold, a journalist-turned-ILP-activist of whom Rosalind disapproves for two reasons. A notorious "sensualist," he has a long history of casual sexual relationships. Equally damaging to his reputation in Rosalind's eyes, he is a gradualist: he not only is an ILP activist but also has publicly claimed that the socialists should seek the support of the Liberal Party in order to gain parliamentary representation for the ILP. He tells Leslie: "Why should we want to go away from all the resources of civilisation we've got already? The real fight is with the world as it is, not with some figment of our own brains we can never realise" (95).

Unlike Rosalind, Leslie takes offense at neither of these aspects of Redgold's character. Because she views human sexuality as an arena of individual freedom rather than a matter of property relations, she welcomes the opportunity to explore her own sexual responses, and she assumes Redgold's right to do the same in other relationships. For example, in a highly symbolic scene that epitomizes Dix's concessions to censorship in the publishing industry rather than her endorsement of bourgeois sexual ideology, Leslie buys and then sets free a pair of birds before (we are to understand) she sleeps with Redgold for the first time. "I would like you to break a thousand cages—the cages of men and women. . . . I am only a mere unit in the forces that make for freedom," she tells him (187).

Leslie also encourages Redgold's determination to become a key behind-the-scenes policymaker by working as an M.P.'s private secretary. In other words, scorning the idealization of chastity in political as well as sexual matters, she considers his work with a prominent Liberal politician as both a legitimate and a politically efficacious expression of his labor politics. She admires his willingness to work within the existing institutional frameworks of government—and to negotiate small changes today—rather than holding out for the grand revolution of the future. The same is true of her own career as well: she is willing to do any kind of work that she can find as a free-lance artist, preferring that form of artistic gradualism to the utopian fantasy of having a room of her own and an inheritance of five hundred pounds a year with which to support her artistic aspirations.

Significantly, Redgold's gradualism becomes a source of conflict in their relationship only when he decides that middle-class domesticity is something that he needs to establish for the sake of his candidate's political reputation. Although Leslie is quite happy sharing a flat with another woman, taking short trips to the country with him when they can afford it, and seeing him when they can both spare the time away from work, he now suggests that they marry and rent a villa in the London suburb that his candidate will represent (if he wins the upcoming election). With the salary he will make as an M.P.'s secretary, he argues, Leslie will be able to give up her work in the city and devote herself to her painting and to playing the role of a politician's wife.

While Leslie does not find the work she is doing—drawing advertisements and posters for commercial ventures—satisfying in terms of its aesthetics, she nonetheless values her financial independence. Moreover, she dreads the isolation of suburban life: "It seemed tragic that Redgold's great desire should be to leave London and the free life to box themselves up in a villa in full view of a town full of stuffy people" (229). And she resents Redgold's acquisition of middle-class attitudes toward the division of labor—his eagerness now to turn her artistic vocation into a leisure-time activity and his increasing reluctance to discuss his own work with her. Sensing that both changes in attitude are prompted not only by his new commitment to the middle-class ideology of separate spheres but also by some sort of flirtation with his candidate's beautiful (and upper-class) niece, Leslie disappears the day they were to have married, leaving him a brief note of apology but no forwarding address. When the two finally meet again more than a year later, their situation is quite different: Leslie is preparing to show her artwork at a public gallery, and Redgold, having decided that working for a Lib-Lab coalition entailed too many compromises in a socialist agenda, is once again working as a journalist. Thus, what Leslie wants to tell her friend when she seeks Rosalind out in the novel's final scene is that Redgold is indeed Leslie's comrade now. Instead of being an instance of what Rosalind had once called "selfishness *a deux*," the marriage that Leslie now looks forward to will be a real working partnership. Having once deferred to the leadership of her upper-middle-class friend, Leslie now solidifies her position as the most important "image-breaker" in this novel, the woman who has most effectively broken the Victorian codes of class and gender identity.

It could be argued, perhaps, that the resolution of both women's life stories in *The Image-Breakers* represents a failure, a loss of faith in the efficacy of political activism and a withdrawal into private life. Leslie Ardent is looking forward only to the fulfillment of her romantic and artistic aspirations, not the revolution of 1900. Betrayed politically and sexually by her partner in a free union, Rosalind, who hides from Leslie when she comes to call in the novel's final chapter, is now working in a stained-glass factory, where her efforts to improve the conditions of labor are ignored by both the management and the women on the shop floor. But rather than assuming that the end of *The Image-Breakers* confirms the failure of these women's political "vision and commitment" (borrowing Pierson's phrasing again), I would suggest instead that we understand their actions as a redefinition of politics. Again briefly consider, by way of contrast, *Gloriana*.

Although Florence Dixie legitimizes women's labor in the public sphere in *Gloriana*, the fact that her utopia steers clear of all domestic issues has the ironic effect of reinstating rather than challenging the Victorian doctrine of separate spheres. Politics, according to Gloriana, are national in scope. In Gertrude Dix's view, in contrast, politics begin at home—because the relationship between the public and the private spheres is much more complex than suggested by that familiar Victorian formulation. The revolution isn't somewhere "out there" in the public sector, waiting to be achieved, almost magically, in one mass conversion experience; the revolution will be achieved gradually—one relationship at a time. The closing chapter of *The Image-Breakers* foregrounds Leslie Ardent's determination to achieve this revolution with Redgold.[22] Significantly, however, Rosalind Dangerfield evidences the same commitment to individual activism through her work at the factory. Rather than fantasizing about the socialist utopia (the good place), rather than temporarily disguising herself as a workgirl in order to write an exposé for a middle-class journal (as Beatrice Webb had done in 1888, for example),[23] Rosalind has now *become* a woman worker. She has joined the rank and file on the workshop floor. Whether or not management heeds her constant reminders about the various hazards to these women's health in this industry, and whether or not these women treat her as one of themselves, she will continue to agitate on their behalf. In spite of the fact that she herself disdained all forms of political gradualism and cherished the religion of socialism's high-minded idealism during the earliest days of her activism, she now practices a very modest form of gradualism: the commitment of a single individual to improving the conditions of labor in a single workplace.

This crucial shift of focus, this redefinition of politics—which is so central to the cultural work of the New Woman novel in the 1890s—begins to explain why the late-nineteenth-century feminist-socialist utopianism epitomized by *Gloriana* was not more helpful to Dix and other early-twentieth-century women writers in modeling Britain's future after the turn of the new century. Recent bibliographical studies by critics such as Nan Bowman Albinski and Lyman Tower Sargent establish certain basic facts: the late nineteenth century was indeed the golden age of utopia writing; the number of utopian novels published fell off rapidly during the first two decades of the twentieth century; of those published in Britain between 1900 and 1909, most were written by men and were either antifeminist or antisocialist in character.[24] Without more information, of course, it is impossible to establish any notion of Florence Dixie's influence, positive or negative, on Gertrude Dix. Still, it is worth noting that recent revisionary feminist histories of the period confirm the legitimacy of Dix's skepticism concerning any kind of utopian faith in the eminence of a socialist revolution. Instead of invoking or reiterating Gloriana DeLara's optimism, Leslie Ardent and Rosalind Dangerfield's disillusionment with organized socialist politics anticipates the real historical experience of women such as Eva Gore-Booth, Ada Nield Chew, Charlotte Despard, and Sylvia Pankhurst, who were soon to find themselves "torn between a socialist movement which denied feminism, and a feminist movement which dismissed socialism in the prewar period."[25]

I would like to suggest, in closing, that Dix's redefinition of politics in *The Image-Breakers* also anticipates the subsequent work of women such as Wilma Meikle, Christabel Pankhurst, Marion Phillips, Lucy Re-Bartlett, and Ethel Snowden. Notwithstanding other differences among their views, in works such as *Towards a Sane Feminism* (1916), *The Great Scourge and How to End It* (1913), *Women and the Labour Party* (1918), *Sex and Sanctity* (1911), and *The Feminist Movement* (1913), these early-twentieth-century women writers and political activists reject out of hand the Victorian doctrine of separate spheres, a doctrine that Dixie unwittingly reinstates as she focuses exclusively on the public sphere in *Gloriana*.[26] As the Labour Party shifts its focus of interests between 1910 and 1930 from the industrial conditions of the skilled and unskilled working class to the conditions of working-class life in general, it is women—as Carolyn Steedman notes in her recent biography of Margaret McMillan—who will do the work of documenting, defining, and analyzing these conditions.[27] It is women, in other words, who will be instrumental in reconceptualizing the relationship between the public sphere and the private sphere, the political life and the domestic life. The New Woman novel's contribution to cultural politics at the turn of the century is rarely recognized either by historians of the Left or by literary critics writing about the dominant literary tradition. But if we don't assume that novels are the ephemera of the superstructure, if we don't use categories such as "the New Woman novel" or "the socialist novel" to isolate (and thereby marginalize) certain kinds of cultural production, then it becomes possible to see how a novel such as *The Image-Breakers* challenges familiar explanations of British socialism's journey from fantasy to politics at the turn of the century as it exposes the class and gender biases that kept—and still keep—"the revolution of 1900" from happening.

Notes

1. Stanley Pierson, *British Socialists: The Journey from Fantasy to Politics* (Cambridge: Harvard University Press, 1979), 2–3. Other studies that support Pierson's include Kenneth Brown, *The English Labour Movement, 1700–1951* (New York: St. Martin's Press, 1982), 183, and James Hinton, *Labour and Socialism: A History of the British Labour Movement, 1867–1974* (Amherst: University of Massachusetts Press, 1983), 24–30.

2. Julia Swindells and Alice Jardine, *What's Left? Women in Culture and the Labour Movement* (London: Routledge, 1990), 2. For discussions of turn-of-the-century British socialists' responses to feminism, see Sandra Stanley Holton, *Feminism and Democracy: Women's Suffrage and Reform Politics in Britain, 1900–1918* (Cambridge: Cambridge University Press, 1986); Susan Kingsley Kent, *Sex and Suffrage in Britain, 1860–1914* (Princeton, N.J.: Princeton University Press, 1987); Jill Liddington and Jill Norris, *One Hand Tied behind Us: The Rise of the*

Women's Suffrage Movement (London: Virago, 1978); Caroline Rowan, "Women in the Labour Party, 1906–1920," *Feminist Review* 12 (October 1982): 74–91; and Sheila Rowbotham, *Hidden from History: Rediscovering Women in History from the Seventeenth Century to the Present* (New York: Vintage, 1976), 90–107.

3. Florence Dixie, *Gloriana; or, The Revolution of 1900*, 3 vols. (London: Henry and Co., 1890), 1:6.

4. As quoted by Barbara Taylor in "Socialist Feminism: Utopian or Scientific?," in *People's History and Socialist Theory*, edited by Raphael Samuel (London: Routledge and Kegan Paul, 1981), 160. Other British women socialists who preferred to dissociate themselves from feminism included Margaret Bondfield, Katharine St. John Conway (later Glasier), Margaret McMillan, and Beatrice Potter Webb. Although their view of feminism as a movement for middle-class ladies was shared by ILP leaders such as Philip Snowden and John Bruce Glasier, Keir Hardie was the only major figure in national labor politics at the turn of the century to join women such as Enid Stacy, Eva Gore-Booth, Julia Dawson, and Ada Nield Chew in trying to integrate women's rights into a socialist platform. (See Liddington and Norris, *One Hand Tied behind Us*, 129–51.)

5. See Carol Dyhouse's discussion of the wide currency of this term in socialist-feminist literature during the prewar period in *Feminism and the Family, 1880–1939* (Oxford: Basil Blackwell, 1989), 38. Dyhouse attributes its popularity to the publication of Olive Schreiner's *Woman and Labour* (1911), but Dixie's use of this term in 1890 suggests a much longer history of this usage.

6. Barbara Taylor, *Eve and the New Jerusalem: Socialism and Feminism in the Nineteenth Century* (New York: Pantheon Books, 1983), xv, 284.

7. For further discussion of this scene, see Ann L. Ardis, *New Women, New Novels: Feminism and Early Modernism* (New Brunswick: Rutgers University Press, 1990), 120.

8. For further discussion of the religious fervor of political conversion in late-nineteenth-century socialist writings and of middle-class women's identification with the working class, see Stephen Yeo, "A New Life: The Religion of Socialism in Britain, 1883–1896," *History Workshop Journal* 4 (Autumn 1977): 5–56, and Brunhild de la Motte, "Radicalism—Feminism—Socialism: The Case of the Women Novelists," in *The Rise of Socialist Fiction, 1880–1914*, edited by H. Gustav Klaus (New York: St. Martin's Press, 1987), 28–48.

9. See, for example, Gail Cunningham, *The New Woman and the Victorian Novel* (London: Macmillan, 1978), 10.

10. Nan Bowman Albinski, *Women's Utopias in British and American Fiction* (London: Routledge, 1988), 19, 4. Note, by way of contrast, the long tradition of experimentation and theorizing about domestic revolution in America, a tradition than Dolores Hayden dates back to the Civil War (see *The Grand Domestic Revolution: A History of Feminist Designs for American Homes, Neighborhoods, and Cities* [Cambridge: MIT Press, 1981]).

11. Susan Squier, "The Modern City and the Construction of Female Desire: Wells' *In the Days of the Comet* and Robins' *The Convert*," *Tulsa Studies in Women's Literature* 8 (1989): 72.

12. See Peter C. Gould, *Early Green Politics: Back to Nature, Back to the Land, and Socialism in Britain, 1880–1900* (Sussex: Harvester Press; New York: St. Mar-

56 ANN ARDIS

tin's Press, 1988), for further discussion of the Kyrle Society, the Commons Preservation Society, and other back-to-nature social-improvement organizations with which Dixie might have been familiar.

13. Catherine Barnes Stevenson, *Victorian Women Travel Writers in Africa* (Boston: Twayne, 1982).

14. Brunhild de la Motte mentions in a footnote that Dix was "part of the socialist movement in Bristol" (see "Radicalism—Feminism—Socialism," 47). In "A New Life," Yeo also mentions Dix in a footnote (54 n. 85) referring to Samson Bryher's 1929 *An Account of the Labour and Socialist Movement in Bristol* (Bristol: Bristol Labour Weekly); I have not had access to Bryher's study. .

15. Yeo, "A New Life," 8.

16. See Chris Waters, *British Socialists and the Politics of Popular Culture, 1884–1914* (Stanford: Stanford University Press, 1990).

17. Hinton, *Labour and Socialism*, 60.

18. Raymond Williams, *Culture and Society, 1780–1950* (New York: Columbia University Press, 1958, 1983), 176.

19. Jane Lewis notes that the family-wage argument was "the major bargaining counter of the general labor unions and sweated workers" during this period ("The Working-Class Wife and Mother and State Intervention, 1870–1918," in *Labour and Love: Women's Experience of Home and Family, 1850–1914*, edited by Jane Lewis [Oxford: Basil Blackwell, 1986], 103). See also Hilary Land, "The Family Wage," *Feminist Review* 6 (1980): 55–77.

20. Ardis, *New Women*, 134–35, 159–60.

21. Gertrude Dix, *The Image-Breakers* (London: W. Heinemann, 1900), 55.

22. Pamela Fox's argument—in this volume (chapter 3)—about working-class women's contradictory investment in the romance plot lends support to my reading of the highly sentimental ending of Leslie's story in *The Image-Breakers*. As Fox suggests with regard to Ethel Carnie Holdsworth's fiction, the foregrounding of Leslie and Redgold's relationship in Dix's novel "helps to redefine the scope of politics in working-class culture and of 'political' narrative in working-class writing." The fact that Leslie has now claimed for herself the kind of storybook idealization of a heterosexual partnering that she had ascribed only to wealthy ladies such as her friend Rosalind in the novel's opening scene "unsettle[s] the whole enterprise of working-class writing."

23. See Ann L. Ardis, "Beatrice Webb's Romance with Ethnography," *Women's Studies* 18 (1990): 1–16.

24. Lyman Tower Sargent, *British and American Utopian Literature, 1516–1975: An Annotated Bibliography* (1979), as quoted by Albinski in *Women's Utopias*, 29.

25. Rowbotham, *Hidden from History*, 22.

26. See Sheila Jeffreys, *The Spinster and Her Enemies: Feminism and Sexuality, 1880–1930* (London: Pandora, 1985), for a detailed discussion of these early-twentieth-century feminist theorists.

27. Carolyn Steedman, *Childhood, Culture, and Class in Britain: Margaret McMillan, 1860–1931* (New Brunswick: Rutgers University Press, 1990), 8.

PAMELA A. FOX

Ethel Carnie Holdsworth's

"Revolt of the Gentle":

Romance and the Politics of

Resistance in Working-Class

Women's Writing

Girlhood glides into womanhood, and one falls in love. (Which shows the innate cheek of the working-class, who dare to dream of happiness living from hand to mouth.)—Ethel Carnie, "The Factory Slave," *Woman Worker* (3 March 1909)

For God's sake, women, go out and play.—Ethel Carnie, "Our Right to Play," *Woman Worker* (14 April 1909)

In his 1906 survey of local Lancashire reading habits, the working-class writer James Haslam can scarcely conceal his disappointment with his neighbors' taste for sensationalist and popular tales. He appears most dismayed, however, by the women readers' preferences. "'Romance, romance, romance,'" he complains, "is their monotonous cry. Romance served up in penny batches; romance that depends upon nonsensical scenes, shallow thoughts, spurious philosophy, and unreal life, for its popularity."[1] This essay is concerned with the "cry" for romance that

Haslam and others hear yet typically regret, dismiss, distort, or deny when they study modern British working-class culture. And since that cry emerges as an explicitly feminized desire, I am especially interested in understanding the often circuitous, often suppressed, route it takes in narratives by working-class women themselves—those who managed to produce, as well as consume, fictional texts in pre— and post—World War I England. Romance provides, it seems to me, a most revealing alternate angle of entry into discussions of working-class political narrative; it functions as a complex resistance strategy for women writers, as well as a more obvious reinscription of a dominant convention governing gender, class, and literary relations.

My discussion will focus on the work of Ethel Carnie Holdsworth (1886–1960s?), the South Lancashire "ex-mill girl" who was one of the few working-class women novelists in Britain to sustain a writing career. The daughter of a staunch Social Democratic Federation member, she became an activist for working-class causes on her own terms, producing more novels, stories, poems, and journalistic reportage than most of her male contemporaries. Though initially tagged the "Lancashire fairy" by the *Woman Worker*'s prominent editor Robert Blatchford, Carnie Holdsworth quickly put that title to rest with her gutsy, militant pieces protesting the very structure and inequities of the capitalist system.[2] In addition to steering the *Woman Worker* in a more radical direction during her short stint as contributor and editor, she also incorporated her experiences as a textile worker into narratives that ran the gamut from children's stories to popular novels to proletarian propaganda fiction.

Yet Holdsworth's literary output has been strikingly ignored or mishandled by most critics otherwise eager to embrace working-class writers (and distressed by the absence of women in those ranks) because it defies assumptions about working-class politics and literary practice.[3] Her writing is difficult to characterize—typically dramatic and passionate but widely varying in form and style, linked primarily by themes of oppression and romantic love. Its feminist orientation has stimulated some recent interest in her work as a whole: Edmund Frow and Ruth Frow have published a helpful biographical piece detailing Holdsworth's early political convictions; H. Gustav Klaus includes reference to her novel *This Slavery* in his essay on "neglected" 1920s socialist fiction; and P. M. Ashraf incorporates several extensive readings of Carnie Holdsworth's novels in a comprehensive survey of British working-class literature.[4] Much remains to be done, however, to do justice to the complexity of Holdsworth's political and literary visions, particularly her sense of the meeting ground between class and gender. After sketching out the historical and cultural contexts at issue here, I will address two quite different novels, *Miss Nobody* (1913) and *This Slavery* (1925), to suggest ways in which romance can be viewed as a manifestation of and response to the parameters surrounding Holdsworth's position as a woman in a working-class community and in a fledgling "community" of male working-class writers.

Feminist theorists and critics from Mary Wollstonecraft to the present have had a particular and obvious stake in viewing heterosexual romance as one linchpin of patriarchal systems. Whether cultural myth, plot device, or popular genre, romance seems a convenient, intimate register of cultural codes and can either be critiqued as a method of producing feminine subjects or be identified as an openly contradictory script and thus a potential site of resistance.[5] Yet for working-class women— as both readers and writers—romance can never be fully available as an "intimate" register of cultural practices. They begin at a different place in their relation to that convention and, in a sense, commit a transgressive act merely by desiring the romance script itself: its plot is *not* a "cover" for their other "anxieties" and "desires," as Tania Modleski argues about romance readers generally;[6] it *is* their anxiety and desire. In order to be addressed adequately by feminist studies, working-class women's troubled (and perhaps troubling) investment in romance needs to be explored in the specific context of working-class culture and its accompanying literary tradition.

During the early decades of the twentieth century in Britain, it was predominantly middle-class women who felt the daily strictures of (and protested against) romantic codes of behavior. Working-class women were more typically denied access to those codes by their own cultural experience. While the cinema and popular novels encouraged diverse female audiences to identify with an array of romance heroines, working-class mothers made sure their daughters understood that romance was purely a fantasy with little relevance to their lives and that marriage was primarily an economic relation, rather than a fulfillment of love, to be performed as a perfunctory ritual (if at all).[7] Unlike their middle- and upper-class counterparts, who frequently suffocated at the hands of fathers, brothers, guardians, and mothers while playing out the real-life role of romance heroine, working-class women suffered chastisement or ridicule within their community if they merely attempted to try on the role.[8] Romance, then, functions at least in part as an emblem of privilege, an experience reserved for others. Its value is linked to the high premium placed more generally on private "space" (both literal and psychological) at a time when the conflation of public and private spheres was especially visible, and painful, in working-class lives. As I hope to illustrate below, the presence of romance in working-class women's texts ultimately serves as a means of registering the desire for a seemingly unobtainable individual subjectivity that is posed against an inescapable collectivity. The romance plot comes into play not only to convey a longing for relations based in tenderness, rather than exploitation, but also to represent a utopian private arena in which one is valued for one's *gendered* "self" alone.

This suggestive connection among romance, individualism, and rebellion becomes especially challenging when it serves to unsettle the whole enterprise of working-class writing. Like the middle-class strata of socialist fiction treated by other chapters in this volume, modern British proletarian fiction traditionally operates as a masculine genre, largely concerned with "public" and transformative experience. As reviews and manifestos from 1908 through the 1930s gradually formulated a set of working-class literary aims or directives that emphasized men's defiance at (or near) the point of production, the entire private sphere—whether in the form of modernist angst or penny-novel love affairs—soon became branded as both feminine and bourgeois.[9] Contemporary Marxist critics tend to accept and reproduce such criteria, perceiving the romance plots that do exist within earlier working-class novels as either a regressive capitulation to popular taste or a sentimental substitute for the "real" political narrative. Offering the converse of a strictly feminist perspective, they consider romance an entirely alien register, foreign to a genuine working-class subject position. Jack Mitchell, for instance, celebrates Robert Tressell's *The Ragged Trousered Philanthropists* (1914) as a breakthrough "revolutionary" text precisely because it centers the novel on work rather than "love." Others, like Carole Snee and Graham Holderness, either wince at the clumsy and overblown rendering of romance in novels such as Walter Greenwood's *Love on the Dole* (1933) and Lewis Jones's *Cwmardy* (1937) (and, in Snee's case, use it as one yardstick of bourgeois values) or attempt to reread and/or rewrite the passages or subplots so that they safely promote an alternative message.[10]

Romance thus becomes a forbidden category not only for working-class women who operate generally as female subjects within a specific class culture but also for those who are producers of class-conscious narratives. Its persistent, if modified, appearance in their fiction arguably enacts another kind of transgression, recasting the genre itself. When the working-class woman writer makes use of the private realm, she finally works to reappropriate what can be called a master narrative of protest within this body of writing by allowing a more self-conscious critique of gender relations, as well as the expression of outlaw desires surrounding those relations. Exposing the patriarchal, as well as pleasurable, dimensions of the private bonds between men and women, the romance plot becomes one means of expanding the political terrain in the proletarian novel. Although it is hardly an "intimate" category or convention, then, it is not altogether "alien" either. It provides a recognizable mechanism for addressing a very real component of women's lives. But writers like Carnie Holdsworth found themselves in a difficult position as they attempted to negotiate an appropriate form for their specific concerns. Their incorporation of romance remains quite an anxious act.

Miss Nobody, Carnie Holdsworth's first novel (published under the name Ethel Carnie), is a fascinating representative of the political tensions that characterize her writing (as well as a most interesting companion text to *This Slavery*.) Juxtaposing urban and pastoral sites, along with realist, proletarian, and "folk" narrative, it defies simple categorization. The novel most clearly draws on the nineteenth-century social narrative model, complete with cross-class marriage, unexpected inheritance, murder trial, and blissful domestic and political closure. Yet Carnie Holdsworth's revision of that model—specifically, her working of the romance plot—is as revealing as her imitative gestures. As with any romance text, plot details assume an especially critical role in directing this narrative, guiding our reading of its conflicting aims.

On the one hand, *Miss Nobody* offers a considerable sobering of romance ideology by focusing on the persistent absence or failure of romantic love in working-class life. Carrie Brown, a Manchester oyster-shop girl,[11] spends her spare time absorbed in Tulip Novelettes while surrounded by, and in some cases experiencing, domestic violence, sexual harassment, and abandonment. Orphaned by a mother who is in the workhouse and a roguish father who fled abroad, she has survived through pragmatism and measured wariness of male promises. Her character has a distinctly "New Woman" air: we learn immediately of her "bold courage," "original mind," and support for the suffragettes, all of which are subsequently reflected in her chastisement of male companions on a tram. "Men, aren't you?" she taunts, as they beat an accompanying animal into submission.[12] But though she is capable of viewing popular romances like "The Duchess of Digglemore's Diamonds" with self-conscious amusement, quite aware of the disparity between their heroines' lives and her own, she is unable to shake their appeal as an avenue of momentary escape and transformation ("Instead of the gritty floor of the oyster-shop she trod soft Persian carpets upon which lovers knelt to propose in long-winded poetical sentences as sweet as barley-sugar . . . Carrie herself was the Duchess for the time being" [6]). Even as she resigns herself to a loveless marriage with Robert Gibson, a prosperous farmer, she continues to read romance fiction with lingering hope.

Although Carrie's more naive responses are juxtaposed with the narrator's wry and jaded perceptions, the novel stops short of suggesting that romantic love is an impossibility and/or delusion—it argues only that romance exists in less mythic, inflated forms. *Miss Nobody*'s romance plot actually fails to be "romantic" in any conventional sense until the last pages of the narrative. Unlike many middle-class heroines, who often covertly exercise their greatest liberties during the extended period of wooing imposed by the narrative structure, Carrie endures a "courtship" that lasts approximately one week, during which time both parties primarily weigh the material benefits of marriage: Gibson eyes her trim waist and considers her efficiency in the kitchen, whereas Carrie dwells on her quickly fading good looks and never-ending battle with mountains of oysters. She decides that "to be a good wife . . . in return for the position and freedom he would give her . . . would surely be a fair exchange" (45–46). Predictably, the marriage soon grows stultifying: Carrie comes to understand the contradictions of life as a "leisured" woman when the "freedom" from her workplace becomes burdensome and alienating. Yet in the middle of the narrative, Carnie Holdsworth summarily drops the combined romance-marriage plot and introduces a more recognizably proletarian schema: Carrie abandons the relationship, signs on at a textile factory, and organizes a successful strike for higher wages (the "Battle for Ninepence"). However, this too proves unfulfilling, and eventually she is drawn back into the marriage—*after* Gibson's position is initially weakened via a murder charge (which instigates his own parallel imprisonment) and her position is strengthened materially via an unlikely inheritance from her long-lost father. After this melodramatic turn in the narrative, *Miss Nobody* closes with sincere commitment and understanding between the two, so that love and marriage emerge as neither a potboiler fantasy nor a service contract but as a rewarding partnership between equals. The novel's (uneven) challenge to traditional romance ideology contests traditional gender roles, but it does not pretend to deny the importance of love itself.

This reconfiguration of the romance trope additionally complements the critique of *middle-class* culture that is suggestively launched by the narrative through its periodic pastoral settings. Much like Holdsworth's most popular novel, *Helen of Four Gates* (1917), *Miss Nobody* makes oblique attacks on privatized social structures, affirming collective experience by demonstrating the price of its absence. Carnie Holdsworth goes to great lengths to indict the isolating effects of rural middle-class existence, which valorizes propriety (along with property). The country village of Greenmeads, site of much of the narrative action, is thus surprisingly insular and sterile, an ironic contrast to Carrie's daydreams. On her initial crowded tram ride out of Manchester, Greenmeads represents the utopian possibility of an expansive and private state. "Looking through the window, splashed with the rain of the previous day, she saw fields of waving meadow grass, infinite spaces of tender blue sky bending down to them. The sky fascinated Carrie. It looked so different here in the country from the narrow, hand's-breadth between the grey houses as she viewed it in slack moments from the door of the oyster-shop. . . . 'To think of all that space being here, and none of us knowing of it,' she said aloud, then, being a practical person, looked into her shabby purse of the uncertain clasp to see if her ticket was quite safe" (7).

Carrie's self-conscious anxiety about legitimately crossing this border is well-taken, for once married and settled there, she continually experiences displacement and is permanently branded with an alien status. She initially seeks out such an existence to escape the monotony of her own class territory, yet once settled into Greenmeads, she achieves an individual subjectivity very different from the one for which she had literally "bargained." She is indeed set apart but precisely because she continues to experience herself as a (different) *class* subject. Her position as a union organizer at the textile factory—the role she adopts after her flight from her husband's farm—thus reacquaints her with the potentially empowering dimensions of communal experience (and introduces another kind of utopian "space"). "Some thirty girls and women worked in the long, whitewashed rooms, and when they were really serious, singing some old hymn tune, or a popular ditty of the day, there was a sense of brave, beautiful fellowship about them, transforming them from so many cranks in a mighty machine into living souls. . . . Carrie loved this life better than domestic service. She felt herself one of many— weak and insignificant enough alone, but wonderful, strong, beautiful, along with them" (160, 166). On one level, Carrie's transformation from would-be bourgeois romance heroine to working-class hero sets the seal on Carnie Holdsworth's privileging of proletarian experience.

The plot's further machinations, however, create another ideological twist by short-circuiting this transformation. In the end, Carrie deliberately forfeits her hero status to emerge finally as a (compromised) heroine: Carnie Holdsworth's own narrative in effect completes the novelette that Carrie leaves behind in Greenmeads with the page still turned down, resuming and finishing its disrupted story. Though she enjoys the solidarity with other women workers, Carrie grows tired of the work itself; her subsequent firing and brief but grueling experience at a Christmas card factory lead her once again to flee Manchester. On her way back to the country, she encounters several other options that, if acted on, would dramatically alter both her own life and Holdsworth's narrative model. For instance, a vagabond invites her to join him on the road, yet she rejects this picaresque role as too dangerous and solitary for a woman. Directly afterward, a socialist in a laundry van offers her a ride and enigmatic political rhetoric, both of which she also rejects. What she accepts, as outlined above, is the position of fulfilled wife and mother in an entirely different class community. Hardly an antidote to popular romance, the novel thus finally reinscribes a great deal of its underlying fictions, at least concerning class mobility. For romance functions here as both utopian and realistic fantasy—a dream of what can exist within the present system but outside Carrie's own particular class-bound world. Holdsworth's handful of supportive commentators all remark on the admirable "independence" of her female protagonists, yet it must be stressed that their independence should be read as a specific kind of autonomy that actually signals the ability to detach oneself from (stigmatizing) class markers and confinements. In some senses, *Miss Nobody* most obviously endorses the vision of the middle-class social novel it often imitates, engineering romance and marriage between classes to stave off radical change. Safely ensconced in the countryside by the narrative's end, Carrie exits from the oppressive industrial economy without having to dismantle it. She settles for individual escape by gaining another, ultimately more desirable, class subjectivity—she becomes Mrs. Somebody.

Viable as it is, the above critique will not get us very far if we fail to recognize that Carrie's choice can be viewed as an act of transgression as much as of regression. Although *Miss Nobody* clearly predates the period of more self-consciously prescriptive working-class fiction, it displays the beginning tensions running through early-twentieth-century efforts. The text's unorthodox privileging of individualism, combined with (and primarily articulated through) its valorization of romance, purposefully resists the dictates of working-class culture. Voicing a dangerous interest in control and privacy—modes of experience out of the reach of most working-class women of her time—this strain of Carnie Holdsworth's writing allows her one method of working out her complex, embattled response to working-class subjectivity. She creates a taboo script that tries to have it all ways. The novel incorporates a composite of episodes from the evolving male working-class narrative forms as if to establish its own validity before commenting on the latter's incompatibility with female working-class narrative strategies. Overrun with contradictions, Holdsworth's text insistently opens up new possibilities of opposition while foreclosing on others; its protagonist exercises the right to create a different set of class borders for herself, problematic as they may be. *Miss Nobody*'s concluding situation and line—"Are not our dreams the lamps on a rainy road?"—represent a daring plot choice: to celebrate cross-class love over working-class unity.

The apprehension that marks Carnie Holdsworth's early fiction is more fully evident in her later novel *This Slavery* precisely because it makes such a strikingly dramatic concession to proletarian literary expectations.[13] A "propaganda" text that stirred debate in the labor press, the novel is at once her most compliant and most resistant effort. Here, she offers a direct, fairly predictable treatment of urban working-class life, charting the effects of economic depression and a bitter strike on a textile mill community named Brayton. The dedication page sets the tone for the novel as a whole: "To my Mother and Father, slaves *and* rebels . . . with a Daughter's affection and a Comrade's greetings." Maintaining Carnie Holdsworth's focus on female experience, *This Slavery* contains and aligns that experience much more in accordance with a masculine narrative model. The novelist's trademark independent women are, this time, strong-minded about the "right" issue: class warfare. The Martin sisters, Hester and Rachel, may respond differently to the pressures of working-class life, but both emerge as the novel's most committed worker-rebels. Holdsworth's manipulation of the romance plot, however, continues to interrogate, as well as facilitate, her class-conscious agenda. In this text, cross-class romance represents an out-and-out betrayal of working-class values, clearly remedying *Miss Nobody*'s (presumed) political slippages. Nevertheless, the novel also succeeds in subverting its own surface narrative of class defiance.

This Slavery lends itself easily enough to affirmative leftist readings, which ignore the romance subplots in favor of its more recognizable political concerns. P. M. Ashraf, for example, argues that the novel's significance lies in its sophisticated treatment and foregrounding of revolutionary practice: "In *This Slavery*, the problems of political education, of a mature leadership, of reformism, of mastering revolutionary theory

and the lessons of a sharpening conflict in industry are not character
traits but part of the story." She centers her analysis on Rachel, who
actually recedes into the background over a portion of the narrative but
is the more openly (and traditionally) militant of the two sisters. From
Ashraf's perspective, Rachel "is much the most serious rank and file
leader in this period of fiction" with "at least some notion of the dialectic
of class struggle."[14] I too cheer on Rachel's refreshing role as a speaker
and strike leader who confronts the mill owner, struggles to read *Das
Kapital*, and spends time in prison for the cause—especially since she
so clearly supersedes the novel's prototypical socialist-union figure, Jack
Baines. But in the haste to claim Rachel as a new, improved version of
the proletarian fictional hero, Ashraf neglects to mention other more
problematic aspects of Rachel's character, specifically her involvement
in a love triangle that includes Baines and Hester. This omission creates a distorted picture not only of Rachel as a female figure but also of
the novel as a whole, whose political and romantic plots are undeniably
interwoven.

To address that connection most productively, we need to shift our
attention to the other protagonist, Hester. Her role in the text's most
substantial "romance" plot ostensibly works to illustrate another dimension or sphere of class struggle. An erstwhile painter and classical
musician, Hester is the sensitive, artistic member of the family, the one
who initially succumbs much more readily than Rachel to the bleakness
of working-class existence. A romantic entanglement with Baines gets
thwarted early on, leaving her vulnerable and alone. Much like Carrie
Brown, she accepts a wealthy businessman's marriage proposal in a des-
perate attempt to "gain freedom," only to discover that she prefers her
own class world. Hester's marital relationship lacks even a hint of sincere affection and soon thrives on antipathy as she is forced to become
part of the enemy class in her husband's war on the mill hands. Yet this
heroine also gradually transforms into a hero of her own kind and, unlike her counterpart in *Miss Nobody*, never turns back: Hester becomes
a spy within her home, surreptitiously helping the strikers rebel against
her husband, Sandy, and eventually openly joining their fight. (Among
other methods of sabotage, she writes the "doggerel" that the striking
workers sing to pass on information from the inside.) Whereas Carrie
unapologetically reaps the benefits of cross-class romance, Hester revels
in her reclaimed working-class solidarity—and, as proof, she dies by
police bullets, becoming a martyr to her people. Her seemingly more
legitimate romance with Baines, which works to frame the narrative

as a whole, is simultaneously resolved in the closing chapter (though in a compromised way and with an obviously compromised future) to confirm her class loyalty.

But the novel accomplishes much more than Holdsworth's testimony to working-class women's revolutionary mettle. Its title becomes the powerful constellation site for an alternate set of classed and gendered meanings that rewrite the text's classic story of resistance: "this slavery" turns out to be quite a pervasive condition triggered by, but not limited to, an exploitative capitalist system. To begin with, the romance plots take on the additional function of gender critique in *both* class spheres. Carnie Holdsworth's condemnation of courtship-marriage as a patriarchal, as well as bourgeois, institution *distinctly harmful to women* is more clearly laid out in the scenes involving Sandy, who treats Hester as one of his countless prized possessions to be displayed and controlled. His condescending impulse to rehabilitate the town's "diamond in the rough," together with his smothering household of material goods, eventually imprisons Hester just as a jail cell confines Rachel (for street agitation) during the same portion of the narrative. Their marriage represents far more than a crudely symbolic class "defection" on Hester's part, as Ashraf surmises. In much the same way, Baines prizes her seeming "difference" from other working-class women while simultaneously pressing her to conform to his own ideal. From the start, he seeks to make her a particular kind of proletarian object of desire, which the course of the narrative brilliantly deconstructs. He clearly prefers Hester's ethereal, traditionally feminine qualities to Rachel's tougher character, but when Hester appears to decline his offer of marriage—and soon after becomes Sandy's wife—he scorns her "softness." Holdsworth's political daring in this regard is most evident in the strike-negotiation scene: drawing the two together again as representatives of opposing camps, the episode reads like a confrontation between the stock male working-class hero and an entirely new female model. Baines condemns Hester's class betrayal, sputtering: "*I am a member of a defensive organisation which may turn into an attacking vanguard.* You—are lost!"[15] Yet she proves to represent the true vanguard by branding his trade-union politics as another form of sellout, including among its strategies the scarcely disguised subjugation of women (along with petty wage increases and hero worship).

At the same time, the analysis that Hester begins to spin out as she constructs her self-defense speaks to a final, much more muted strain of critique in the novel, one that betrays Carnie Holdsworth's own fascination with romance ideology and, in connection, her lingering sense of shamefulness surrounding working-class identity. *This Slavery*'s working-class tableau is punctuated by moments of enormous yearning and deprivation that finally seem to endorse Hester's bid for individualism even as her attempt to achieve it through class mobility is questioned and ultimately undermined. The novel opens with an instance of what I designate as "exposure" scenes in twentieth-century working-class narrative—scenes, from a variety of texts, that feature a literal or figurative exposure of working-class identity (often of the body itself), revealing the "dirtiness," "vulgarity," or sense of unworthiness that working-class characters strive to conceal.[16] This example combines three characteristic elements: a wish, a gap, and a stain. Longing for the spare time to paint, and despairing over her weary fate as a "working girl," Hester sits by the dying fire repairing a "tremendous hole" in her sock that she had attempted to hide earlier but "had found peeping over her clog-top" (6). When Baines makes a surprise visit and the light is suddenly turned on, she is caught not only with a bare leg exposed (the ostensible comic focus of the scene) but also, more important, with her winder's belt still wrapped around her body and a damning "smudge of blacklead on one soft, delicate curve of . . . pale cheek" (9). The episode neatly captures the self-contempt that often coexists with a defiant class consciousness in working-class experience and that finds its expression in fear of having one's class identity revealed (usually to another member of the working class, such as Baines above). Hester is repulsed by both the fundamental dirtiness of her class world and the persistent struggle necessary to survive and change it. She confides to Rachel, "It's all so sickening. . . . To have to fight for everything—bread, love, everything—like beasts" (18).

The narrative's final turns clearly invite us to join Rachel in finding such a perspective unsatisfactory. We are also, I would argue, asked to understand it and, further, to envision it as another valid form of class resistance—as, to borrow a term from the novel, the "revolt of the gentle" (19) against their own enforced degradation. Hester's shame derives from "a sensitive perception that to be poor amongst the poor was to have the soul slain, bit by bit, until nothing was left to creep on the earth but a bent body from which the light had faded" (33). Rachel hopes that this "fine sensitive disdain" will eventually "break" so that her sister will demonstrate that "surrender is not infinite and that the revolt of the gentle is more to be feared than that which spends itself" (19). But Hester's persistent faith in a self-determined, singular, and privileged identity—"I . . . am still—Hester Martin, wild though crushed, solitary though jostled and herded" (38)—is already in itself a kind of rebellion, posing a countervoice that does in fact bear out those middle-class readings of her character, such as Sandy's, that the narrative so derides. Hester indeed seems a "sensitive plant" who shouldn't "class" herself "with them" (86). Her self-styled role as thwarted artist cannot shake all of its associations with bourgeois, bohemian culture because the promises afforded by that culture clearly remain compelling to the writer of this novel. Despite Holdsworth's periodic attempts to recast the role so that Hester embodies the "Soul of the People" (243), the author cannot conceal its inherent attractiveness as a *valued* position of difference.

It seems entirely fitting, then, that Hester serves as the vehicle for romantic daydreams that also become tentatively validated over the course of the narrative, underwriting the text's covert theme of individualism. Although she tries to deny her susceptibility to romance's seductions and later lives out its contradictions, she cannot bear to have the ideal sullied, calling it "the great primitive, sacred impulse, the only romance that touches with angel-hands the grovelling ignominy of a slave's life" (16). The novel thereby naturalizes heterosexual love, suggests that it is not a mere patriarchal or capitalist "plot." The discourse creating Hester and Baines's single love scene makes a similar point. They "said in the vernacular . . . things that had been said in old Baby-lon, classic Greece. . . . They stepped over the borders of a county into the universal land of poetry" (13–14). To be sure, such observations are immediately prefaced by a considerably grimmer view of male and female relations ("Nature made her inexorable appeal, in the sordid trap of monotonous streets where slaves lived, eager to let none escape her" [10]). Yet Hester's evolving presence in fact justifies the longing for free-dom from "sordid" class ties, a freedom that romance ideally guarantees. Her mother perhaps provides the most persuasive endorsement of the romance myth when she offers the following interpretation of a love poem: "we are only ourselves, and know ourselves, when somebody loves us—just for ourselves—and we feel free, then" (225). The voice of working-class pragmatism and the opponent of romance ideology throughout most of the narrative, Mrs. Martin comes to recognize the connection between romance and subjectivity quite late in the novel; though the final turn of events quickly overshadows it, her declaration makes all too clear the relationship between gender construction and the seductive illusion of self-determination. In such a schema, a fixed class identity is exchanged for a fixed gender identity, making available to the working-class woman a seemingly exclusive (and certainly exclusionary) position.

Hester's link to the character Bob Stiner, another marginalized member of Brayton's working-class community, supplies the final pieces to this counternarrative. Stiner is distinguished not so much by aesthetic refinement as by an extreme, violent anger about his existence (along with a penchant for poetry and alcohol). Another closet romantic, he emerges as a revealing "mad" double for Hester, clinging stubbornly to his outcast status within his own class culture while also seeking collectivity. He roams the town muttering to himself, occasionally scrawling revolutionary messages on sidewalks and walls, and is shunned by most of his own class (except Hester and Rachel) for his inexplicable flights of fancy. His repeated chance meetings with Hester play up their relation as "soul mates."

But their tie is most dramatically exposed in his fateful search for a bouquet of violets. A measure of Stiner's alternately pathetic and endearing efforts to romance his estranged wife, the search represents another mode of resistance that, like Hester's, violates norms of working-class experience. The ragged bouquet he chooses indeed mocks his aspirations. Both his wife's and Mrs. Martin's "unsentimental" taunts seem to echo throughout the scene, sneering at his efforts to adopt a different class cultural code. When he is tragically killed in a scuffle between a policeman and a striker, Stiner finally demonstrates the larger tragedy of the parameters that confine working-class practices (and that are maintained from within as well as without). His aborted mission registers dissatisfaction with, and despair at ever escaping, a burdensome class existence. That transgression ultimately explains the "indirect and ironic relation" posed between his "quest of violets" and the policeman's simultaneous "quest of trouble" (198): in working-class culture and its accompanying fictional texts, the quest for romance is, quite assuredly, a "quest of trouble" that disrupts established conventions.

This Slavery thus haltingly weaves together another story that cannot help but conflict with its own larger project, continually calling into question its very interpretation and validation of working-class experience. Interestingly, when the novel was criticized by the *Sunday Worker* for making the "usual love situation" serve as "the pivot of the machinery of the whole tale," Carnie Holdsworth retorted that love, like "the bread struggle," is central to existence.[17] To her credit, she publicly defended romance (and all that it represents) as a viable political issue in working-class fiction. Yet she also clearly felt a need to mask or offset those dimensions that threatened her own status as a class-conscious woman and writer. As Hester says when Sandy mocks working-class people's propensity "to tell all sorts of yarns," "perhaps the true story they don't tell would be less popular but more terrible" (86).

Written during a particularly volatile and at times militant period of British working-class history, women's texts such as *Miss Nobody* and *This Slavery* reflect the enormous pressures shaping working-class cultural production. As my discussion has attempted to demonstrate, romance serves as one underestimated and crucial component of those texts, accomplished with considerable ambivalence and seeming sleight of hand. The trivialization of private, emotional trends in fiction coincided with the overall masculinization of the Left, creating a risky climate for political women writers who departed from the norm. The increasingly heated conflict between Marxism and Labour Party socialism, for example, which served as a critical backdrop to the fiction produced from the turn of the century on into the thirties, was itself a gendered debate: Labour socialism, considered "ethical" rather than "scientific" and associated with Keir Hardie's slogan "socialism is much more an affair of the heart than of the intellect," was denounced by the British Communist Party as an essentially feminized political movement.[18]

The spirit of the times also, of course, affected male working-class writers. Yet the instability of romance in working-class experience is in some ways made use of more openly and easily by men, who are not quite as implicated in its effects and exclusions. They enjoy the power to legitimize romance by pressing it to serve a more strictly socialist agenda in their fiction. In novels such as C. Allen Clarke's *The Knobstick* (1893), Harold Heslop's *The Gate of a Strange Field* (1929), and Lewis Jones's *We Live* (1939), romance comes to signify the possibility of a different social system that allows for "civilized" bonds of intimacy at the same time that it meets material needs. At once resisting and desiring the very "right" to claim feminine status, the female texts convey another kind of vexed relationship to writing and to the romance convention. They seek a "right to play" that for women can represent either liberation or confinement (or both), depending on class positioning. More than a deliberate intervention into gender relations and a gendered literary practice, romance serves the critical function of allowing a more veiled critique of working-class subjectivity through its alternate expressions of dissatisfaction, longing, and refusal. It is finally in the *intersection* of such gestures and desires that romance helps to redefine the scope of politics in working-class culture and of "political" narrative in working-class writing.

Notes

1. James Haslam, *The Press and the People: An Estimate of Reading in Working-Class Districts* (Manchester: Manchester City News, 1906), 15–16.

2. See "Factory Intelligence," March 1909, "The Factory Slave," March 1909, and "The Tree of Knowledge," December 1909, as well as her ardent feminist pieces, "Our Right to Play," April 1909, and "Modern Womanhood," August 1909. For a brief account of Carnie Holdsworth's years with the *Woman Worker*, see Edmund Frow and Ruth Frow, "Ethel Carnie: Writer, Feminist, and Socialist," in *The Rise of Socialist Fiction, 1880–1914*, edited by H. Gustav Klaus (New York: St. Martin's Press; Brighton: Harvester Press, 1987), 251–66.

3. Ironically, she merits a line in Standish Meacham's historical study *A Life Apart: The English Working Class, 1890–1914* (Cambridge: Harvard University Press, 1977), but even there she is mistakenly identified as a "middle-class social worker" due to her "right to play" stance in the *Woman Worker* (28).

4. See Frow and Frow, "Ethel Carnie"; H. Gustav Klaus, "Silhouettes of Revolution: Some Neglected Novels of the Early 1920s," in *The Socialist Novel in Britain: Towards the Recovery of a Tradition*, edited by H. Gustav Klaus (New York: St. Martin's Press; Brighton: Harvester Press, 1982), 88–109, especially 94–97; and P. M. Ashraf, *Introduction to Working-Class Literature in Great Britain, Part II: Prose* (Berlin: VEB Kongress-und Werbedruck Oberlungwitz, 1979), 176–95.

5. For the former tendency, see such classics in the field as Elaine Showalter, *A Literature of Their Own: British Women Novelists from Brontë to Lessing* (Princeton, N.J.: Princeton University Press, 1977); Sandra Gilbert and Susan Gubar, *The Madwoman in the Attic: The Woman Writer and the Nineteenth-Century Literary Imagination* (New Haven: Yale University Press, 1979); Judith Lowder Newton, *Women, Power, and Subversion: Social Strategies in British Fiction, 1778–1860* (Athens: University of Georgia Press, 1981); and Rachel Blau DuPlessis, *Writing beyond the Ending: Narrative Strategies of Twentieth-Century Women Writers* (Bloomington: Indiana University Press, 1985). For the latter position, see Tania Modleski, *Loving with a Vengeance: Mass-Produced Fantasies for Women* (Hamden, Conn.: Archon Books, 1982); Janice Radway, *Reading the Romance* (Chapel Hill: University of North Carolina Press, 1984); and Leslie Rabine, "Romance in the Age of Electronics," in *Feminist Criticism and Social Change*, edited by Judith Newton and Deborah Rosenfelt (New York: Methuen, 1985), 249–67.

6. Modleski, *Loving with a Vengeance*, 30.

7. Jane Lewis notes the pervasive lack of enthusiasm surrounding the marriage ceremony in many working-class neighborhoods and suggests that the ideology of motherhood, which received quite a renewed boost in the Edwardian period, was due in part to bourgeois anxiety about frequent common-law

marriages and separations among the working class. See *Women in England, 1870–1950: Sexual Divisions and Social Changes* (Bloomington: Indiana University Press, 1984), 11.

8. Indeed, in autobiographical writing produced by working-class women at this time, susceptibility to romance ideology is associated with guilt, danger, and a sense of thrill, as well as outright scorn. See, for instance, Mrs. Layton's "Memories of Seventy Years," in *Life as We Have Known It*, edited by Margaret Llewelyn Davies (London: Hogarth Press, 1931), 1–55, in which she admits to her "fascination," as a domestic servant, with "trashy" serial tales but notes that memories of her mother made her "give up" the habit (26–27). See also Hannah Mitchell, *The Hard Way Up* (London: Virago Press, 1977); Women's Cooperative Guild, *Working Women and Divorce* (1911; reprint, New York: Garland Publishing, 1980); and Elizabeth Roberts, *A Woman's Place: An Oral History of Working-Class Women, 1890–1940* (Oxford: Basil Blackwell, 1984). Interestingly, even in Haslam's survey, the women respondents' enthusiasm for love stories is qualified by a preference for tales about "proper love" involving aristocrats rather than workers (16). For a contemporary look at the relation between romance and working-class women, see Angela McRobbie's "Working Class Girls and the Culture of Femininity," in *Women Take Issue*, edited by Women's Studies Group, Centre for Contemporary Cultural Studies (Boston: Routledge and Kegan Paul, 1978), 96–108. While focusing on the girls' desire for romance, McRobbie also notes their mothers' influence in subverting romance ideology.

9. The "statement of aim" adopted by the Writers' International in the early 1930s perhaps offers the most obvious evidence of such a stance (see *Left Review* 1 [December 1934]), yet see also important earlier articles in *Plebs*, which advocated the development of a "fighting culture for a fighting class": "The Workers' Culture" (February 1922) and "Marxism and Literature" (October 1922). A seemingly minor piece in *Left Review* also helps to illustrate this point. In "Factory Library," Ann Gresser contrasts a "boss-run" library, which offered women employees romance and "sex" stories, with a worker-run library, which eliminated romance entirely in favor of books that "helped to make Trade Unionists, Communists, and militant wworkers" (1 [February 1935]: 177–78).

10. See Jack Mitchell, "Early Harvest: Three Anti-Capitalist Novels Published in 1914," in *The Socialist Novel in Britain*, 67–88; Carole Snee, "Working-Class Literature or Proletarian Writing?," in *Culture and Crisis in Britain in the '30s*, edited by Jon Clarke et al. (London: Lawrence and Wishart, 1979), 165–91; and Graham Holderness, "Miners in the Novel: From Bourgeois to Proletarian Fiction," in *The British Working-Class Novel in the Twentieth Century*, edited by Jeremy Hawthorn (London: E. Arnold, 1984), 19–32.

11. Though the shop is quite modest, Carrie apparently owns it. This places her among the more "respectable" in her class even as it fails to bring her any real economic security.

12. Ethel Carnie, *Miss Nobody* (London: Methuen, 1913), 1.

13. Despite the novel's publication date, H. Gustav Klaus speculates that *This Slavery* was written a decade or so earlier; he notes its occasional references to prewar historical events and political figures and, interestingly, what he perceives to be a "strong emphasis on suffering and brutalisation" associated with

a "distinctly prewar working-class sensibility" (94). But as my essay argues, the novel is in fact noteworthy for its faith in working-class solidarity and a narrative structure characteristic of later, class-conscious fiction.

14. Ashraf, *Working-Class Literature*, 195, 194.

15. Ethel Carnie Holdsworth, *This Slavery* (London: Labour Publishing Co., 1925), 144.

16. For a comprehensive discussion of the interworkings of shame, exposure, and resistance in British working-class texts, see my doctoral dissertation, "Recovering the 'Narrow Plot of Acquisitiveness and Desire': Reproduction, Resistance, and British Working-Class Writing, 1890–1945" (University of Washington, 1990).

17. *Sunday Worker*, 5, 26 July 1925. I am indebted to H. Gustav Klaus's essay "Silhouettes of Revolution" for bringing this crucial exchange to my attention.

18. As Stuart MacIntyre has shown, Labour socialism's optimism and emphasis on winning for workers a pleasurable way of life (in addition to better wages) appeared naive, reformist, and "weak." See his extensive examination of the splits between Labour socialism and Marxism among sectors of the British working class in *A Proletarian Science: Marxism in Britain, 1917–1933* (Cambridge: Cambridge University Press, 1980), 47–65; 106–26. MacIntyre's research offers suggestive evidence of the gendered dimension to this conflict, but he fails to pursue the implications.

MAROULA JOANNOU

"The Woman in the Little House":

Leonora Eyles and Socialist Feminism

Margaret Protests, a novel by Leonora Eyles, who is remembered, if at all, as a well-known journalist and a respected "agony aunt" rather than as a writer of fiction, may be located in nineteenth-century utopian traditions of writing.[1] Set in the slums of East London, Eyles's book subverts the Victorian and Edwardian slum novel by taking over some of its familiar elements and giving them a feminist specificity.

I wish to show how Eyles inherited and extended feminist traditions that have existed within socialist politics and to explore some of the tensions and contradictions that arose in her attempt to express feminist ideas as part of a socialist project. Eyles was not only concerned with questions of class in *Margaret Protests*; she also sought to focus on and to connect different aspects of struggle of crucial importance to women, such as motherhood and concern for the environment. The protest to which her title refers is double-edged, directed both against the excesses of industrial capitalism and against masculinist ideas and assumptions within a socialist culture. Before I discuss *Margaret Protests* and Eyles's other writings in more detail, I shall make some general observations about socialist and feminist approaches to neglected and forgotten works.

The enterprise of socialist literary criticism has its own temporalities and histories, which fall largely outside the scope of this essay. However, the retrieval of lost texts and writers, which has constituted an important aspect of feminist critical enterprise, has also been a major strand within socialist critical practice. Socialist critics have made a priority of questioning the hierarchies of literary value by focusing on writing by working-class authors or with working-class subject matter. Indeed, the revival of interest in texts as diverse as Charlotte Perkins Gilman's *The Yellow Wallpaper*, Lewis Grassic Gibbon's *A Scots Quair*, Lewis Jones's *Cwmardy*, and Kate Chopin's *The Awakening* is due to the efforts of feminists and socialists who have taken these novels, and others like them, as good examples of a literary culture that may embody values radically opposed to the dominant literary culture.[2]

H. Gustav Klaus has been the prime mover of initiatives that have questioned the existing constitution of the literary field by unearthing and analyzing lost works, a task that has gathered momentum in recent years. The publication of several compilations of essays, including Klaus's *The Socialist Novel in Britain*, *The Literature of Labour*, and *The Rise of Socialist Fiction, 1880–1914*, Jeremy Hawthorn's *The British Working-Class Novel in the Twentieth Century*, Ken Worpole's *Dockers and Detectives*, and Andy Croft's *Red Letter Days*,[3] has usefully augmented our understanding of the rise of socialist fiction, the literature of London's East End, and worker-writers like the Tyneside novelist Jack Common. These excavations have brought to light a rich and varied seam of socialist and working-class fiction from the nineteenth century and earlier, of considerable complexity and interest. These works allow us to glimpse a long-ignored literary culture that profoundly alters our sense of history and literature. But in arranging for forgotten texts to be republished, socialists have, by and large, proved much less successful than their feminist counterparts.[4] Many socialist writers remain out of print and unknown, a fact that places tight constrictions on any counter-hegemonic project of retrieval. As Graham Holderness has put it, until "working-class novels from the nineteenth and early twentieth centuries are reprinted and educationally mobilised on a much larger scale, there can be no effective general recovery to shift radically the political balance of the literary tradition."[5]

How does the work of socialist critics concerned with working-class writing relate to feminism? The type of criticism that Klaus, for example, represents is political criticism originating from deep socialist conviction. His work is characteristic of a kind of intervention in cultural politics impelled by the desire to defend as well as explicate. The relationship of the critic to the text, a relationship that Klaus exemplifies, is essentially custodial, the critic exercising a kind of careful trusteeship over works of importance. Klaus's attitudes to literature are shaped by his attitudes to class. As the literary is subsumed into the political in his criticism, what matters about a text is often the class of the writer and what the text has to say to the class-conscious reader of our time. What I wish to contest, however, is the way that Klaus and others with whom he is associated reproduce through their own literary practice many of the most deeply ingrained and least constructive traditions of the labor movement. Although their literary criticism is neither overtly sexist nor misogynistic, it nonetheless perpetuates a chain of assumptions that contain the subordination of women at their center. One example is the concept of the working class to which Klaus subscribes, the traditional concept of the working class aggregated, for the most part, in urban communities and deeply conscious of and prizing highly particular aspects of its own culture and experience. The aspects of working-class experience that are valued include the cult of masculinity, which is often confused with working-class militancy. In giving primacy to male experience rather than to female, this concept clearly marginalizes and excludes women.

Ken Worpole's *Dockers and Detectives* provides another example of an attempt at cultural reconstruction "of some particular patterns of reading and writing during the past fifty years that conventional literary criticism has ignored."[6] Worpole concentrates on detective stories and escape stories, on writing from London's Jewish East End, and on working-class writers like James Hanley, Jim Phelan, and George Garrett. To be fair, Worpole volunteers the information that many women, including working-class women, feel estranged from popular vernacular writing because it clearly emanates from a world from which they have been historically and culturally excluded. "They feel, no doubt correctly, that it reflects a certain kind of working-class male bravura which, by definition, is oppressive." Nevertheless, Worpole's deep commitment to the working man obliges him to defend, critically, vernacular realism "because of its narrative strength and popular accessibility to the language of everyday life."[7]

What have working-class women read? Worpole admits that women do not read stories of male bravura. What have they written? Since the writers, like Phelan and Hanley, whom Worpole chooses to discuss are invariably male, we have no way of knowing from his account. Moreover, since he does not even consider the question worth exploring, the reading and writing experiences of working-class women are a structuring absence in his study. Consequently, one is left with the impression of working-class culture, and of the popular fiction of the last fifty years, as a tradition of laboring men reading celebratory accounts of male prowess—precisely the image evoked by his title, *Dockers and Detectives*.

To take a final example, David Smith's discussion of Ellen Wilkinson's *Clash*, a novel set in part in a northern mining village after the General Strike, illustrates how gender-based notions of appropriate subject matter for a political novel hover below the surface of the male critic's writing. In *Socialist Propaganda in the Twentieth-Century British Novel*, Smith begins his analysis of *Clash* by quoting Wilkinson: "It's no use my pretending that I'm more interested in A's falling in love with B and the possible reaction of C, than in politics, because I'm not. There isn't really anything I care as much about as politics, and there's no use in pretending there is!"[8] These comments, which were not made in reference to *Clash*, are cited by Smith to justify his own view that *Clash* is not really a romantic novel—although that is exactly what it might seem to an unprejudiced reader. The implication is that romance somehow drains the novel of its political content. Far from constituting the essence of Wilkinson's novel, the presence of romantic and sexual interest amounts, for Smith, to a distraction from serious matters. What the critic clearly lacks is any understanding of how heavily sexual politics touched on Wilkinson's own life. As Betty Vernon's biography makes clear,[9] Wilkinson's personal dilemmas and choices (the conflicts arising from her view that a democratic and liberated sexual politics is attainable only as part of a more general political struggle) are clearly refracted in the dilemmas and choices of Joan Craig in her semiautobiographical novel.

There is no reason, in principle, why socialist critics who are male should not be able to produce work with a satisfactory focus on women. Why, then, is the practice clearly so far removed from the possibility? No work of socialist criticism, for example, has yet included discussion of Leonora Eyles, a highly popular and versatile socialist writer of the 1920s. I do not believe that Eyles has simply escaped the attention of those male socialist critics, whose knowledge of the 1920s is exhaustive. Nor do I believe that she is simply considered to be too poor a stylist for discussion. The fact is that male socialist critics have consistently proven far more adept at recognizing male aspirations than female and have consistently failed to recognize the implications, for those thinking creatively about human possibility, of much imaginative writing by women. Yet it should be obvious, as Ethel Mannin pointed out in 1937, that women also dream.[10] But collections like *The Socialist Novel in Britain*, despite their ritual disclaimers to the contrary, do not usually admit women's writing that does not reflect the more traditional concerns of the labor movement. Indeed, when these collections speak of radical imperatives or aspirations, the imperatives and aspirations of men are assumed to be the same as, or to stand in for, those of women. Since *The Socialist Novel in Britain* is subtitled *Towards the Recovery of a Tradition*, feminists might well ask to whom tradition belongs.

Feminist historians have drawn attention to the ways in which socialist traditions have systematically suppressed the voices of women. Barbara Taylor's groundbreaking study of the nineteenth-century cooperative movement, *Eve and the New Jerusalem*, is germane to my own argument. Taylor demonstrated how a scrutiny of the socialist tradition in the light of its contribution to the emancipation of women produces a rather different image from the one dominating most socialists' view of the past. *Eve and the New Jerusalem* outlines the consequences of the waning of the early utopian imagination and the death of the commitment to a new social order premised on equality between the sexes, two important elements in early socialist thinking. "As the older schemes for emancipating 'all humanity at once' were displaced by the economic struggles of a single class, so issues central to that earlier dream—marriage, reproduction, family life—were transformed from political questions into 'merely private' ones, while women who persisted in pressing such issues were frequently condemned as bourgeois 'women's rightsers'. Organized feminism was increasingly viewed not as an essential component of socialist struggle, but as a disunifying, diversionary force, with no inherent connection to the socialist tradition. And thus the present disowns the past, severing connections and suppressing ambitions once so vital to those who forged them."[11] The narrow view of socialism that Taylor so eloquently and authoritatively decries is the narrow view of socialism that is so deeply inscribed in much socialist literary criticism.

Women's writing, which maintains that an essential aspect of a total transformation of society must be the transformation of relations between the sexes, therefore presents a serious challenge to socialist men. Its visionary and utopian elements cannot be unproblematically accommodated within the contracted socialist project that Barbara Taylor and others have shown as having systematically marginalized or excluded visionary and utopian concerns. This being the case, there is clearly a danger that women's writing will be omitted from general discussions of the socialist novel or will be subsumed within such discussions as a tributary of other, more important currents.

That the 1920s was a time of great flowering and creativity on the part of women may be borne out not through lengthy excavations in university library deposits but by a scrutiny of the volumes, currently on booksellers' shelves, that have been reissued by the feminist presses. But works that are clearly of interest to feminism have been excluded from discussion by socialists.[12] Winifred Holtby, for example, does not feature in discussions of socialist writing of the 1920s. Much of the fiction that, in E. P. Thompson's useful phrase,[13] has been rescued from the condescension of posterity relates in only troubled and uneasy ways to the limited range that has been discussed under the rubric of socialist writing of the immediate postwar period. The relationship between feminist and socialist writing would, of course, be a good deal less troubled and uneasy if the definition of socialist writing were broadened along the lines suggested by the critic Kiernan Ryan. Ryan's imaginatively all-encompassing definition of socialist writing breaks decisively with narrow, economistic, and prescriptively class-based definitions of socialism. Ryan begins by uncompromisingly rejecting "the mere fictional reproduction of some ready-made, finalised version of socialist ideology" as totally inadequate to help bring about the "emancipative transformation of the prevailing social relations into a more truly human socialist society." The critic adds, "The essential function and value of fiction as such, and of a *consciously* materialist and dialectical fiction above all, reside in its relentless, uncompromising interrogation of the received in the light of an ever-changing reality, its restless explorations, beyond the given horizon of experience and knowledge—including, where truth and need demand, beyond the hitherto accepted formulations and prescriptions of socialism."[14]

As Carolyn Steedman has reflected, in piecing together the patchwork of her mother's and grandmother's lives for her biographical *Landscape for a Good Woman*, "It was the women who told you about the public world, of work and politics, the details of social distinction."[15] Yet the literature of labor is manifestly a literature in which women do not tell their daughters or their sons about "the public world, of work and politics." On the contrary, the public world of work and politics is frequently represented as a world that women are assumed neither to enter nor to understand. As Steedman shows, the discontents of women, as given in their accounts, are not the discontents of men, and these accounts shatter the glass in which men have all too often been able to see themselves reflected as good providers and protectors of the family. Moreover, these accounts hold up for inspection men who offer no protective care to women and who are engaged in love affairs with the hard traditions of manual labor that can be conducted only in the absence of women. Class consciousness, it turns out, is often, by a sleight of hand, male and not female consciousness and is far removed from feminist consciousness or consciousness of feminism.

To develop the points that I have made so far, I will focus closely on Leonora Eyles, a curious and contradictory figure whose early didactic, polemic novels concern the narrowness of working people's lives and clearly place the author on the side of those whose desire to interpret the world has been matched by a desire to change it.[16] The roots of Eyles's feminism lie in nineteenth-century utopian traditions exemplified by women like Catharine Barmby, a founder of the Communist church, a small religious sect committed to feminist and cooperative ideals. The vision of socialism that is exemplified in her novels rejects an economic and social order based on competition. Moreover, she insists that the relationships of subordination between men and women are no less damaging than the relationships between employers and workers. All this is, of course, deeply troubling to those whose idea of socialism is scientific materialism. My analysis of Eyles's early novels will show how her work generates a set of questions that reflect a feminist critique and sensibility. Furthermore, these questions provide a challenge not only to the canon of literature but *to the literature of labor itself.*

In 1920 the critic R. Brimley Johnson described the postwar literary aspirations of the woman writer: "She is seeking, with passionate determination, for that Reality which is behind the material, the things that matter, spiritual things, ultimate Truth. And here she finds man an outsider, wilfully blind, purposely indifferent."[17] Brimley Johnson did not discuss Eyles's fiction, but his description certainly encompasses the quests of heroines of her early novels. Each of these women—Margaret Wayre, Helen Clevion, and Marcella Laschcairn—struggles to reclaim the identity that a materialistic industrial system has unjustly denied her. In her first novels, Eyles dramatizes the refusal and questioning of that system, not in the name of violent revolution of class consciousness but in the name of a radically other social order that is predicated on the imagination, on liberty, and on beauty.

What would a feminist criticism that wished to illuminate feminist consciousness in socialist writing have to say about Eyles? In the first place, I think that we would have to say, as did Mary Agnes Hamilton in 1922,[18] that Eyles is in many respects an exasperating writer, her potpourri of religious allegory, mysticism, and social reform uneasily conscripting naturalistic detail to a florid, overblown prose style. Yet even at those moments when Eyles's prose style fails to convince (for example, in the lofty, exalted passages of dialogue between men and women, passages with heavy biblical overtones that pretend to naturalism and break all its rules), much can still be found of interest. Eyles's women characters are often principled, strongly independent, and proudly resilient. In the militancy of their unsupported motherhood, Helen in *Hidden Lives*, Margaret in *Margaret Protests*, and Marcella in *Captivity* bravely defy convention. We should note as well that Eyles's fiction in many ways resembles the utopian fantasies of Victorian women novelists,[19] linking the sexual nonconformity and social dissidence within the fiction to a wider feminist and socialist vision. Finally, we would recognize the woman in the little house as a recurring image in Eyles's work. This metonymic projection of woman's isolation is used to stress each woman's distance from the collectivity of other women, to symbolize how patriarchal social relationships confine, divide, and isolate women.

Who, then, was Leonora Eyles? And what is her relationship to this overwhelmingly male tradition of socialist writing? She was born Leonora Pitcairn in 1889 into a well-to-do family of Staffordshire pottery-owners whose fortunes subsequently declined. After the death of both her parents, she was left to the care of a young stepmother, her father's second wife, whom she detested. Leonora ran away to London and from that day never saw her stepmother again. A naive eighteen-year-old exposed to all the potential dangers of the capital city, Leonora tried to cope as best she could, but she often found herself hungry. Having to pay for rent and coal out of the meager wages she earned by addressing envelopes in a basement office left hardly enough money for food. Tempted by an advertisement for domestic servants in Australia, she sold one or two possessions left to her by her mother to raise the passage money and sailed in 1907 with ten shillings in her pocket.[20]

In Australia she appears to have been happy, working hard all day on the land and living in a tent, with her nearest neighbor ten miles away. Later she dated her swift conversion to "revolutionariness" to her days in Australia: "When I had been there a few months I had changed from a timid-mouse sort of person into a fighter." She married A. W. Eyles and resolved at the same time that no man would ever support her. In 1926 she was able to record, with some pride, "And no one ever has."[21] The Australian experiences also gave her firsthand information for a novel, *Captivity*, and the account of Marcella's marriage in *Captivity* may well be based on Eyles's own.

Since her autobiography, *The Ram Escapes*, ends on the eve of her departure to Australia, piecing together the fragments of her life after that is not easy. We cannot be sure why or when Eyles returned to London. By the time she was twenty-four, she already had three small children and was living in a little terraced house in Peckham struggling to make a living for them all. Her husband, "W," having left her when the children were still very young, she was reduced to making factory garments, typing at ten pence per thousand words, and taking on whatever badly paid jobs she could find to do at home. The work exhausted her but hardly brought in enough money to feed or clothe her growing family.[22] On the verge of despair, pushing her pram up Peckham Rye (where William Blake had once seen a tree of angels), she chanced to see an advertisement in the *Times* for a young writer able to write appeals for a childcare organization. Her career as a professional writer began when she was selected from more than five hundred applicants.[23] When war broke out, she volunteered to become one of two thousand women working on munitions in the Woolwich Arsenal.[24] After the war came a period of intensive writing when she wrote most of her books, including her popular crime fiction, and produced millions of words of journalism—writing for George Lansbury's *Labour Leader*, editing the problem page of *Modern Woman* and the woman's page in the *Daily Herald*, and, under the pen name "Martha," taking over from Winifred Horrabin as the woman's page editor of the *Miner* in 1927.

In the expanding market in women's magazines of the 1920s and 1930s, Eyles was able to carve out a niche for herself as one of the country's most respected agony aunts. As Ros Coward has pointed out, the advice column functions as a sort of poor woman's introduction to the world of professional therapy, but the centrality given to sexual problems, the exhortation to reveal the intimate details of sexual life, dates only from the end of World War II.[25] It was through the advice column—a revealing mode of communication largely ignored by socialist historians and cultural critics of the interwar period—that Eyles chose to reach out to thousands of women, as sisters and daughters, mothers and lovers, workers in both the home and the public workplace, and the women read her columns avidly. A committed pacifist after World War I, she argued the case for nonviolent action in the *Labour Leader* and the *Daily Herald* whenever her editor allowed her, although, like many women, she abandoned pacifism at the start of the 1939 war.[26] The popular success of *Eat Well in War-Time* in 1940 was followed by a short-lived problem page in the *Tribune* from April to July 1941, through which she offered advice on nutrition, the problems of evacuee families, birth control, and family relations in war. A convert to vegetarianism and to Theosophy in her later years, she remained a socialist until the end of her life in 1960.

Leonora Eyles's documentary study of working women's lives in Peckham, *The Woman in the Little House*, first appeared in serial form in *Time and Tide* in 1922. *The Woman in the Little House* is a work of social investigation (Maud Pember Reeves's *Round About a Pound a Week* is a good point of comparison)[27] intended to bring women's experience of poverty, poor nutrition, and bad housing to a middle-class readership. The author was attacked by some women who felt that working women were responsible for their own living conditions. Honesty, thrift, and cleanliness, they argued, should not be beyond the reach of any woman, however poor. Her critics pointed out that it was only because she had come from a different social background that she was unhappy. Eyles responded that her neighbors in Peckham ("vaguely dissatisfied, uncomprehendingly bad-tempered") were more dissatisfied than she.[28] Her renewed defense of the woman in the little house was impassioned. "I want her to demand things, to demand life's best bargains, not its remainders; because she deserves the very best from life." The episode confirmed her deep hatred of the kind of leisured, privileged women who had criticized her most vocally. "The dragon fly is beautiful, the ornithorhynchus is unexpected, the cow is useful. What are these women for?"[29]

In 1922 Eyles was at pains to stress that she was no rich woman slumming, no journalist descending into the underworld to jog the conscience of the rich. *The Woman in the Little House* was written from the firsthand experience of one who had lived in that house and known its misery. In that Peckham slum, she had experienced discomfort, ugliness, and irritation. In it, two of her children had been born. For five years the conditions she shared with her young family effectively meant that she had no privacy whatsoever. She wrote: "In bed, in the kitchen, shopping, gardening, always was some-one very near to me, touching me most of the time. I felt sometimes as though I could come to hate these crowding people who were really so dear to me" (54). Indeed, she had worked so hard and known so little pleasure as an adult that she felt miserable if compelled to take a day's holiday.[30]

By 1932, however, Eyles's domestic circumstances had changed for the better. Happily married to David Murray (who was editor of the *Times Literary Supplement* from 1938 to 1944), she had clearly reentered the world of middle-class comfort. The "Life and You" column in the inaugural issue of *Woman's Own* introduced Eyles to her readers as "the woman who understands," referring briefly to her history of personal hardship in order to gain the trust and confidence of potential correspondents.[31] But the "happy snapshots" of Eyles in the library or in the "charming orchard" of her country home in Sussex, in subsequent issues, project a different image and speak of a gracious mode of living that the woman in the little house could never hope to emulate. For despite the firsthand knowledge of working women's conditions, Eyles's writings exhibit the unmistakable hallmarks of a woman cut adrift from her own class. The distaste that she felt for the meanness of East End streets and her deep sense that what the East Enders needed was art, beauty, and poetry confirmed her impressions as those of an outsider and proved her critics to some degree right. However well disposed toward the women she described, she did not, in the final analysis, belong, although her own experience of slum life, and her feminist militancy, clearly distanced her from other middle-class women.

After the war, probably because hundreds of women who read her columns in the *Daily Herald* and the *Labour Leader* wrote to her, Eyles was often asked to speak at trade-union recruiting meetings. The factory women who drifted into these meetings seemed to her utterly worn out, some taking needlework home to complete, although this was illegal. Eyles was deeply moved by their condition and came to believe that women should stay at home and look after their children. Women were being pushed back into the home at this time, and many feminists were fighting for women's right to paid work,[32] but Eyles still defended her position. "They should be free to work away from home or not as they like, but they should not be driven by poverty into factories."[33] For a time Eyles had herself worked for Dr. Barnardo's, the children's charity. Looking through their archives, she had noticed that almost every unruly, neglected, or destitute child was the child of a woman who went out to work.[34] She believed that full equality for women must involve the reconstruction of society so that the needs of women and children were placed at the center of the social agenda. For her it was never just a question of rights to be bargained for or legislation to be won. Motherhood could be made efficient only if the state recognized its importance. She objected to the phrase "the endowment of motherhood," with its clear suggestion of charity or largess. "Women don't want charity. They want and deserve wages."[35]

In 1926 the publication of *Women's Problems of To-day* triggered an acrimonious correspondence between Marie Stopes, the pioneering advocate of family-planning methods, and Eyles. Stopes, who claimed to have "the intimate confidence of hundreds of thousands of working-class women,"[36] objected to the following "reactionary and misleading" statement in Eyles's book: "When men and women are no longer dispossessed the problem of Birth Control will cease to exist."[37] Stopes wrongly supposed Eyles to be associated with the strong Catholic lobby in the Labour Party opposed to birth control. This was far from the case. In fact, Eyles was prepared to offer contraceptive information to

any woman who wanted it and often referred her London readers to
family-planning clinics for advice. As a result of her own unhappy experiences ("married when a child, to a dipsomaniac and kept having
babies"),[38] Eyles feared that birth control might sink women into "the
dreary morass of sex obsession" by encouraging them to believe that
sex was the most important aspect of woman's existence. However, her
belief that contraception might make working-class women vulnerable
to sexual exploitation at the hands of men ("there is so much more in
life than sexual connection, even the modern type with pessary all complete")[39] was always coupled with a deep concern about the plight of
poor women burdened with unwanted children. In 1927 the correspondence between the two grew appreciably warmer as it became clear that
both recognized the urgent need for clinics to be set up to help women
in the mining districts.[40]

　　These feminist and socialist concerns inform *Margaret Protests*, Eyles's
first novel and her most important. A best-seller in 1919, it remained
popular with the reading public as late as the 1960s when it was reprinted as a Portway imprint,[41] a label under which books in demand
in public lending libraries were occasionally reissued. This account of a
woman's voyage through the social and cultural order traces the route
of Margaret Wayre, a young woman who marries "beneath her sta-
tion," and charts her growing disillusionment with a life of domestic
drudgery. The novel highlights the dichotomy between the Victorian
ideal of womanhood and the degrading reality that Margaret experiences. The subtext of *Margaret Protests*, published shortly after Marie
Stopes's *Married Love* and *Wise Parenthood* (1918),[42] is birth control, a
subject about which Eyles had learned from reading Havelock Ellis and
then Marie Stopes.[43] At its simplest, the novel tells how a young widow
is driven by poverty to set up a business dealing in abortion-inducing
medicines in order to support her family. Though her illicit business
flourishes, Margaret suffers deep pangs of conscience about how her
profits are being made. After the death of her young son and the defection of her partner, Kitty, she decides to trek out to the depths of the
countryside to begin her life afresh. It is an extraordinary tale, one that
includes features of melodrama, of the social exploration found in the
industrial and urban novels of the nineteenth century, and of feminist
utopianism. Margaret's is the story of any woman who fights back, who
breaks out of the patriarchal incarceration that decrees rigid roles for
women. The novel vividly dramatizes the possibility of questioning and
refusing those roles.

　　To understand how *Margaret Protests* relates to other slum novels, we need to remind ourselves that the slum novel is almost entirely a product of the male imagination, since most slum novels were written by men. If we were asked to draw up a list of late-nineteenth- and early-twentieth-century slum novelists who immortalized working-class London, and the East End in particular, the names would probably include Walter Besant, George Gissing, Arthur Morrison, William Pett Ridge, Henry Nevinson, Somerset Maugham, Jack London, Edwin Pugh, and Clarence Rook.[44] Women's names do not feature among the lists of writers who mythologized the East End by exploiting, as Besant and others became famous for doing, the romance of the East End, nor are they to be found as authors of the so-called social realism of the 1890s with its booze and bonhomie. Margaret Harkness (John Law, pseudonym) is better remembered as the recipient of Engels's letter explaining his preference for Balzac over Zola than for her novel, *A City Girl* (1887), which sparked Engels's correspondence. Her contemporary Constance Howell is today unknown.[45]

Margaret Protests contains many recognizable features of Edwardian and Victorian representations of urban working-class life; echoes of slum novels such as Morrison's *The Hole in the Wall* or Nevinson's *Neighbours of Ours* will be obvious. Yet the novel has a number of features that clearly set it apart from such representations. Extending and developing the traditions of radical protest exemplified by writers such as William Blake, who used industrial artifacts like the factory or the mill as powerful symbols of oppression, Eyles, as we have seen, found an iconography better suited to expressing the servitude of woman. The elements of overt social protest in the novel center on the little house as a supreme symbol of women's subjugation. In *Hidden Lives*, her second novel, the little house is personified; the slum Ruthers Row is "twelve small cottages, with earth floors and gaping walls, their heads propped despondently in the smoky air, their feet ankle-deep in ashes and garbage" (8).

The usual distinctions between the workplace and the home are questioned in her writing. For women, the workplace is the home, and the home the workplace, and we are continually reminded of this fact through the careful choice of social-realist detail in *Margaret Protests*. In this novel, the only men at home during the day are the very young, the sick, or the old, and the only well-dressed men to be found in the labyrinth of streets in South London, in which *Margaret Protests* is set, are harbingers of trouble of some sort. Many women writers—such as Kathleen Woodward, whose autobiography, *Jipping Street*, tells of growing up female and working-class in prewar Bermondsey, or Kathleen

Dayus, whose *Her People* tells of life in Birmingham early in this century—have provided illuminating insights into the working-class experience.[46] However, Eyles belongs to the select company of novelists
for whom the concentration on women's lives is such that the working
class *is* effectively female. Margaret Harkness, Constance Howell, Olive
Birrell, Emma Leslie, and Isabella Ford had all written of slum conditions before her.[47] But a writer who used her anomalous identity as a
refugee stranded between cultures and classes and as a mother of three
to describe slum life from the perspective of a working mother is a rarity
indeed.

The following extract from *Margaret Protests* is taken from a point
midway in the narrative when Margaret has returned to Peckham to
take an observer, Falcon Smith, on a tour of the area. The fact-finding
journey through the East End—bounded by The Elephant and Castle,
Camberwell Green, and Walworth Road—corresponds to the literary
exploitation of unchartered London from the Victorian writers James
Greenwood and George Sims onward.[48] However, we should note that
it is a woman's first-person narrative that is the center of interpretation.
This constitutes a departure from the conventions of the mid- and late-
Victorian classic journeys of exploration, in which we would expect the
burden of exposition to fall upon a man.

> We went away leaving Mrs. Quinn dishing up the "stoo" so that
> Mr. Quinn could fall on it the moment he came in—and Falcon
> Smith, with a deep breath, said, as he stood on the pavement:
>
> "Where can we get a taxi?"
>
> "Not here, I'm afraid. We'll have to get the tram to Camber-
> well Green".
>
> So we went along little shabby streets to the tram—past green
> grocers who shouted their wares aggressively, past the usual fried
> fish shops, past butchers' shops with meat piled in the open win-
> dow, where frowsy looking women pawed and mauled it.
>
> We said nothing until, passing one of these shops, where we
> could hear the man arguing with a woman about a piece of bone
> which she thought ought not to "count"—I said, bitterly:
>
> "That's the sort of thing women live for—that's working
> women's life—haporths of bone! pennorths of cabbages, pen-
> norths of meat! Washing dirty clothes—in tiny sculleries where
> they can't get enough water at work to wash a doll's handkerchief
> decently! Drying them in smuts until they're grey and everything's
> grey. Fretting and worrying because 'he' likes 'stoo' and Doll likes

bloaters. Oh, can't you see the appallingness of it! And then men have the impudence, the cruelty to say that women are petty! Good heavens, can you take a man from selling farthing candles behind a little village counter, and make him a successful Chancellor of the Exchequer? Then how can you take a woman from dirty washing, cooking food, and all the petty, material things you can think of, and expect her to be big?"

"You feel this very much," he said quietly.

"Yes, I do. I'm hot about it. That house of Mrs. Quinn's—it was mine in replica. Except for this, Mrs. Quinn is quite a skilful housewife. I never was. So my house was probably worse than that, on washing days especially. Then—Mrs. Quinn hasn't the living to earn. There's a 'abby there, as beast of burden, you known. So there again her place is probably better than mine." (207–8)

Whereas the detail of this passage, with its emphasis on ugliness, its ill-kept sordid shops and "frowsy looking women" who "pawed and mauled" meat, is clearly reminiscent of turn-of-the-century naturalism, we should also notice that it contains inflections indigenous to neither turn-of-the-century naturalism nor the slum novel, inflections that have been clearly imported to serve feminist ends. Were we, for example, to come across Margaret's labored explanations about the lives of the poor (statements that are ostensibly addressed to Falcon but are clearly intended for the consumption of the reader) elsewhere, the message that our reading of the Victorian slum novel has habituated us to expect would be different. Having apprehended the horrors of the slums, we would expect to be asked to do all within our power to bring the horrors that we had witnessed to an end.

Margaret's speech is predicated not on the question of poverty in the midst of plenty, which preoccupied the Victorians, but on "the woman question." Its purpose is to question deep-rooted ideas relating to "natural" female inferiority by attaching the working-class woman's spiritual impoverishment to the material conditions to which she is subject. Just as a man cannot be transformed from a seller of farthing candles over the counter into a successful chancellor of the exchequer, Margaret argues, so a woman cannot be taken from "dirty washing, cooking food and all the petty, material things" and then expected to be big. Consciousness of gender, the awareness of belonging to an oppressed group, pervades the passage and becomes the key organizing principle of the work, the central difference on which turn all other psychological, moral, and social distinctions. Eyles here makes us aware not of the fact that women are corrupt but of how they have come to be corrupted. She sees, more-over, men and women imbricated in material circumstances and with each other, and she sees also the pitfalls that may destroy a politics of resistance that, if it is to exist at all, must grow out of the intimate relationships lived within an oppressed community. The solidarity that she seeks to build does not exist naturally but must be constructed. In seeking to build such a solidarity, Eyles clearly inherits and continues the feminist traditions that have existed within socialist politics.

The detail that we are given about Mrs. Quinn, Margaret's neighbor, is carefully selected to avoid condescension. Margaret points out spe-cific facts that have emotional significance for women. We are told that Mrs. Quinn is a better manager, a more skillful housewife, than Mar-garet, whose own house is a replica of Mrs. Quinn's. Yet if it is easy to detect a note of sisterhood (if that term is not too modern in its connotations), it is also easy to detect the imposition of artificial values upon working-class characters. Eyles will never allow her working-class women characters to express hopes, ideals, or aspirations that might detract from our understanding of working-class conditions as inexo-rably tragic or pathetic. The differences in background that separate her from the working-class women she describes thus ensure that whatever bonds of sympathy might exist between the two, her writing discloses not the closeness but the distance between the author and the women she describes.

The opening paragraphs of her second novel, *Hidden Lives*, although lacking Eyles's characteristic focus on women, introduce us not to a London slum but to an industrial town in the Midlands, also situating us at a kind of horrified distance from ugliness. "To the right stretched the town shawdruck, a horror of desolation, of brokenness. Always when Francis Reay crossed the shawdruck he closed his eyes for an instant, and had a vision of Job the Patient, tormented by pain and ill counsel-lors, sitting among the potsherds of his ancient city; but the sky above Job was a burning blue, to which he might have turned for cheer. The sky above Shellpit was hidden by the dank smokes and vapour of many industries that stripped the beauty from the stunted trees, making men's souls and bodies stunted and unbeautiful" (7).

Here the corruption that hangs over Shellpit is specified as industrial in character. The sky above Shellpit is concealed by "the dank smokes and vapour of many industries." Thus a cancerous and deeply ominous aspect of urban existence is introduced, a landscape insidiously, hid-eously, altered and corroded through the processes of industry. Indeed, in a literal sense the shawdruck (an industrial waste tip) *is* the waste of industry and the power of the passage traceable to its reinforcement by metonymy. Standing in for the industry that is the *raison d'être* of the urban slums, the shawdruck is seen with a double perspective. It is part of a specific mode of production, a material fact, and it is a phantasm that becomes the waking nightmare of the clergyman, Francis Reay. In his troubled imagination, the waste tip of a small town in the Midlands is compared to the devastation of an ancient biblical city. Such is the magnitude of the disaster for humanity that it represents.

Eyles's insistence that the shawdruck is part of an economic system is a recognition of the power of the industrial colossus that dwarfs and dominates the lives of those who live under its shadow. The emphasis on illusion in the passage makes the shawdruck something of a chimera, a figment of the imagination of a sick society that may one day awake to the possibilities of other things. Eyles's own hatred of the advanced capitalist processes of production is evoked through omniscient narration. Words such as "stunted" and "stripped" and the clumsy "unbeautiful" underscore the narration and produce in the reader a sense of moral abhorrence, a hard condemnation of industrialism that is almost Dickensian in character. At the same time the explicit parallel with Job, the good man overtaken by calamities not of his own making, the archetype of patience under misfortune, produces a notion of industry as a kind of alien force weighing down a helpless people. It is a monster that can be vanquished but not economically contested. It cannot be transformed, or repossessed and reorganized for the common good. There follow only two possible responses to the catastrophe. One is the idea of escape, a solution in several of Eyles's novels; the other is stoic endurance of the kind exhibited by the majority of urban slum dwellers.

The rhetoric of passages like these carries us beyond realism to focus on the unbridgeable chasm that separates the world as intended by God and the world defiled by human beings. The presence in the text of specific images like the shawdruck or the woman in the little house, to which a whole complex of meanings attach, continually alerts us to questions of good and evil and of right and wrong. The narrative logic of these works leads to the conclusion that human suffering is inextricably linked to the man-made industrial world. There are strong utopian elements in Eyles's early novels, and the utopian mode predominates at the end of *Margaret Protests*, when Margaret sets off with her young family to live in rustic simplicity in a place so remote that money does not change hands, a place in which exploitation is unknown. "A fantastic thing—a woman with two children, in the twentieth century, setting out to find an ideal world in England—was it too fantastic, too visionary? Was I mad? Ought I instead of setting off along the country lanes to-morrow to be locked up in an asylum where dreamers so often end, crushed?" (325).

What choices exist for Margaret, cursed with a feckless husband, an unhappy marriage, and then unexpected widowhood? The text strongly implies that the choice between urban degradation and the good life away from the city is open to any-woman or every-woman. At least it is open to her once she has come to understand how sterile and self-deluding is the notion that material progress alone will improve women's lives. The ending of *Margaret Protests* is not intended to offer a literal answer to the problem of women's exploitation. Instead Eyles appropriates the discourses of utopian enthusiasm to express an intensity of aspiration for which there is simply no secular language available. In *Margaret Protests*, Eyles symbolically affirms every woman's potential to cut free of bondage and, through her own determined efforts, to build her own New Jerusalem, as Margaret does at the end of the novel, arriving at "the House Made without Hands," a place where, at last, the good do not suffer, and the purest of human emotions may be displayed.

The tone of protest in Eyles's early novels conveys a feminism that, in concentrating and powerfully rendering the injustices suffered by women, is intended to heighten the desire of women to take control over their own lives. Yet it also leads Eyles to simplify what is complex, and in so doing, she clearly displays the weakness of the inexperienced novelist. For the tendency to naturalism, to present women as the hapless victims of circumstances, is a major recurring problem in her fiction. Sarah, the arsonist in *Hidden Lives*, Annie, the prostitute in *The Hare of Heaven*, and Kitty, the thief in *Margaret Protests*, are all unconvincing character studies that reveal the limitations of this kind of sympathy. Perhaps only in *Captivity*, a novel in which the vivid details of a man's drunkenness convey what this means for the woman nearest him, is simplification avoided. Eyles's hatred of the industrial system also led her into some of the same pitfalls that trapped the early Chartist writers. As Martha Vicinus has explained, "This insistence upon a better future, rather than exploring and validating the here and now, no matter how grimy and degraded, prevented authors from treating seriously contemporary working-class life and from developing character and conflict within the existing world."[49] Eyles cannot strike a balance between the requirements of artistic form and those of feminist politics.

The quest for "authenticity," a leitmotiv in Eyles's fiction, results in fixed patterns of behavior for her women characters, patterns that send Margaret in *Margaret Protests*, Helen in *Hidden Lives*, and Marcella in

Captivity into the depths of the countryside. Leonora Eyles's key criticism of industrial society is largely the same as her criticism of patriarchal society: that it forces women to deny their feminine natures. The freedom that her women desire, when closely analyzed, is really a desire for freedom to display a nature that is more serene and beautiful than industrial society will permit. And the flight of her characters from the city to the country gives the impression that women may find happiness only by turning their backs on the industrial world. The femininity to which Eyles's characters aspire and the Victorian ideal of unblemished womanhood, it would seem, are in many respects alike. Eyles fails to question the origins of her ideal of womanhood, and in the end, her writing represents an escape from, rather than an assault on, patriarchal values.

Moreover, hatred of the industrial world produces a travestied picture of the London slums. If the slums were an abomination, for the author to write without disapprobation about what goes on there is impossible. To suggest that slum dwellers can still lead reasonably human lives, to describe factories as if some good might come from them, would be to imply that the slums themselves are justified. Yet capitalism is contradictory, and its social relations no less so, and such complexities cannot be presented in terms of juxtaposition—*either* the slums of Shoreditch *or* the moors of Bedstone in *The Hare of Heaven, either* Ruthers Row *or* the mountains of Laschcairn in *Hidden Lives, either* outcast London *or* rural paradise in *Margaret Protests.* In fact, the demolition of Ruthers Row (and its replacement by any of the woman-based alternatives in the novels, whether Lady Carradon's village homes or Helen's Bethesda, a refuge for working women) is made possible only by the affluence generated by the productivity of factories. The garden city of Eyles's vision is not a utopia but has its own well-documented problems: the deracination and anguish that occurs when old communities are broken up and Londoners find themselves dispersed over an unfamiliar countryside. Such contradictions are obscured and concealed by an exclusive emphasis on the passive and downtrodden aspects of life in the East End, an emphasis in which the sense of community, the neighborliness and warmth, that we find in discursive accounts of life in the East End in this period is missing.

The novelist's focus on the middle classes, often professionals like the doctor Helen Clevion, reinforces the reader's sense of the urban poor as the objects of compassion or reform. Though middle-class characters may live in working-class neighborhoods, they manifestly do not share the working classes' living conditions. Seldom in any of Eyles's novels do working-class characters talk of more than "stoo" or "bloaters," and there is often a thinly veiled pity for their limited intellectual capacities. That Eyles sees the working class as having no collective voice or class-based sense of identity is exemplified in the dramatic clash in *Hidden Lives* between Jonathan Ruthers, the classic Victorian landlord who notes that "what people want to call the submerged tenth are only fit to be submerged" (138), and Helen Clevion, the classic reforming Victorian heroine who believes that the working classes deserve better than his hovels. There is not the slightest suggestion in this dramatic confrontation that the "submerged tenth" should speak for themselves.

In 1922 Eyles became conscious of the simmering working-class discontent that was manifested in a series of major strikes and urban disturbances. She responded in domestic and personal terms: "I firmly believe that the only thing to get at the root of the industrial unrest today is happiness in the little homes. This unrest, if one studies it from the point of view of the restless ones, is so much less political than domestic and neurotic." She added, "If something is done to make the women better in health and spirits, the men will simmer down, for the women set the note of a nation as they do of a home." The unrest gave her a welcome opportunity to canvass support, from *Time and Tide*'s respectable and socially concerned female readership, for the state endowment of motherhood "as a national service, to be paid for as the army and navy or the civil service are paid for."[50] Seriously worried by the prospect of cracks in the social fabric in the period leading up to the General Strike, she appealed to women to stay calm: "Revolution in its finest and constructive sense—will begin in the homes of the people."[51]

Toward the end of 1925, a series of articles titled "Oh That I Knew Where I Might Find Him" began to appear regularly in the *Daily Herald*, continuing throughout the first few months of 1926. Curiously juxtaposed to another regular feature in the newspaper, the daily column "From the Workers' Point of View," each religious piece contained a personal account of the different churches, chapels, and religious meetinghouses that the writer had visited in her quest for God. The author was none other than Eyles, for whom Anglicanism, nonconformity, Catholicism, Quaker meetings, and socialist Sunday schools had all at some time provided hope and enlightenment. The end of the spiritual journey of the woman for whom socialism seems to have been meaningful only if informed by a particularly literal kind of Christianity was to come much later, with Theosophy. In 1926 Eyles was genuinely alarmed at the prospect of bloodshed and was acutely conscious of how far removed she, as a woman, was from the sources and centers of economic and political power. From this perspective, to remind the labor movement of the presence of God made excellent sense. Today when one reads the lofty Victorian earnestness of these religious pieces, written in a daily paper of the labor movement at a time of almost unprecedented political crisis, one is left wondering whether they tell more about the state of the labor movement in 1926 or about Leonora Eyles.

Notes

1. Leonora Eyles, *Margaret Protests* (London: Erskine Macdonald, 1919). An agony aunt is a woman who offers advice on domestic, emotional, and sexual problems, in answer to readers' letters sent to a newspaper or magazine.

2. It should be noted that both realism and the novel genre itself have come under attack from socialist and feminist critics as forms of writing irretrievably contaminated by bourgeois ideology. For discussion of these issues, see Fredric Jameson, *The Political Unconscious: Narrative as a Socially Symbolic Act* (London: Methuen, 1981), or Toril Moi, *Sexual/Textual Politics* (Brighton: Harvester Press, 1985). Although I recognize the importance of such arguments, I do not have the space to deal with their complexities here.

3. H. Gustav Klaus, ed., *The Socialist Novel in Britain: Towards the Recovery of a Tradition* (New York: St. Martin's Press; Brighton: Harvester Press, 1982); idem, *The Rise of Socialist Fiction, 1880–1914* (New York: St. Martin's Press; Brighton: Harvester Press, 1987); idem, *The Literature of Labour: Two Hundred Years of Working-Class Writing* (New York: St. Martin's Press; Brighton: Harvester Press, 1985); Ken Worpole, *Dockers and Detectives: Popular Reading, Popular Writing* (London: Verso, 1983); Jeremy Hawthorn, ed., *The British Working-Class Novel in the Twentieth Century* (London: Arnold, 1984); Andy Croft, *Red Letter Days: British Fiction in the 1930s* (London: Lawrence and Wishart, 1990).

4. Socialist fiction, including works by women, has been reissued under the Merlin Radical Fiction series starting in 1990. Rex Warner, *The Wild Goose Chase* (London: Boriswood, 1937); Walter Brierley, *Sandwichman* (London: Methuen, 1937); Margaret Harkness [John Law, pseud.], *Out of Work* (London: Sonnenschein, 1888); Ella Hepworth Dixon, *The Story of a Modern Woman* (London: Heinemann, 1894). A series of talks by Andy Croft on BBC Radio in 1990, based on *Red Letter Days*, attracted an audience of a quarter of a million.

5. Graham Holderness, "Miners and the Novel: From Bourgeois to Proletarian Fiction," in *The British Working-Class Novel*, 19.

6. Worpole, *Dockers*, 9.

7. Ibid., 47.

8. David Smith, *Socialist Propaganda in the Twentieth-Century British Novel* (London: Macmillan, 1978), 44.

9. Betty Vernon, *Ellen Wilkinson* (London: Croom Helm, 1982).

10. Ethel Mannin, *Women Also Dream* (London: Jarrolds, 1937).

11. Barbara Taylor, *Eve and the New Jerusalem: Socialism and Feminism in the Nineteenth Century* (London: Virago, 1983), xvi.

12. The women writing in the 1920s, including Ethel Carnie, Ethel Mannin, Mary Agnes Hamilton, Gabrielle Vallings, Ellen Wilkinson, and Amabel Williams-Ellis, had, of course, strong connections with the organized labor movement and wrote explicitly political fiction. See Ethel Carnie, *General Belinda* (London: Jenkins, 1924), and *This Slavery* (London: Labour Publishing, 1925); Ethel Mannin, *Venetian Blinds* (London: Jarrolds, 1932); Mary Agnes Hamilton, *Follow My Leader* (London: Cape, 1922); Ellen Wilkinson, *Clash* (London: Harrap, 1929); Gabrielle Vallings, *The Forge of Democracy* (London: Hutchinson, 1921), and *The Tramp of the Multitude: A Triptych of Labour* (London: Hutchinson, 1936); Amabel Williams-Ellis, *The Wall of Glass* (London: Cape, 1927).

13. E. P. Thompson, *The Making of the English Working Class* (Harmondsworth: Penguin, 1968), 13.

14. Kiernan Ryan, "Socialist Fiction and the Education of Desire: Mervyn Jones, Raymond Williams, John Berger," in *The Socialist Novel in Britain*, 166–67.

15. Carolyn Steedman, *Landscape for a Good Woman: A Story of Two Lives* (London: Virago, 1986), 33.

16. There are over twenty titles listed under Leonora Eyles's name in the British Library catalog. I am here able to refer selectively only to *Margaret Protests* and to the following works: *Captivity* (London: Heinemann, 1922); *Eat Well in War-Time* (London: Gollancz, 1940); *For My Enemy Daughter* (London: Gollancz, 1941); *Hidden Lives* (London: Heinemann, 1922); *The Hare of Heaven* (London: Melrose, 1924); *Unmarried but Happy* (London: Gollancz, 1947); *The Ram Escapes: The Story of a Victorian Childhood* (London: Nevill, 1953); *The Woman in the Little House* (London: Grant Richards, 1922); *Women's Problems of To-day* (London: Labour Publishing, 1926).

17. R. Brimley Johnson, *Some Contemporary Novelists (Women)* (London: Parsons, 1920), xiv–xv.

18. Mary Agnes Hamilton, review of *Captivity*, in *Time and Tide*, 12 May 1922, 448–49.

19. See Nan Bowman Albinski, *Women's Utopias in British and American Fiction* (London: Routledge, 1988).

20. Eyles, *The Ram Escapes*, 197–200.

21. Eyles, *Women's Problems of To-Day*, 56, 11.

22. Eyles, *The Ram Escapes*, 159–60.

23. Ibid., 11.

24. Eyles, *For My Enemy Daughter*, 44–45.

25. Rosalind Coward, *Female Desire: Women's Sexuality* (London: Paladin, 1984), 137. *Modern Woman* was founded in 1925, *Woman's Journal* in 1927, *Woman's Own*, which amalgamated *Home Notes* and *Woman's Day*, in 1932, *Mother* in 1934, and *Woman* in 1937.

26. Eyles, *For My Enemy Daughter*, 48.

27. Maud Pember Reeves, *Round About a Pound a Week* (1911; reprint, London: Virago, 1979).

28. Eyles, *The Woman in the Little House*, 26.

29. *Time and Tide*, 14 April 1922, 360.

30. Eyles, *Women's Problems of To-day*, 11.

31. *Woman's Own*, 15 October 1932, 40.

32. See Jane Lewis, "In Search of a Real Equality: Women between the Wars," in *Class, Culture, and Social Change*, edited by Frank Gloversmith (Brighton: Harvester, 1985), 212.

33. Eyles, *Women's Problems of To-day*, 11.

34. Eyles, *The Woman in the Little House*, 63.

35. Ibid., 161.

36. Marie Stopes to Leonora Eyles, 28 May 1926, PP/MCS/A84, Stopes Collection, Contemporary Medical Archive Centre (hereafter cited as CMAC), Wellcome Institute for the History of Medicine, London. I wish to thank Lesley Hall for drawing my attention to this correspondence.

37. Marie Stopes to Leonora Eyles, 21 May 1926, PP/MCS/A84, CMAC.

38. Leonora Eyles to Marie Stopes, 20 December 1927, Add. Mss. 58680–738, 58702, vol. CCVI, British Library (hereafter cited as BL).

39. Leonora Eyles to Marie Stopes, 22 May 1926, Add. Mss. 58701, vol. CCLIII, BL.

40. Marie Stopes to Leonora Eyles, 28 December 1927, PP/MCS/A84, CMAC. The first family-planning clinic outside London was set up during the seven months of the miners' lockout in 1926 in the colliery district of Cannock Chase and was visited by some 140 miners' wives. See Peter Fryer, *The Birth Controllers* (London: Secker and Warburg, 1965), 253.

41. There is no entry for this imprint in either the Cambridge University or the British Library catalog.

42. Marie Stopes, *Married Love: A New Contribution to the Solution of Sex Difficulties* (London: A. C. Fifield, 1918), and *Wise Parenthood: The Treatise on Birth Control for Married People, a Practical Sequel to "Married Love"* (London: G. P. Putnam's Sons, 1918).

43. Leonora Eyles to Marie Stopes, 20 December 1927, Add. Mss. 58680–738, 58702, vol. CCVI, BL.

44. Walter Besant, *All Sorts and Conditions of Men: An Impossible Story* (London: Chatto and Windus, 1882); George Gissing, *The Nether World* (London: Smith and Elder, 1889) and *Thyrza* (London: Smith and Elder, 1887); Arthur Morrison, *A Child of the Jago* (London: Methuen, 1896) and *The Hole in the Wall* (London: Methuen, 1902); William Pett Ridge, *Mord Em'ly* (London: Pearson, 1898); Henry Nevinson, *Neighbours of Ours* (London: Arrowsmith, 1895); Somerset Maugham, *Liza of Lambeth* (London: Fisher Unwin, 1897); Jack London, *The People of the Abyss* (London: Macmillan, 1903); Edwin Pugh, *A Street in Suburbia* (London: Heinemann, 1895); Clarence Rook, *The Hooligan Nights* (London: Richards, 1899).

45. Margaret Harkness [John Law, pseud.], *A City Girl* (London: Vizetelly, 1887); Constance Howell, *A More Excellent Way* (London: Sonnenschein, 1889). For Margaret Harkness, see John Goode, "Margaret Harkness and the Socialist Novel," in *The Socialist Novel in Britain*, 45–67. For Constance Howell, see Brunhild de la Motte, "Radicalism—Feminism—Socialism: The Case of the Women Novelists," in Klaus, *Rise of Socialist Fiction*, 28–49.

46. Kathleen Woodward, *Jipping Street* (1928; reprint, London: Virago, 1981); Kathleen Dayus, *Her People* (London: Virago, 1982), and *All My Days* (London: Virago, 1988).

47. Olive Birrell, *Love in a Mist* (London: Smith and Elder, 1900); Emma

Leslie, *The Seed She Sowed: A Tale of the Great Dock Strike* (London: Blackie, 1891); Isabella Ford, *On the Threshold* (London: Arnold, 1895). On Ford, see Chris Waters's essay in this volume.

48. James Greenwood, *A Night in a Workhouse* (London: *Pall Mall Gazette*, offset, 1866); George R. Sims, *How the Poor Live* (London: Chatto and Windus, 1883).

49. Martha Vicinus, "Chartist Fiction and the Development of a Class-Based Literature," in Klaus, *The Socialist Novel in Britain*, 23.

50. *Time and Tide*, 14 April 1922, 360.

51. Eyles, *Women's Problems of To-day*, 13.

PART TWO

Sexuality and Science:

Constructions of

the Other

SHIRLEY PETERSON

The Politics of a Moral Crusade:

Gertrude Colmore's *Suffragette Sally*

Rebellion against tyrants is obedience to God.—Emily Davison

The above aphorism, attributed to the suffragette Emily Davison by her biographer, Gertrude Colmore, eloquently expresses the revolutionary tone of Davison's life as well as her allegiance to a higher power. Most rhetoric of the British women's suffrage movement followed this model of impassioned political and religious propaganda in both tracts and fictional productions. One question raised then, as well as now, concerns the distinction between propaganda (politically and historically inflected writing) and high art (writing that somehow transcends its political and historical moment). Subsequent critical methods such as "new criticism" calcified this distinction into bad and good writing, respectively, while aesthetic standards accompanying high modernism also denigrated propagandistic and historically referential works as too didactic. In this essay, I offer an alternative way of evaluating such propagandistic works, not as lesser or greater than their current status in the "Great Tradition" but as works that successfully express the passion of the struggle against human oppression without refusing their historical and cultural relevance. I consider this project a rebellion against another form of tyranny—canonical standards; I do not appeal to a higher authority other than the belief that we owe it to our feminist forerunners to evaluate their literary contributions on their own terms.

Feminist critics involved in the reconstruction of the canon have often inadvertently reinforced the status quo. For example, Elaine Showalter, in *A Literature of Their Own* (1977), continues to validate canonical aesthetic standards at the expense of women's political writing. She hails the British women's suffrage movement as a historical and literary period that galvanized women writers in a uniquely political fashion.[1] She praises them for their courageous rejection of Victorian reserve, yet she goes on to devalue the literary importance of their works. "Relatively little of this work is distinguished as fiction, but it is of immense interest historically; it provided the link between the ambivalent altruism of the [nineteenth-century] feminists and the self-contained theories of the postwar female aesthetic."[2] Showalter draws attention to a body of literature that critics have generally overlooked,[3] but her assumption of formalist aesthetic standards that exclude these works from "distinguished" literature again raises a question of crucial importance to women's position in modern literary culture. Ironically, these apparently unexamined aesthetic standards reinforce an orthodox tradition and an ideology that suppressed women's political voice in the first place.[4] The works of these writers are certainly of historical interest, as Showalter says, but her unquestioned acceptance of these standards actually diminishes the relevance of women's political writing to both literary and historical criticism as well as to social change.

Critical methods that resist the polarization of art and politics found in formalist criticism are available. For instance, Judith Newton and Deborah Rosenfelt's revisionist Marxist project calls for a "materialist-feminist" approach to politically motivated literary works. Under the terms of materialist-feminist criticism, literary works are always seen as conditioned by the cultural and ideological systems of belief that produce them. "Since we live within the myths and narratives about history, there can in fact *be* no reflections of it. Literature, rather, draws upon various ideological productions of history or discourses about history to make its own production. What a literary text does not say, therefore, becomes as interesting as what it does say. The discourse suppressed tells as much as the discourse expressed, for omission throws the margins of a text's production into relief, allowing us to see the limits and the boundaries of what it posits as the real."[5]

From this perspective, we might consider suffragist literature as more than a mere "link" between what Showalter considers the more important historical-literary periods. Instead we can examine suffragist literature (or any historically referential works) as cultural artifacts that both employ and challenge conceptions of gender and class difference *within* the "myths and narratives" of history, a discourse that is always, to some extent, what Hayden White calls "verbal fiction."[6] In other words, although these works are historically specific in that they were produced in response to a particular historical struggle, they clearly do not objectively record that struggle. Rather, as hybrids of fiction and history, they document women's intervention in the cultural, ideological, historical, and *literary* processes that give us our own identity. For this reason alone, we cannot adequately evaluate them according to canonical aesthetic standards. We should ask instead which values these writers do articulate in the form and content of their works.

This essay takes a materialist-feminist approach to *Suffragette Sally* (1911), Gertrude Colmore's "forgotten" novel about the women's suffrage movement.[7] Republished in 1984 as *Suffragettes: A Story of Three Women*, this novel is an important restoration to the subgenre of suffragist fiction.[8] From a materialist-feminist critical perspective, I examine the conditions surrounding the production of this novel, the relationship of the author to the suffrage movement, the author's use of narrative forms, and the specific ideological agenda behind the work itself. I contend that the novel reveals contradictions and tensions stemming from the competing political ideologies within the suffragist movement; the novel was in fact written for the converted who, after all, did not require justification for women's suffrage but did want reassurance that the extreme and controversial militant agenda was politically and morally correct.

The origins of Colmore, known also as Mrs. Harold Baillie-Weaver, are uncertain. It is clear that she died in 1926 having published twenty-three works (in both England and America) and gaining, according to the *Times* obituary, "an attached constituency of readers."[9] Not surprisingly, this politically conservative publication provides no information about her feminist involvement, featuring instead her husband's connection with the Theosophical Society and both of their contributions to the antivivisectionist movement.[10] Although *Suffragette Sally* (probably her most popular novel) receives mention, its radical content does not. Instead, her works are described as a reflection of her "gentle, refined personality." Ann Morley and Liz Stanley note the ironic contrast of this description with another in *The Vote*, the organ of the Women's Freedom League. That obituary memorializes Colmore as "a forcible convincing speaker" with a "clear and logical mind."[11] Undoubtedly, the disparity between these two recollections of the author reveals more about the ideological agendas of the publications themselves than it does about Colmore.

From her death in 1926 until her novel's republication as *Suffragettes: A Story of Three Women* in 1984, Colmore remained obscure, and we still have only a sketchy history of her activities. In the introduction to *Suffragettes*, Dale Spender notes that Colmore was educated in Frankfurt-am-Main, Paris, and London and belonged to the Pioneer Writers' Club. One of six daughters, she remarried after the death of her first husband, Henry Arthur Colmore Dunn.[12] Colmore expresses her deep devotion both to her father and to Dunn in the moving dedication of her *Poems of Love and Life* (1896), "written chiefly in the four years that passed between the death of the one and the death of the other."[13] She took her pen name, G. Colmore, from this mourned first husband. Interestingly, the ambiguous gender of this name was apparently exploited by *Suffragette Sally*'s original publisher (Stanley, Paul), which referred to the writer as "he" (whether with or without her approval is unclear).[14] Yet she was not an unknown entity in literary circles. Writing in 1911, a *Times* reviewer of *Suffragette Sally* compliments Colmore on her "ability in former novels."[15] She had in fact been publishing novels since 1888.[16]

More recently, Morley and Stanley's collaborative detective work through the suffrage archives in London and Manchester has revealed a solid link between Colmore and the movement itself. Although Morley and Stanley cannot find a direct connection between Colmore and the suffragette Emily Wilding Davison, they do document an indirect connection through Grace Roe, a suffragette who for a time took charge of suffragette headquarters in London while the leadership was in jail or exile. A mutual friend of Colmore's and Davison's, Roe describes Colmore as "a tried and trusted member of feminist organizations, a regular contributor of time, money and energy—and of stories. [She] was also a fairly well-known author outside feminist circles."[17] In addition to poetry and essays, Colmore published novels, some of which dealt with current controversies such as female alcoholism (*The Angel and the Outcast*, 1907), antivivisection (*Priests of Progress*, 1908), and venereal disease (*The Thunderbolt*, 1919). In the latter two works, she also raises ethical questions about human medical experimentation, cogently arguing that the ends do not justify the means. "There is something more precious . . . than knowledge," she insists, and that is "the spiritual progress of man."[18]

The moral and spiritual imperative clearly audible in the above passage also informs *Suffragette Sally* and *The Life of Emily Davison* (1913).[19] In this sense, these works corroborate Martha Vicinus's claim that the women's suffrage movement was more than just a political campaign. It aimed to "forge a new spirituality, based upon women's traditional idealism and self-sacrifice but intended to reach out and transform not only the position of women in society, but that very society itself."[20] Deriving its energy and commitment from the spiritual idealism associated with the private sphere of Victorian England, the suffrage campaign became the political manifestation of feminism's arrival in the modern age. As valuable documents of that spiritual and political conjunction, *Suffragette Sally* and *The Life of Emily Davison* should be read together. Even though *The Life* was written two years after the publication of *Suffragette Sally*, I would like to briefly consider *The Life* first to demonstrate the fluidity of form between Colmore's biography and fiction. The generic separation of historical and literary writing is not distinct in these works; thus, it is difficult to categorize them satisfactorily according to convention.

The Life of Emily Davison illustrates Colmore's tendency to blend fact, fiction, and myth in pursuit of a moral, rather than objective, reality. Published shortly after Davison's death in 1913, *The Life* employs a nonfictional biographical narrative form, although much of it is clearly imaginative. The "facts" Colmore provides about Davison's life include her involvement with the Women's Social and Political Union (WSPU), numerous arrests and imprisonments, hunger strikes and forced feedings, a suicide attempt in prison, an unusually brutal prison ordeal in which she was hosed down for barricading her door, her concealment in a heating duct in the Houses of Parliament, the Black Friday demonstration, and finally the spectacular and bizarre suicide in which she flung herself in front of the king's horse on Derby Day, 1913.

The biography also incorporates religious and mythical motifs common to suffragist writing, as this description of Davison illustrates: "Innately religious, with keenly and nobly conceived ideals and an imagination touched by the spirit of devotion, [Davison] was as fully convinced that she was called by God, not only to work but also to fight for the cause she had espoused, as was Joan of Arc when she led the army of France."[21] Whereas Joan of Arc foreshadows Davison's martyrdom for the cause, she also exemplifies the conflation of history and myth in Colmore's narratives. Originally a historical character, by 1911 Joan of Arc had become a mythical female hero who combined for suffragettes the militant conviction of spiritual righteousness and physical martyrdom with a fortuitous ambiguity. Lisa Tickner has examined this powerful combination: "[Joan of Arc] offered an identification which was neither that of the domestic feminine ideal nor of its obverse, the hysterical fanatic. . . . Her political and ideological instability made her more, not less, adaptable to the different factions of the suffrage campaign. She was the touchstone that spiritualised militancy and linked it with that to which it was in all other respects utterly opposed: an Evangelical ideal of femininity that accorded women moral pre-eminence. . . . She was the paradigm for militant virtue compounded with feminine audacity. Everyone could have their own Joan."[22]

Joan of Arc would not be canonized until 1920, but in 1911 she was already well on her way. It was as difficult then to separate the historical from the mythical Joan of Arc as it is today to distinguish the historical from the mythical Marilyn Monroe or Elvis Presley: they have become invested with the values of the culture that produced them (and continues to reproduce them) to the point that they transcend their own historical moment. They are now conveniently vague symbols. Davison too became such a symbol. If the truth about her is still as elusive today as it was to the suffragists immediately after her death, it is perhaps because, as Morley and Stanley suggest, she immediately became an integral part of the public spectacle, the image, and the myth that constituted the suffrage campaign.[23]

Morley and Stanley classify Colmore's biography as "hagiography," a narrative strategy designed to document Davison's martyrdom and thereby canonize her in the interests of the movement she served.[24] I would add that this mythologizing process constitutes an integral part of the movement's literary and historical project. Employing White's terminology, I maintain that Davison is "re-emplot[ted]" within the narrative events of history through the narrative form of hagiography, one of several story types that "we conventionally use to endow the events of our lives with culturally sanctioned meanings."[25] Thus, through hagiography, Colmore can exalt Davison beyond the moral complexities of her death to the status of Redeemer: she "died that other women might find it possible to live truer, happier lives."[26] At the same time, Colmore's biography redeems Davison from the taint of suicide by way of a fundamental principle of Victorian and early modern feminism: that the body must be sacrificed "in order that [the] spirit might triumph."[27] On a very practical level, this bio/hagiography surely helped reconcile Davison's suicide in the mind of the typical suffragist operating within the moral matrix of Christianity. If this biography is intended to consecrate the movement's first martyr, Colmore's use of this narrative form was as much a political as a literary decision.

In *Suffragette Sally*, Colmore uses this same blend of fact and fiction to represent events and participants associated with the militant branch

of the suffrage organizations. The novel also invokes religious metaphors similar to those in *The Life* to emphasize the suffrage campaign
as an evangelical quest or holy crusade. Like Elizabeth Robins's earlier
and better-known suffragist novel *The Convert* (1907), *Suffragette Sally*
is a roman à clef, populated by thinly disguised suffragettes[28] in the
vanguard of suffrage militancy, the WSPU. Such well-known figures
in suffrage circles as Christabel Pankhurst, Annie Kenney, Emmeline
Pethick-Lawrence, Charlotte Despard, and Lady Constance Lytton all
find fictional counterparts in this novel of political-spiritual conversion.[29] The historical allusions in the novel include Pankhurst's and
Kenney's arrests in 1905 for demanding votes for women during a speech
by Sir Edward Grey (an incident designed to inaugurate the militant
campaign), the WSPU's 1908 deputation to Parliament, and the Black
Friday demonstration in November 1910, after which many suffragists
reported brutality from police and bystanders. These characters and
events would have been readily recognizable to readers of the time, particularly readers of *Votes for Women*, which enthusiastically promoted
this novel.

Comparisons with *The Convert*, however, keenly illustrate the rapidly
shifting political climate during the brief four-year span separating these
two works. The optimistic tone of the 1907 novel had deteriorated by
1911 into cynicism toward an increasingly duplicitous and underhanded
Liberal government. As a result, *Suffragette Sally* was published during a period of intrigue, disillusionment, and violence. Several incidents account for this demoralization. In 1910, members of the moderate National Union of Women's Suffrage Societies (NUWSS) and the
WSPU persuaded Liberals to form a Conciliation Committee to draft
a bill for female suffrage, and the WSPU called a temporary truce while
the bill passed through its second reading in the House of Commons.
However, Prime Minister Herbert Henry Asquith (an antisuffragist)
derailed the bill by recessing Parliament. Protests ensued, most notably
the Black Friday debacle. During 1911, another truce was called while
the bill was once again presented, only to be stalled with Parliament's
recess. When Asquith returned with a Reform Bill for extended male
suffrage with the "possibility" of limited female suffrage, the suffragists
and suffragettes split, the former supporting the bill and the latter con-
demning it. The subsequent escalation of militant activity was met with
the defeat of the Conciliation Bill in 1912.[30]

In this context, we might read *Suffragette Sally* as sheer propaganda—
that is, a "call to arms"—for the WSPU's redeployment. It records the
crisis mentality of the movement and the intensified climate of violence,

a climate represented best in the campaign's ultimate ordeal: the prison hunger-strikes and the consequent force-feeding policy enacted by the Liberal government. This policy, carried out from 1909 to 1914, further infuriated the suffragettes, who keenly interpreted this violation of the body as an extension of their political disembodiment. It carried great symbolic power, which suffragists did not fail to exploit in visual and literary form.[31] Combined with the religious metaphors already at work, this ordeal operates as a narrative rite of passage in Colmore's novel, transforming the suffragette convert into a martyr-hero through suffering at the hands of a brutal oppressor. To say that suffragettes perceived this phase of the struggle as a virtual holy war is not to overstate the effect of this symbolism.

In addition to the political tension informing the novel, we can trace another form of tension to the narrative crisis at the turn of the century, a crisis that would shortly develop into what we now consider modernism's search for new forms to express the nature of reality. Often these narratives become paradoxes of form and content not unlike the suffrage movement itself, a paradox that Vicinus explains as a "radical break with the Victorian women's movement" but also "its culmination."[32] In other words, these narratives derive many of their conventions from the Victorian period while simultaneously resisting those conventions. One way this conflict erupts is in narrative forms about women who try to reconcile romantic desires (the subject matter of nineteenth-century bourgeois realism) with the modern demand for political voice. Conventional realistic closure offered marriage or death for female protagonists, neither of which satisfied the political urgency of the plot. Consequently, as Rachel Blau DuPlessis maintains, early-twentieth-century feminist writers began "writing beyond the ending" of the nineteenth-century realistic novel to devise an alternative closure to the (en)closure offered to women by the conventional novel.[33]

We can detect some of this innovation in the tension between *Suffragette Sally*'s realistic form and its ideological content. Colmore begins each chapter with a passage from a Victorian writer, offering a tribute to the realistic style and middle-class morality she advocates while affirming the view of the Edwardian period as Victorian feminism's "culmination." Yet in its political viewpoint, the novel makes a "radical break" with that feminism. Its valorization of the WSPU expresses an extreme view (even within the suffrage struggle) that certainly undermines the traditional recuperation of the female protagonist in the marriage-death ending. On the one hand, the text seems to reconcile the romantic and political quests through the middle-class protagonist's union with a man who supports the militant suffragists. On the other hand, the epony-mous working-class protagonist, Sally, finds love incompatible with her commitment to the movement. She chooses the suffrage cause, the con-sequence of which is death. Thus, the novel both resists and reiterates the traditional marriage-death plot through the political dimension of the novel. I want to elaborate further on this point, though, because the different results of these two protagonists' romantic desires fuel another underlying tension that I would attribute to the inscription of class differences in the novel.

The complex issue of class in Colmore's novel erupts in the space between text and subtext. Through the novel's three protagonists, Col-more foregrounds one of the major assertions of the suffragists and of many subsequent historians: that the suffragist movement (and by extension feminism) operated across class lines despite its middle-class image. I suggest, however, that the novel's competing ideologies (repre-sented in the three central characters) actually deconstruct this egali-tarian impression to expose the political purpose of the novel itself, which is not to advocate a classless society but to shape the ideology of working-class women to that of the middle and upper classes.

As the feminist historians Jill Liddington and Jill Norris have per-suasively argued, the suffrage movement owed more to working-class women than scholars have typically acknowledged.[34] Working-class suf-frage organizations (often referred to as "radical") promoted a more labor-intensive agenda than did their offshoot, the militant WSPU, but clearly played as significant a part in the overall campaign. Likewise, the constitutional-liberal suffragists (the NUWSS) substantially con-tributed in a quieter and less visible way by advancing the cause through legislative channels. Historians concur as to the superior visibility of the militant suffragettes, yet there is little consensus as to whether the WSPU (clearly the preeminent wing of the movement in this novel) advanced or retarded the progress of the campaign during the period just before World War I. While riveting public attention to the women's cause, WSPU violence no doubt partially eroded Liberal Party support for the Conciliation Bill.

While Colmore apparently intends for her three central characters to dramatize the movement's broad spectrum of class involvement, the novel's own political agenda suggests another reading. The novel consti-tutes a defense of WSPU policy and an exaltation of militant philosophy over concurrent liberal and radical thought. Because of this agenda, I suggest that the novel be approached not only as inspirational reading for suffragettes but also as a textbook of the militant ideology specifically articulated by the WSPU; ironically, this attitude bears a troubling resemblance to the same ideology that devalues this novel today by applying standards rooted in the status quo. For example, the WSPU projected an image of a classless sisterhood while simultaneously conducting itself as an autocracy. Indeed, it has been well documented that middle-class women composed its leadership and that its central spokesperson, the ultrapragmatic Christabel Pankhurst, expressly emphasized the importance of upper- and middle-class women to the cause. Stated bluntly, they could exert more power.[35]

Nevertheless, it was in the WSPU's interest to present a public image of sisterly solidarity. Thus, read as a product of WSPU ideology, the novel's narrative polarizes women, as disenfranchised citizens, against men, as powerful components of patriarchal society, yet it mutes the difference between working-class women and their upper-class sisters. One wonders why Colmore, whose awareness of class differences was so acute, cooperated in this project.[36] One explanation might be that Colmore—a middle-class feminist with connections and allegiances to both the WSPU and the more moderate NUWSS—was not so much out to dismantle the system as to establish an equitable place for women within it. In this respect, she closely resembles her Victorian feminist predecessors who, as Ann Ardis notes, did not question "the middle class's right to monopolize the responsibilities of citizenship."[37] Moreover, this oversight may simply reflect the powerful ideology of the WSPU, particularly at a time when suffrage for any class of women seemed increasingly remote.

The novel's three protagonists signify the primary divisions within the multifarious suffrage movement. Sally Simmonds is working class, Edith Carstairs belongs to the bourgeois middle class associated with the constitutional suffra*gists*, and the aristocratic Lady Geraldine Hill voices the principles of the militant suffra*gettes*. Their common bond is disenfranchisement, but Sally's nearly complete ignorance of the suffrage movement in the novel's opening spotlights the extreme political, economic, and social marginalization of the working-class woman. The novel's philosophical debate concerns the most politically expedient and morally acceptable way to combat the three women's shared oppression: through polite constitutional persuasion (disparaged as a political extension of the Victorian woman's power to "influence") or through subversive militant action.

Sally's portrayal as the working-class hero-martyr best illustrates the tension between text and subtext. At the beginning of *Suffragette Sally*, we see her doubly victimized through both her class and her sex. She works as a servant to the aptly named Bilkeses, who exploit her in their own gender-specific fashions: "The mistress scolded, but the master kissed" (11). Sally escapes the depression of servitude and sexual humiliation by religiously (a key word here) attending the meetings of the women's suffrage movement. The enlightened atmosphere of the meetings contrasts with Sally's bleak home life while glaringly exposing her working-class mentality. The "fine ladies and gentlemen" who speak at the suffrage meetings inspire and comfort Sally, but at the same time they signify her own difference from them. Sally responds to them in typical "convert" fashion, admiring the individual speakers and comparing their words to "preaching, only that there was no mention of God or heaven or hell." Her acquaintance with Lady Henry (Geraldine) Hill enthralls her even further, convincing her that "women, however poor, however put upon, had a right to have a say in the things which mattered most to them" and that they would "stand together; she and Lady 'Ennery 'Ill" (15–16).

Sally and Geraldine's friendship operates as linchpin to the novel's proposed classless society of women, and their disciple/priestess relationship implies the specifically feminine nature of this brand of religion. But their relationship also asserts the superiority of the upper-class ideology to that of an intellectually impoverished working class. As the convert, Sally must be transformed into a martyr according to the clearly admirable principles of the "fine ladies and gentleman" who are her role models. Although her martyrdom exalts her to sainthood, it paradoxically insinuates the working-class woman's expendability in the larger scheme of women's struggle for political identity.

One of the novel's key incidents seemingly contradicts this devaluation of the working-class woman by reproducing an actual attack on the government for discriminating against working-class women. This incident draws on the experience of Lady Constance Lytton, who gained fame in 1910 for exposing prison policies that provided preferential treatment to upper-class women such as herself. After an arrest and immediate medical release (she suffered from a heart condition), Lytton underwent another arrest under an assumed name. During her subsequent imprisonment, her heart condition went undetected, and she was consequently force-fed until gravely ill. Once authorities discovered her identity, she was released to a horrified public, shocked at the spectacle of the brutalized "lady." In the novel, Lady Hill receives similar preferential treatment until she assumes an alias. In prison as "Anne Heeley," she celebrates the sense of solidarity and sisterhood surrounding her: "It was wonderful how class distinctions fell away, or rather how naturally she adopted the attitude of the class to which she now belonged: the class of prisoners. She was no longer Lady Henry Hill, but one of a body of women, at the command of another woman, absolutely subject to the prison authorities, completely at the mercy of the law's machinery. Similarity of conditions created a sense of fellowship; there is an *esprit de corps* even amongst prisoners, and Geraldine was imbued with it" (109). The "body of women" who share Geraldine's imprisonment ironically signify the physical nature of the martyr's sacrifice, for the forced feeding that concludes this initiation is a repulsive physical ordeal that its victims often compare to rape.[38] Nevertheless, Geraldine's refined and condescending perception of this "class of prisoners" seems a mark of class privilege that underscores her difference from ordinary prisoners rather than her identification with them. Again, she functions as an exemplary figure, at one point "lay[ing] a healing touch" on another woman, suggesting a divinity difficult to separate from her aristocratic social position as a "lady" (109).

Interestingly, Colmore here shifts the narrative focus to Sally for a closer look at the forced feeding itself. In doing so, she delicately shields readers from the physical violation of the refined, aristocratic Geraldine by handling it offstage. By contrast, Sally undergoes the forced feeding in grim detail, becoming in this final rite of passage the novel's martyr-hero. She also functions as a Christlike scapegoat for all women (the same metaphor Colmore would later use for Davison). Yet despite this spiritual transformation, Sally remains Geraldine's disciple, a subordinate social position perpetuated even after they both endure the ultimate test of dedication. Whereas Sally achieves sainthood through her consequent death, Geraldine's power to inspire and, as Anne Heeley, to heal brings her close to deification. She is "the lady of all ladies," who makes prison worthwhile for women like Sally. "It was compensation, consecration, and reward" (283). Although this relationship certainly extols the compensatory power of female friendship within patriarchy, it also retains the hierarchical arrangement that conditions their lives from the beginning, implying that within the class of women, some are still more equal than others. This attitude, of course, seems to replicate the WSPU organizational pattern and philosophy.

If the class issue remains vexed in this novel, another strand of the narrative makes a very important point regarding heroic myths in the formation of feminist politics and also in the reformulation of novel-istic closure. Here, Colmore appears to be speaking more for herself as a writer than as a spokesperson for the WSPU. Edith Carstairs is a young middle-class woman whose commitment to constitutional suffragist politics coexists with a romantic imagination, both of which impede her clear apprehension of women's role in the suffrage movement. Edith somewhat reluctantly works for the constitutional suffragists while entertaining dreamy excursions into a romantic fantasy world. In contrast to the iconic version of female medieval heroism, Joan of Arc, Edith initially projects any heroic potential in herself onto imaginary "knights, princes, [and] heroes" who display "chivalry, loyalty, honour, courage and romance" as their virtues (18). But her romantic involvement with one of these latter-day knights, a Liberal member of Parliament named Cyril Race, dispels the romantic myth and triggers her conversion to the militant ideology advanced by Lady Hill. Simultaneously, she rejects the role of romantic heroine for that of a female hero. This rejection implies that the romantic myth of conventional literature dangerously reduces women from autonomous *heroes* in a quest for self-actualization to what Carolyn Heilbrun describes as ancillary *heroines* in a male heroic quest.[39] Edith's story illustrates the incompatibility of the political quest with the role of heroine. She must instead become the hero of her own story, a task analogous to that of the suffragist. In this respect, Colmore is "writing beyond the ending" to redefine the female heroic myth within the historical context of the suffrage movement, a period ripe for such a redefinition.

The pivotal point in Edith's heroic transformation is her acceptance of the militant philosophy. Edith, Sally, and Geraldine accidentally meet early in the story at the seashore, where Geraldine evokes for the younger women one of the principal metaphors of the suffrage movement to illustrate and justify the militant position over the less-forceful constitutional one. "'Have you ever watched the tide come in?' asked Geraldine. 'When it's far out, a long way from the shore it ripples along gently, as the woman's movement did for fifty years; a very lady-like tide; and nobody heeds it—nobody on the shore I mean. But when it gets to the beach, and the slope is steep and there are stones and rocks which stem the force, the irresistible force of it, then the smooth waves change to breakers, and the nearer it comes to its destined goal, the fiercer the conflict'" (43). Edith tries to ride the "lady-like" tide while maintaining a safe distance from the rocky terrain of militant feminism. She washes between the two competing ideologies before finally siding with Sally and Geraldine. Her subsequent arrest for disrupting a government official's speech (reminiscent of Christabel Pankhurst's initial arrest) brings Cyril "Race-ing" to her rescue. His political influence saves Edith from prison, but it also ends their blossoming romance. The political "race" is, after all, his priority as well as his province. Edith regrets losing

Race's affection until she witnesses his behavior during the Black Friday demonstration.

That infamous November afternoon in 1910 inaugurated the government's new no-arrest policy. Rather than immediately carting protesters off to jail, as had been done in the past (which meant relatively few injuries), the police on this day deliberately manhandled the protesters and effectively gave license to onlookers to do the same. On Black Friday, Edith finds herself in Parliament Square in the midst of the turmoil when Cyril Race emerges, in an agitated state, from a little crowd of women. Having just helped defeat the Conciliation Bill, Race turns away from Edith in embarrassment only to twist his ankle and fall. The image of Race limping away completely dispels any romantic residue from Edith's vision and frees her to pursue her conscience unimpeded by love or loyalties to the Liberal Party. Since the novel operates on Victorian novelistic conventions, however, closure requires a marriage. Therefore, Edith quickly replaces Race in her romantic vision with another, more politically suitable, admirer she has formerly overlooked. This suitor stimulates her recognition of the heroic virtues in herself: she now has "happiness and confidence and strength" (316). The female hero has supplanted the heroine.

In a concluding author's note, Colmore wrote that "the end of this book" could not be written until the tide came in. Indeed, it would be seven more years before the woman's vote became a reality, and then for only some women.[40] The death of a woman like Sally Simmonds would hardly have swayed the government to reconsider its position. Historically, the official response to Emily Davison's death, a response that expressed more sympathy for the king's horse and jockey than for the woman, would seem to support such speculation. It would take a nearly apocalyptic event, World War I, and a new prime minister, Lloyd George, to sway the government from its intransigent position and gain women the vote. It is ironic that this concession, ostensibly a reward for women's loyalty and patriotism, may well have excluded women like Sally on the basis of its property and age restrictions.[41]

The two works discussed here represent just a small portion of Colmore's contribution to literature, but they effectively demonstrate her passionate devotion to the "Cause" and her belief in the power of language to politically transform the sex-gender system. I find great value in this philosophy for many of us working as academic feminists today. While we become increasingly sophisticated in the refined terminology of feminist theory, we run the risk of losing touch with the political realities of women's lives. At the risk of sounding anti-intellectual (which is unintentional), I still maintain that depoliticizing feminist criticism is self-defeating. Even one of the most intellectual and canonical of feminist writers, Virginia Woolf, admittedly repelled by the spectacle of female social reformers, realized the interdependence of artistic and political expression. She argued that "the rose and the apple have no political views" but that the artist's freedom to present a vision of them depends on political circumstance.[42] This allegiance to artistic and political expression strikes me as the underlying principle of Colmore's work, strongly implied in the unhesitating polemical style of an artist with moral and political conviction. Therefore, I urge us to read the works of Colmore and her contemporaries in the suffragist movement to foster a stronger understanding of our own feminist rhetoric and the forces operating within our equally complex political arena. If it is true that we can never completely escape our historical moment, nevertheless we can certainly learn from our literary and historical foremothers the strategies to negotiate the tide of our own time.

Notes

1. Elaine Showalter, *A Literature of Their Own: British Women Novelists from Brontë to Lessing* (Princeton, N.J.: Princeton University Press, 1977), 216–39.

2. Ibid., 218.

3. Credit also goes to Jane Marcus in her introduction to Elizabeth Robins's *The Convert* (New York: Feminist Press, 1980), to Susan Gibson, "Love and the Vote: Fiction of the Suffrage Movement in Edwardian England" (Ph.D diss., University of Massachusetts, 1974), and to Susan Higgins, "The Suffragettes in Fiction," *Hecate* 2 (1976): 31–47.

4. See Ann L. Ardis, *New Women, New Novels: Feminism and Early Modernism* (New Brunswick: Rutgers University Press, 1990). Ardis argues that the division between life and art promoted in the 1890s was partially a response to didactic "New Woman" novels (generic forerunners of suffragist novels). The result was to remove "literature to the margin of culture—and the New Woman novel to the margin of that margin" (54).

5. Judith Newton and Deborah Rosenfelt, eds., *Feminist Criticism and Social Change* (New York: Methuen, 1985), xxiii.

6. Hayden White, "Historical Text as Literary Artifact," *Tropics of Discourse* (Baltimore: Johns Hopkins University Press, 1978), 82.

7. Gertrude Colmore, *Suffragette Sally* (London: Stanley, Paul, 1911). Republished as *Suffragettes: A Story of Three Women* (London: Pandora, 1984). Subsequent references are to the 1984 edition.

8. I object to the title change because it removes the focus from the novel's working-class protagonist, whom Colmore clearly intended as the martyr-hero. For other suffragist novels, see also Elizabeth Robins, *The Convert* (1907); May

Sinclair, *The Tree of Heaven* (1918); Mabel Collins and Charlotte Despard, *Out-lawed* (ca. 1908); Mrs. Humphry Ward, *Delia Blanchflower* (1914); H. G. Wells, *Ann Veronica* (1909); Rebecca West, *The Judge* (1922); and Virginia Woolf, *Night and Day* (1919).

9. *Times*, 27 November 1926, 15.

10. In her will, Colmore left money both to animal-rights groups and to the Theosophical Society. See *Times*, 9 January 1927, 17. Also see Ann Morley with Liz Stanley, *The Life and Death of Emily Wilding Davison* (London: Women's Press, 1988), 98.

11. Quoted in Morley and Stanley, *Emily Wilding Davison*, 98. See *The Vote*, 10 December 1926, 360.

12. Dale Spender, introduction to Colmore, *Suffragettes*, 7.

13. Gertrude Colmore, *Poems of Love and Life* (London: Gay and Bird, 1896).

14. Spender, introduction to Colmore, *Suffragettes*, 6.

15. *Times Literary Supplement*, 4 May 1911, 178.

16. Morley and Stanley, *Emily Wilding Davison*, 188, lists all of Colmore's works.

17. Quoted in ibid., 173.

18. Gertrude Colmore, *Priests of Progress* (New York: B. W. Dodge, 1908), 262.

19. Gertrude Colmore, *The Life of Emily Davison: An Outline* (London: Woman's Press, 1913).

20. Martha Vicinus, *Independent Women: Work and Community for Single Women, 1850–1920* (Chicago: University of Chicago Press, 1985), 252.

21. Colmore, *The Life*, 20.

22. Lisa Tickner, *The Spectacle of Women: Imagery of the Suffrage Campaign, 1907–14* (Chicago: University of Chicago Press, 1988), 209–10.

23. Morley and Stanley, *Emily Wilding Davison*, 173.

24. Ibid., 77.

25. White, "Historical Text," 87–88.

26. Colmore, *The Life*, 60.

27. Vicinus, *Independent Women*, 252.

28. The term *suffragette* distinguishes the militant suffrage supporters from the nonmilitant *suffragist*. Originally a disparaging term coined by the *Daily Mail* in 1906, it was later adopted by Christabel Pankhurst, who found it more forceful than *suffragist*.

29. Spender, introduction to Colmore, *Suffragettes*, 4.

30. Diane Atkinson, *Votes for Women* (Cambridge: Cambridge University Press, 1988), 29–36.

31. See Tickner, *The Spectacle*, 104–8.

32. Vicinus, *Independent Women*, 251.

33. Rachel Blau DuPlessis, *Writing beyond the Ending: Narrative Strategies of Twentieth-Century Women Writers* (Bloomington: Indiana University Press, 1985), 3–4.

34. Jill Liddington and Jill Norris, *One Hand Tied behind Us: The Rise of the Women's Suffrage Movement* (London: Virago, 1978).

35. Ibid., 206–7.

36. See, for instance, the treatment of the working-class woman in *Priests of*

Progress or in Colmore's poems "On the Pavement" and "In a Cell" (in *Poems of Love and Life*), which concern the plight of the prostitute and the homeless mother who commits infanticide.

37. Ardis, *New Women*, 15.

38. Showalter, *Literature of Their Own*, 222.

39. Carolyn Heilbrun, "The Woman as Hero," *Texas Quarterly* 8 (1965): 132.

40. The vote applied only to women over thirty who occupied, or were the wives of men who occupied, premises of not less than a five-pound annual value.

41. See Atkinson, *Votes for Women*. Although the role that women's war work played in gaining the vote is debatable, one thing is clear—their war work "made it easier for politicians to support a bill" for women's suffrage (39).

42. Virginia Woolf, "The Artist and Politics," *Collected Essays*, 4 vols. (London: Hogarth Press, 1966), 2:230.

LESLEY A. HALL

Uniting Science and Sensibility:

Marie Stopes and the Narratives

of Marriage in the 1920s

One of the great benefactors of the age.—A.J.P. Taylor, *English History, 1914–1945*

A work of enormous importance in English cultural history.—Samuel Hynes,
A War Imagined: The First World War and English Culture

A.J.P. Taylor's opinion of Marie Charlotte Carmichael Stopes (1880–
1958), Ph.D., D.Sc., follows contemporary claims for her as "the working woman's friend" and "poet artist and dreamer as well as prophet
and saint."[1] However, "quite unbalanced in her egomania and conceit"
was the verdict of fellow birth-control advocate Stella Browne, who was
far from unique in perceiving Stopes as egocentric and authoritarian
monster rather than saintly heroine.[2]

Stopes's life, work, and influence were complex and full of contradictions.[3] Revolutionary in many ways, she could also be profoundly
conservative. Her arrogant complaints when she thought she was not
being given due credit for her achievements are far from endearing, yet
in the midst of a hectic life, she could write kindly, helpfully, and at
length to a distraught stranger. It is not simply a question of the public
persona differing from the private but of several, conflicting, versions

of both. Stopes's flamboyant "media presence" embodied these contradictions: was her "crusade" merely personal aggrandizement, or was the publicity she accrued essential for spreading her "New Gospel"? (Even Stella Browne conceded the publicity value of Stopes's 1923 libel suit against Halliday Sutherland.)[4]

Whatever her personal qualities, Samuel Hynes reminds us that her innovative marriage manual, *Married Love* (1918), was "one of the documents that shaped post-war imaginations."[5] A successful scientist, author of books on botany, coal, and Japan, as well as writer of poetry and plays, Stopes finally achieved the fame she craved with *Married Love*, and the similarly popular works *Wise Parenthood* (1918), *Radiant Motherhood* (1920), and *Enduring Passion* (1928).[6] These writings outsold contemporary best-selling fiction and, with her influential journalism, generated what she herself described as "an avalanche of demand, enquiry, and appeal."[7]

Stopes would have been the first to claim herself a feminist, concerned for the good of other women. She was prosuffrage, though she did not at first support the militants as did her mother, Charlotte Carmichael Stopes, and she was active in campaigns admittedly beneficial largely to the middle-class professional woman like herself: separate taxation, the right to retain her maiden name, the abolition of marriage bars on women's employment. She was not one of those high-achieving women who regards herself as an exception, assigning the vast majority of her sex to a subsidiary and domestic role.

A little biographical background on this second-generation "New Woman" cannot be avoided in the consideration of her writings. Her mother, one of the earliest university-educated women in Scotland, was a scholar of some repute.[8] Married to an amateur scientist some years her junior, Charlotte Stopes was a supporter of feminist causes and a pillar of the Rational Dress Society. Marie, adhering to this creed, never wore corsets under her floating and rather "artistic" garments, eschewing the severely tailored suits that might have been expected of a "lady scientist." (She is reported to have been, also, very "feminine" in manner.)[9]

After a school career of no great academic distinction, Marie Stopes chose to study botany and geology at University College in London, a mixed (rather than single-sex) institution, and then specialized in paleobotany, the study of plant fossils. There are interesting ambiguities in this choice of subject. Nature study had long been regarded as suitable for women, and although botany was becoming an increasingly professionalized science, it was one that bore no danger of being "unladylike," unlike the study of animals or the "hard" sciences such as physics and chemistry. Yet Stopes made this perhaps rather "feminine" field of study the basis of a career that still looks remarkable.

She went—alone—to study in Munich for her Ph.D. She received a Royal Society fellowship to investigate living plant fossils in Japan. Her work took her down coal mines and involved her in industrial questions. She held academic appointments, including the first-ever university lectureship in paleobotany at University College, London, and undertook government-funded research on coal and coal products. Moreover, she held such posts while married, not only during the war but after it.[10]

In 1911 the Canadian government invited her to study the coal beds of New Brunswick. While in North America, she met the Canadian botanist Reginald Ruggles Gates. Stopes was over thirty and had one disastrous emotional experience behind her: an intense relationship with a Japanese fellow student in Munich had disintegrated when she visited Japan. Although adamantly determined to continue her career, Stopes must be assumed to have been growing anxious about her prospects of marriage and motherhood. She married Gates, who returned with her to England, where she shortly afterward achieved a post significantly superior to her husband's.

Botany was believed at that time to be an excellent approach to the difficult topic of sex education. How practically useful the knowledge of stamens, pistils, and pollination was in the marriage bed is demonstrated by the fact that this marriage between two university lecturers in the subject was a sexual disaster. It was only, apparently, an inexplicable failure to conceive after several years of wedlock which finally drove the unsuspecting Stopes to investigate. She embarked on a study of the books, dealing with sexual questions, held in that restricted collection still known as "Cupboard" in the British Museum Reading Room. Concluding that the union had never been consummated, she sued for annulment (Ruggles Gates refused to divorce her and had—perhaps understandably—provided no grounds whereby she could divorce him). In 1916 the marriage was dissolved.[11]

In later life Stopes claimed that *Married Love* was born out of this debacle. "In my first marriage I paid such a terrible price for sex-ignorance that I feel that knowledge gained at such a cost should be placed at the service of humanity."[12] In fact she had already written a philosophical and idealistic treatise on marriage in about 1910, never published and now lost.[13] Her subsequent course of study provided valuable practical underpinnings for a manuscript that circulated among her friends and publishing firms from about 1915. But it was not until 1918, with a subsidy of two hundred pounds provided by the aviator and birth-control advocate Humphrey Verdon Roe (whom Stopes subsequently married), that the work was published. *Married Love*, explicit (for its time), easy to read, short and to the point, and offering what readers perceived as beautiful idealism, became a best-seller.[14]

Stopes dealt with her subject vividly and dramatically, with poetic imagery that comes off far more successfully in this context than in her poetry. Hynes, in *A War Imagined: The First World War and English Culture*, remarked on the skillful way in which Stopes leads her readers to the basic facts they needed to carry out her prescriptions, by a carefully judged move from the soothingly "poetic" mode of her initial rhetoric on marriage to the reassuringly "scientific" mode of her imparting of sexual information. Sheila Jeffreys likewise contends that by adding "sexual and emotional scenery" to the "arid descriptions of the sexologists," Stopes made "a religion of sexual intercourse."[15]

The book was certainly perceived by its first readers as both "beautiful" and "lucid" in setting forth facts formerly obscured. It can be accurately described as a book that genuinely changed lives, having the kind of impact on its readers and its society that few novels—perhaps *Uncle Tom's Cabin* or the works of Dickens—have ever achieved. Hynes suggests that in shaping "post-war imaginations," it belongs with *Eminent Victorians*, *The Economic Consequences of the Peace*, and the Parliamentary Acts granting political rights to women.[16]

Sheila Jeffreys' trenchant attacks on what she considers the antifeminist tenor of the new marriage advice and birth-control movement of the 1920s, and her perception of Stopes as a propagandist for a crypto-patriarchal model of heterosexual marriage closing off the other options recently opened up for women, have had considerable influence.[17] While according recognition to the "care for the woman . . . her right to sexual pleasure and . . . to bodily integrity" found in *Married Love* itself,[18] and paying tribute to Stopes's recognition of "the horrifying realities of un-regulated heterosexual life for women," Jeffreys criticizes her prescriptions for marriage as applying "sexual first aid" rather than "breaking the mould."[19] Stopes has also been decried as a eugenicist without any consideration of how her position related to contemporary debates on "breeding" in an era when eugenic ideas were miasmically pervasive.[20] Although she indeed advocated some eugenic measures, at one point in her only published novel, *Love's Creation*, she forthrightly condemned crude individualistic social Darwinism. Much of the "C3 problem" in her view was due to social, not genetic, factors.[21]

Her views on lesbianism were indeed deplorable, even for the period. She referred to it in *Enduring Passion* (1928) as "unnatural," a "vice," and "corruption," explaining that her objections to the practice were based on "vital scientific argument untinged with any of the simple, old-fashioned repudiations." It was her view that "women can only *play* with each other and *cannot* in the very nature of things have natural union or supply each other with the seminal and prostatic secretions which they ought to have, and crave for unconsciously." So important were these secretions that Stopes even advocated that unmarried women take glandular extracts to supply the lack.[22]

In enthusiastically advocating the joys of heterosexuality, however, she was by no means promoting traditional concepts of the conjugal relationship. In *Married Love* and its sequels, Stopes was invoking an entirely new vision of marriage. Her work for the dissemination of knowledge of birth control and amenities for its provision, although also a humanitarian concern for mothers overburdened with children they could not afford, was closely bound up with this rewriting of marriage. What Stopes aimed at—and, I would argue, in many cases achieved—was making the marital relationship more pleasant for women and one in which they enjoyed greater power. The woman-centered character of her views on sex in marriage is particularly apparent in comparison with those of certain other contemporary writers in the marriage-advice genre, for example the Dutch gynecologist Theo Van de Velde, whose widely read *Ideal Marriage* (1926) contains numerous misogynist sentiments. Furthermore, most unusually for the period, Stopes believed that "work or profession and honourable achievement" not only were not incompatible with motherhood but were "highly beneficial" to it, as well as to marriage.[23]

Publishing a serious work on sex in Stopes's day could be risky. Twenty years earlier, the prosecution of Havelock Ellis's *Sexual Inversion* had led him to have further volumes of *Studies in the Psychology of Sex* circumspectly published outside the United Kingdom. In 1923 Dr. Isabel Hutton decided to publish a work on *The Hygiene of Marriage*, a book that now appears very staid.[24] Hutton had qualified as a doctor before World War I, worked in psychiatric institutions, and served with the Scottish Women's Hospitals in the Balkans and Turkey during the war. She was scarcely readily intimidated. Yet in her autobiography she described her "spasms of apprehension in the watches of the night" at imagined "street posters announcing 'Suppression of Woman Doctor's Marriage Book.'"[25] Radclyffe Hall's novel *The Well of Loneliness* (1928) could be banned merely for acknowledging that lesbianism existed even though the book hardly presents the lot of the "invert" as enviable. Though often arbitrarily applied, the constraints upon the serious writer on sexual themes were very real. Well up to World War II, prosecution for obscenity was a genuine risk for the most well-meaning, even medically qualified, writer on sexual matters.[26]

So daring a project demanded the utmost caution. Is it any wonder that the writers of such works emphatically insisted that all they were doing was reinforcing marriage? By carefully circumscribing the conditions under which such things could be practiced, they were able to discuss sexual pleasure, clitoral stimulation and the female orgasm, variant sexual positions, oral sex, and the use of birth control.

Stopes, like other women of her day, was deeply divided and in some ways regressive even as she believed herself to be in the vanguard. Her works blended old and new thinking; this may actually have constituted part of her appeal to her readers. She had an acute sense of audience and, in always lucid prose, shaped her style toward her intended readership, whether this was her scientific peers or the uneducated but basically literate working-class woman. Her advice in *Wise Parenthood* about inserting the cap while "dressing in the evening" is often jeered at: was Stopes in fact flattering her middle-class audience by implying a lifestyle somewhat more upper crust than the one they enjoyed?[27] *A Letter to Working Mothers* (1919) reveals that she was very much aware of the problems that poor women, living in inadequate accommodations far from medical aid, faced in obtaining and using contraception.

Within five years, sales of *Married Love* had passed one-half million, and the book continued selling well into the 1950s.[28] These sales and the voluminous correspondence Stopes received, from both sexes in almost equal numbers, are some indication of how enormously influential her work was. If she did not actually regenerate society through her vision of marriage, she nonetheless made a profound difference in the lives of individuals (and couples). Insisting that wives could and should experience sexual pleasure, she gave clear and explicit sexual advice; and of particular significance, she provided a vocabulary for discussing this sensitive subject. Until it became impracticable, Stopes replied in person to her torrents of correspondence. Several thousand letters, almost entirely from the general public, survive in the Stopes papers held in the Wellcome Institute for the History of Medicine. The British Library retains, besides her extensive correspondence with the eminent, a selection of "General Correspondence" and a further sample of "Readers' Enquiries." Even after most routine inquiries were dealt with by subordinates and form letter, Stopes continued to take a deep personal interest, annotating letters with instructions for response and contributing postscripts and even entire letters if she found a case particularly interesting.[29] In turn, readers' reactions to the books influenced subsequent editions.

Married Love and its sequels contain and suggest stories, and adumbrate theories, but above all they were practical guides and were welcomed as such. Stopes did not merely hypothesize or theorize change; she endeavored to bring it about, through the regeneration of individuals (or couples). At the very least, her works assisted in negotiating the problems of a changing society in which tradition was no longer a reliable guide.

Unexplored ambiguities, however, lurk within her depiction of marriage. The man is presented as the aggressor, the pursuer, who has to study his wife's subtle rhythms of desire and then evoke their fullest potential for blissful erotic harmony by playing the part of tender wooer. Woman is assigned innate mystery desirable even in the intimacy of marriage. "The beauty which is always at hand . . . must inevitably attract far less than the elusive and changing charms." Thus the wife should be "always escaping."[30] Rhetorically valuable as these romanticized visions may have been in persuading couples to reconsider their sex lives, they also held the capacity to undermine Stopes's beliefs in the wider potential of her sex, however much she advocated untraditional qualities such as male sensitivity.

Her contemporaries may have been so thrilled by her work, with its beguiling style and helpful information unobtainable elsewhere, that they hardly noticed such ambiguities. The following are characteristic comments in correspondence from ordinary readers: "may God prosper your noble work . . . I felt as though I was having a heart to heart chat with you"; "my heart has often burned within me to thank you in some adequate way"; "your life, dedicated as it has been to the relief of suffering, attests to a fearlessness and sincerity inspiring to behold"; "until I recently read your books I had not any knowledge of what the words 'marriage rite' meant"; "thank you for your wonderfully helpful books, which I think every married woman ought to read"; "your sex owes you a deep debt of gratitude for your heroic frankness on the subject"; "your book mentions and explains many desires and ideals which I had but which through modesty alone I could not tell my husband."[31] In two volumes of her autobiography, Naomi Mitchison, a product of intellectual and scientific circles, mentioned the gratitude with which she discovered and read the work. The "elementary techniques" advocated were "not the kind of thing young people talked about" at the time of

World War I but were in her view responsible for "a marked increase of happiness." [32]

Stopes's advocacy of birth control, intrinsic to her vision of marriage, was not mere propaganda: in 1921 she and Roe set up a birth-control clinic in North London. Her life became relentlessly hectic as she lectured on birth control, continued to write advice works as well as journalism and a film script promoting birth control, oversaw a growing number of Mothers' Clinics, dealt with her increasing correspondence, and became involved in a highly publicized libel case. Her first pregnancy resulted in stillbirth, but in 1924 (at forty-three), she gave birth by cesarean section to a son, Harry Stopes-Roe. She thus demonstrated her achievements in the traditional female sphere as well as in those areas in which she was already distinguished.

Still, she had other ambitions that had not yet been fulfilled. Well before her post–*Married Love* notoriety, she was writing fiction,[33] and all her life she wrote poetry (managing to avoid any contamination by poetic movements later than the Georgians), as well as plays, film scripts, children's books, and a libretto. In 1928 Stopes finally published her novel *Love's Creation*, under the pseudonym "Marie Carmichael," Carmichael being her mother's maiden name.

Since she worked on the novel over a period of twelve years, *Love's Creation* presumably had some particular significance for Stopes.[34] It seems to have had its inception at about the time she was working on early drafts of *Married Love*. In her biography of Stopes, Ruth Hall has entitled the chapter on this gloomy phase of Stopes's career, after the annulment of her first marriage, "Alone in the Wilderness." Although this may follow Stopes's own mythmaking, the time was clearly a dark patch. She had achieved professional recognition, but paleobotany was a restricted field and not a scientific sphere in which newsworthy advances were being made, recognizable even to the lay public. She was in her late thirties, without husband or child, and the war was at its height. There was more that she wanted to say—and in other areas. She did this, with remarkable success, in *Married Love* and its sequels. But in 1916 *Married Love* was being pronounced unpublishable on grounds of legality and public acceptability. At one stage Stopes would seem to have contemplated conveying her revelations about marriage in fictional form.[35]

Love's Creation, however, is less exclusively concerned with issues of marriage than *Married Love* or Stopes's subsequent works. In a riposte to the *Times Literary Supplement*'s review, Stopes alleged, somewhat disingenuously, that the novel had been written long before she had even heard the word *sexology*.[36] She was determined to dissociate the novel

from the writings with which the name "Dr. Marie Stopes" was irretrievably linked. She claimed that the ideas put forward (principally
through Kenneth Harvey) in *Love's Creation* were "the first publication
of a large cosmic theory . . . a development of geological and paleonto-
logical researches" about which she had never "made any statement for
publication. . . . The hero's theory is absolutely new."[37] (It is not clear
why she did not publish this as a work of scientific speculation, perhaps
in the "Forum Series" or the "Today and Tomorrow" volumes, which
attracted many contemporary thinkers.)

There were, of course, rather straitened limits on how sexual matters could be dealt with in "serious" literature at this time. Rebecca
West wryly lamented in her essay "The Tosh Horse" that respectable
elderly ladies in genteel seaside resorts were devouring the highly erotic
best-sellers of writers such as Ethel M. Dell while works such as D. H.
Lawrence's *The Rainbow* were being banned.[38] This phenomenon of the
speakable and the unspeakable had not escaped Stopes, and she wrote
perceptively on the matter in *A Banned Play and a Preface on the Censorship* (1926). She argued: "The Lord Chancellor approves, or at any
rate officially sanctions . . . the portrayal on the stage of men's illicit
amours and intensity of lust [while] vice, so long as it is presented in
terms of the strong man's *over*-sexuality and the frail woman's yielding
to his domination, is approved, unthinkingly accepted and consequently
is not banned." But her own play, *Vectia*, based on her first marriage, had
a plot depending "on the under-sexuality of a man." In consequence,
"The play is considered improper and is banned!"[39] She was therefore
acutely conscious of what was and was not acceptable in literature.

Stopes's friend and colleague Mary Stocks, who was active in the
Labour movement and editor of the *Women's Leader*, as well as involved
in setting up birth-control clinics, wrote her a letter that contains an in-
sightful critique of the novel in manuscript form as it stood about a year
before its publication. Stocks felt that the two heroine-sisters, Lilian and
Rose Amber, represented two sides of Stopes, whom Stocks considered
"far more than most people a dual personality."[40]

In the novel, Lilian—serious, humorless, lacking in intuition, and
socially conventional—is the scientist. After Kenneth's initial horror at
the thought of a female in the laboratory, their union is depicted as an
idyllic meeting of like minds, even though they are both of the class
that Stopes knew (personally and from her readers) to be particularly
liable to problems of marital adjustment. Lilian's death is presented as
a tragic blow to Kenneth and not as a welcome relief from sexual disaster. Nevertheless, it provides Kenneth with an opportunity to be both

softened and strengthened by suffering, to give up his steady university position and travel, and finally to achieve major scientific insights, described at length.

Rose Amber, the younger sister, is more of a womanly woman. Aware that many of the things she does, which people might ascribe to sweet womanly ways, are in fact "work," she still seems to have been born nurturing and supportive. There is no indication that she has been socialized into this role of "Angel in the House" or that her gifts are developed through the events of the plot. Discussing vocations with her sister, Rose Amber argues that the study of psychology, in order to work out how to have healthy relationships, is the next important phase in human evolution. She feels that her "work" lies in that area. However, she ends up in the domestic sphere. After consoling Vera, the divorced wife of Harry, who is nonetheless chivalrously sheltering her in her distress (deserted by her lover, and dying), Rose Amber herself marries Harry. This union turns out catastrophically because of Harry's insatiable uxorious passions, which fail to awaken—a failure, it is implied, due to this very overheated intensity—reciprocal passion in his wife. The marriage is fortunately terminated when Harry accidentally plunges over a cliff, to which he has gone searching for corroborative evidence for unjustified jealousy. Rose Amber then marries Kenneth and inspires his scientific career. Given the chilly reception that his colleagues accord his theories, it is just as well that she is a rich widow.[41]

What Stocks did not say was that surely Kenneth also represents Stopes, or a side of her. Kenneth's experiences in the East mirror her own. A scientist who starts out as rather an example of the "ungrown man," described by Edward Carpenter in his influential *Love's Coming of Age* (1896),[42] Kenneth needs to unite science with sensibility, symbolically consummated through his marriage to Rose Amber. This conventional ascription of science and logic to the male, and sensibility and intuition to the female, tends somewhat to undercut any potentially more radical message.[43]

Stopes herself was often seen as uniting scientific knowledge with womanly sympathy; yet how far did she (perhaps unconsciously) conceptualize science as male? To be fair, no one describes Lilian as having a male intellect: she is a woman and a good scientist. Stopes would certainly not have explicitly endorsed the view that the higher part for woman consisted in supporting and inspiring the questing male intellect. But Lilian lacks her sister's subtle attunement to the life of the emotions, and it is Rose Amber who makes all the difference to their grim lodgings by adding little feminine touches. During their courtship, Kenneth associates Lilian with coolness, ice, polar regions. The very names of the two sisters contain contrasting floral symbols: lilies for chastity, roses for passion.

Stopes's own life was unconventional, and in *Married Love* and its sequels she was rewriting traditional narratives of marriage. Yet her novel seems to underwrite conventional and traditional models of marriage to a depressing extent. Nothing in *Love's Creation* demonstrates what *Married Love* propounded: that far from being the end of romance and adventure, marriage was only the beginning. Rose Amber's first marriage is certainly, in terms of *Married Love*, a glaring example of what not to do. From her conversation with Kenneth in the final chapter, it appears that they are going to do all the right things, but we do not see whether they do achieve "The Glorious Unfolding."[44]

Stopes appears to be stuck with the same old plot, unable to get past it. Is it her own imaginative failure or a problem to do with the very form? She is hardly the first woman novelist whose work reflects conventional assumptions contradicted by her life. Susan Leonardi has shown that the contemporary group of "Somerville novelists" had similar problems.[45] Stopes was taking standard narrative conventions without, it would seem, thinking through the messages they conveyed, messages possibly even contradicting the ideas she was explicitly and consciously presenting. The science and sensibility that Stopes managed to blend with success in her works of marriage advice fail to cohere so happily in this novel, exposing underlying contradictions. *Love's Creation* raises interesting questions about the difference between preaching a program for change and the imaginative conception of what change might look like.

It seems odd that Stopes placed the novel with John Bale and Danielsson, who published her textbook *Contraception* and other medical works but lacked expertise in fiction publishing. She later ascribed the book's lack of success at least partly to this, but the reasons for her initial decision (and theirs) are unfortunately obscure.[46] She must have been conscious that the work would get more exposure in association with a well-known name, and her identity was not kept secret, but when reviewers treated the book as yet another work by "Dr. Marie Stopes" she was infuriated, even while complaining that earlier pseudonymous works had suffered neglect.[47]

Love's Creation sold badly and never achieved more than one edition.[48] In the same year, *Enduring Passion* became another runaway best-seller. In contrast to the huge amounts of correspondence about her other works, she received very few letters commenting on *Love's Creation*.

Those letters she did receive came from friends and literary acquaintances who had personal or professional motives for reading the book, not from the general public, and there were fewer remarks about the novel than might have been forthcoming out of sheer courtesy, recalling the good old social tenet "if you can't say anything nice, don't say anything at all." There was little press coverage, even given the publicity-inspiring association with a notorious name. When *Love's Creation* was reviewed it seems to have been dismissed with a short notice.[49] One of Stopes's correspondents suggested that the moral panic generated by the *Sunday Express*'s attack on Radclyffe Hall's *The Well of Loneliness* might have made libraries and booksellers cautious.[50] But *Love's Creation*, described in one review as "old-fashioned," actually looks rather tame compared with other books of the year.[51] Possibly its unimpressive reception had much to do with expectations of what a novel by Marie Stopes ought to be dealing with and ought to be like. It may also have had something to do with the novel's juxtaposition of diverse, even contradictory, interests, which elsewhere Stopes either kept distinct or successfully emulsified.

It is thus perhaps not altogether surprising that Stopes is a "neglected novelist." The neglect or condemnation of her better-known and highly influential nonfictional works is less easy to understand in this era of the recuperation of women writers. Dale Spender gives surprisingly scant attention to Stopes in her *Women of Ideas*: one parenthetic allusion in the chapter on Margaret Sanger, which would have infuriated Stopes, since Sanger was her hated rival, and a brief comparison with Annie Besant (quoting Constance Rover's *Love, Morals, and the Feminists*) in the chapter on the Pankhursts.[52] One need not subscribe to Mollie Stanley Wrench's rather fulsome view of Stopes as "poet artist and dreamer as well as prophet and saint" to feel that such cursory treatment does less than justice to a figure whose impact on her contemporaries was considerable.[53]

Is there, perhaps, unacknowledged snobbery against her chosen genre, one that specifically aims to generate action? In the First Marie Stopes Memorial Lecture in 1971, Laurie Taylor remarked on the overlooking of the "theoretical significance" of ideas conveyed in "a guidance manual for newly weds."[54] Works of advice are not considered "literature" and are very much of their particular time. Books on household management, cookery, etiquette, and domestic health, as well as sex manuals, have very often been written by women, with implicit or explicit agendas on woman's place. Even more than women's fictional writing, they are a despised and neglected genre. Self-help advice manuals await further study: their blend of conservative with radical messages for wide acceptability, their relationship to social change, are questions that need addressing. Did readers assimilate the whole agenda of *Married Love*, or did they read it as they would a cookbook or etiquette guide, seeking a "recipe" for some particular contingency?

Stopes's popularity owed much to the way she provided a marriage discourse acceptable to large numbers of people of both sexes, raising broader questions of the problems involved in "popularization." However, she should surely be exculpated from accusations of knowing collusion with the patriarchal imposition of "compulsory heterosexual" norms. Both she and her more recent critics have perhaps failed to consider the many other forces, economic and social, compelling women of that era into marriage and reducing their choices within it.[55]

Stopes's lack of attention to existing gender-power relations and her assumptions that they could be resolved within the private sphere with transformative results for society as a whole compromised her radical message even while rendering it easier to swallow. Her vision of the sexual relationship and its potentialities owed much to the writings of Edward Carpenter (1844–1929),[56] but she divorced her vision from Carpenter's wider program of far-reaching social reform (just as she divorced birth control from neo-Malthusian politico-economic doctrines) while she added the practical information that readers craved. She severed sex reform from its long association with overt agendas of political and social subversion and assimilated it to a depoliticized personal realm.[57]

Her appeals to science may now strike us as perhaps naive in their belief that it was value-free, a safe ally for the aspiring woman. Emphasizing the importance of "womanly" qualities of sensibility can resemble a recommendation that women stick to their traditional roles. But on a less far-reaching philosophical level, Stopes, her writings, and what she meant to thousands, even millions, of women were enormously important. She aided many marriages and helped innumerable women to cope, which may not be revolutionary but was immensely valuable to those concerned, increasing the sum of human happiness. Her very name became a kind of euphemistic metonym for contraception and legitimized erotic pleasure.

Above all, she made it possible to talk about female reproductive choice and sexual pleasure, foremothering debates of continuing relevance. Modern debates about reproductive technology and its control may focus on different issues, but they involve the same questions of the autonomy of the individual female and her control over her own body. Stopes reconceived the traditional relation of woman to the domains of private and public by allocating her a role in public, extradomestic life while asserting that her reproductive decision-making was a private, individual affair. She formulated notions of self-defined female sexuality, with sexual pleasure for the woman not simply a possible gratifying by-product of the male's pleasure but something to which she was entitled. Her perception of female desire as an autonomous force, rising and falling in "love-tides," was surely a radical revision of concepts that considered female desire merely engendered by that of the male. In addition, she provided women with a language for speaking about sexual and reproductive issues, not only in the intimacy of the marital relationship but also in the public domain. Without Marie Stopes—and her less-flamboyant contemporaries in the same field—we might not be arguing these issues today, or even be in a position to argue them.

Notes

I should like to thank Daphne Patai for providing me with a copy of *Love's Creation*. My work on this essay owes a great deal to discussions (postal and face to face) with Daphne Patai, Angela Ingram, Susan Squier, Roberta Clarke, and Mary Joannou. I am particularly grateful to June Rose for our conversations on Stopes, her assistance in locating reviews and comments by Stopes's correspondents on *Love's Creation*, and a view of her new biography *Marie Stopes and the Sexual Revolution* (London: Faber and Faber, 1992). I am also indebted to Dr. Ann Summers of the Department of Manuscripts at the British Library for all her assistance.

1. A.J.P. Taylor, *English History, 1914–1945* (Oxford: Oxford University Press, 1965), 165; Mrs. EW to Marie Charlotte Carmichael Stopes (hereafter cited as MCS), PP/MCS/A245, Stopes Collection, Contemporary Medical Archives Centre (hereafter cited as CMAC), Wellcome Institute for the History of Medicine, London; Mollie Stanley Wrench to MCS, 26 June 1928, Add. Mss. 58491, Stopes Collection, Department of Manuscripts, British Library (hereafter cited as BL).

2. F. Stella Browne to Havelock Ellis, 6 March 1922, Add. Mss. 70539, Havelock Ellis Papers, Department of Manuscripts, BL. Stella Browne had been active in the birth-control and sex-reform movements for many years before Stopes gave both these topics and herself a high public profile.

3. Biographical information has been drawn from Ruth Hall, *Marie Stopes: A Biography* (London: Andre Deutsch, 1977) (published as *Passionate Crusader* in the United States), from my own nonbiographically orientated but extensive

research in the massive surviving collections of Stopes's papers in the British Library and the Wellcome Institute, and from discussions with June Rose, whose biography, *Marie Stopes*, is illuminating on Stopes's construction of the narrative of her own life.

4. F. Stella Browne to Havelock Ellis, 2 June 1923, Add. Mss. 70539, Ellis Papers, BL.

5. Marie Stopes, *Married Love: A New Contribution to the Solution of Sex Difficulties* (London: A. C. Fifield, 1918); Samuel Hynes, *A War Imagined: The First World War and English Culture* (London: Bodley Head Ltd, 1990), 368.

6. Marie Stopes, *Wise Parenthood: The Treatise on Birth Control for Married People, a Practical Sequel to "Married Love"* (London: G. P. Putnam's Sons, 1918); idem, *Radiant Motherhood: A Book for Those Who Are Creating the Future* (London: G. P. Putnam's Sons, 1920); idem, *Enduring Passion: Further New Contributions to the Solution of Sex Difficulties, Being the Continuation of "Married Love"* (London: G. P. Putnam's Sons, 1928).

7. Stopes, *Enduring Passion*, 20; and see also Lesley A. Hall, "The Stopes Collection in the Contemporary Medical Archives Centre at the Wellcome Institute for the History of Medicine," *Bulletin of the Society for the Social History of Medicine* 32 (1983): 50–51; Billie Melman, *Woman and the Popular Imagination in the 1920s: Flappers and Nymphs* (New York: St. Martin's Press, 1988), 3; and Peter Eaton and Marilyn Warnick, *Marie Stopes: A Checklist of Her Writings* (London: Croom Helm, 1977).

8. Charlotte Stopes's study of the declining legal position of British women over the centuries is mentioned by Dale Spender, *Women of Ideas and What Men Have Done to Them from Aphra Behn to Adrienne Rich* (London: Routledge and Kegan Paul, 1982), 280.

9. See Hall, *Marie Stopes*: a friend's aunt who attended one of Stopes's Mothers' Clinics saw her there on one occasion, being very "fluttery" (personal communication).

10. Jane Marcus makes the unwarranted assumption, in *Virginia Woolf and the Languages of Patriarchy* (Bloomington: Indiana University Press, 1987), 176, that Woolf was utopian in imagining a married woman working in a scientific laboratory in the 1920s. Women and scientific careers during this period are discussed more generally in my unpublished paper "Women in Medicine and Biomedical Science, 1914–1945," presented at the conference "Women in Britain, 1914–1945," held at the University of Sussex, 10–13 April 1992.

11. Ruggles Gates's statement about the affair (Add. Mss. 59848) was deposited in the British Library Department of Manuscripts by his widow (he married again twice but had no children). Understandably bitter, he contradicts Stopes's version, though his statement, written many years after the event, contains certain implausibilities. It seems unlikely that Stopes would have acted as cynically as Gates implied (for example, that she was using contraception from the outset of their marriage and that she was promiscuously unfaithful to him), but it is plausible that she could have convinced herself that they had had no "true marriage" in spite of technical consummation.

12. Stopes, *Married Love*, author's preface, xiii.

13. Alluded to in a letter from Maurice Hewlett to MCS, 26 [February/March

1911] (conjectural dates apparently penciled in by MCS), Add. Mss. 59496, BL, alludes to this.

14. Eaton and Warnick, *Marie Stopes*; Melman, *Woman and the Popular Imagination*, 3.

15. Hynes, *A War Imagined*, 366–69; Sheila Jeffreys, *The Spinster and Her Enemies: Feminism and Sexuality, 1880–1930* (London: Pandora Press, 1985), 157.

16. Hynes, *A War Imagined*, 369.

17. Jeffreys, *The Spinster and Her Enemies*, 157–58. In Frank Mort, *Dangerous Sexualities: Medico-moral Politics in England since 1830* (London: Routledge and Kegan Paul, 1987), and Johanna Alberti, *Beyond Suffrage: Feminists in War and Peace, 1914–1928* (London: Macmillan, 1989), discussions of the complex issues surrounding sexuality in the 1920s are heavily and somewhat uncritically influenced by Jeffreys' thesis.

18. Sheila Jeffreys, "Sex Reform and Anti-feminism in the 1920s," in *The Sexual Dynamics of History: Men's Power, Women's Resistance*, by London Feminist History Group (London: Pluto Press, 1983), 177–202.

19. Jeffreys, *The Spinster and Her Enemies*, 158.

20. For charges that she was a eugenicist, see, for example, Stephen Trombley, *The Right to Reproduce: A History of Coercive Sterilisation* (London: Weidenfeld and Nicolson, 1988), 79–82, and Angela Holdsworth, *Out of the Doll's House: The Story of Women in the Twentieth Century* (London: BBC Books, 1988), 95–96. On eugenic ideas at the time, see Lesley A. Hall, "Illustrations from the Wellcome Institute Library: The Eugenics Society Archive in the Contemporary Medical Archives Centre," *Medical History* 34 (1990): 327–33, which includes a bibliography of recent works; see also R. A. Soloway, *Demography and Degeneration: Eugenics and the Declining Birthrate in Twentieth Century Britain* (Chapel Hill: University of North Carolina Press, 1990).

21. "Marie Carmichael" [Marie Stopes], *Love's Creation* (London: John Bale, Sons, and Danielsson, 1928), 340–43. Her view was encapsulated in the title of *A Letter to Working Mothers on How to Have Healthy Children and Avoid Weakening Pregnancies* (London: Published by the author, 1919): too many pregnancies too close together depleted the mother's vitality and diverted her energies from the proper rearing of the children she already had. See also Stopes, *Radiant Motherhood*, chap. 17, "Baby's Rights," 171–82, in which she attributes "the mental and physical aberrations which are today so prevalent" to "the secret revolt and bitterness which permeates every fibre of the unwillingly pregnant and suffering mothers."

22. Stopes, *Enduring Passion*, 41–43, 45–48; see also Marie Stopes, *Sex and the Young* (London: Gill Publishing Co., 1926), 53–56.

23. Stopes, *Radiant Motherhood*, 157–59.

24. It is targeted for attack by Sheila Jeffreys in "Sex Reform."

25. Isabel Hutton, *Memories of a Doctor in War and Peace* (London: William Heinemann, 1960), 216–17.

26. *Love without Fear*, by Eustace Chesser, a gynecologist and psychologist with a Harley Street practice, was prosecuted, albeit unsuccessfully, for obscenity in 1942.

27. Stopes, *Wise Parenthood*, 31.

28. Eaton and Warnick, *Marie Stopes*.

29. Hall, "The Stopes Collection"; see also Lesley A. Hall, *Hidden Anxieties: Male Sexuality, 1900–1950* (Cambridge: Polity Press, 1991), for a more detailed analysis of the response of her male readers.

30. Stopes, *Married Love*, 67, 70. See chap. 5, "Mutual Adjustment," 38–54, and chap. 7, "Modesty and Romance," 66–71.

31. Mrs. AR, Mrs. GR, PP/MCS/A212, Mrs. HW, Miss DMW, Mrs. FMW, Mrs. MW, PP/MCS/A245, Mrs. DEW, PP/MCS/A249, CMAC.

32. Naomi Mitchison, *You May Well Ask: A Memoir, 1920–1940* (London: Victor Gollancz, 1979), 69–70; see also idem, *All Change Here: Girlhood and Marriage* (London: Bodley Head, 1975), 157.

33. She submitted at least two manuscripts, "A Man's Mate" (1910) and "Winged Egoism" (1915), to Macmillan (Sotheby's catalogue for the Macmillan archive—withdrawn from sale to go to the British Library). She also endeavoured to exploit the publishing contacts of her friend Mollie Stanley Wrench (MSW to MCS, 5 February 1917, Add. Mss. 58491, BL).

34. Stopes to her journalist friend Mary Abbott, 23 August 1928, PP/MCS/A2, CMAC. The writer Maurice Hewlett objected to the name "Rose Amber" in a manuscript by Stopes that he read in 1916 (Hewlett to MCS, undated [c. 1916], Add. Mss. 58496, BL).

35. Mentioned in the typescript version of her reminiscences of Maurice Hewlett (published in somewhat different form in *John O'London's Weekly*, 8 March 1940) (Add. Mss. 58496, BL).

36. *Times Literary Supplement*, 19 July 1928, 538. Stopes was reading in "Cupboard" from late 1913 and was in touch with Havelock Ellis, Margaret Sanger, and other sex reformers during these years. Rose's *Marie Stopes* sheds considerable light on how "innocent" Stopes was at this stage of her career.

37. Ibid.; she expressed similar sentiments in a letter to the editor of *Nature*, 22 August 1928 (Add. Mss. 58704, BL).

38. Rebecca West, "The Tosh Horse," in *The Strange Necessity: Essays and Reviews* (London: Jonathan Cape, 1928), 319–25.

39. Marie Stopes, *A Banned Play and a Preface on the Censorship* (London: John Bale, Sons, and Danielsson, 1926), 10–11. However, although Stopes was prepared to concede, indeed defend, the "natural desires" of normal healthy womanhood, she still swerved away from presenting a "nice" woman as sexually knowledgeable, even on a purely theoretical level; Vectia is enlightened about the true state of affairs in her marriage by her neighbor and platonic admirer, Heron.

40. Stocks to MCS, 27 August 1927, Add. Mss. 58540, BL; see also Mary Stocks, *Still More Commonplace* (London: Peter Davies, 1973), 18–28, for her own account of Stopes and further comments on *Love's Creation*.

41. No one mentions the Deceased Wife's Sister Act, 1907 (enabling marriage to a sister-in-law, previously illegal), though Stopes remembered it in her *Marriage in My Time* (London: Rich and Cowan, 1935), 12–13, as being a source of heated controversy; and see E. S. Turner, *Roads to Ruin* (London: Michael Joseph, 1950), 98–121, on this much-disputed issue. Such marriages were far from universally accepted even when legalized.

42. Edward Carpenter, "Man the Ungrown," *Love's Coming of Age* (1896; re-

print, London: George Allen and Unwin, 1930), 51–59; his works greatly influenced Stopes.

43. Roberta Clarke, in a personal communication, has suggested that Rose Amber "equals" Stopes's second husband, Humphrey Verdon Roe, for many years the ideal supportive spouse. Although this is plausible, and perhaps illuminating about the transmutation of "life" into "art," it is nonetheless remarkable that Stopes made her fictional characters fulfill conventional roles that her life contradicted.

44. "The Glorious Unfolding" is the title of the concluding chapter in Stopes, *Married Love*.

45. Susan J. Leonardi, *Dangerous by Degrees: Women at Oxford and the Somerville College Novelists* (New Brunswick: Rutgers University Press, 1989).

46. Her copious correspondence with the publishers (Add. Mss. 58526, BL) includes nothing about *Love's Creation*. To John Farquharson, "Business Manager for Authors," she claimed that the pressure had come from their side (22 March 1934, Add. Mss. 58524, BL).

47. See her letter to the editor of *Nature*, 22 August 1928 (Add. Mss. 58704, BL).

48. She made some effort to get a cheap edition brought out in the early 1930s, but John Farquharson indicated that publishers were likely to undertake this only if a new novel generated further interest. See his letter to MCS, 31 May 1934, enclosing letter of 23 May 1934 from Rich and Cowan, Publishers, to this effect (Add. Mss. 58524, BL).

49. Short or collective reviews were found in *Nation and Athenaeum* (30 June 1928), *Evening News* (6 July 1928), *Times Literary Supplement* (12 July 1928), *Spectator* (21 July 1928), and *Morning Post* (14 August 1928), as well as the notice in *Nature* (4 August 1928) that so aroused her ire (see note 37).

50. Mary Abbott suggested that "Sunday-Express-itis and all that 'Well of Loneliness' pother" might explain "the attitude of Boots Library" (letter to MCS, 27 August 1928, Add. Mss. 58497, BL), but Rebecca O'Rourke, in *Reflecting on "The Well of Loneliness"* (London: Routledge, 1989), 92, states that "the initial impact" of the *Sunday Express*'s attack on Hall and her book "was to increase interest and sales."

51. *Spectator*, 21 July 1928, 112. It seems to be commonly assumed that *"Life's Adventure"* by "Mary Carmichael" in Virginia Woolf's *A Room of One's Own* (1928; reprint, Harmondsworth: Penguin, 1970), 79–93, is "really" *Love's Creation* by "Marie Carmichael." See, for example, Marcus, *Virginia Woolf*, 175–76. This must work by almost total reversal, with Woolf describing what Stopes failed or never set out to achieve in the first place. Woolf's use of the name "Mary Carmichael" follows her previous allusions to the old ballad "The Queen's Maries"—"There was Mary Beaton, and Mary Seton, and Mary Carmichael, and me." If she had known of Stopes's novel, and had had any inkling of Stopes's famous litigious touchiness, would she have used this name instead of, perhaps, "Mary Hamilton"? Anyway, where Stopes really belongs is surely at the beginning of the same chapter, among other women writing not in the traditional female form of the novel but in areas previously closed to them.

52. Spender, *Women of Ideas*, 371, 407; of all Stopes's many works, only *Wise Parenthood* is cited in the bibliography.

53. Mollie Stanley Wrench to MCS, 26 June 1928, Add. Mss. 58491, BL.

54. Laurie Taylor, "The Unfinished Sexual Revolution," First Marie Stopes Memorial Lecture, 12 March 1971, published in *Journal of Biosocial Science* 3 (1971): 473–92.

55. Martin Pugh, *Women and the Women's Movement in Britain, 1914–1959* (London: Macmillan, 1992), provides a useful overview.

56. Carpenter, "Marriage: A Forecast," *Love's Coming of Age*, 110–29.

57. Taylor, "The Unfinished Sexual Revolution," however, makes a start toward "placing" Stopes in those debates of the period, associated with such figures as Wilhelm Reich and D. H. Lawrence, concerning the broader social implications of sexual repression and liberation. "The Unfinished Sexual Revolution" is a fine but little-known article, which I myself came across only during the late stages of revision of this essay.

SUSAN SQUIER

Sexual Biopolitics in *Man's World*:

The Writings of Charlotte Haldane

"What would the effect be on society if human beings could determine in advance the sex of their children?"[1] Six years before Aldous Huxley's *Brave New World* (1932), sixty years before amniocentesis and the selective abortion of female fetuses, a feminist radical published a novel dramatizing the results of such a scientific advance.[2] Charlotte Haldane's *Man's World* (1926) portrays a society in which women are reduced to biology, categorized by their reproductive roles, and ruled by a coterie of racist male scientists through a network of cybernetic surveillance and biologically based control.[3]

Despite her prescient analysis of the gendered threat of reproductive technology, Charlotte Haldane is more likely to be remembered now for her sixteen-year marriage to the British geneticist J.B.S. Haldane. Perhaps this is because the tale of their meeting has the popular appeal of the romance genre: a young woman journalist planning to write a novel on a scientific theme seeks out the scientist whose writings inspire and educate her. They fall in love, and after a celebrated divorce case, they marry.[4] Finis? Hardly, since marriage was no more conclusive in Charlotte Haldane's life than it is in feminist fictions. Escaping the constriction of the romance plot, separating from and later divorcing J.B.S. Haldane, Charlotte Haldane went on to work as a prolific journalist, novelist, political essayist, and editor of the anti-Fascist magazine *Woman Today*.

   Charlotte Haldane was a woman of deep contradictions: a self-declared lifelong feminist who wrote an "antifeminist classic" supporting vocational motherhood and blaming suffragists and spinsters for the devaluation of mothering; a severe critic of anti-Semitism and racism whose first novel concerns a white-only eugenic society led by the "particularly Jewish" visionary Mensch; a vocal champion of the meliorist project of scientific control who used that same first novel to dramatize the dangers of state government by scientists.[5] How could a woman of such conflicted and turbulent allegiances produce a novel critical of scientifically based reproductive control and, only a year later, the pro-natalist tract *Motherhood and Its Enemies* (1927)? One answer would be to say that Haldane's dystopian novel reflects the discursive and historical pressures faced by feminists in the early modern period. It oscillates, in a way characteristic of female modernism, between critique of and collaboration with the modern scientific project, dramatizing the oppressive potential, for women, of the scientific control of reproduction while constructing its plot and characters in terms of the dominant scientific discourse. The novel thus records the interactions of a feminist radical with her context: the scientific, social, and literary milieu of early-twentieth-century Britain.

   Biology was a powerful language in which to express the changing sense of the human condition at the turn of the twentieth century.[6] In the wake of Darwin and Mendel, biologists increasingly called on theories of evolution, degeneration, and heredity to draw parallels between the development of the human race and the development of other species.[7] The dominant discourse of biology spawned other, more focused discourses linking the reproductive histories of individuals to the fate of the human race: eugenics, sex reform and sexology, and vocational mothering.

   Founded in 1907, the Eugenics Education Society sought to advance "the science which deals with all influences which improve the inborn qualities of a race; also with those which develop them to the utmost advantage."[8] Although its membership was always small, the influence of the Eugenics Society increased with World War I, when the population decline caused by battlefield deaths renewed the popular interest in aggressive policies of both positive and negative eugenics.[9] Pioneers in the new scientific field of sexology, among them Francis Galton, founder of the Eugenics Society, studied human sexuality as part of the scientific project of "the discovery, description, and analysis of 'the laws of Nature.'"[10] Celebrating the consolidation of sexology as a scientific discipline at the Third Annual Congress of the World League for Sexual

Reform (1929), Dr. Magnus Hirschfeld identified the sexologist's proper terrain as the fields of "sexual biology, sexual pathology, sexual ethnology ['the sexual life of the human race from prehistoric times up to our own'] and sexual sociology." [11]

Sexologists constructed new taxonomies of sexual pathology, prominent among them the category of the *intersex*, a term used for a condition of gender nonconformity ranging from the social (i.e., "mannish" behavior in a woman) to the physiological (i.e., individuals who appear outwardly to correspond with one sex but whose sexual organs are appropriate to the other sex).[12] Some biologists in the 1920s used such categories to argue for universal potential bisexuality, but when the biological data were applied to society by the sexologists, they were typically used to police gender boundaries and shore up the differences between so-called normal male and female behavior and appearance.[13]

Common to these discourses inspired by late-Victorian biology was the new sense that human sexual behavior, and perhaps even the human species itself, might be capable of scientific and/or social reconstruction. Yet despite this shared assumption, neo-Darwinians, eugenicists, sexologists, and sex reformers ignored the constructed nature of the *gender* distinction central to their investigations. As Sheila Jeffreys has shown, the sexologists and sex reformers built their "progressive" sexual program on an antifeminist foundation. They used scientific discourse to validate three unscientific (and tiresomely familiar) misogynistic notions: that there are innate, biologically based, immutable differences between the sexes (especially in the realm of sexual behavior); that ideal sexual relations are male-dominant, female-submissive; and that the womanly ideal is wholly embodied by motherhood.[14]

Although contraceptive education was an important goal of the sexologists and sex reformers, who supported the scientific separation of sexuality from reproduction, many sexologists also vigorously promoted the notion of vocational or "racial motherhood," holding that to produce healthy children was a woman's duty to the nation and the race.[15] This biologically based construction of woman's "proper role" recycled feminist rhetoric to masculinist eugenic ends, exalting motherhood at the price of female diversity.

The late-Victorian and early-modern fascination with biology also reinvigorated the reproductive fantasies that have played a prominent role in utopian and dystopian fictions since Thomas More's *Utopia* (1516) and Francis Bacon's *The New Atlantis* (1627), both of which experimented with notions of selected breeding.[16] H. G. Wells drew on that utopian tradition to explore different modes of reproduction in his turn-of-the-century writings, but the notion of scientifically controlled reproduction achieved cultural prominence with J.B.S. Haldane's *Daedalus; or, Science and the Future* (1923), which in the first year after publication sold fifteen thousand copies and went through five printings.[17] Indeed, the climate of scientific enthusiasm in the first three decades of the twentieth century made the notion of reproductive control seem, if not yet fully practical, something more than just a fantasy. While novelists and social theorists considered the social impact of scientific techniques for controlling reproduction, biologists and embryologists were experimenting with techniques of mechanically induced parthenogenesis, embryonic grafting, tissue and cell culture, and prenatal sex determination.[18]

The contemporary cultural fascination with biology led to a deep interest in the question of the mechanism of sex determination in the early 1920s. Charlotte Haldane published a column on the social impact of prenatal sex selection in the *Daily Express* six months after J.B.S. Haldane predicted extrauterine gestation in *Daedalus* and before Charlotte sought him out as scientific adviser for her first novel. In "The Sex of Your Child," Haldane explores current developments in the scientific project "to probe, reveal, and ultimately to control the forces behind the phenomena of existence." The column forecasts the issues to be raised by a technique for prenatal sex determination, only to foreclose them by the scientific parameters defining the debate. Haldane predicts that such a technique will result in major changes in the social organization of race and gender. The ability to produce male babies will give crucial support to colonialist projects, whereas the ability to choose the sex of children will eradicate gender-based social inequality: the "surplus women" problem will disappear, and every woman will be able to become a mother.[19]

These meliorist predictions ignore the links between gender and war, the implicit racism in the construction of the colonizing project, and the phallocentrism of the assumption that only women who are legally married may become mothers and that unmarried women are problematic because "surplus." Haldane's response to the possibility of prenatal sex determination is overwhelmingly positive because she sees in it a biologically based control that can be exercised on both the individual and the group, the physiology and the psyche, to ensure that "male" and "female" continue to be distinctly different categories. Once prenatal sex determination is possible, Haldane predicts, children will no longer be burdened with parental resentment for being "the wrong sex" and society will no longer be burdened by the "intersex".

Haldane gave her fullest treatment to the issue of the intersex in *Motherhood and Its Enemies* (1927). This volume advances certain limited feminist positions, among them contraceptive access (for married women), subsidized motherhood, and increased research into, and use of, anesthetics in childbirth. Yet those feminist interventions rely on a disturbingly antifeminist distinction between mothers and "abnormal" women (spinsters, war workers, suffragists, and feminists).[20] Central to Haldane's argument in *Motherhood* is an attack on the intersex woman, whom she blames for male-female "sex-antagonism." Haldane holds that competition among women, rather than sexual oppression, has caused the particular "problem of sex" that concerns her: "the [debased] position of motherhood in the modern world" (146, 8).

Motherhood and Its Enemies grounds tendentious social observations in the purportedly authoritative discourse of biology and constructs female sexuality as almost totally limited to reproduction. Haldane condemns the intersexual woman not for her homosexuality but for her failure to have children, which she claims poses a grave threat to the human race. Jane Lewis has suggested that such a privileging of motherhood may have been unavoidable at the time. "[Few] women would have dared to speak against motherhood when the quality and quantity of population was considered to be of such great national importance."[21] Yet if Haldane's volume idealizes motherhood, it also criticizes eugenics as potentially open to racist and class-based abuses, asserting that "as certain ordained and even lay preachers of eugenics prove, this science holds potentiality of great danger" (238).[22] Despite its pronatalist bias, *Motherhood and Its Enemies* shares the concern of *Man's World*: the scientific control of female reproduction threatens female agency and autonomy.

Man's World (1926) dramatizes Haldane's assertion in "The Sex of Your Child" that the discovery of a technique of prenatal sex selection could change the relations between sexes, nations, and races. Yet the nature of that change, as well as the way the novel resolves the "problem" of the intersex, articulates a powerful critique of the scientific project "to probe, reveal, and ultimately to control the forces behind the phenomena of existence."[23] Critics disagree on whether Haldane's novel is utopian or dystopian. I question the very possibility of reconstructing a unitary authorial intention for *Man's World*. To my way of thinking, a more useful approach to the novel—the approach I take in this essay—

is to consider it as a record of the conflicts in Haldane's own response, as a feminist, to the dominant discourse of modern science.

Remarkably, half a century before Michel Foucault, *Man's World* dramatizes how reproductive technology can produce power and knowledge for a patriarchal state through control of the (female) body.[24] The novel's premise is the invention of a technique of prenatal sex selection. Developed by a geneticist well versed in animal husbandry, the "Perrier exercises," performed regularly by the pregnant woman, are her way of advancing the state goal: the progressive development of the white race "by the scientific mastery of man's instincts . . . to propagate his species" (10). Although designed to empower the pregnant woman (to produce sons), the Perrier exercises transform female choice into female necessity. They enable the state to choose the sex of each generation and so use the scientific search for enlightenment to further its patriarchal, nationalist, and racist-colonialist mission.

Haldane's fictitious state is dedicated to the perpetuation of the "entire white race," a task that recalls the theory of the survival of the germ plasm. Promulgated by the nineteenth-century German zoologist August Weismann, this theory held that a "particular sort of protoplasm . . . was transmitted substantially unchanged from generation to generation via the germ-cells, giving rise in each individual to the body-cells (soma) but itself remaining distinct and unaffected by the environment of the individual."[25] This early articulation of the genetic basis of heredity was later embraced by eugenics groups, concerned with inherited racial purity, as an answer to those who pressed the influence of environment over heredity.[26] As it was portrayed by biologists of the day, the theory was unconsciously, if not intentionally, gendered male, a gender bias that Haldane's dystopia fully exploits.[27]

Haldane's novel not only portrays the sexism integral to eugenics in the late twenties but also anticipates the rise of Nazi eugenics within the decade. In 1933, the counselor of Germany's Reich Ministry of the Interior would justify the Eugenic Sterilization Law, passed by Hitler's cabinet, by evoking the purity of the racial bloodline. "We want to prevent . . . poisoning the entire bloodstream of the race."[28] A similar mythology of the purity of the blood gives structure to the dystopian state of *Man's World*: modeled on the human cell, its central city is named Nucleus, and its official propagandists have "translated the terms of the social organization into those of the human body [which stands] symbolically for the entire white race" (63).

Anticipating the abuses of the Nazi doctors, Haldane's fictitious state uses biomedical science to produce racial division and white supremacy.

The state relies on a worldwide network of "communication and direction," on a surveillance and control group called the "Ears," "founded strictly on the principles laid down by their psycho-pathological researchers," and on a technique for race-specific chemical warfare known as Thanatil, targeted to "that enzyme which produces the black pigment in negroes, and which, when attacking the tyrosine ester of Thanatil absorbed by the dusky skin, gradually liberates the poison till the central nervous system is invaded, causing paralysis and death" (63–65).

Haldane's narrative of the political uses found for the Perrier exercises dramatizes the gendered objectification that contemporary critics have argued is integral to the scientific method.[29] Although the Perrier exercises testify to woman's power (for the woman's physical work produces the desired-sex fetus), once governments realize the method's potential to consolidate "Man Power," the prenatal production of male fetuses takes top priority (36). Boys are needed, the narrator explains, to perpetuate patriarchy, the patrilineal class system, and industry.

The disproportionate value placed on masculinity in Haldane's dystopia translates into a biologically based vision of gender roles. Women are divided into three categories according to their reproductive activity. Vocational mothers are selected by state committee to participate in "a career which had its grades like all others." They devote their lives to "the theory, as well as the practice, of race-production" (55).[30] "Neuters" occupy themselves with the professions, and "entertainers" serve men sexually and aesthetically—as dancers, actors, singers, poets, and novelists—and smile "perpetually" (130). These categories are rigid and impermeable. Women must choose their category at puberty, and at that point the other two are permanently closed to them by the intervention of state-enforced science. "Either you become a mother or you must be immunized" (127).

Haldane's novel chronicles two tales of individual, body-centered resistance to the compulsory reproductive categories enforced by this scientific state. There is Christopher, whose mother, mourning the loss of a daughter born "abnormal," refuses to practice the Perrier prenatal exercises during his gestation. As a result, he is born "intermediate sexually" (296). Resisting conscription into the ranks of the professionally and biologically "normal" males, Christopher prefers to be a musician and philosopher rather than a scientist and to remain celibate rather than mate with an appropriate female partner.

The second resister is Christopher's sister, Nicolette, who refuses to choose between motherhood and the two other socially enforced women's roles, a Neuter professional or an Entertainer. Instead, with

her brother's help, she procures an antidote to the state-enforced ster-
ilizing "immunization," planning to become pregnant *not* according to
state policy but by her own free actions.

Both attempts at resistance fail, not because they are defeated from
without but because they collapse from within. Haldane's representation of the power over human bodies produced by her fictional reproductive technology reveals that the very terms within which resistance
arises may transmute it into an effect of the power it seeks to dislodge.
Christopher's opposition to heterosexual normality is hollowed out and
possessed by the normalizing discourse it opposes. With fatal consequences, he internalizes the restrictive categories of Nucleus, which label
some people normal and others deviant depending on their sexual and
reproductive behavior. He comes to see himself in the terms of the
dominant society: as one whose "submasculinity" prevents him from
contributing to the improvement of the race (297). Unable to find support for his beliefs either from Nicolette or within himself, Christopher
commits suicide by flying too high in his airplane. He crashes for lack
of oxygen, a Daedalus turned Icarus.

Nicolette's resistance is directed not at gender roles but at sexuality,
defined narrowly as reproduction. The state controls women's reproductive lives through the Motherhood Council, which assesses the women's
fitness to be mothers in terms of their genetic makeup, character, and
education and assigns reproductive partners—"mates"—to the women
permitted to reproduce. Nicolette resists this state regulation of motherhood, arguing that it reduces female liberty, and chooses instead to
regulate her reproductive life herself.

Freedom is an elusive condition in Haldane's biologically determinis-
tic society. Although Nicolette's resistance does not end tragically—as
does Christopher's—she suffers a kind of death, for she is co-opted by
the patriarchal and instrumentalist values of "Man's World." She falls in
love with Bruce Wayland, chief experimental scientist of Nucleus, and
her resistance is transformed to loyalty. Pregnant by her scientist-lover,
who calls her his little "mother-pot," Nicolette comes to think of herself
as but an instrument for producing "his" son (295). High-placed in government, Bruce recasts her pregnancy as an act not of defiance but of
submission to the state ethos of auto-experimentation: "an experiment,
although . . . unusual and a bit risky" (239). Accepting the romantic-
reproductive-scientific contract, Nicolette both objectifies herself and
accepts the objectification of others.[31]

Thus, power produces resistance that turns into power—both
Nicolette's socially constructed, limited power as a mother-to-be and

the patrilineal power soon to be enjoyed by the archetypal masculine subject who will be (re)born from her womb. Pregnant, Nicolette affirms not just experimental science but also the specifically *vocational* motherhood she previously resisted, whose central concern is the creation of a son through the Perrier technique of prenatal sex selection.

To argue that Haldane's novel embodies the oppressively gendered implications of prenatal sex selection is not to say that Haldane consciously planned to write a dystopian novel. Rather, the novel may have been intended, and was certainly received, as a feminist utopia. Critics praised "the wife of the well-known Cambridge biologist" for enriching "the literature of Utopia" while they ironically emphasized the novel's feminist agenda, as "a protest of modern woman against opposition to her ideals."[32] The novel betrays an ambivalent response to the scientific project, nowhere more vividly than in the character of the scientist Bruce Wayland. Bruce must have been conceived of, at least to some degree, positively, for he is modeled on J.B.S. Haldane and is explicitly associated with the two scientific activities that first attracted Charlotte Haldane to her husband-to-be. As she recalled in her autobiography, *Truth Will Out*, J.B.S. was "a biologist who specialised in making experiments on himself with some substance called acid sodium phosphate. His imagination seemed to equal his physical courage. With humorous audacity he was . . . making startling predictions about the biological future of the human race, including a fantastic but matter-of-fact account of the growing of a human foetus in the laboratory. 'This is my man!' I thought instantly" (16–17). Yet despite this initial attraction to J.B.S., and the ectogenesis and auto-experimentation with which he was associated, *Man's World* dramatizes the oppressive foundations of these scientific activities. Haldane also shows the frightening side of Bruce Wayland, in both the early scene in which Wayland defends ectogenesis to the vocational mothers of Nucleus and the later scene in which he protests his ban from the laboratory where he engages in auto-experimentation.

The early scene, in which the vocational mothers of Nucleus discuss ectogenesis, contrasts dramatically with Huxley's ungendered treatment of the topic in *Brave New World*. It reveals Haldane's fear that the new technology will displace women from their reproductive (and social) roles. A visiting geneticist, who has developed the technique in his work on cattle, asks the mothers how they think "the suggestion of human ectogenesis will be generally received." The response he receives is unequivocally negative. "You will be the most unpopular man in the world" (59). Yet despite the women's horror at the notion of "a sort of

human termite queen from whom the entire race shall be bred," Bruce
Wayland joins the geneticist in impassioned defense of the reproductive technology on eugenic grounds. He states: "Ectogenesis provides
the means to select on the most strictly accurate lines. The number of
mothers chosen diminish year by year. Until at last, those who supply
the race are the supreme female types humanity can produce" (61–62).
Claiming a stance of scientific objectivity not yet shaken by the revelations of Nazi biomedicine, Bruce Wayland shows frightening indifference to the reduction of women to breeders.[33]

Haldane continues her attack on scientific objectification in the debate
between Wayland and the company director, who bans Bruce from further auto-experimentation. The very parameters of this debate express
the limitations of instrumental rationality: either Bruce can do what he
wants with his body and continue auto-experimentation, or the company director can do what the company wants with Bruce's body and
Bruce cannot continue with his dangerous auto-experimentation. But
no matter which form of instrumentality prevails—scientific or industrial—the outcome is the same: Bruce's body is objectified and alien-
ated, constructed as something to *use* rather than to *be*. Indeed, the
scene dramatizes the breakdown of that very opposition between scientific and industrial instrumentality, for as Sandra Harding has pointed
out, since the nineteenth century, science itself has "increasingly been
organized along industrial lines."[34]

If we tease out the implications of auto-experimentation and ectogenesis—the scientific procedures that first drew Charlotte to J.B.S.
Haldane and with which her character Bruce Wayland is associated—we
discover that both activities express an ideology privileging scientific instrumentality or, as Bruce puts it, viewing "all living and striving . . . [as]
amenable to experiment" (62). Both procedures embody notions characteristic of Western post-Enlightenment rationality and shared by both
industrial and reproductive technology: a notion of a mind/body split,
which valorizes mental experience and denigrates physical experience;
and a notion of the autonomous individual, which, coupled with the
notion of the body as property, has been marshalled to support acts of
bodily objectification as diverse as prostitution, organ selling, surrogate
motherhood, and transsexual mutilation.

Charlotte Haldane's pseudoscientific utopian novel falls short of the
critique of instrumental reason that I have sketched out above, in part
because it relies on scientific discourse to advance the cause of female
agency and autonomy. But there is another reason why Haldane's novel
eludes the clear-cut criticism of the scientific project, a criticism that

contemporary feminist readers might desire: her position as a woman writer working in a literary field that was all too often constructed as a "man's world" as well.

The ambivalence toward science betrayed by Haldane's novel is rooted not only in Haldane's personal experience but also in her position as a woman writer in relation to literary modernism, as a brief comparison of *Man's World* and *Brave New World* will demonstrate. Although both works offer representations of reproductive technology, in particular of J.B.S. Haldane's notion of ectogenesis, they articulate distinctly different critiques of the modern scientific project. Gender, the crucial analytic category for Charlotte Haldane's novel, figures little in Huxley's dystopia; instead, *Brave New World* focuses on class. Thus Huxley excoriates science as the handmaiden of a feminized mass culture, whereas Haldane warns of its potential for a restrictive and oppressive control of women.

In *Brave New World*, Huxley articulates the high modernist criticism of mass culture as debased and feminized, a theme shared by such diverse male modernist works as E. M. Forster's *Howards End* and D. H. Lawrence's *Women in Love*. From the novel's opening scene—when the director of the Central London Hatchery and Conditioning Centre jokingly remarks, "Embryos are like photograph film . . . they can only stand red light"—Huxley portrays the ultimate result of industrial rationality: the standardization of the human product.[35] In their passive uniformity, Huxley's ectogenetic embryos reflect the techniques of mechanical reproduction (the cinema, the camera) that have produced modern mass culture.[36] Reprints of one another, they produce and consume in a world devoid of high art or pure science, activities Huxley constructs and valorizes as subversively masculine.

Huxley's novel, despite its horror at the feminized modern industrial world, never problematizes gender as a category of experience or analysis. Thus he portrays ectogenesis as affecting women no differently than men. Both sexes donate gametes (women, eggs; men, sperm), which the factory combines and modifies and from which it produces babies to standardized and factory-generated specifications. "Standard Gammas, unvarying Deltas, uniform Epsilons. Millions of identical twins. The principle of mass production applied to biology."[37] Huxley's vision is gender-uniform and uniformly dismal: women and men alike are debased by the factory method, since biological mass production serves mass culture.

Although *Man's World* betrays none of the fear of a feminized mass culture that is characteristic of male modernism, Haldane's work does embody the characteristic traits of female modernist writing: *attention to the experience of marginality*, in its consideration of the problem of the intersex; *concern with gender politics*, in its portrayal (in contrast to *Brave New World*) of the gendered implications of such reproductive technologies as ectogenesis and prenatal sex selection; *strategic use of a decentered perspective*, in its use of two protagonists of opposite sex (Christopher and Nicolette), one of whom resists while the other capitulates; and *the split focus or doubled gaze resulting from conflicting identification*, in its ambivalent representation of scientific instrumentality as a force both sexually appealing (to Nicolette) and life-threatening (to Christopher).[38]

To those structural and thematic traits of female modernist writing, we can add a fifth trait shared by late-Victorian and modernist woman writers: *the use of scientific language to advance the feminist cause of female agency and autonomy*. As Jane Lewis has observed: "By the late nineteenth century it was already necessary to demonstrate a scientific approach in order to gain full recognition. . . . The use of biological analogy, in particular, proved very popular in explaining all kinds of social problems."[39] Haldane's novel reflects this trait as it negotiates the conditions for expression with the hegemonic discourse of science.

Tracing the development of the scientific state from control over reproduction (via birth control, then sex predetermination) to control over women, *Man's World* ends with a chilling assertion by Bruce the scientist: "There will always be Christophers, and they will always suffer. But it's the experiment that counts for us, not the result" (299). Poised between celebration and critique of the scientific control project, *Man's World* is—to contemporary feminist readers who respond to its prescient political analysis—a profoundly troubling dys/utopia.

Discursive regimes, like flesh-and-blood ones, eventually come to an end. Charlotte Haldane gradually became disillusioned with the analytic power of science.[40] But before she abandoned the scientific worldview, she experimented once again with mobilizing scientific discourse for her own political purposes. This time, however, her goals were a potent and conflicting mix of socialism, antifascism, and feminism.[41]

In 1939, Haldane took on the editorship of *Woman Today*, a paper published by the Women's Committee for Peace and Democracy. *Woman Today* had a monthly circulation of more than twenty-five hundred, mostly sold through Left Bookshops, and boasted the support, among others, of M.P. Ellen Wilkinson and the novelists Rosamund Lehmann and Rebecca West.[42] Using the domestic discourse of the woman's magazine to advance the causes of antifascism and socialism, *Woman Today* printed a steady stream of leftist fiction and features, including Sylvia Townsend Warner's series "Women of Yesterday" (Harriet Beecher Stowe, Rosa Luxemburg, Countess Markievicz, and Josephine Butler), short stories by Naomi Mitchison, and monthly editorial essays discussing topics ranging from women's role in the Spanish Civil War to the Chinese women's movement. Reflecting Haldane's long-standing interest in the area, the magazine also published essays on scientific topics, such as Dr. Barbara Holmes's discussion of the early forays into estrogen-replacement therapy, "The Gland That Controls Your Sex."[43]

An article by Haldane herself perhaps best illustrates how the magazine used the discourse of science for left-wing political purposes, often muting its feminism in the process. Entitled "'They Were Two Hours from Death, but I Was Not Afraid': The Inside Story of My Husband's Experiment," the piece records how J.B.S. Haldane and four other members of the International Brigade experimented on themselves to determine why British submariners died in an accident on the submarine *Thetis*.

The essay recycles themes familiar from *Man's World*—the bravery of auto-experimentation, the social centrality of science—but with a crucial difference. Haldane begins by promising to reveal "what it feels like to be married to a scientist who occasionally experiments on his own body to find out things for the benefit of humanity," and the narrative strategies of the woman's magazine sugarcoat her subject, producing an idealized portrait of the scientist.[44] If the feminist critique has dropped out, however, the leftist critique has replaced it. In an ironic return to—and deconstruction of—the notion of enlightened government by scientists, a notion central to *Man's World*, Haldane praises the "scientific tradition" as "one of the noblest conventions of mankind" while she denies that a link exists between science and the post-Enlightenment state. Instead, Haldane constructs science not as gendered oppressor but as ungendered site of resistance, and she shows scientists working not to consolidate (masculinist) state power but to reduce the human abuses (industrial and military accidents, illnesses) produced by capitalism. She rejects the glorification of auto-experimentation as the pinnacle of human self-sacrifice and bravery, exalting instead the greater bravery of ordinary citizens. Implicitly rejecting the notion of a scientific elite controlling a debased and passive citizenry, she puts aside the specifically feminist analysis of her earlier critiques of science, instead urging

"the common men and women of this country" to work together with
scientists "to overthrow this system and to bring in Socialism, Peace,
True Democracy, and a really Brave New World" (3).

From *Man's World* to "a really Brave New World," Haldane's writings
in the years leading up to fascism embody a variety of complex, even
frustratingly inconsistent, ways of defining and responding to social
injustice. In *Man's World*, she articulated a vigorous feminist critique
of the scientific control of woman's reproductive power, whereas in
Motherhood and Its Enemies, she collaborated with the scientific construction of woman-as-mother in order to combat the greater eugenic threat
to woman's maternal agency. Finally, as editor of *Woman Today*, Haldane mobilized the rhetoric of conventional wife- and motherhood to
leftist, anti-Fascist ends. Often contradictory, always engaged, Charlotte
Haldane's writings stand as a fascinating record of one radical woman's
changing responses to the sexual biopolitics of a turbulent era.

Notes

I am grateful to the editors for their helpful comments on an earlier version of
this essay.

1. Charlotte Haldane, *Truth Will Out* (London: George Weidenfeld and
Nicolson, 1949), 15.

2. Feminist and leftist critique of the uses of amniocentesis to identify and
abort female fetuses is extensive. See, for example, Les Levidow, "Sex Selection in India: Girls as a Bad Investment," *Science as Culture*, pilot issue, 141–52,
and Michelle Stanworth, ed., *Reproductive Technologies: Gender, Motherhood, and
Medicine* (Minneapolis: University of Minnesota Press, 1987). For another discussion of "feticide," see Gena Corea, *The Mother Machine: Reproductive Technologies from Artificial Insemination to Artificial Wombs* (New York: Harper and
Row, 1985).

3. Peter Firchow mentions Haldane's novel in his essay "Science and Conscience in Huxley's *Brave New World*," *Contemporary Literature* 14 (Summer
1975): 301–16, but the fullest treatment appears in Elizabeth Russell, "The Loss
of the Feminine Principle in Charlotte Haldane's *Man's World* and Katharine
Burdekin's *Swastika Night*," in *Where No Man Has Gone Before: Women and Science Fiction*, edited by Lucie Armitt (London: Routledge, 1991), 15–18. See also
Nan Bowman Albinski, *Women's Utopias in British and American Fiction* (London: Routledge, 1988). Charlotte Haldane, *Man's World* (London: Chatto and
Windus, 1926).

4. Charlotte Haldane uses the romance genre to tell the story of her marriage
to J.B.S. Haldane in *Truth Will Out*, 14–24. J.B.S. Haldane's biographer also

uses the romance genre to describe their courtship. See Ronald Clark, *J.B.S.: The Life and Work of J.B.S. Haldane* (London: Hodder and Stoughton, 1968), 73–77.

5. Sheila Jeffreys has described Haldane's *Motherhood and Its Enemies* (London: Chatto and Windus, 1927) as an "anti-feminist classic." See Jeffreys, *The Spinster and Her Enemies: Feminism and Sexuality, 1880–1930* (London: Pandora Press, 1985), 174.

6. The term *biology* was coined at the beginning of the nineteenth century by Gottfried Reinhold to refer to the study of human existence and was later extended to mean "the scientific study of living things." See Peter Morton, *The Vital Science: Biology and the Literary Imagination, 1860–1900* (London: George Allen and Unwin, 1984), 11, and M. Abercrombie, C. J. Hickman, and M. L. Johnson, eds., *The Penguin Dictionary of Biology* (London: Penguin Books, 1951, 1980), 41.

7. For a discussion of the way literature dealt with the Darwinian notions of evolutionism, degeneration, eugenics, and heredity, see Morton, *Vital Science*; for a discussion of the contradictory impact of the work of sexologists in the last decades of the nineteenth century and the first three decades of the twentieth century, see Jeffrey Weeks, *Sexuality and Its Discontents* (London: Routledge, 1985).

8. In 1926, the year Charlotte Haldane published *Man's World*, the Eugenics Education Society changed its name to the Eugenics Society (Sir Francis Galton, cited in Lesley A. Hall, "Illustrations from the Wellcome Institute Library: The Eugenics Society Archive in the Contemporary Medical Archives Centre," *Medical History* 34 [1990]: 327).

9. Daniel Kevles, *In the Name of Eugenics: Genetics and the Uses of Human Heredity* (Berkeley: University of California Press, 1985), 85; Jane Lewis, *The Politics of Motherhood: Child and Maternal Welfare in England, 1900–1939* (London: Croom Helm, 1980), 16.

10. Magnus Hirschfeld spoke of Galton as one of sexology's "great pioneers"; see Hirschfeld, "Presidential Address: The Development and Scope of Sexology," in *Sexual Reform Congress*, edited by Norman Haire (London: Kegan Paul, Trench, Trubner and Co., 1930), xiv. Weeks, *Sexuality*, 64.

11. Jeffreys identifies this conference as the "high point" of the field of sexology, which after 1930 came under attack by the rising Nazi movement in Europe and suffered from the combined effects of the rise of fascism, the economic depression, and the drift to war in England (*The Spinster*, 186–87). Corroborating Weeks's observation that "sexology is . . . an heir to the post-enlightenment faith in scientific progress," Hirschfeld closed his presidential address by claiming, "Francis Bacon's famous saying, 'Knowledge is power,' is also true in this field" (*Sexuality*, 70; "Presidential Address," xv).

12. Weeks, *Sexuality*, 67–69; Jeffrey Weeks, *Sex, Politics, and Society: The Regulation of Sexuality since 1800* (London: Longman, 1989), 104–17.

13. Weeks, *Sexuality*, 87–88. The tendency to extrapolate from animal to human sexual characteristics produced an entertaining confusion even in the contemporary biological literature, as in the following passage from a classic text on reproductive physiology: "There exist [among men and women] all transi-

tional forms from the most masculine male to the most effeminate male, and, on the other side, from the sapphist and the virago to the most feminine female; but in man the characters of one sex are always dominant, though the degree of dominance varies through considerable limits" (Francis H. A. Marshall, *The Physiology of Reproduction*, 2d ed. [London: Longmans, Green, and Co., 1922], 690–91).

14. Jeffreys, *The Spinster*, 128–46.

15. Weeks, *Sex*, 128–31; Jeffreys, *The Spinster*, 134–36. Angela Ingram examines the dangerous political consequences of the notion of vocational motherhood in "Un/Reproductions: Estates of Banishment in English Fiction after the Great War," in *Women's Writing in Exile*, edited by Mary Lynn Broe and Angela Ingram (Chapel Hill: University of North Carolina Press, 1989), 326–48.

16. Morton, *Vital Science*, 97, and Darko Suvin, *Metamorphoses of Science Fiction: On the Poetics and History of a Literary Genre* (New Haven: Yale University Press, 1979), 103.

17. H. G. Wells, *The Time Machine: An Invention* (London: Heinemann, 1985), *The War of the Worlds* (London: Heinemann, 1906), *The First Men in the Moon* (London: Newnes, 1901); Clark, *J.B.S.*, 70; J.B.S. Haldane, *Daedalus; or, Science and the Future* (London: Kegan Paul, Trench, Trubner and Co., 1923). I discuss the debate over ectogenesis in my book, in progress, on the representational origins of reproductive technology, "Babies in Bottles."

18. Among the important research being done by early-twentieth-century biologists and embryologists was Jacques Loeb's discovery of the technique for mechanically induced parthenogenesis in sea urchins (1899), Alexis Carrel's development of a technique for keeping frog embryo nerve tissues alive outside the body (1907), W. E. Castle and John C. Phillips's work transplanting the ovaries of guinea pigs (1909), and Hans Spemann's discovery of techniques for embryonic grafting (1918). See Gordon Rattray Taylor, *The Science of Life* (London: Thames and Hudson, 1963), 255–62; see also Mordecai L. Gabriel and Seymour Fogel, eds., *Great Experiments in Biology* (Englewood Cliffs, N.J.: Prentice-Hall, 1955), 204–8.

19. Charlotte Burghes [Haldane], "The Sex of Your Child," *Daily Express*, 2 July 1924, 6–7. For clarity and convenience, I refer to the author as Haldane rather than Burghes, her name by her first marriage. Haldane predicted: "The question of colonisation will be reviewed in a new light. Colonial nations that cannot at present produce sufficient males to populate their vast territories may then be able to do so" (6).

20. Jeffreys, *The Spinster*, 174–75. In *Motherhood*, Haldane defines the "intersexual woman" as one who "[deviates] more or less markedly from the feminine form towards the anatomical and physiological characteristics of the masculine sex" (158). Despite this biologistic construction, Haldane focuses on "intersexual" women's *behavior*, which she blames for reducing the social standing of mothers: "In the past few years, particularly since the war, when their [intersexuals'] advertised activities threw into the background the less spectacular exertions of mothers . . . their influence has grown alarmingly" (156).

21. Lewis, *The Politics of Motherhood*, 221.

22. Haldane continues: "Let the class-conscious or race-proud individual . . . attain any influence in this matter, and those whom he fears or hates (the same

thing) will fare hardly. One would require a certificate of psychological purity even in the case of certain scientists before one would entrust them with so dangerous a profession as that of human geneticist" (*Motherhood*, 238).

23. Haldane, *Truth Will Out*, 15; Burghes [Haldane], "The Sex of Your Child," 6.

24. Michel Foucault has defined "four great lines of attack along which the politics of sex advanced . . . combining disciplinary techniques with regulative methods": the sexualization of children, the hysterization of women, the control of birth, and the psychiatrization of perversions. *Man's World* anticipates the latter two control strategies. Michel Foucault, *The History of Sexuality*, translated by Robert Hurley (New York: Vintage Books, 1980), vol. 1, *An Introduction*, 145–47. See also Michel Foucault, *Discipline and Punish: The Birth of the Prison*, translated by Alan Sheridan (New York: Vintage, 1979), and Hubert L. Dreyfus and Paul Rabinow, *Michel Foucault: Beyond Structuralism and Hermeneutics* (Brighton: Harvester Press, 1982).

25. M. Abercrombie, C. J. Hickman, and M. L. Johnson, *The Penguin Dictionary of Biology*, 7th ed. (London: Penguin Books, 1980), 129–30.

26. Kevles, *In the Name of Eugenics*, 70–71.

27. Julian Huxley's representation of the germ-line theory in *The Science of Life* offers an instance of such unconscious gendering. According to Weismann's theory, the germ plasm would be perpetuated in, and through, the bodies of women as well as men. Yet in Huxley's coauthored textbook, the line drawing illustrating the way "the germ-plasm in each generation produces bodies (soma)" unmistakably represents three white men. See H. G. Wells, Julian Huxley, and G. P. Wells, *The Science of Life* (London: Cassell and Co., 1931, 1938), 441.

28. Quoted in Kevles, *In the Name of Eugenics*, 116–17, 195–96.

29. There is a burgeoning body of feminist scholarship on this issue. Among the best recent works are Evelyn Fox Keller, *Reflections on Gender and Science* (New Haven, Conn.: Yale University Press, 1985), Sandra Harding, *The Science Question in Feminism* (Milton Keynes: Open University Press, 1986), Mary Jacobus, Evelyn Fox Keller, and Sally Shuttleworth, eds., *Body/Politics: Women and the Discourses of Science* (New York: Routledge, 1990), and Ludmilla Jordanova, *Sexual Visions* (Brighton: Harvester Wheatsheaf, 1990).

30. Like the early-twentieth-century hygienists, Haldane's hypothetical state has reconstructed "the sexual" as "the racial," by conflating reproductivity with sexuality. See Frank Mort, *Dangerous Sexualities: Medico-Moral Politics in England since 1830* (London: Routledge and Kegan Paul, 1987), 186.

31. Here I extend Carole Pateman's analysis of male sex-right as integral to post-Enlightenment liberal society. In Haldane's novel, collaboration with the scientific control of reproduction has reduced woman to experimental subject, thus robbing her of agency, whether biological or social. See Pateman, *The Sexual Contract* (London: Polity Press, 1988).

32. *Berliner Tageblatt* and *Labour Magazine*, reprinted as part of the advertising matter for *Man's World*, in Haldane, *Motherhood*.

33. In 1937, Katharine Burdekin memorably fictionalized the Nazi reproductive reduction in *Swastika Night* (New York: Feminist Press, 1985), edited by Daphne Patai. Russell, "Loss of the Feminine Principle," discusses the parallels

between Haldane's and Burdekin's dystopian visions of societies in which men have ultimate control over women's (reproductive) bodies.

34. Harding, *The Science Question*, 70.

35. Aldous Huxley, *Brave New World* (New York: Harper and Row, 1932, 1946), 6; Andreas Huyssen, *After the Great Divide: Modernism, Mass Culture, Postmodernism* (Bloomington: Indiana University Press, 1986).

36. "During the 1920s and '30s, rather than approaching film as an art, Huxley saw film primarily as another product of technology, mass-produced and mass-oriented; as entertainment, a passive leisure-time activity which, instead of stimulating creativity, induced mindless quiescence" (Virginia M. Clark, *Aldous Huxley and Film* [Metuchen, N.J.: Scarecrow Press, 1987], 7). For a good study of Huxley's critique of Taylorism and Fordism, see Peter Edgerly Firchow, *The End of Utopia: A Study of Aldous Huxley's Brave New World* (Lewisburg, Pa.: Bucknell University Press, 1984).

37. Huxley, *Brave New World*, 4.

38. See Susan M. Squier, "Virginia Woolf's London and the Feminist Revision of Modernism," in *City Images: Perspectives from Literature, Philosophy, and Film*, edited by Mary Ann Caws (New York: Gordon and Breach, 1991), 99–119.

39. Lewis continues, "The ideas formulated by scientists and mediated by the medical profession formed the framework within which all women, including active feminists . . . had to work" (Jane Lewis, *Women in England, 1870–1950* [Bloomington: Indiana University Press, 1984], 82).

40. This happened at roughly the same time that she fell out of love with J.B.S. As she recalled in her autobiography: "Having absorbed as much as my untrained mind could master of the scientific outlook on life, I began, at first slowly, with emotional resistance to admitting my disillusionment, but gradually more rapidly, to lose my interest in science. This coincided with my realisation that my second marriage was not going to give me the satisfactions, especially the children, which I had hoped for from it. So I began to look for intellectual and emotional compensation in other directions" (*Truth*, 33).

41. Between 1934 and 1944, Haldane worked as an undercover agent for the Communist International Brigade (in the Spanish Civil War) and, during World War II, as a journalist in the Soviet Union. See Haldane, *Truth*, especially chap. 7, "Communist International."

42. Like Haldane's writings before it, *Woman Today* is (as its title indicates) a battleground for different constructions of woman. The inaugural issue of the journal under Charlotte Haldane's editorship carries congratulatory messages from a number of women who would have been anathema to the Charlotte Haldane of *Motherhood and Its Enemies*, in particular Florence White, of the National Spinster's Pensions Association, and Rebecca West, whose endorsement lauds Haldane herself "as one of the finest figures that the woman's movement has brought forward" (March 1939). Later, the distinct feminist emphasis in the fiction and many of the features (such as Sylvia Townsend Warner's series on women in history) would war with the complacent construction of women as proud wives of brave men. My discussion of *Woman Today* is based on research in the Haldane archives of the D.M.S. Watson Library, University College, London, and on the microfilm copies of *Woman Today* held at the British Library (Colindale).

43. *Woman Today*, October 1936, 4, 10, 12; March 1937, 6, 14; April 1937, 5, 12; June 1937, 6, 12; September 1937, 5, 8, 9–10, 13–14; January 1939, 1–5, 16–17; February 1939, 3, 9–10, 11, 16–17; July 1939, 2–3, 8–9.

44. Charlotte Haldane, "'They Were Two Hours from Death, but I Was Not Afraid': The Inside Story of My Husband's Experiment," *Woman Today*, August 1939, 2.

SHOSHANA MILGRAM KNAPP

Real Passion and the Reverence for Life:

Sexuality and Antivivisection in

the Fiction of Victoria Cross

On the first night of a romantic elopement, before the honeymoon has properly begun, Eva discovers that Eric, her new husband, is cruel to animals: he beats and berates a dog whose only crime is excessive affection. Eva's love for her husband is irremediably destroyed. She feels, in its place, empathy with the suffering dog and imagines the dog's dread of death and his pain, which she sees as a foreshadowing of her marriage. She escapes from her husband, taking the dog with her; over a year later, she and the dog are still living happily together. A good man is hard to find; Eva chooses instead to live with woman's best friend. Such is the story line of "A Novel Elopement" (1921), which focuses its condemnation of a man's mistreatment of animals not primarily on the sufferings of the animal itself, but on the man's projected deprivation of a woman's right to a full and independent life.

Animal welfare, as a moral and political issue, has been the focus of two sorts of reformist groups: the traditional humane movement dedicated to eliminating cruelty to animals because it symbolized and inspired cruelty toward humans; and the more radical, more explicitly ideological movements, particularly in the late-Victorian period and thereafter, that decried animal experimentation as part of an institutionalized scientific and technological antilife force.[1] The two approaches—the personal and emotional versus the political and institutional—are both relevant to the long-standing intimate connection between feminism and animal welfare, a connection that itself can be seen as following both tendencies.

The traditional, humane, emotional trend asserts that women's victimization resembles the animals' victimization, that is, that their pain is seen as unimportant or even desirable and that women, who share the animals' fate, are thus far more likely than men to empathize with animals' suffering. Women have been viewed as more primitive, more instinctive, and thus more sensitive to the experience of beings who are closer to nature. The more radical, political, institutional expression of the woman-animal connection holds that women, as victims of oppression, are more likely to care about the experience of the powerless and disenfranchised. In modern times, moreover, science has been accused of justifying and perpetrating the domination and appropriation of women; medical technology in particular is seen as invasive and demeaning.[2]

Sexuality, inherently a shaping element in women's pain and subordination, is relevant to the parallels drawn between women and animals. Echoing and transforming Freud's "A child is being beaten" (which meant a male child) in her chapter title "A Woman Is Being Beaten," Coral Lansbury discusses the sadistic objectification of women by men —in metaphor and in life—as parallel to the mistreatment of animals; male readers and spectators experienced sexual pleasure through torturing and dominating both animals and women. Carol Adams, who draws parallels between meat eating (the fragmentation and consumption of animals) and the objectification of women (again, in metaphor and in life), appears to be saying that, in these situations, "a woman is being eaten."[3]

Within the spectrum of writers who draw analogies between the mistreatment of animals and the mistreatment of women and who care about alleviating human and animal suffering, Victoria Cross is notable for attempting to blend the two approaches rather than to choose between them—much as she wishes, for certain purposes, to view the nonhuman animals as part of the same community as the human animals. She is thus concerned, simultaneously, with individual and social reform, presenting the former in a story such as "A Novel Elopement" and the latter in the utopian novel *Martha Brown, M.P.* In a similar spirit of reconciliation, she also attempts to see sympathy, passion, and sexuality not as dividing lines between men and women but as the inspiration for a common ground. Yes, women are often abused (physically, emotionally, sexually, politically), as are animals, by men—but healthy, passionate spirits can triumph, privately and in concert, over bad ideas, bad habits, bad laws. Women are not merely and universally victims, and men are not merely and universally villains. In her worldview, the sexes need not be opposites.

With regard to sexuality, Victoria Cross promotes a transformative vision; instead of seeing women as sexually mistreated because they are often treated and abused like animals, Victoria Cross celebrates animal sexuality—genuine passion and freedom—as a kind of ideal. Whereas, as Lansbury observed, prostitutes were often conceptualized as animals, Victoria Cross, in *Martha Brown, M.P.*, presents an England in which the eradication of prostitution is both the effect and the cause of a burgeoning animal-like sexual passion.

Throughout her forty-year career, Victoria Cross celebrated the power of sexual passion as life's chief reward. In her view, cruelty to animals was not only immoral but also unattractive because it destroyed, along with life itself, the zest and joy that give life its savor. Rising to prominence as the "New Woman" author of *The Woman Who Didn't*, a response to Grant Allen's *The Woman Who Did*, she wrote some twenty-five novels, from 1895 to 1937, promoting passion and the reverence for life, in a variety of expressions. Among her books are *The Night of Temptation*, *The Eternal Fires*, *Over Life's Edge*, *Hilda against the World*, *A Girl of the Klondike*, *Life of My Heart*, and many others (all of which feature the sort of exotic settings and erotic events that the titles imply).

Annie Sophie Cory (1868–1952), also known as Vivian Cory and V. C. Griffin, seems to have chosen the pseudonym "Victoria Cross" as a complicated joke: she deserved the Victoria Cross for her valor, and she hoped to make (Queen) Victoria cross through her candor.[4] Her name, in other words, identified her as both a hero and an outlaw. Although she now qualifies for inclusion in a volume of radical writers who have been forgotten, she was published worldwide and was well known in her time as an exponent of passionate sexuality. As evidence of her notoriety in this context, consider the statements of two formidable authorities on romantic passion: Oscar Wilde and the mother of a teenage girl. While serving as hostess of a tea on the Riviera, in 1928, the mother was invited by one of her guests to attend a party at which Victoria Cross was to be present:

> "Victoria Cross!" exclaimed the hostess in horror. She could not have appeared more horrified had her friend uttered aloud the name of some unmentionable disease, and at once her expression became

one of condemnation. "In that case I'm afraid I can't come. You see," she added, "Yvonne's only seventeen."

"But does that make any difference?" asked the genuinely surprised guest.

"Well, dear, Victoria Cross . . . I mean, she wrote all those dreadful books. I read them, naturally, after I was married. But *Three Weeks*! Hardly a book for a girl of Yvonne's age."

Gently I informed the mother that Mrs. Elinor Glyn was responsible for *Three Weeks*.

"Perhaps," I said, "you're thinking of *Five Nights*?"

"Surely," she snapped, "it's the same thing? Except that *Five Nights* sounds even worse."

Victoria Cross! The woman whose novels were read behind locked doors; who had at one time been accused of poisoning the purity of British homes with her sordid writings—a veritable Noel Coward of the nineties![5]

Oscar Wilde is equally assured in his assessment of Victoria Cross's power, and far more enthusiastic. "If one could only marry Thomas Hardy to Victoria Cross," Wilde told Frank Harris, "he might have gained some inkling of real passion with which to animate his little keepsake pictures of starched ladies."[6]

Victoria Cross left, by design, little public record of the "real passion" in her own experience. Born in India and educated there and in England, she was the sister of Adela Florence Cory Nicolson (1865–1904), who wrote *The Garden of Karma*, *Stars of the Desert*, and *Indian Love* (collections of poems, chronicles of interracial romance) under the name "Laurence Hope." Hope's passionate love poems, which were rumored to have been based on her affair with an Indian prince, were, most likely, fantasies. Nonetheless, some have attributed the death of her husband, at the age of sixty-one, not to illness but to shock and grief; her suicide by poison, two months later, has been seen as an indication of guilt and regret. Somerset Maugham indicated, in *A Writer's Notebook*, that "The Colonel's Lady" was suggested by her life and death.[7]

The life story of Victoria Cross is less overtly melodramatic but is nonetheless enigmatic. She lived much of her adult life in Europe, with Heneage Griffin, a wealthy uncle, who cosigned most of her book contracts. Was her Uncle Heneage her lover? Her inspiration? Her collaborator? Her victim? She left such questions unanswered. She took steps to conceal his private papers, and hers. Even when the threat of censorship made the film of her novel *Five Nights* front-page news in 1915, she declined to step forward. Annie Sophie Cory preferred to live as Victoria Cross, in contact primarily with readers. She died in Italy, naming as her "universal heir" Paolo Tosi, a diamond dealer who is said to have been her lover.[8]

Although her identity was masked and the events of her life have been concealed, her sensibility is inimitable and compelling. Nowhere else can a reader find such a fascinating gallery of sexually passionate women: a schoolgirl who becomes, in a dream, the bride of Apollo and is allowed to rejoin her lover only after providing for the future of their baby demigod (*The Eternal Fires*, 1910); an actress-dancer-playwright who marries an evil man in exchange for his promise to produce her play but who later tramps seven miles through the Italian mountains to infuse her blood into her anemic lover (*Paula*, 1896); an artist, androgynous in manner and appearance, who makes her lover jealous of her friendships with both men and women but who saves his life, in Port Said, by submitting for a week to the desires of a gang of men (*Six Chapters in a Man's Life*, 1903); a scholarly aesthete who secretly becomes the lover of an Indian prince and, after his death, kills their child to free herself to marry a man she loves even more (*Anna Lombard*, 1901); a demure, repressed wife who expresses her natural sensuality only when she assumes the identity of a demimondaine to attract (or regain?) her husband's affections (*A Husband's Holiday*, 1932); and Martha Brown, citizen of a truly exotic country, a thirtieth-century England in which women are the ruling sex (*Martha Brown, M.P.*, 1935): Martha is a novelist, playwright, reformist politician, founder of schools, mother of four (two pretty boys and two sturdy girls), and lover of four (an older man with a powerful mind, a fun-loving younger man with an appealing body, a tempestuous artist who lives in Italy with one of the children, and a dependent husband who lives in the suburbs with the other three). Readers responded to these characters with shocked suspicion or sincere admiration.

There was, however, more to Victoria Cross's advocacy of passionate sexuality than the promotion of permissiveness; her position, on the contrary, amounted to a new religion. She celebrated love as a combination of affection and natural passion, stressing the bond between body and spirit. She addressed the same points when she dealt with the topic of the treatment of animals, and she integrated her political advocacy with her literary description of human emotions. Although, in keeping with her tendency to avoid the public eye, she was not herself an activist in the cause, she regularly contributed money and—through such fiction as "A Novel Elopement," "To Sup with the Devil," and *Over Life's Edge*—expressed her convictions through her writing.

Victoria Cross's lengthy passages depicting sexual desire and activity are abstract but intense, extensive, and absolutely central to the events. Although reviewers typically decried the excessive attention to "a certain side of our nature," the books sold extraordinarily well all over the world. Perhaps the mothers who removed the books from their daughters' hands intended, secretly, to read the books themselves. Her presentation stressed the path from affection (based on perceived kindness) to passion. Although the emphasis is on passion, affection is the starting point, and she conceives of both emotions as natural, inevitable, appropriate, and quasi-sacred.

For the man who is in love with Eurydice Williamson, the "woman who didn't" (in Victoria Cross's first novel): "The gentleness, the reverence, the consideration that ran through all my thoughts regarding her, and that I had sedulously encouraged and cultivated for her sake, had been like delicate flowers growing on the sides of a volcano and co-existent with the subterranean flames." Although love begins with gentle reverence, it does not end there. Victoria Cross continues: "And as in an eruption of the volcano, the flowers perish, are annihilated and obliterated in the flow of boiling lava, so now all those holier, more tender impulses sank submerged under the liberated tide of the underlying passion."[9]

In "The Kiss in the Wilderness," kindness to animals is specifically identified as the trigger of respectful reverence, a prerequisite (necessary if not sufficient) for love. On the road between Jericho and Jerusalem, Christine Smith feels esteem for Sheik Lasrali when she observes his kindness and tenderness to animals, but her esteem becomes love only when she also perceives "that strange wild magnetism, that irresistible call and challenge to the senses," the "one supreme joy and consolation for all the sufferings of life, the joy of simple, natural unrestrained love."[10]

That this sort of passionate involvement is indeed natural, though so often constrained and imperiled, is an important point. In *A Husband's Holiday*, Jeanette reclaims her true identity only by disguising her appearance and altering her manner in an attempt to seduce her own husband. "She was mistress to all the arts of fascination and seduction; it was no trouble to her, no effort to make use of them because they arose naturally from that great well of intense feeling within her. In moments when she might have seemed to others exaggerated, artificial in her intensity of passion and emotion, she was in reality only revealing her natural self: throwing open her heart and its secret stores. It was Jeanette, quiet and repressing herself, acting up to what she thought a wife should be, who was the more artificial woman of the two. In this life now Rosalie might have to paint her skin and hide her physical self under a disguise, but mentally a mask had been thrown away."[11] The natural self, the self without the mask, the fully passionate and unreservedly sexual self, is also described by Victoria Cross as, at its best, the animal self.

Kindness to animals is the index of general kindness and, as such, inspires reverence and affection. When passion appears, it too can be associated with animals: to be a passionate person is to be as ardent, intense, and uninhibited as a passionate animal. In *Electric Love*, both aspects of love (respect and passion) are presented in association with animals. Lena, to begin with, is reassured by Rinyi's kindness to animals: "He loved animals, those weak defenseless things that can only suffer without appeal man's barbarities. That was enough for her. She was wise enough to know that the man who loves animals and treats them well is fundamentally good and can be always trusted, just as the man who is cruel to them and denies them their rights, is rotten all through and should be shunned and fled from."[12]

Lena moves on from mild affection to passion, through a dream of herself as a lioness awaiting her mate.

She mounted to the top of the peak and from there, with uplifted head, she sent forth a long reverberating roar that rolled far and wide like a roll of thunder over the lower plain. Then she listened. Faint out of the distance came an answering cry and then another from nearer and then another louder and stronger as the advancing animal approached, covering miles in its swift leaping steps. She called again sweetly this time, her voice full of love, and the answer came beck from very near. Then her eyes, strong to see for a distance of eighty miles, descried a lithe and sinuous form bounding forward over the level yellow plain. It was her mate, and she knew him at that distance, knew his voice, and she cried again with melting tenderness. Tense and quivering with love and longing she stood there waiting for him, and he saw her too, her graceful outline against the sky, the sun on her smooth golden flanks. And his great muscles carried him to her like the wind, and he was up close upon her now, on the rock beside her, gorgeous in the sun, beautiful in the wild strength and grace of his form. And from under his forehead of short, tawny fur, blazed upon her with the fires of love two great shining plates of gold; the light-filled eyes of the desert lion. He was close, very close, to her panting, trembling form, and those glorious eyes looked straight into hers. (30)

One can see why the mother of seventeen-year-old Yvonne did not want her daughter to spend an evening chatting with Victoria Cross.

But along with the evocation of the natural power and the powerful nature of sexual passion, there is also an insistent and pervasive assertion of the connection between the body and the spirit. The body is not merely body. The painter Trevor Lonsdale, in *Five Nights*, reflects on his love for his model, "Yet it would be wrong to say that those lines alone had captured me, for had they enclosed a stupid and commonplace mind they would have stirred me as little as if they themselves had been imperfect." [13] Naranyah, the Indian student in *Self and the Other*, says, "The love of the soul, the light of the mind that plays through the worship of the senses, that breaks and bends and subdues, and uses the body as its instrument and exponent, as the brain uses the voice—that is what fills and fires one's life and one's being." [14]

A late novel, *Martha Brown, M.P.*, contains an eloquent passage on this subject. The artist Carlo explains to Martha that his current lover, a beautiful fisher-girl, is the equivalent of a pillow, a weak and inadequate substitute for Martha herself. "In you there is a whole spiritual domain. Your mind, your spirit, all your thoughts and wishes and ideas, your sentiments, they must all respond to me. . . . But in that girl there is no soul to call to. As I have said, it is like clasping a beautiful, warm pillow and nothing more." [15]

The same novel contains one of Victoria Cross's trademark love scenes: romantic passion in a lovely, wild, and unusual location. Martha and Carlo spend the night in a silver cavern, which is filled each night with pulsing waves and unearthly singing sounds—an experience that frightened the pillowlike fisher-girl but that delights and arouses Martha. "So far, it had been a crescendo of melody as the water rose and rose, reaching its climax at high tide, when all the drums beat madly as the waves rushed in, hurling themselves against the cliffs with a tremendous boom, and the air, forced out of its million recesses, fled, crying and lamenting into space, but after that, as the great ocean prepared to draw itself back and the tide fell, came a beautiful and slow *diminuendo*. The drums pulsed more faintly and at rarer intervals, the sweet singing sounds, the violin sounds, all melted into a soft decline" (106). The passage appears to describe, at once, a musical performance, a natural phenomenon, and a sexual act.

The power of passion has the inevitability of nature and the emotional specificity of human experience. The sexual symbolism, moreover, is so overt that it seems clearly intentional, perhaps even deliberately amusing in its directness. Speaking to Martha of the "symphony of sound," Carlo points out, "There is practically an organ in every cavern" (104). One can see why Oscar Wilde thought that this sort of "real passion" was just what was needed for Hardy's "starched ladies," and why Yvonne's mother was nervous.

Contemporary reviews were frequently even more alarmed and hostile than Yvonne's mother. *Reedy's Mirror* referred to *The Eternal Fires* as "putrescently prurient," the *Athenaeum* spoke of the "repulsive realism" in *The Religion of Evelyn Hastings*, and the *New York Times* considered *Anna Lombard* to be "brazen," "nauseating," and "far more disgusting" than Zola without even trying.[16]

The source of their discomfort is surely no mystery. Janet Hogarth's essay entitled "Literary Degenerates" aimed straight at Victoria Cross, whose first story had just appeared in the *Yellow Book*. "Tolstoi, at his worst, is almost preferable to the flood of literature professing to lay bare the mysteries of sex with a daring only possible to a shameless depth of ignorance. Few people are without the germs of possible disease; but are the confused and morbid imaginings, which the sane hide deep within their breast, to be offered to the world as the discovery of a privileged few? To be silly and sinful is not necessarily to be singular. We commend this consideration to the authoress of *Theodora*."[17]

The "mysteries of sex," the generally hidden "confused and morbid imaginings"—even the reviewers who relished the vividness of Victoria Cross's imagination were troubled by the frank treatment of passion. The *New York Times* advised her to exercise restraint: "There is much beauty in the book, much to appeal to the imagination, much power and discrimination and sense of color in the use of language. But Victoria Cross has a bad case of adjectivitis and would do well to make unsparing use of the blue pencil. She would do better still to remember that the holiest of human passions demands always a little reticence upon the printed page and that in descriptions of love it is necessary for an author to go warily lest he take unwittingly that unforgivable step which separates by so narrow a space the sublime from the ridiculous."[18] The character of the objections—the demand for reticence, the fear of ridiculousness, the threat of the unforgivable step—suggests that Victoria Cross literally trespassed, ventured into foreign territory, took matters beyond the civilized pale.

Regarding *The Religion of Evelyn Hastings*, the *New York Times* commented, "Heretofore her stories, both short and long, have dealt mainly with the passion of love, of which she writes with color and warmth and with an earnestness which helps to make amends for her lack in that discretion which is by far the better part of literary valor."[19] Observe that Victoria Cross herself is somehow on trial, that her moral status has been challenged, that she is being warned not to "cross" the line and become a "fallen" writer.

Victoria Cross professed to be serenely intransigent, responding to negative criticism with untarnished self-regard. "People who are jealous of me always hurl at my writings the reproach that they are immoral. From my own point of view I have never written a single immoral line in my life. I am immensely proud of my books and would read them aloud to a jury of Bishops with the greatest pleasure any time."[20] Her self-confidence, however, may have been based on her awareness, from the beginning of her career, of her vulnerability to attack on moral grounds. She was forced to work hard to develop appropriate defenses because her fiction encountered persistent and virulent moral slurs. Reviewers were free with cautionary advice.

B. A. Crackanthorpe's essay "Sex in Modern Literature," like Hogarth's "Literary Degenerates," cited Victoria Cross and her story "Theodora" as exemplars of a deplorable trend:

> Instead of walking on the mountain tops, breathing the pure high atmosphere of imagination freely playing around the truths of life and of love, they force us down into the stifling charnel-house, where animal decay, with its swarms of loathsome activities, meets us at every turn. . . . Revolting as it is that it should be possible for a girl to project herself into the mood of a man at one of his baser moments, faithfully identifying herself with the sequence of his sensations, as was done in a recent notable instance. . . . It is only by insisting on the essentially spiritual element in sex, by accepting it as the direct manifestation of a divine law, that it can be rescued from the camp-followers of literature and lifted back into that pure region which is its natural home.[21]

For Victoria Cross, the animals themselves lived in that "pure region." Viewing, as she did, animals as something other than brutes in the pejorative sense, Victoria Cross portrayed her characters as treating animals with kindness and as fully embracing their own animal selves—to their credit and with joy as their reward. She thus refused to see "animal decay" as a legitimate term of opprobrium, and she rejected the grounds on which Crackanthorpe and others attacked her work.

To be an animal, in sexual matters, was a positive attribute. In *Martha Brown, M.P.*, Victoria Cross presented the sexual reforms (and consequent health) in her women-dominant utopia as the result of replacing human law with animal law:

> Another great factor in the health of the country was the passing away of prostitution. For centuries this had existed, and it had come to be looked upon as the necessary accompaniment of civilization! Very primitive races, savages, animals did not know it. But now that woman had made herself so absolutely free, now that she had demanded and attained the right to live as happily as an animal, the need and use of prostitution had naturally declined. And to the naturally weakened and dying custom the women had given the knock-out blow by their laws. . . . They had looked around and seen that amongst the animals, where love is unlimited and free, it does not exist. With characteristic boldness, they had taken the reins off woman, and the bit out of her mouth, and turned her loose. . . . Though love is free among the animals, they have this one law, by which they all abide, that the female will never mate except from her own wish and will. This law alone seemed strong enough to keep them well. (36–37)

For Victoria Cross, there is no "animal decay" as such—only animal health and purity.

Accepting the charge and the mission of delineating the spiritual element in sex, the function of sexual passion as a manifestation of divine law, and the essential purity of what the impercipient might see as loathsome and corrupt, Victoria Cross made a special point, in her treatment of animals and the antivivisection cause, of showing that cruelty to animals was not only an act of aggression toward a weaker creature but also an index of moral evil, a failure of moral integrity, a mark of the passionlessness and lethargy that constitute moral death. To mistreat animals, in other words, is to remove oneself from consideration as a moral being. To do so in the name of science, moreover, is even worse than to do so casually or arbitrarily. The scientific justifications for animal research are seen as worse than irrelevant. In her view, to explain the mistreatment of nonhuman animals as the means to an end is itself an admission that the means are reprehensible. The end, furthermore, is a mere pretext in that the experiments—unreliable confirmations of invalid hypotheses by incompetent scientists—serve no purpose. Nothing is learned. Nothing is gained. Vivisectionists simply acquire practice in cruelty, which they can then further apply in their treatment of human animals. Her condemnation of the mistreatment of animals is based not on a notion of animal "rights" but on what becomes of human beings when they act with cruelty, on what they kill in themselves when they harm animals.

In her fiction, the consequences of the mistreatment of animals are both psychological and practical. Psychologically, Eric, the new husband in "A Novel Elopement," shows himself incapable of understanding and valuing his wife, Eva, when he mistreats the dog. He seems, to her, to have become a different person. "Somewhere between the Church and the farmhouse the Eric she loved had vanished."[22] She feels the dog's pain and fear and senses that she too is the victim of Eric's cruelty. "She had never meant to marry such a man. Had he shown himself before the ceremony as he had at the supper here, she would never have married him. Her hands turned cold, and her knees shook. She sank down in a chair by the fire. She had never realized the prison side of marriage. . . . In that moment she longed to be free of that room, free of her marriage as the dog outside longed to be free of his chain. . . . Eva had given to Eric not only love and admiration, but also the natural joyous passion of awakened girlhood. Now all these were equally dead" (77–78).

While Eric sleeps, Eva escapes through the farmhouse window and runs to the dog. "No Juliet felt more eager to join her Romeo than this girl did now to get to the suffering animal and soothe its pain" (87). Eva and the dog, whom she names Joy, become inseparable. "He understands *her* far better than Eric ever had, and at any moment he would lay down his life joyfully for her sake" (98). Through the thoughtless cruelty Eric displays toward the dog, he forfeits Eva's love and is replaced in her affections by a dog who shows the loyalty that Eric lacks.

In other works of fiction dealing with this subject, Victoria Cross dispenses punishment with even more gruesomely poetic justice: the perpetrators suffer the fate of their victims. In "The Vengeance of Pasht," a young medical student, experienced in animal experimentation, shows his insensitivity by pressing his advances on a young woman, the daughter of an Egyptologist. He pursues her to the temple of Pasht, a god with the body of a woman and the face of a cat, only to be crushed by Pasht's statue.[23]

In "To Sup with the Devil," the lab assistant—horrified at the experiments in starving, choking, and mutilating animals—ultimately locks the vivisectionist in the "lethal chamber" designed for the animals. Jenkins, who wanted to be a lab assistant because he likes working with animals, begins by feeling pity for the animals' suffering—and anger at the medical researcher who heedlessly tortures them—but he is finally moved to action by a lecturer who speaks of the effect of such experiments on young medical students.

> They are told that callous man who is sinking his knife between muscle and bone cutting the nerves of the poor moaning victim is doing *right* and a great man. Thus they are initiated into the devil worship. Supposing the young students, overcome by the revolt of all their natural instincts against it, faint at the revolting sight. They are carried out of the classroom and revived. By the order of the professor they are brought back and *made* to witness the lingering torments of the animals on the operating-table. They are being hardened. Day by day they are trained thus and gradually their normal feelings begin to change. From sickness and revolt at the horrors they see done, they come to a liking for them, a wish to participate in them, they become abnormal. Their brains having been shocked at the most sensitive age, they become deflected from their true balance. Those feelings of justice, mercy, sympathy and pity which distinguish the worthy human being disappear and the normal young man who commenced his medical course is at the end of it an abnormal ill balanced creature with that impulse toward cruelty we notice in the monkey highly developed and the qualities of man carefully trained out of his crooked brain.[24]

Knowing what he does of the medical researcher's actions and character, Jenkins has no qualms about killing him in order to save a few thousand helpless animals from torture and death. "The great deed for which he had lived night and day was done, swiftly and successfully accomplished. . . . So now if he had to die on the scaffold for this night's work he would die proudly for he knew that the work was good. One liar, one duper of the public, one traitor to his country, *one* monster of cruelty, if but one, has been put out of existence" (215). The doctor, in Jenkins's view, deserves to die, and in just that way: the door to the lethal room is closed, and the gas is turned on.

In *Over Life's Edge*, the protector of the animals, the executioner in the name of sympathy, kindness, and passion, is a woman, Violet Cresswell (note the initials, which are the same for Victoria Cross, and the name "Violet," which was the nickname of Laurence Hope). Violet, a writer who fled notoriety and allowed herself to be assumed dead, lives alone in an isolated cavern. One day Dudley, the man she loved when she was in the "world," discovers her hiding place; she allows him to remain, but she is unwilling to return with him to the life she found tiresome and artificial. When a shipwreck brings a Dr. Smith to her island, she risks her life to save him. But on hearing his cheerfully unrepentant confession of unnecessary experiments on animals human and nonhuman, she says she can no longer allow him to live, and she has her companion kill him.

> Could she ever close her eyes in sleep knowing that he, by her instrumentality, was working in his laboratory, preparing from the agony of dying animals his serums, that would later transfer their agonies, or other deeper ones, to the human race?
>
> No, better this horrible duty of extinguishing one life than partnership in the martyrisation of thousands. . . .
>
> There was not even the sense of acting as an avenger to excite and warm her heart; no fervours of righteous vengeance to sustain her. . . . Had she rescued an ordinary murderer, or anyone who had grievously injured her in the past, she would have readily forgiven, and as readily saved him. To the past belongs all past wrongs, and to her view, judgment, punishment and vengeance were in the hands of God alone. It was only plain, cold, stark duty that called her now; and it was not punishment for past, but prevention of future wrongs that she had to deal with.[25]

Murdering a vivisectionist on principle is entirely appropriate for a woman who abandoned civilization, and a successful career, in order to live in an unencumbered state of nature. "Don't you see my life here is like an animal's? I feed and live at the hand of the Creator, as the animals do, hence the freedom, the feeling of mixing, and being one with the elements" (39), hence too the passion, the joy, the juice of life, "full of a perfect calm, no worried, weary brain, no strained eyes, no jangled nerves, no heart aching from the cruelty, the ingratitude, the treachery of one's fellow creatures, no brain seared by their unkind speeches, no yearning after things beyond one's reach; nothing but melody, beauty, and peace" (20).

Violet Cresswell seems designed to speak for the writer: Violet left the "world" when her mother died, and Victoria Cross dedicates the novel to her own mother, who had died a few years earlier. Having chosen for herself the life of an animal, she takes the life of a man who harms animals. She represents passion at its purest, purity at its most passionate. The elements of her experience—her retreat to the cavern, her love for Dudley, her execution of Smith—are consistent, of a piece.

Although Victoria Cross appears to have been supremely self-confident, she did not ignore the comments made for and against her work; her insistence on the soulfulness of sex and the sexiness of the soul may have been, in part, an answer to her critics. Throughout her books she tried—to quote a familiar passage from a novel by one of her contemporaries—"to point out the salvation that was latent in . . . the soul of every man. Only connect! That was the whole of her sermon. Only connect the prose and the passion, and both will be exalted, and human love will be seen at its height. Live in fragments no longer. Only connect, and the beast and the monk, robbed of the isolation that is life to either, will die."[26]

Only connect. The monk—and the beast. Thomas Hardy—and real passion. Seventeen-year-old Yvonne—and Victoria Cross. The human —and the animal.

Notes

1. Susan Sperling, *Animal Liberators: Research and Morality* (Berkeley: University of California Press, 1988); Nicholas Rupke, ed., *Vivisection in Historical Perspective* (New York: Methuen, 1987).

2. Mary Daly, *Gyn/Ecology: The Metaethics of Radical Feminism* (Boston: Beacon Press, 1978); Barbara Ehrenreich and Deirdre English, *Complaints and Disorders: The Sexual Politics of Sickness* (Old Westbury, N.Y.: Feminist Press, 1973); Sperling, *Animal Liberators*; Rupke, *Vivisection*.

3. Coral Lansbury, *The Old Brown Dog: Women, Workers, and Vivisection in Edwardian England* (Madison: University of Wisconsin Press, 1985); Carol J. Adams, *The Sexual Politics of Meat: A Feminist-Vegetarian Critical Theory* (New York: Continuum, 1990).

4. Edward Lauterbach and W. Eugene Davis, *The Transitional Age: British Literature, 1880–1920* (Troy, N.Y.: Whitston, 1973), 81.

5. Sewell Stokes, *Pilloried!* (London: Richards, 1928), 71–72.

6. Frank Harris, *Oscar Wilde: His Life and Confessions* (New York: Covici, Friede, 1930), 331.

7. For appreciations of Laurence Hope, see Thomas Hardy, "Laurence Hope," *Athenaeum*, 29 October 1904, 591, and Otto Redfield, *Indian Dust: Studies of the Orient* (New York: Lane, 1910), 203–16. For a balanced view of the rumors and the facts, see Lesley Blanch, *Under a Lilac-Bleeding Star: Travels and Travellers* (London: John Murray, 1963), 184–208. Concerning Maugham's short story "The Colonel's Lady," inspired by the rumors about Laurence Hope, see W. Somerset Maugham, *A Writer's Notebook* (1949; reprint, Westport, Conn.: Greenwood, 1970), 80.

8. Gwyn Lewis, "Heart-throb of the 20's Leaves All to Mr. Tosi," newspaper clipping, 1953(?), shown to me by Anthony Griffin, great-nephew of Heneage Griffin.

9. Victoria Cross, *The Woman Who Didn't* (London: Lane, 1895), 63.

10. Victoria Cross, "The Kiss in the Wilderness," in *The Beating Heart* (New York: Brentano's, 1924), 36.

11. Victoria Cross, *A Husband's Holiday* (London: T. Werner Laurie, 1932), 82.

12. Victoria Cross, *Electric Love* (New York: Macaulay, 1929), 28–29.

13. Victoria Cross, *Five Nights* (New York: Mitchell Kennerley, 1908), 105.

14. Victoria Cross, *Self and the Other* (New York: Hewitt, 1911), 124.

15. Victoria Cross, *Martha Brown, M.P.* (London: T. Werner Laurie, 1935), 90–91.

16. "Muck and Mysticism: New Books," review of *The Eternal Fires*, by Victoria Cross, *Reedy's Mirror* 207 (26 May 1910): 16; review of *The Religion of Evelyn Hastings*, by Victoria Cross, *Athenaeum*, 25 February 1905, 237; William L. Alden, "London Literary Letter," review of *Anna Lombard*, by Victoria Cross, *New York Times*, 1 June 1901, 395.

17. Janet Hogarth, "Literary Degenerates," *Fortnightly Review* 57 (1 April 1895): 592.

18. "Studies of Women," review of *Six Women*, by Victoria Cross, *New York Times*, 15 December 1906, 869.

19. "Real Life in Fiction," review of *The Religion of Evelyn Hastings*, by Victoria Cross, *New York Times*, 24 October 1908, 613.

20. Victoria Cross to Mr. Harris (als), 20 July 1909, Special Collections, Virginia Polytechnic Institute and State University, Blacksburg.

21. B. A. Crackanthorpe, "Sex in Modern Literature," *Nineteenth Century* 31 (April 1895): 614–15.

22. "A Novel Elopement," in *The Beating Heart*, 76.

23. "The Vengeance of Pasht," in *The Beating Heart*, 116–27.

24. "To Sup with the Devil," in *The Beating Heart*, 206–7.

25. Victoria Cross, *Over Life's Edge* (New York: Macaulay, 1921), 192–93.

26. E. M. Forster, *Howards End* (New York: Random, 1921), 186–87.

PART THREE

In Search of a

Moral Life

ANGELA INGRAM

"In Christ's Name—Peace!":

Theodora Wilson Wilson

and Radical Pacifism

King Edward's new policy of peace was very successful and culminated in the
Great War to End War. This pacific and inevitable struggle was undertaken in
the reign of His Good and memorable Majesty king George V and it was the
cause of nowadays and the end of History.
—W. C. Sellar and R. J. Yeatman, *1066 and All That* (1930)

Are you quite sure that war is the only way out?
—Theodora Wilson Wilson (1916)

In their manic parody of the Whig version of history, Walter Sellar and
Robert Yeatman—old-fashioned subalterns in the 1914–18 war—offered
in 1930 as useful an "explanation" of the war and its consequences as any
complexly argued (and anguished over) analysis of the liberal crisis of
conscience that made war "inevitable."[1] It seems not unreasonable to
say in the early 1990s, looking at Europe, at parts of Asia and Africa,
and at the Middle East, that the "Great War to End War" continues to
be "the cause of nowadays." That it marked "the end of History" is,
perhaps, a moot point, History having been constructed for us by those
who, less honest than Sellar and Yeatman (and certainly less funny),
would have us believe that war is inevitable. There are histories within

History, of course, often spoken by voices so little heard that they seem beyond the reach of "objective" analysis, academic mythmaking, or even subalternesque parody. This essay is a part of one of those histories.

Nine months after the Central Powers and the Entente powers went to war in August 1914, the Hungarian pacifist Rosika Schwimmer urged the fifteen hundred delegates at the International Congress of Women at The Hague to send envoys to the rulers of Europe to discuss peace. The delegates, from belligerent and from neutral countries, had initially agreed on two propositions: "That international disputes should be settled by pacific means"; and that "the parliamentary franchise should be extended to women." With these, as with the more revolutionary resolutions for a permanent and just peace, the congressional delegates could concur. Over Rosika Schwimmer's call for immediate *action* there was some consternation: such a procedure was unprecedented and diplomatically illogical (also, of course, dangerous). Rosika Schwimmer, who knew "diplomacy" well enough to become, later, the first female ambassador in European history, understood, also, the weaknesses of precedent and logic. She told the delegates: "Brains—they say—have ruled the world till to-day. If brains have brought us to what we are in now, I think it is time to allow also our hearts to speak." Her resolution passed on the second vote.[2]

What Rosika Schwimmer meant by "what we are in now" is perhaps most simply illustrated by noting that a hundred miles south of The Hague, the novelty of the new weapon having passed, "a major gas attack on 1 May failed to take a yard of ground, despite the only rudimentary gas masks available to the defenders." The ground not taken was in the Ypres salient where, between 22 April and 30 May 1915, sixty thousand British, thirty-five thousand German, and ten thousand French uniformed men were killed or wounded. It was one of the smaller battles of the war.[3]

What "brains" did from the outset was declare the rightness of the war. Three days after the expiration of Britain's ultimatum to Germany, H. G. Wells wrote in the *Daily Chronicle*: "Every sword drawn against Germany is a sword drawn for peace. . . . Never was war so righteous as war against Germany now. Never has any state in the world so clamoured for punishment." An 8 August *Daily News* editorial cited a response by one "sweet old lady" who said, "God reigns." In "The War to End War," published in the 14 August *Daily News*, H. G. Wells asserted: "Into this war we have gone with clean hands, to end the rule of brutal and artificial internationalism for ever. . . . we will fight, if needful, until the children die of famine in our houses, though every ship we have is at the bottom of the sea." Victorious, England would reckon with "the private dealers in armaments and with all this monstrous stupid brood of villainy that . . . brought this catastrophe upon the world."[4]

The oft-told tale of the effectiveness of this sort of language is too depressing to rehearse here. Appreciable numbers of upper- and middle-class men did feel invigorated, their notion being that Britain "needed" a war. Historians often illustrate this rather general psychosis by referring to the "grateful" patriotic letters of F. H. Keeling (published to great acclaim in 1918) or to Rupert Brooke's "Now God be thanked, Who has matched us with His hour / And caught our youth, and wakened us from sleeping." Young men could now escape "as swimmers into cleanness leaping / Glad from a world grown old and cold and dreary." Entitled— for some reason—"Peace," Brooke's sonnet seems to have "caught" the thinking of many at the time.[5]

Women who resisted appeals to support the "holy war" faced the problem of how to act and how to speak. As Jane Addams said in 1915, "Even to appear to differ [was] . . . the supreme test of woman's con-science." They must have felt (as must some men) a sense of being "languageless" as clerical and secular establishments effortlessly manipu-lated the language of family loyalty and religious devotion. There are early indications that some women felt, simply, that their actions should speak. In July 1914, the socialist Louise Saumoneau called on "women to stop the impending carnage, to form a 'living barrier against murderous barbarism.'"[6] Sylvia Pankhurst received a letter from Lucy Thoumaian, who summoned her "to join a thousand women who [Thoumaian] would muster to make their way to the Front and fling themselves be-tween the contending armies." Nothing came of this plan, which Sylvia considered splendid but impractical. Dorothea Hollins wrote to news-papers, suggesting that "at least a thousand" women go to the Front "as a Peace Expeditionary Force, to stop the War," but despite several meet-ings, "no action" resulted.[7] She later sent a greeting to the International Congress of Women, enclosing a ring that she asked be given to "any German delegate . . . who might care to have *it as a symbol of the future friendship we hope for between* the women of England and of Germany when this terrible war is at an end."[8] Such appeals seem symptomatic of the frustration of isolated resisters, especially, perhaps, women, ap-parently bereft of any means, of any tools, linguistic or otherwise, with which to build peace once war was started.

Governments can perpetrate war only if populations subscribe to or can be coerced into supporting belligerency. To envision a sort of "anti-army" at the site of battle is to reckon that if the people lead (and soldiers are also people), the leaders will, indeed, follow. Direct action at home suggests a belief that if the people can be persuaded to think, they will resist following the leaders. Faith in the effectiveness of such peace actions bespeaks a kind of radicalism one might not consider especially native to the pre-1914 life of the hero of this story—Theodora Wilson Wilson (TWW) (1865–1941).

The eldest daughter among ten children of an old Cumbria family, TWW attended Stramongate Friends' School and the new Croydon High School (whose first headmistress, Dorinda Neligan, became an active suffragist). When her father died in 1881 she returned home but later, with one of her sisters, studied for two years in Germany. For about twenty years she taught at the Fellside Sunday School where, from the late 1880s, she superintended the infants' division, and she started the "Evening Home" for working-class girls. Once she accompanied to court in Liverpool a child charged with "trespassing" on land she had believed to be a public right-of-way. She kept poultry and wrote a pamphlet about it.[9] In 1907 she became the first president of the Stramongate Old Girls' Association. In Kendal, TWW presided for many years over the Women's Auxiliary of the Westmorland Liberal Association, and in 1904 she was a founder of the South Westmorland chapter, working for its successful candidate in 1906. (Her brother Philip won a London ward.) In 1910 Philip and her brother-in-law W. H. Somervell had her help in their Westmorland campaigns. (One might add that in 1918 she spoke "in the Labour cause" against Somervell.)[10]

By the turn of the century she had published at least a couple of stories—"Studies in the Westmorland Dialect"—and in 1901 came her first novel, *T'Bacca Queen* (republished in 1908 as *The Factory Queen*). A sometimes startlingly realistic depiction of the lives of working people contending with exploitation and landlordism (and attendant alcoholism), it was followed by several more Cumbrian novels concerned with labor and other economic and political issues of the nineteenth and early twentieth centuries. By 1906 she was publishing, in *Chambers* and *Punch* for example, stories about, but not only for, children: prewar stories range from "The Alarum," a "romantic" but moving indictment of cruelty to children, to lighthearted *Punch* material in which TWW's sense of a child's point of view of adult idiocies is incisive as well as humorous. She gained a name for her Bible stories.

There was one other very important factor in her life. Though she moved to London after her mother's death in 1909, her ties with West-morland remained intact (partly because she liked visiting Cumbrian farmhouses to absorb "local colour" for her books). In 1913 or 1914 she joined, "by convincement," the Kendal and Sedburgh Monthly Friends' Meeting.[11] She could hardly have chosen a better time.

TWW must often have given talks for liberal causes before August 1914. But now, she *spoke*. In a brief speech in September 1914, she said:

> Almost as soon as the war broke out I felt almost as if I had been converted—as if God had given me a great new vision. Now, that was not because I happened to belong to the Society of Friends. I believe that He has given the same vision to tens of thousands in other churches. I hope that we shall lay upon the Conference Committee the further burden of endeavouring to organize deputations to the towns and villages where there are no Friends' meetings. We have spoken of sacrifice. I believe that, if our message is accepted in any serious degree in the country, we shall be faced with persecution. If we put our vision so strongly . . . that men pause before they join the army, what then? This is a thing which we must very seriously and prayerfully consider. . . . If it were possible for us to have a great campaign to project the wonder of this Conference to the troubled hearts of many tens of thousands of Christians up and down our Empire, I think that God would be with us.

At a time when "the country" claims that God is on the side of soldiers, and asks young men and their families for the utmost sacrifice, an appeal like this, even to hospitable folk, suggests how difficult it is to allow "our hearts to speak." Following TWW, Mary E. Phillips, an Anglican, suggested a "regiment of men . . . walking from town to town . . . [to] our clergy of the Church of England, and to the ministers of other denominations, telling them that you were going forth on this peace crusade." She thought thousands of people were "only waiting to receive an invitation to come together to join such an army of peace."[12] TWW used ideas like these in *The Last Weapon* and *The Weapon Unsheathed*, but before she returned to stories to find a larger audience, she took on other kinds of peace work. The first was to help found the Fellowship of Reconciliation (FOR).

At Cambridge, on 28 December 1914, 130 women and men met, says Lilian Stevenson, their first chronicler, "to discover together how the way of love and service, as shown in Jesus, could be followed in every relationship of life, and human society could be thereby radically transformed." The founding committee's "early statement of principle" said:

That Love, as revealed and interpreted in the life and death of Jesus Christ . . . is the only power by which evil can be overcome and the only sufficient basis of human society.

That, in order to establish a world-wide order based on Love, it is incumbent upon those who believe in this principle to accept it fully, both for themselves and in their relation to others, and to *take the risks involved* in doing so in a world which does not as yet accept it. That, therefore, as Christians, we are forbidden to wage war, and that our loyalty to our country, to humanity, to the Church Universal, and to Jesus Christ, our Lord and Master, calls us instead to a life-service for the enthronement of Love in personal, social, commercial, and national life.

Proclaimed at a time when the promise of Christianity and international socialism had almost entirely failed, and when even international feminism had faltered badly, the FOR's internationalism reflects a risk taking that matches its recognition that "the revolutionary principle of Love must be unflinchingly applied, however impracticable it might appear at the moment; individuals and groups must go forward without waiting for the whole community."[13] TWW had, of course, already recognized the possibility of persecution were the vision to be "put . . . so strongly . . . that men pause[d]" before enlisting. Membership on the FOR founding committee gave her one cooperative context from which to speak. Very soon, there was another.

By late 1914 it was clear that the scheduled International Woman Suffrage Alliance (IWSA) congress could not take place in Berlin. Dr. Aletta Jacobs and other Dutch suffragists proposed meeting in (neutral) Holland, suggesting that in times of "so much hate" women had to show that they retained their "solidarity" and were "able to maintain mutual friendship." Outvoted by IWSA officers, Aletta Jacobs invited a few women to meet in Amsterdam in mid-February to plan a congress "to discuss the special problems" arising from the war.[14]

So while Admiral Sackville H. Carden prepared to start bombarding Turkish forts to begin the disastrous Dardanelles campaign and while Sir John French counted the one hundred thousand artillery shells he would order fired at Neuve-Chapelle (to show the French army that the British Expeditionary Force could do things thoroughly),[15] twenty-six Dutch women, four German women, four Belgian women, and five British women met to discuss internationalism. Of the British five, TWW is the least frequently mentioned in any subsequent accounts of Amsterdam and of The Hague Congress. However, Chrystal Macmillan, in her 1915 "History of the Congress," wrote:

> It is interesting to note that the presence of two members of this preliminary meeting namely Frida Perlen of Stuttgart, and Theodora Wilson Wilson of Keswick both of whom were prevented by the official authorities in their respective countries from attending.the Congress was an important factor in the introduction of the resolution originally entitled, "To urge a Truce". Over this resolution on the preliminary programme it was that so much controversy was waged. Not a few of those who wished to attend the Congress said they would not think it worth to go if it had not been for this resolution since it was the one which asked for action to be taken towards ending hostilities. On the other hand it was because of this resolution that many women refused to attend the Congress or even to express any sympathy with it.[16]

It is but one of the many wonders of this extraordinary coming together of women in the spring of 1915 that the "vision" of a middle-aged Quaker lady from an historically Liberal family should find a reflection in the thinking of a socialist Jewish feminist from Stuttgart. The resolution they drafted asks, not surprisingly, for honest speech and for action. "Considering that the people in each of the countries now at war believe themselves to be fighting, not as aggressors but in self-defence [*sic*] and for their national existence, this International Congress of Women urges the Governments of the belligerent countries, publicly to define the terms on which they are willing to make peace and for this purpose immediately to call a truce."[17] (How might the world be different if *this* had been "the cause of nowadays"!)

The Congress incorporated an amended resolution into its definition of "The Peace Settlement," dropping the call for an immediate truce. The sense of urgency felt by TWW and Frida Perlen emerged in Rosika Schwimmer's plea that envoys visit national leaders as soon as the Congress ended. In London, Evelyn Sharp—another of the 180 British delegates "prevented" from going to Holland—wrote: "Not now, says the *Daily Graphic*, 'while their husbands and sons and brothers are fighting and dying a hundred miles away!' . . . [T]he *Sunday Pictorial* . . . adds that 'The ladies who would sit with German women for the purposes of theoretical discussion show a strange want of imagination and of public decency, and a ridiculous sense of unreality.' Not now! Then, in heaven's

name, when? . . . [I]t is fear that really runs through this outcry . . . lest
the women might perhaps be right, . . . might perhaps make this war
really 'the last war', instead of merely talking about it as an unattainable
ideal very useful as a recruiting cry."[18]

In her presidential address at the Congress, Jane Addams paid tribute
to the heroism of women from belligerent countries for meeting at a
time when individuals "merged" themselves "into [their] country's existence. . . . Even to appear to differ from those she loves in their hour
of affliction or exultation has ever been the supreme test of woman's
conscience."[19]

The British women who were stopped by officials at Tilbury, their
tempers no less than their consciences tested by press ridicule and by
German-hating reactions to the torpedoing of the *Lusitania* on May 7,
held to their purpose. They arranged interviews with the prime minister and the foreign minister for Jane Addams, Aletta Jacobs, and an
Italian delegate, Rosa Genoni, who then participated in meetings to
establish what became the Women's International League (WIL), the
British branch of the Women's International League for Peace and Freedom (so named in 1919). For at least 1915–16, TWW was on the WIL
Executive Committee, thus becoming "officially" linked with other extraordinary women who retained their international perspective during
and after the war.[20]

Christian pacifism, feminist pacifism, internationalism. Heady stuff. But
TWW's vision had to exist in other contexts too. The first part of 1915
was, we are told, "a special time of hate in Britain." Burgeoning atrocity
stories "reinforced the conviction that, although the end of the struggle
might be farther off than had originally been expected, no resolution of
the conflict was acceptable short of total victory."[21]

Government propaganda could now point to the shelling and zeppe-
lin bombing of the East Coast and, after April, of London, to Germany's
declaration of an unrestricted war zone all around the British Isles, and
to Germany's use of tear gas in January and chlorine gas in April (just
before Britain started using it). Rushed out a few days after the sinking
of the *Lusitania*, the Bryce Report on alleged German atrocities was,
in part, utter nonsense (some of its stories were "recycled" from earlier
wars),[22] but taking it in conjunction with the material evidence—however much that might have been officially exaggerated—conventional
patriots might well have thought England was fighting Evil incarnate.

Although the press most sensationally urged support for the war, the religious establishment was perhaps more persuasive. (As Sir Joshua Power, the armaments manufacturer in TWW's *The Last Weapon*, knows, to have government and people support his plan to make Hellite—the most powerful force ever invented—"he must have the Church behind him, or the scheme broke in his hands.")[23] The bishop of London was instantly a militant "patriot"; the thinking of others was more gradually militarized. The bishop of Chelmsford, for example, counseling against "bitterness in spirit," acknowledged that "Christ bled and died" for German and Briton alike, but by June 1915 he asked his clergy to "urge all men of military age, as a religious duty, to take their stand with their brothers at the Front."[24] The archbishop of Canterbury urged "willing sacrifice" to defend "the very foundations of civilized order in Christendom," and he blessed soldiers and sailors; although he "would not say that 'this was a holy war, as he had been criticised for using those words, . . . he did say [the] cause was a sacred one. Every man who fought in it was a hero and every man who died in it was a martyr.'"[25]

In November, the *Times Recruiting Supplement*, its cover resplendent with an illustration of St. George and a letter from King George "To My People," offered "Messages of Hope and Encouragement" from bishops and rabbis, politicians and writers, the Salvation Army and Sir Hiram Maxim. The messages are as single-mindedly militarist as one might expect—and must have bruised the good humor of the most generous-minded pacifist.[26] The aim was to promote the Derby Scheme—a plan for all men between eighteen and forty-one to "attest" that they would enlist when ordered to. But there were not enough hundreds of thousands of men attracted by Rupert Brooke's notion of "into cleanness leaping"; the most desirable—physically fit bachelors—were the least responsive, so in early January the first Military Service [Bachelors] Bill was introduced in the Commons. Said Sir John Simon, resigning from the Cabinet over the matter, "Does anyone really suppose that once the principle of compulsion has been conceded that you are going to stop here?"[27]

Pacifists (and others) had anticipated compulsion at least as early as 15 August 1915, Registration Sunday, when all citizens between fifteen and sixty-five were legally "required" to give canvassers details about themselves, their occupations, and their "skills useful to war work."[28] Some of the people who had demonstrated against compulsion that day met on 10 January 1916, formed the National Council Against Conscription, and also sent a deputation to the Commons (where the bill was being debated). Sylvia Pankhurst—"elected to both," of course—described the deputation as "mainly bourgeois, middle-aged, and elderly,

black lace mantles and black silk skirts trailing and rustling," and among
them was "Theodora Wilson Wilson, calmly ecstatic."[29] A nice phrase.
TWW had, indeed, been given her vision; its literary embodiment was
at that moment being printed by the radical publisher C. W. Daniel.[30]

The Last Weapon is a story for just those people expected to respond
to the pointing finger of Earl Kitchener (minister of war, 1914–16), to
hundreds of posters, to thousands of pamphlets distributed before conscription. The Education Acts of 1870 and 1902 had brought almost
nationwide literacy; cheap books and weeklies, cigarette cards and postcards, popularized tales of the glorious Empire and of Christian heroes
whose patriotism was no less thrilling than their religious superiority
was triumphant.[31] The nineteenth-century "peace" such youngsters were
enjoined to celebrate was, of course, a fable—based on the frequent
colonial wars the British army committed, on military domination in
India, and on lethal naval power. As C. K. Ogden and Mary Sargant
Florence pointed out in *Militarism versus Feminism* (1915): "From earliest
childhood the modern infant is nurtured in an atmosphere of war. . . .
History proper begins when lists of warriors and dates of battles can be
conveniently memorised. About 90 per cent of the population escape
with a few such lists and leave school at thirteen or fourteen with a
vague memory of a few outstanding warriors and of martial exploits
chronologically arranged."[32]

Here, I think, was TWW's intended audience. The upper and upper-
middle classes were, in general, imbued with a sense of "duty"; it would
seem that the "better" the education, the more likely the child was to
subscribe to what I call Brooke-ism.[33] Boys who were apparently destined for the factories or the mines and girls who viewed munitions
making as an escape from domestic service were the "targets" of government propaganda and were, logically, the people TWW wrote for
and to.

She offered them radical revisions of what they had been told constituted patriotism, Christian service, and heroism. A perceptible middle-
class "tone" by no means silences the voices of working-class characters;
it partly utilizes the appeal of recruiting posters in which middle-class
women "say GO!" and middle-class children ask: "Daddy. What did
you do in the Great War?" It might, indeed, be useful to regard the
Weapon books as written subversions of the poster art that drew on feelings about "ordinary people" as well as on myth and allegory.[34] The
characters come from every class; in every class are enlightened and be-

nighted people. Although TWW's sorrow at the apostasy of "official" Christianity is perhaps most frequently expressed, her critique is of the whole Establishment. Talking to the arms manufacturer's wife in *The Last Weapon*, a young pacifist says, "Oh well, . . . of course you are involved in the evil system." Whether it is a crime to "allow oneself to be involved in a system," she concedes, is "puzzling," but she disagrees that, in being crucified, Jesus "failed," because if people had "been willing to love the world to death, the world would have been saved long ago! And so—we are all guilty of this war!" (102–3). This kind of recognition of general complicity is, often, rather moving; it is intrinsic to a vision, ecstatic or not, rooted in a sort of pragmatic compassion. The pacifist adds: "Only—what an awful thing it will be if—we are right! I simply can't endure to think of that sometimes—What all the nice people will do when they find out it was a delusion! The people are being slaughtered by the million—not by an earthquake, or something clean like that, but by one another!" (105–6).

The Last Weapon begins in the Courts of Heaven, where a heavenly Child accepts the "Christ God's" commission to visit earth so that he can understand the prayers issuing thence, prayers like the following: "O Mighty God! . . . We thank Thee that we are not as others—even as this enemy! Are not our hands clean in this great conflict and our ways honourable?"; "They have killed my boy . . . O God . . . Avenge me on their noblest—No. No! Merciful Father, forgive! Make not another woman's heart desolate as mine!"; and "Gentle Jesus. Stop this war . . . before my Daddy has to kill anybody—please!" (9–11). This outcry fills some three pages and seems rather extravagant, though no more so than newspaper headlines or a diocesan declaration that "ejaculatory prayer" was proper for soldiers and might prove "at least as wholesomely effective for good as the German malediction must prove baneful to those who were taught to ejaculate it."[35]

The manipulation of language is "taught" in the Halls of Fear, a recognizably Miltonic hell, where Despair and Cruelty, splendid in black and crimson (and the dully glowing gems of capitalism), prostrate themselves before the gorgeous Prince of Fear, who lucidly explains Fear's perversion of the Sermon on the Mount. The "Father of Lies" can, to his own glory, tell the truth about the shooting of "deserters," the use of gas, the isolation experienced by pacifists. Because, ruled by Fear, people believe his lies, it is true that "everything they think they are fighting for is being destroyed, even as they fight!" (20–22).

The images and the language are very much on the order of a morality play, and the subsequent journeys of the Child furnish numerous "good angel–bad angel" scenes, while the absolute contradiction implicit in the image of "Christ with a bayonet" is frequently voiced by those who have directly experienced what Fear ultimately spawns. A "regular" soldier back from eight months in the trenches puts the case as well as any: "If these Christians had jumped clean out of their skins with horror when this war started, they could have stopped the whole bang business, and stood a better chance of getting things set straight than ever we soldiers could do!" Asked why they haven't, he explains that army men believe in their jobs but "parsons . . . don't . . . and when their chance comes, they're *not* there." When his old Sunday school teacher boasted of winning recruits, the soldier said, "It doesn't somehow go down to hear a man sing at the top of his voice:—

Sufficient is Thine arm alone
And our defence is sure.

and know that all the time he is saying in his inside, 'But we should be dished if we hadn't our army and our navy!' If I set up for believing in an Almighty God, I wouldn't insult him like that!" (41–42).

Using allegory, TWW can situate absolute evil in the Halls of Fear, and so present people as fearful, puzzled, weak, conceited, greedy— and *always* forgivable. The device of the Child allows the focus to shift from pleasant villages in Imperia (England) to devastated villages near the Front, from the plush houses of the arms manufacturer to churches where recruiting sermons reverberate, from the trenches to the wounded soldiers at home and to the wanderings of Peace Pilgrims. The Child's mission is to encourage people to throw down the weapons of Fear and "take up" the Last Weapon of Fearless Love—which has been offered "for more than nineteen hundred years" (185).

The last "earthly" weapon is a "force" that is named Hellite by a Neutralia scientist who offers the formula to Imperia; since "business is business," he will take it to Ironland should Imperians have scruples. It is "swift as lightning. . . . Set free in any direction, it disperses itself through the air and blasts everything within its range—which can be practically limitless. It can as easily destroy ships, armies, fortifications, cities, as the whole vegetation of a country." It will end the war in a week, perhaps a day, "or the very threat of the use of Hellite may be sufficient." He offers them "the greatest Peace-making power the world has ever known"; their enemies must accept Imperia's peace terms or "deliberately submit themselves to annihilation" (52–53). This prophetic, Wellsian description of atomic force does not immediately persuade the arms manufacturer's guests: a cabinet minister, a newspaper publisher, a

Great Church Ruler, a nonconformist leader, and the Empire's wealthiest duchess—a group that, with Sir Joshua, fairly represents the nation's rulers. Sir Joshua reminds them of the "excellent news" of Imperia's success "in driving [the] enemy to his knees through [the] gradual starvation of the civil population" by means of the blockade. But Hellite will be "quick" not "slow Hell" (58).

The factual substance of *The Last Weapon* relies on press reports (which include parliamentary debate), on "alternative" sources like *Jus Suffragii*, whose editor, Mary Sheepshanks, published as much as possible from neutral and belligerent countries, and obviously on the experience of TWW herself and of other members of the FOR and WIL.[36] It is all most revealingly authentic, and one can assume only that it is the simple religious "colouration" that saved the book from the censor until a large cheap edition was "seized" in 1918.[37] A story that opens in the Courts of Heaven perhaps did not even merit further perusal, and, in any case, TWW was best known for Bible stories and for children's stories.

Wandering through Imperia and Ironland, the Child finds women working for peace, and capitalists and the ruling classes pursuing their ends more assiduously than the Child knows they do "even in times called peace" (69). He sees acts of insane violence and of heroic "brotherhood" in the trenches (some of this draws on Philip Gibbs's dispatches from the Front and on accounts of the 1914 Christmas truce),[38] attends a prowar meeting, and goes to what sounds like the memorial service for Keir Hardie, the Labour pacifist who "didn't fight men. . . . He fought systems" (135).

Propaganda must appeal to what people know, or think they know, as much as to what they feel, or have been told they should feel. In this respect *The Last Weapon* is powerful propaganda, as well as a good story and an accurate account of the country at war. The Peace Pilgrims might at first seem rather fantastical, but pacifists who spoke around the country were periodically attacked. A "riot" in July 1915, in which the FOR's Edith M. Ellis, Henry Hodgkin, and Henry Harris were confronted by "street roughs" and "quite a decent Canadian soldier" amid stone throwing and fighting, probably gave TWW "copy" for the scene in which one Peace Pilgrim is punched in the face by an enraged woman and another is blinded by stones.[39]

As well as historical accuracy, TWW's propaganda has a sort of ethical honesty that grounds the vision in the hurt bewilderment that most people probably felt—no matter that their papers and their parsons exhorted them to joyful "sacrifice" of male relatives and of physical comfort (such as it was) for the war effort. Such bewilderment prompts the man whose stones hit "Bottom Dog" to go and demand he be prosecuted. Denied this retribution, he reveals that one of his sons has just been killed and the other blinded. The scene very simply demonstrates the relationship between nationally sanctified violence and individual violence and demonstrates too that if countering violent "retribution" with reconciliation is visionary, it may also be practical. "I see," says the man, "that it's a devil's trick to get us poor fools to hit back! It only keeps the cursed business going on for ever! . . . If you don't hit back— then it's a stopper—it dries up." Not one to chastise poor fools, Bottom Dog, asking a "kindness," sends the man home to tell his son that "he answered the call he heard." Bottom Dog adds, "I answered the call I heard, and . . . we are both wounded in the service. The King knows all his privates, and all the difficulties, and if we get off the track, He'll understand" (121–22).

Both *Weapon* books insist on revealing the contradictions of a language that must serve irreconcilable "visions." Undoubtedly, TWW knew of the most perfect instance of such contradiction. When, in 1916, members of the No-Conscription Fellowship (NCF) Committee were tried for publishing the pamphlet "Repeal the Act!," the public prosecutor, Archibald Bodkin, pronounced: "War will become impossible, if all men were to have the view that war is wrong. There will be no soldiers to carry it to its logical conclusion." Logically, the NCF made a poster of this, with attribution. The government prosecuted the journalist-printer who "intend[ed] to display it"; and the journalist's defense demanded the "author of dangerous words" be arrested. The NCF publishers of the *Tribunal* "offered maintenance to [Bodkin's] wife and children if he felt it his duty to prosecute himself." Bodkin didn't; the potential poster-displayer was given ninety-one days or a fine of £120.[40] To contend with such official "thinking" is one purpose of *The Last Weapon*; another is to address the well-meaning patriotism of people lacking the wit to appreciate the NCF's subversiveness. Two scenes in the book illustrate this well.

When the Peace Pilgrims are attacked in Sir Joshua Power's home-town, his wife rescues them. Her son, George, just back from the trenches where he successfully bayoneted an "Enemy" soldier, has, she believes, lost his senses. "We explained that he was not in the least to blame, because war is war, and he only did his duty. . . . Our preacher . . . explains to George that he is absolutely guiltless of the crime—I mean, he explains that there was no crime. . . . But nothing helps." The youngest Pilgrim agrees to talk to George, silently praying she can think of *some*thing to say: "'Have you come to tell me that I am a hero, and that I did my duty nobly?' he asked suspiciously. 'Oh no!' she said simply, 'I have come to tell you that you are a murderer.'" And she leads him through a Quaker version of the "talking cure," praying with him, still "very simply," until he says, "It is good to know the truth" (107–13). Plain words plainly spoken—language that is unsophisticated in the true sense of the word—are, even now, moving. One can only imagine what their effect might have been on people used to reading on almost every page of every newspaper every day the sophisticated contradictions of a society determinedly pursuing war.

A later scene analyzes how these two kinds of language work— to everyone's ·confusion. At a church meeting to honor a young man who has "lost" his arm and "won" a military service medal, Sir Joshua (nebulously) releases news of Hellite: it "will make an end for ever of armaments, battleships, trenches, bleeding and mutilated sons, broken-hearted wives and mothers. All the ideals we have struggled after for generations may now be realised." If the "enemy" does not accept "our" terms, Hellite will wipe them out fairly quickly. The people are ecstatic: boys home; money saved. Then the war hero rises to recount his experiences: trenches full of "rot"; an old peasant shot for sheltering wounded "enemies"; bayonets much used and dripping; a soldier—someone they knew—whom he had to shoot for falling asleep. The platform guests are uneasy; George Power, erstwhile insane murderer and now gratefully sane and pacific murderer, listens intently. The hero reminds fellow parishioners that he once planned to preach that "God so loved the world that He *gave*," but then he "acted upon the assumption that God so loved the world that He *slew*." Now they must choose between Sir Joshua's "last weapon" and the "Power of Fearless Love." There is commotion, contempt. "He daren't have said that if he hadn't got his discharge!" Predictably—but it does not lessen the drama—George stands up: "I have not got my discharge! Let me speak the truth too! The Last Weapon is not Destruction and Death—It is Love and Life! . . . I also choose the winning side! I also refuse to slay my brother!" His father, speechless, turns "deadly white."

The minister must speak. He is a gentle soul, much influenced by ideas like those of the bishop of Chelmsford and the archbishops. TWW understood such folk, recognized how bemused and misled essentially "decent" people were. She showed compassion for those she thought would be—as she says of the souls, stripped of their uniforms, on the "other side"—"unutterably sorry." Like Lady Power's stumbling "I mean," the minister's too lays bare the futility of using language in a conventionally thoughtless way. He says: "Friends, . . . I confess that I am not clear what to say to you tonight. I fear that the powers of Heaven and Hell are working at this meeting, and I would rather not take either side—that is—I mean—Sir Joshua's pronouncement has come as a great surprise, and perhaps something of a shock to us all." Getting Sir Joshua's confirmation that Hellite will not be used before the enemy has had a chance to agree to an "honourable Peace" and finding himself unable to comment on "our beloved fellow-member's" speech, the minister pronounces the benediction (170–75).

Such benedictions, TWW knew, only momentarily comforted people beguiled and betrayed by Sacrifice, Patriotism, and other unexamined abstractions. Her vision, here, remains "unfulfilled," an inscription of the deepening sense of helplessness in late 1915. The use of Hellite is made moot by the rumor that Ironland has the formula and by the assassination of the Neutralian scientist. The mob killing of the war hero and of George Power leaves Sir Joshua mentally "incompetent." The Child flees back to heaven in despair.

The year 1916 brought Britain conscription, the persecution of conscientious objectors, the war's first "significant" naval battle, and the "big push" on the Somme, a push that was "a calamity," in the words of a fairly representative historian who adds: "What cannot be conveyed is the swift death or long agony sustained on a vast scale by men who joined the army in the early enthusiasm of recruiting, had trained with inadequate resources under barely adequate instructors, and had approached—with mingled hope, enthusiasm, misgiving, dedication—this moment of high endeavour. For many it was a short moment indeed. Of the 60,000 men who went over the top in the first waves, half had become casualties in the first 30 minutes. Of the 120,000 who attacked altogether during the day, casualties were again almost 50 per cent."[41] At Verdun, the Germans and French attacked and counterattacked each other from February until December; the "official" casualty count was 720,000 men killed or wounded.[42]

TWW responded to the horror of 1916 by working: she served on the WIL Executive Committee, at some time she was on the NCF Committee, and certainly her FOR work must have increased.[43] In late autumn C. W. Daniel published her sequel to *The Last Weapon*. *The Weapon Unsheathed: A Spiritual Adventure* is set far more "on earth" than its predecessor; the focus is on human activity, on human motives for continuing the war. Hellite being "lost" (but formulas never are), the Prince of

Fear "discovers" Selfite; he is joined by a "woman" whose several names are Righteous Indignation, Righteous Vengeance, and, most truly, Self-Righteousness. Truth, Liberty, and Purity are in chains.[44]

The Last Weapon was "A Vision"; the sequel is "A Spiritual Adventure" because it risks asking readers to contemplate how the pacifist vision might be translated into action. And to some extent it is a working out of the resolution that TWW and Frida Perlen drafted in 1915. Many people are timid: an elderly character says, "We Peace-folk . . . repeated the parrot cry: 'This is not the time to speak.'" A young woman who doesn't "understand all that visionary [pacifist] stuff" urges her fiancé to enlist and help smash the Ironlanders and get their trade. On this second anniversary of "Blood Day" (4 August 1914), however, he favors a different sort of "practicality." He will stop working for the government, he says. "And, well—the fact is, I want to get across the Ironland on an adventure of Goodwill—Love—anything you care to call it." As one of the "butchers-in-chief" whose flyers have been "shedding destruction on Ironland," he will make "one great adventure in the cause of Peace. . . . I want to find out the truth" (39–41).

One adventure traced here is that of the well-named Sir Percival. But there are others. The Child's mission now is to spread the watchword "Love Omnipotent" and the prayer "In Christ's Name, Peace!" Derived from TWW's own vision and the FOR's "Statement of Principle" (if we can distinguish) and from the revolutionary work done at The Hague and by the WIL, the NCF, and the Women's Peace Crusade, the story shows these workers' ideas becoming reality for increasing numbers of people. It is fantastical; it is also a salute to the peace movement and to the courage of resisters.

Here, as in *The Last Weapon*, wartime distortion of language is stressed. A prison chaplain tells a jailed Peace Pilgrim of a national day of repentance; cheered to think that the church regrets its support for the war, she is downcast to learn that people will be urged to repent "pride, sabbath-breaking, drink, immorality, worldliness, greed"—but not murder.[45] The young king of Imperia, converted to pacifism (his name, of course, is Arthur), stuns his ministers by announcing he will be true to his title of Defender of the Faith, though it might cost him his throne. When he asks which coronation gift to keep, the Bible or the Sword Imperial, the Great Church Ruler begs time to consider.

An airplane flight is perhaps the clearest illustration of the adventure—which, after all, is to see the truth, speak it plainly, and *act* on it. Sir Percival and his wife, Eirene, for whom he names his plane, fly over Ironland dropping leaflets, or "sky petals," which bear the watchword and the prayer: "Love Omnipotent! In Christ's Name, Peace." Defending planes shoot down the *Eirene*, killing its pilots. The Ironland princess, once King Arthur's fiancée, sends two messengers in the repaired plane to deliver the leaflet to him. The *Eirene* is shot down again—for Arthur's "safety." Thus do "defensive" belligerents deal with Peace.

Then a Peace Army of women settles between the opposing forces in Ironland, and the soldiers refuse to go on killing. (Thus is the 1914 vision of Dorothea Hollins and others realized.) After Hellite is "rediscovered" in a form that can destroy the Imperian navy, Ironland begins an invasion. The Peace Following—shepherds and shopkeepers, doctors and students, our old Peace Pilgrims—place themselves between "defending" guns and invading forces. Men on both sides lay down their arms. Watching soldiers fraternize, an officer "disgustedly" says: "Look at that! . . . Once let the men get together, and they will never fight again!" (159–63, 171).[46]

The *Times Literary Supplement*, which gave *The Last Weapon* five noncommittal lines, devoted a twenty-line paragraph to the sequel. It noted the *Eirene*'s "adventure," the Peace Following, and the Peace Army—their "uniform" described as representative of a story of "rhapsodic pacifism" in which "the peace enthusiasts win the day." The paper added, "But their victory does not seem of much importance after such a medley of fantastic and theatrical emotionalism."[47] The reviewer ignored, for example, the accurate description of "Number One Field Punishment," in which resisters, "handed over" to the army and refusing to fight, were, with other rule breakers, "crucified" on the wheels of gun carriages within enemy firing range. There is no word of TWW's critique of a system that, built on inequity and greed, spawns a horrible prison system, poverty and starvation, and the corruption of labor and of colonized peoples, with Indian soldiers much exploited in trench raids because they are so usefully "dark" and thought to be good at stabbing people quietly. These things are perpetuated, as one weary cynic in the novel says and the *Times Literary Supplement* does not, in the name of women and children because war for "trade, possessions, concessions and top-dogginess generally" does not appeal to those "who do the bulk of the fighting and get the bulk of the knocks" (83).

The "truce of God"—"what Government dare break it?"—becomes a formal peace. Such an event, perhaps, was envisioned by TWW and Frida Perlen in Amsterdam in 1915. The notion is simple, to be sure, as befits a story whose premise is "What if?" And some who were there might not have thought it "fantastic." In 1981, a British soldier who was seventeen in 1914 said of the Christmas Truce: "If the truce had gone on and on, there's no telling what could have happened. It could have meant the end of the war. After all they didn't want war, and we didn't want war and it could have ended up by finishing the war altogether." A German soldier, in 1964, considered it "wonderful . . . that the thought of Bethlehem brought these men together. They heard the voice of 2000 years back, but the rulers did not hear, and so the war went on for four years and millions of young men had to die." And a World War II pilot wrote: "There remains for all time an enormous 'if' from that date. If only all the soldiers along the Western Front . . . had come out and refused to go back to the slaughter. If only this precious peace had spread, the whole of history might have been different."[48]

It was a very simple and a very problematic "if," as TWW well knew. The Chief Minister in *The Last Weapon* recognizes he has "driven liberty from the land," bringing himself into "open conflict with some thousands of men and women, who, in the face of the direst obliquy [*sic*], had refused to be engulfed in the war enthusiasm. Their position was so simple that they were popularly known as the 'Wonts.'" Deemed "the last thing in cowardly futility," the Wonts, he knows, are "the sappers and miners under the throne of the War-god, . . . daringly spreading very dangerous constructive ideals, claiming that though they were Wonts to war, they were aggressive Goodwillers to Humanity" (101–2).

There were too few Wonts in belligerent countries at the end of 1916. TWW kept on working, observing in a pamphlet, "The Red Sea did not part *until the forward march began.*"[49] As honorary secretary of a Special Committee for Peace, in November she distributed a pamphlet, "Are You Quite Sure That War Is the Only Way Out?" It encouraged holding meetings, singing carols, and canvassing signatures for a peace memorial urging the government to "seek the earliest opportunity of promoting negotiations with the object of securing a just and lasting Peace." (Germany was renewing peace "feelers.") It ended with the following reminder: "That it is possible to negotiate a reasonable Peace without killing off the youth of Europe; That though the way of war has failed, the way of Jesus Christ remained untried." For the Prince of Peace's birthday, TWW suggested, "Let this cry and this prayer rise from all hearts: IN CHRIST'S NAME—PEACE."[50]

That the pamphlet was printed by the National Labour Press publicly marks, I think, TWW's adherence to a more specifically socialist Christian pacifism. Like her joining the Friends, this expansion of her vision couldn't have happened at a more appropriate time. Since March 1916, the ILP in Manchester had been printing a free broadsheet, the *New Crusader*, written and edited by Wilfred Wellock, a pacifist, socialist, and

Independent Methodist minister. The print run was about ten thousand, and by the summer a collection of *New Crusader* articles came out in book form.[51] Wellock not only wrote and spoke for peace: when married men became liable for conscription, he refused both the exemption due him as a minister and "alternative" service. Inevitably, his local tribunal handed him over to the military authorities, and on 15 February 1917, he was court-martialed and sentenced to two years of hard labor. Ten days later he received a letter from his wife. He recalled: "The last issue of the New Crusader had been paid for with a balance over, and . . . Theodora Wilson Wilson (a London Quaker) on hearing of my arrest and imprisonment had written for permission to produce the Crusader as a weekly in London. I expressed my gratitude and said 'by all means continue!'"[52]

Thus did Providence, military compulsion, and, of course, access to "start-up" money give TWW yet another métier. And in the month the Royal Flying Corps called "Bloody April," when the British attack at Arras left nearly three hundred thousand killed and wounded men,[53] TWW distributed "an enlarged form of the paper established by Mr Wellock" with a letter headed "The Christian Peace Crusade" and with a free children's supplement, the *Explorer*. It cost a penny a week.

TWW was the proprietor of the *New Crusader* (renamed the *Crusader* in 1919) until 1923 and was de facto editor until Wellock's release in April 1919. Her first issue (17 April 1919) includes editorials, book reviews, and news "From Abroad," including praise for Jeannette Rankin's vote against the declaration of war in the United States Congress. Fourteen "Fearless Pacifist Books," published by C. W. Daniel (who printed the paper), are advertised. A brief article about the Wellocks urges readers to start "afresh with renewed energy to make the paper . . . a mighty success, and a real hot weapon of love and brotherhood, to melt away hard hate, fear, and grasping competition, so that 'In Christ's name—Peace!' and all that such a motto involves, may ring through the world."[54]

The first *Explorer* incorporates stories, a call for suggestions on how to spend money now used on war and war preparations, and a request for postcards bearing the name of "the first man we read of in the Bible who refused military service, even for the defence of women and children." An editorial to "Fellow Explorers" explains that the idea of the paper "came into [TWW's] head because of the war" and asks, "Why do we have wars at all?" Suggesting they might work it out together, she invites the children to tell her what they think: "I am not having you on. I honestly believe that if the Kingdom of Jesus Christ is to come on earth . . . it is the boys and girls who will have to set themselves diligently to discover the way." And she wasn't having them on. She asked for "funny" mottoes about making the world better *and* quoted Seneca: "A brave spirit struggling with adversity is a spectacle for the gods."[55]

The "cause of nowadays" was halted at the eleventh hour on the eleventh day of the eleventh month, 1918. The war was not ended, of course, when guns stopped being fired on the Western Front. The blockade remained in effect until 12 July 1919, and the deliberate starvation of civilian populations, now swelled by demobilized soldiers, continued apace. In addition to the continued killing, the "settlement" to be imposed on Germany seemed to make a future war very likely, as those demanding to know war aims back in 1915 had feared.[56] Knowing that war is never inevitable, eight days before the convening of the Versailles Conference in January 1919 TWW began serializing in the *Crusader* a sequel to *The Wrestlers*, her pacifist and anti-tsarist novel that C. W. Daniel had published in 1916.[57]

The sequel, "August Pendragon," begins on 1 August 1914 and ends after demobilization and the release of conscientious objectors. We follow a group of young people, their parents and acquaintances to the battlefront and into peace work, war work, resistance, and prison. We relearn the arguments of the *Weapon* books—without divine and hellish aid, with as full a knowledge of the war as was available, and with a pretty good understanding of what "peace" would bring. Pacifism and its antithesis are played out among a variety of war's victims: atheist socialist workingmen and bemused vicars; county officials "hooking" recruits; itinerant Quaker women preaching peace; young men driven insane by following orders in the trenches; a vicar's wife who believes that to urge Sunday school pupils to enlist is to do God's work. The voices of these and others are moving, funny, terrible; their search for some unclouded vision—the first chapter is entitled "Eyesight"—is a record of the struggles of people whose society rewards myopia. August, the attractive hero (who would seem too lovely to be true did not his irreverent cousin call him "Boy Beautiful"), comes slowly to realize that he must resist and that it will be "a great fight."[58] He goes to prison, and his father's house becomes a center for peace work and propaganda—like its actual FOR and NCF counterparts.[59]

More robustly than in the *Weapon* books, TWW analyzes the failures of international socialism and organized religion and the general complicity of women. August longs to believe women will resist, but his cousin Jill says: "It is woman who is the real war-maker—who sets . . . soldiers up on high as little tin gods—you wouldn't go if women didn't really back you. . . . We are the excuse. . . . No civilized man would kill another today unless it were to protect women and children!" This clear-sighted young woman, "packing [herself] away" for the duration while recognizing her "feelings have always been true, but [her] arguments—despicable,"[60] does nursing at home and then drives ambulances in France. There she meets and comes to love a French officer and, with him (August's "great fight" inspiring her), realizes that dedication to the "Carpenter of Nazareth" *is* the fight. Her husband, disowned by his parents, is shot for resisting, and Jill goes home to bear their child. This little boy's insistence that the adults help him play with his building blocks gives the last chapter its title—"The Builders."

As well as being among the first "postwar" novel-length English war stories, "August Pendragon" is a clear warning to the war's adult survivors and to those too young to have been conscripted—the seventeen- and eighteen-year-olds who might be expected to fight in the next war. It is a history showing us how we got to "what we [were] in" in 1919 and how to change things. A simple and actually rather exciting tale, it is told with humor and an acute sense of the self-delusion that sustains the status quo. When Jill, abandoning "despicable" arguments for true feelings, determines to have a child with a man she knows will be shot as a "traitor," she overturns the notion, quasi-official in Britain, Germany, and France before and after 1918, that any children were valuable only because dead soldiers had to be "replaced." When the young Quaker, embarking on a sure route to jail, says, "We must go out . . . and preach the Gospel, which really means Love and Internationalism—and we can't admit that we have a single enemy in the world, so that at least is a relief!"[61] it sounds simple, even simplistic. But in the context of 1914–18, of 1919, of 1939, or of the 1990s, one might want to read it as a call to revolutionize human relations.

TWW ended the serial on 2 January 1920. An adjacent editorial column in the *Crusader* noted a talk refuting those who thought "the kingdom of God" a vague term rather than a reality and commented, "The great thing to believe and understand is that the whole universe is on the side of those who attempt to translate this Reality into the actual social conditions of this world."[62]

Believing and understanding in this manner, TWW continued translating her "reality." The autumn 1919 railway workers' strike inspired her to organize the Shareholders Movement, whose members affirmed,

"The claims of the workers to wages making it possible . . . to live a full and free life came before the claims of the Shareholders to dividends." An early Shareholders list shows hundreds of names, and a 1921 article on the "new movement for social amelioration" indicates that it "enlarged to include other enterprises also."[63] The same impulse to restructure institutions put TWW on the Committee to Oppose Military Training in Schools—one of three committees established at the NCF's last meeting in late 1919. The committee, however, found it "impossible to form a quorum" on three occasions in 1920; indeed, the historian Martin Ceadel tells us that "socialist pacifism remained unorganized" at this time.[64]

Nevertheless, the *Crusader* group became a matrix for different branches of the left-wing peace movement during the 1920s.[65] Like the FOR, the group established links with European pacifists but by early 1921 were finding an unmet "desire for mobilisation" of "the C.O. movement." To focus that desire, they circulated an "Affirmation against War," and on 24 February, a few hundred absolutist pacifists met at the Penn Club, London. All had signed the affirmation, "the originator of which"—wrote W. J. Chamberlain, who presided—"was Miss T. W. Wilson, who had been one of the foremost women workers for peace during the war." The slogan of the first concerted antiwar movement—in Germany, naturally enough—was *Nie Wieder Krieg!*, and Chamberlain remembered that those at the Penn Club were "confirmed in their resolve to adopt the slogan . . . by the exhibition of posters . . . which had been sent to Miss Wilson by friends in Germany."[66] Thus was born the "No More War" Movement (NMWM), with whose help in 1923 the War Resisters International (WRI) was founded.

On the NMWM's Provisional Committee and then the Executive Committee, TWW saw her original antiwar affirmation fashioned into a more inclusive statement. Chamberlain gives this version: "War is a crime against humanity. I am therefore determined— (1) Not to take part in any war, international or civil; (2) To work for Total Disarmament, the removal of all causes of war, and the establishment of a New Social and International Order based on the Pacifist principle of Co-operation for the Common Good."[67]

In 1937, eight months after the NMWM merged with Dick Sheppard's Peace Pledge Union, TWW wrote C. W. Daniel, "It is tragic about Canon Shephard [*sic*], but he died as one would like to die, in harness, and I feel that the Cause will go on stronger than ever." Daniel agreed that Sheppard's early death was tragic.[68] "But," he wrote, "men may come and men may go but the *truth* goes on for ever."[69] Daniel had just published TWW's *Those Strange Years*, which one advertisement called "a tremendous challenge in this tragic year of 1937" and "a vivid novel written by one who remembers for those who don't."[70] At the end of "August Pendragon," TWW had appended a note: "This story . . . will be elaborated with a view to book publication. It has now run for a year and that is long enough." *Those Strange Years*, inscribed "To all who follow on" and ending "For the children," redeems that promise, affirming the earlier vision and reaffirming the warning, with greater knowledge of what the war had entailed and of what it had led to.

This story too has certainly run "long enough." There must be thousands like it, wherever governments have used war to "settle differences." TWW is too little remembered, even for her children's books, which were recently characterized as "worthy predecessors of Arthur Ransome's 'Swallows and Amazons' stories."[71] And there is much more of her "history" still to discover, especially among those organizations she helped "originate."[72] The Women's International League for Peace and Freedom, whose envoys began their work when Rosika Schwimmer suggested it was "time to allow also our hearts to speak," in 1990 celebrated seventy-five years of such work. The International FOR, one of the first peace groups to send observers to Iraq, as well as to Israel, Jordan, and Palestine before and after the slaughter of 1991, celebrates its seventy-fifth anniversary in 1994. War Resisters International continues its work to support and honor all who resist war, early or late. At a WRI dinner in 1991, a former navy reservist recalled watching military "victory" parades and thinking: "Is this about peace? No, the people who really fought for peace are in the brig."[73] These organizations continue, in their different ways, to ask TWW's question: "If we put our vision so strongly . . . that men [as well as, of course and alas, women] pause before they join the army, what then?"

What then? TWW was not merely radical for her time; she was, one trembles to suggest, radical in terms of our foreseeable future. Near the end of *The Weapon Unsheathed*, on the day that peace is formalized, someone says: "The weapon is unsheathed! . . . It has cut off the top of a tree and sent a lot of poisonous fruit to the ground to rot. But the roots are still there, deep down in our social life. We have a rare lot of grubbing to do yet!" (179–80).[74] I shouldn't like to attempt a better definition of radical pacifism than that.

When Theodora died in November 1941, the German army was mounting its second offensive against Moscow, and the British army was starting its attack in the "Western Desert." Wilfred Wellock wrote in *Peace News*:

> There has just passed from our midst one of the most ardent, untiring, consistent, and thorough-going pacifists of our time.
>
> The name of Theodora Wilson Wilson may not be very familiar to the new generation of pacifists, but to the older generation, and especially to Christian pacifists, it was a household word. During the last war, when conscientious objectors were going to prison in their thousands, Theodora Wilson was a tower of strength and a leader whom the women pacifists of the time will never forget. . . .
>
> The pacifist cause has never had a truer or more sincere and wholehearted servant.[75]

We are fifty years on from Wilfred Wellock's tribute. The roots are still there, deep down, and we have, indeed, "a rare lot of grubbing to do yet."

Notes

1. W. C. Sellar and R. J. Yeatman, *1066 and All That* (1930; reprint, Penguin, 1967), 121.

2. International Congress of Women, *Bericht—Rapport—Report* (Amsterdam: International Women's Committee of Permanent Peace, [1915]), 174 (hereafter cited as *Report*).

3. Trevor Wilson, *The Myriad Faces of War: Britain and the Great War, 1914–1918* (Cambridge: Polity Press, 1986), 128, 129.

4. Newspaper articles excerpted in Irene Cooper Willis, *England's Holy War: A Study of English Liberal Idealism during the Great War* (New York: Alfred Knopf, 1928), 88, 89, 90–91.

5. For Keeling, see Arthur Marwick, *The Deluge: British Society and the First World War* (1965; reprint, New York: W. W. Norton, 1970), 36. For Brooke, see, e.g., *The Collected Poems of Rupert Brooke* (New York: Dodd, Mead and Co., 1927), 111.

6. Quoted in Judith Wishnia, "Feminism and Pacifism: The French Connection," in *Women and Peace: Theoretical, Historical, and Practical Perspectives*, edited by Ruth Roach Pierson (London: Croom Helm, 1987), 108.

7. E. Sylvia Pankhurst, *The Home Front: A Mirror to Life in England during the First World War* (1932; reprint, London: Cresset Library, 1987), 64–65, 64n.

8. *Report*, 206.

9. Two entries before the long listing of titles under "Wilson, Theodora Wilson" in the British Museum Catalogue (vol. 259, col. 70) is the following: "Wilson (T. Wilson), Authoress of 'The Royal Road to Poultry Rearing'. Poultry keeping for women, for pleasure and profit. pp 66. Cable Printing and Publish-

ing Co: London [1899] 12 [Cable Series of Farm and Household Books, No 5.]" The British Museum's cataloguing notwithstanding, this entry must refer to TWW, whose niece Margaret Somervell has written me that when she was a child, "it fascinated [her] to go with [TWW] to feed [TWW's] hens." She added: "My mother helped her with them before her marriage [in 1895]. In the end the hen business failed" (personal communication, 11 July 1989).

10. Basic information is from *Burke's Genealogical and Heraldic History of the Landed Gentry*, 16th ed. (London: Burke's Peerage, 1939), 2463–64, and from the following obituary notices: "A Westmorland Novelist," *Cumberland and Westmorland Herald*, November 1941; "Death of Kendal Authoress," *Westmorland Gazette*, 15 November 1941; and "Theodora Wilson Wilson," *The Friend*, 21 November 1941, 539. I am very much indebted to TWW's niece, Margaret Somervell, and to Tessa Wilson of the Kendal Civic Society, Christine Strickland of the Kendal Public Library, Frank Shaw of the *Cumberland and Westmorland Herald*, and Colin Porteous and David Butler, both of Kendal, for their generous, patient, and often lengthy responses to my ill-informed inquiries about one of their own.

11. Records at Friends' House, London, and those of the Kendal Friends' Monthly Meeting differ as to year. David Butler, of the Kendal Friends' Monthly Meeting, told me (19 October 1991) that the Monthly Meeting Register of Members shows that TWW joined the Kendal and Sedburgh Meeting on 29 January 1913; Friends' House records show that she became a member in 1914. For information and photocopies of numerous pamphlets and other materials relating to TWW, I am forever grateful to Sylvia Carlyle, Librarian at the Library of the Religious Society of Friends, Friends' House, London (hereafter cited as Friends' House). Without her generosity and gleeful interest, parts of this essay could not have been written.

12. Quoted in *Friends and the War* (London: Headley Bros., 1914), 98–100, a publication of addresses delivered at a conference of members of the Society of Friends and others at Llandudno, 25–30 September 1914. Thanks to Sylvia Carlyle for this reference.

13. Lilian Stevenson, *Towards a Christian International: The Story of the International Fellowship of Reconciliation* (London: IFOR, 1929, revised 1941), 1, 2–3 (emphasis added). See also John W. Graham, *Conscription and Conscience: A History, 1916–1919* (1922; reprint, New York: Augustus Kelley, 1969), 204–5.

14. *Report*, xxxvii–xxxviii; Jill Liddington, *The Long Road to Greenham: Feminism and Anti-Militarism in Britain since 1820* (London: Virago, 1989), 94–95; Anne Wiltsher, *Most Dangerous Women: Feminist Peace Campaigners of the Great War* (London: Pandora, 1985), 223.

15. S.L.A. Marshall, *World War I* (New York: American Heritage Press, 1964, 1971), 149–50; Wilson, *Myriad*, 122–25.

16. *Report*, xl.

17. *Report*, 281. A radical suffragist, Frida Perlen (1870–1933) had, with Mathilde Planck (the other Stuttgart representative of the Suffrage League), telegraphed the Kaiser on 3 August 1914, asking him to stop the war. She rejected the Bund Deutscher Frauenvereine's cooperation with the government, and after The Hague Congress she helped establish one of the German Committees

for a Lasting Peace in Württemberg, which, a government official said, "consisted . . . of nothing more than the political ambitions of Mesdames Perlen and Planck and two more world-stormers." The authorities feared radical pacifists' influence on schoolteachers. See Richard J. Evans, *The Feminist Movement in Germany, 1894–1933* (London: SAGE Publications, 1976), 216–23. There is scant information about Perlen in German, let alone in English.

18. Quoted in Wiltsher, *Dangerous Women*, 100.

19. *Report*, 18.

20. *Report*, 317–18; Jane Addams, Emily G. Balch, and Alice Hamilton, *Women at The Hague* (New York: Macmillan, 1915); Wiltsher, *Dangerous Women*, 107–8; Liddington, *Long Road*, 105–6.

21. Wilson, *Myriad*, 182.

22. Almost all accounts of British propaganda make this point. In addition to those cited, see H. C. Peterson, *Propaganda for War: The Campaign against American Neutrality, 1914–1917* (Norman: University of Oklahoma Press, 1939), especially 53–70.

23. Theodora Wilson Wilson, *The Last Weapon: A Vision* (London: C. W. Daniel, 1916), 56.

24. Quoted in Wilson, *Myriad*, 178.

25. *Times*, 27 May 1915, 10e, 7 July 1915, 6e, and 9 July 1915, 10c.

26. *Times Recruiting Supplement*, 3 November 1915.

27. Simon quoted in R.J.Q. Adams and Philip P. Poirier, *The Conscription Controversy in Great Britain, 1900–1918* (Columbus: Ohio State University Press, 1987), 143; J. M. Winter, *The Experience of World War I* (New York: Oxford University Press, 1989), 118; Denis Winter, *Death's Men: Soldiers of the Great War* (1978; reprint, London: Penguin, 1979), 31–36.

28. Adams and Poirier, *Conscription*, 98. See also Pankhurst, *Home Front*, 214.

29. Pankhurst, *Home Front*, 285–86.

30. Charles William Daniel (1871–1955) began publishing in 1902 with a view to opening people's minds to reforms in taxation, eating habits (he was a vegetarian), religion, politics, literacy, and medicine. Works he published include those of Leo Tolstoy and José Ortega y Gasset, Emma Goldman and D. H. Lawrence, Mary Everest Boole and T. S. Eliot. He was imprisoned in 1916 for publishing a radical pacifist pamphlet and was fined in 1918 for *Despised and Rejected*, Rose Allatini's pseudonymous pacifist novel with homosexual heroes. Among other books by TWW, he published an Esperanto version of her allegory of social evils, *The Search of the Child* (1916). A full account of Daniel's consistent "philosophical anarchism" remains to be written. Meanwhile, there are the following pamphlets: "A Tribute to the Memory of Charles William Daniel" by Denise Waltham (1955) and "The Centenary of a 'Crank' Publisher: Charles William Daniel (1871–1955)" by Daniel's great-nephew, Jeremy Goring (1971), both privately printed, and Nicolas Walter's 1989 unpublished talk "C. W. Daniel: The Odd Man." Copies of these were sent to me by Mary Sweetlove. The Daniel archives are to be deposited in the International Institute of Social History, Amsterdam. I'd know little of this were it not for the extraordinarily friendly help of Mary Sweetlove, Daniel's niece, to whom my initial letter of inquiry was sent by Jane Miller, present co-owner of C. W. Daniel Company.

Like Mary, I look forward to a detailed biography of her remarkable uncle, a man who, as Jeremy Goring says, "through the medium of the printed word put one mind in touch with another."

31. See, for example, John M. MacKenzie, *Propaganda and Empire: The Manipulation of British Public Opinion, 1880–1960* (Manchester: Manchester University Press, 1984), 17–19.

32. Mary Sargant Florence, Catherine Marshall, and C. K. Ogden, *Militarism versus Feminism: Writings on Women and War*, edited by Margaret Kamester and Jo Vellacott (London: Virago, 1987), 118.

33. Denis Winter, *Death's Men*, 31, 63.

34. See, for example, J. M. Winter, *Experience*, 183ff.

35. *Times*, 1 July 1915, 10c.

36. For *Jus*, see Sybil Oldfield, *Spinsters of This Parish: The Life and Times of F. M. Mayor and Mary Sheepshanks* (London: Virago, 1984), 185–87.

37. In a letter to C. W. Daniel in 1937 (see note 69), TWW says the edition was 20,000; *Friend*, 22 March 1918, reported that the police "pulped" 18,000 copies.

38. Philip Gibbs, *The Soul of the War*; Malcolm Brown and Shirley Seaton, *Christmas Truce: The Western Front, December, 1914* (New York: Hippocrene Books, 1984); and see Denis Winter, *Death's Men*, 26–27.

39. H. G. Wood, *Henry T. Hodgkin: A Memoir* (London: Student Christian Movement Press, 1937), 163–65; Vera Brittain, *The Rebel Passion: A Short History of Some Pioneer Peace-Makers* (Nyack, N.Y.: Fellowship Publications, 1964), 81.

40. See Jo Vellacott, *Bertrand Russell and the Pacifists in the First World War* (New York: St. Martin's Press, 1980), 66–67; Graham, *Conscription*, 191–92, 197–98.

41. Wilson, *Myriad*, 323

42. J. M. Winter, *Experience*, 140.

43. Wiltsher, *Dangerous Women*, 242 n. 7; Graham, *Conscription*, 182.

44. Theodora Wilson Wilson, *The Weapon Unsheathed: A Spiritual Adventure* (London: C. W. Daniel, 1916), 31–37.

45. There were repeated calls for such "repentance." See *Times*, 27 May 1915 and ad nauseam.

46. At Christmas 1915, British soldiers had strict orders not to repeat the fraternization of 1914. A few officers were court-martialed for disobeying; one soldier remembers being threatened with the death penalty. See Brown and Seaton, *Christmas Truce*, 195–203.

47. *Times Literary Supplement*, 17 February 1916, 83, and 8 February 1917, 71.

48. All quoted in Brown and Seaton, *Christmas Truce*, 191–92.

49. "To All Women," FOR pamphlet, 1916(?), 7, Friends' House. Thanks to Sylvia Carlyle for this reference.

50. Pamphlet, Friends' House.

51. Andrew Rigby, *A Life in Peace: A Biography of Wilfrid [sic] Wellock* (Bridport, Dorset: Prism Press, 1988), 21–22, 129; Wilfred Wellock, *Off the Beaten Track: Adventures in the Art of Living* (Tanjore: Sarvodaya Prachuralaya, 1961), 41.

52. Wellock, *Off the Beaten Track*, 41, 44.

53. Wilson, *Myriad*, 452–53.

54. "A 'Prisoner of Jesus,'" *New Crusader*, 19 April 1917, 1.

55. "Editorial," *Explorer, Supplement to "The New Crusader." For Boys and Girls*,

19 April 1917, 1, 2, 3. The papers are in Box D/30 at Friends' House. Thanks to Sylvia Carlyle for finding and copying them for me.

56. See C. Paul Vincent, *The Politics of Hunger: The Allied Blockade of Germany, 1915–1919* (Athens: Ohio University Press, 1985).

57. *The Wrestlers—Father, Mother, Son* is at once a movingly romantic adventure story about extraordinary spiritual and physical courage, a realistic critique of tsarist Russia, and an account of what one might call "the growth of a pacifist's mind."

58. *Crusader*, 15 August 1919, 11. There is a complete run of the *Crusader* in the Swarthmore College Peace Collection, McCabe Library, Swarthmore College, Swarthmore, Pennsylvania. "August Pendragon" runs from 10 January 1919 to 2 January 1920. I am most grateful to Wendy Chmielewski, Curator of the Swarthmore College Peace Collection, for photocopying the entire serial for me.

59. See, for example, Graham, *Conscription*, chap. 5.

60. *Crusader*, 2 May 1919, 5, and 7 November 1919, 11.

61. Wilson, "August Pendragon," *Crusader*, 15 August 1919, 11.

62. "Mr. Clutton Brock on 'Vagueness,'" *Crusader*, 2 January 1920, 11.

63. Herbert H. Horwill, "A Quaker Social Movement," *Constructive Quarterly* 9 (June 1921): 318–31. Thanks to Sylvia Carlyle, Friends' House, for copies of three pages of material relating to the Shareholders Movement.

64. NCF Trustees Annual Report (typescript), January to December 1920, Swarthmore College Peace Collection. I am very grateful to Wendy Chmielewski for providing me with this report. See also Martin Ceadel, *Pacifism in Britain, 1914–1945: The Defining of a Faith* (Oxford: Clarendon Press, 1980), 53, and Graham, *Conscription*, 342.

65. Wellock, *Off the Beaten Track*, 45.

66. W. J. Chamberlain, *Fighting for Peace: The Story of the War Resistance Movement* (London: No More War Movement, [1928]), 118, 124. And see Ceadel, *Pacifism*, 72.

67. Chamberlain, *Fighting for Peace*, 124.

68. Canon H.R.L. (Dick) Sheppard (1880–1937) was ordained in 1909; in 1914, he served as an army chaplain. Appointed vicar of St. Martin-in-the-Fields (Trafalgar Square, London), he drew large wartime congregations and, soon after, an even wider audience when his services were broadcast by the BBC. An increasingly convinced pacifist, he wrote a letter to the press in October 1934, inviting men to send him postcards stating, "We renounce war and never again, directly or indirectly, will we support or sanction another" (quoted in Caroline Moorehead, *Troublesome People: The Warriors of Pacifism* [Bethesda, Md.: Adler and Adler, 1987], 123). He soon had some one hundred thousand "pledges," and in July 1935, at a London meeting of seven thousand people, the Sheppard Peace Movement was begun. Soon renamed the Peace Pledge Union (PPU), and joined by women who signed the pledge, it attracted an extremely distinguished group of sponsors and speakers, opened a bookshop, and began to publish *Peace News*. Sheppard, who had been asthmatic since childhood, died at his desk in October 1937. One hundred thousand people filed past his coffin in St. Martin's; the PPU continued his work. See Moorehead, *Troublesome People*, 122–28; Robert Graves and Alan Hodge, *The Long Week-End: A Social History of*

Great Britain, 1918–1939 (1941; reprint, New York: W. W. Norton, 1963), 328–29; and Vera Brittain, *Testament of Experience: An Autobiographical Story of the Years 1925–1950* (1957; reprint, N.p.: Wideview Books, 1981), 164–88.

69. In mid-1990 Mary Sweetlove, C. W. Daniel's niece, discovered some two dozen letters (most from TWW but a couple from Daniel to TWW) relating to *Those Strange Years*. With quite remarkable generosity, she sent them to me— another kindness in a series of several over three years.

70. Sylvia Carlyle found this in an issue of *Peace News*, Friends' House.

71. From a letter to Friends' House, 15 September 1989.

72. Stories of peace workers are slow in getting out (unless the workers did other things deemed "noteworthy"). For example, Eileen Egan notes that Dorothy Day gained widespread recognition in the United States and a "wide range of readers" when her writings were collected, but these comments preface a collection of the writings of Muriel Lester (1884–1968), far less known although an International FOR Ambassador from 1933 to 1958. Thanks to Richard Deats, Lester's work is now accessible to contemporary readers. See Deats, ed., *Ambassador of Reconciliation: A Muriel Lester Reader*, foreword by Eileen Egan (Philadelphia: New Society Publishers, 1991). Sandi E. Cooper's *Patriotic Pacifism: Waging War on War in Europe, 1815–1914* (Oxford University Press, 1991), is a richly detailed, scholarly account of numerous workers and thinkers but, because no one can do all the work, is necessarily silent on many others. Moorehead's *Troublesome People*, a splendid account of "what modern pacifists are actually like" (xiii), is already remaindered. Moorehead poignantly both declares her objective *and* suggests some reasons for the disdain that millions feel for pacifists: "I wanted to show how, for all the threads that link pacifists to their roots and to their mentors, for all the contacts that bind them to each other all over the world, pacifism is basically the most lonely of beliefs, held for the most part in private, and sustained in isolation, often in the face of powerful opposition. . . . There is a stubbornness, an obduracy, about pacifism that can be infuriating; it can also be heroic, admirable" (xiii).

73. *AFSC-TAO: News from the American Friends Service Committee*, July 1991, 4–5; navy reservist quoted in "Activist News," *Non-Violent Activist*, July/August 1991, 17.

74. This character is almost certainly modeled on Clifford Allen, chairman of the NCF, who was jailed, to the ruination of his health, as a conscientious objector. TWW "made" him prime minister; His Majesty's Government later gave him a peerage.

75. Wilfred Wellock, "Theodora Wilson Wilson," *Peace News*, 28 November 1941, 3.

ANDY CROFT

Ethel Mannin:

The Red Rose of Love and

the Red Flower of Liberty

Shortly after the outbreak of war in 1914, the children of Ethel Mannin's boarding school were asked to write an essay on "Patriotism." Though not yet fourteen, Mannin wrote a passionate attack on king and country, hoping to impress her favorite teacher, a member of the Communist Party. But if her teacher was impressed, her headmistress was certainly not. Mannin was lectured on the wickedness of her ideas in front of the whole school and was made to kneel all morning in the school hall. Suffering for both a noble cause and for the teacher she worshipped clearly nourished her adolescent sense of the dramatic and gave her a taste for martyrdom; on Empire Day 1915, when the whole school was expected to march into the playground and salute the Union Jack, she refused.

> The revolutionary in me emerged once more. I would not salute the flag. My Flag was the Red Flag, according to the creed set forth by my father, and the communist teacher who had admired my essay deriding patriotism. I made this declaration with my little frightened heart beating like mad, but all the time hammering in my head the memory of my talks with my father, and with my adored Miss X. I think I would have died then and there rather than salute any flag but the Red Flag. I was threatened with expulsion. But I

was prepared to face all the fearful odds for the ashes of my fathers and the temple of my gods. So whilst the rest of the school marched through the playground and saluted the Flag—the girls' salute a ladylike waving of handkerchiefs—I knelt again in the hall with my beating heart and my hurting knees and my terrific sense of martyr-dom for a splendid cause. I freely forgave my Miss X that she must march past with her class and salute like any capitalist or "jingoist." She dared not risk getting "the sack." My young heart bled for her. She looked at me as she passed through the hall with her class. I saw that she was wearing the red rose I had given her that morning when I arrived at school. The red rose of love, the red flower of liberty.[1]

This story is very Ethel Mannin. The solemn prose quivering with moral indignation—this could have been one of her own early romantic hero-ines. Though she was to later write about her own life in rather different ways, she was constructing her childhood here in political terms, her education a political education, her adolescence a steadfast growing into political maturity, from rebellion to revolution.[2] Already in 1930 she was drawing on the emotional categories that her many readers would come to recognize—youth, rebellion, martyrdom, idealism, and love—in order to convey a political idea.

Today the sentimentality of this passage sits perhaps uneasily with its politics; in the 1990s, liberty, love, and socialism are hardly synony-mous. Or perhaps the politics seem quite as unrealized, as superficial, as romantic as the writing. To those who argue that British literary cul-ture was for a few years in the 1930s overwhelmed by a sentimental and ridiculous attachment to communism, Ethel Mannin's writing ought to be a gift.[3] And yet you will look in vain for any consideration of Ethel Mannin's fiction in the orthodox literary histories of that period.[4] Per-haps because to address this popular best-seller would be to breach the assumption that the literary culture of the 1930s was a tiny, elitist one, talking to itself instead of to a reading public. Her novels suggest that the developing social concerns and political responsibilities of British novelists, publishers, and readers clearly ran wider and deeper than is usually suggested; it was not the "entry" of intellectuals into politics so much as the unavoidable presence of contemporary events in almost all aspects of British cultural life—even in the world of romantic fiction.

To consider the political and creative development of Ethel Mannin in these years is to go far beyond the limits of the generation of the Auden Group, to which so much attention has been paid and around which so many histories of the "Red Decade" are still constructed. Ethel Mannin never went to Oxford or Cambridge and had published fourteen books before she discovered Marxism. Though she called herself a "revolutionary," Ethel Mannin was never a member of the Communist Party, a membership that is usually necessary for inclusion in the dismissive myths of Stalin duping the intellectuals (though her unbridled enthusiasm for the Soviet Union—for a few years at least—went farther than most). A consideration of Ethel Mannin's fiction in the 1920s and 1930s and its developing political consciousness, clarity, and engagement might therefore begin to reopen the question of the relation between politics and literature between the wars—and since. For unlike many of her now more famous contemporaries, Ethel Mannin never completely abandoned the political commitments of the 1930s, continuing to write with critical pride about her youthful revolutionary politics. In her late seventies, she still described herself as a Republican and a "Tolstoyan anarchist," still "preaching communism," still welcoming the likely collapse of capitalism, still giving qualified support to the Soviet Union ("a more egalitarian society"), and by then an enthusiast for Mao's China ("that the whole of the far East, and South East Asia, will eventually go communist I do not doubt; it will do so because of the extremes of poverty that prevail for the multitudinous masses and for which communism offers a solution, which nothing else does").[5]

The Road to Romance

Ethel Mannin was born in Clapham in 1900, one of three children. From her mother she claimed what she liked to call her "zest for life"; from her father, a letter sorter in the local post office, she learned a lifelong commitment to a passionate socialism.[6] At the boarding school, Miss X introduced her first to Tennyson, Coleridge, Shelley, and Keats and then to Olive Schreiner, Wells, Gissing, and Wilde. She started writing poetry herself, and before she was thirteen she had published stories in *Lady's Companion* and *Reynold's News*. At fifteen, after reading Shaw and Morris, she announced to the world that she was a vegetarian. In her autobiographies at least, she never hesitated in her determination to be a writer.

I had something to say, and everyone must hear, hear, and know that I was different—ah yes, different, with something in me, in spite of my shyness and my stupidity at other things. Shy and

dull, and agonisingly self-conscious . . . when I was writing I became someone, I was transformed, power was in me, the power of
words . . . I lived in a secret world untill I was fifteen. All the time I
was walking anywhere I would be mentally writing a story. If I had
to break off to come out for a moment into the real world, I would
always pick up the story where I last left it off in my mind. It was
a sort of endless serial. . . . Whenever possible I would be writing
on paper. I wrote endlessly, foolscap sheets, exercise books, on the
backs of circulars. . . . It was a flame that burned in me.[7]

But in 1915 she left school to start work as a shorthand typist in the city
at Charles Higham's advertising agency, taking home just twenty-three
shillings a week. Then Charles Higham gave her a remarkable opportunity. Since all his best copywriters were away at the war, he invited
her to try her hand at writing advertising copy. She did so and, with a
bit of coaching, was soon writing copy for the firm's biggest clients. At
the age of sixteen, she was given the job of editing the house journal.
At seventeen, she was editing the *Pelican*, a theatrical paper owned by
Higham, going to first nights, smoking Turkish cigarettes, and falling
in love. By the time she was nineteen, she was married to Jack Porteous,
a copywriter at Higham's. At twenty, she was pregnant.

During her pregnancy she continued writing, selling serialized romantic novelettes like *The Road to Romance* at a guinea per thousand
words in order to meet the rent.

"Oh, Joan," she cried, "if you aren't the luckiest, luckiest girl in
the world!"

She rushed to the side of the bed and lifted a fold or two of the
silken loveliness which lay outspread there before her.

"Orange blossom and white shoes and satin sachets and everything," she breathed, and turned a flushed, excited face up to the
beautiful girl who stood at the end of the bed, watching her with
rather a grave smile.

"I do envy you, Joan," Muriel added, with the ghost of a sigh, "it
must be simply lovely getting married!"

"It must be wonderful getting married to someone you love,"
Joan Sutherland said slowly, "but getting married like I am, to
someone you don't know—have never seen—it's awful!" . . .

Muriel Harding looked at her friend in horrified amazement.
"You mean that you are not going to marry Sir Martin after all?
Oh, Joan, but you must now, you know!"

Joan shook her head, and her lips tightened. "I can't, Muriel! . . .

how would you like to be married to a man just because he happened to be the son of your father's bosom friend!"

"But the money?" Muriel protested, "your father left it to you on condition—"[8]

Calling herself Ethel *E*. Mannin (after her much admired Ethel M. Dell), she entered a novel-writing competition in 1922 with a story about a girl who, as she put it, "loved not wisely but too well." The novel, *Martha*, won second place and was published by Leonard Parsons in 1923. Martha is an orphan working as a scullery maid in the infirmary where her mother died giving birth to her. Martha marries a handsome young doctor, but when she rejects him sexually, he rapes her. She runs away, finds work in a laundry, and falls in love with a handsome young Christian Socialist; however, David deserts her when she becomes pregnant, and the baby dies. Meanwhile the handsome young doctor has died, leaving her a small fortune. She becomes a successful playwright and decides at the end of the novel to marry a handsome young farmer. "If she could make Allan Frayne happy—that would be worth while. Married to him, and in the care of his home and children, she would deaden the ache of her hunger for David, and she would make him happy. . . . And married to him, the intolerable loneliness would disappear. There would be more babies to take the place of the dead child of love. Happy babies born within the sanctuary of marriage."[9]

Four more novels followed in the next four years: *Hunger of the Sea* (1924), set among the fishing villages of Hastings on the Sussex coast; *Sounding Brass* (1925), about the rise and fall of an advertising king who sacrifices worldly success for love and beauty; *Pilgrims* (1927), about the hopeless love of an unworldly young Dutch painter; and *The Green Willow* (1928), a novel of childhood. Enjoying remarkable sales, these were unremarkable novels, generic and conventional. In *Hunger of the Sea*, for example, Mary (like the novel) has difficulty distinguishing between the "romance" of the fishermen's lives and her romance with the rough, handsome Jan.

> "Now give me a kiss, sweet," and he turned her face up to his.
>
> She wanted to resist, but the blueness of his eyes held her, and the spirit of romance came surging back, washing away everything but the thrill of being with him, in his arms, his lips fastening greedily upon hers.
>
> It was with an effort that she said at last, "I must be going." . . . She rose and groped for her hat and coat. She remembered that other night . . . Jan rose abruptly and caught her wrists. "You can't

go—now," he said shortly, and swung her into his arms, his hands pressing about her face. "You can't go," he cried. "Don't be a fool, Mary, you can't go now."

He stopped her answer with kisses that bruised her lips. More than anything in the world she wanted to stay.[10]

Ethel Mannin was by now a celebrity. Her opinions were sought on everything from marriage and motherhood to fashion and the theater. Writing stories for *Nash's Magazine*, the *News Chronicle*, the *Grand Magazine*, and *Everyman*, she collected two volumes of short stories, *Green Figs* (1931) and *Dryad* (1933). She met writers like Gilbert Frankau, Douglas Goldring, Beverley Nichols, Somerset Maugham, and Arnold Bennett, dancing through the 1920s to Paul Whiteman's band at the Hammersmith Palais de Danse, at Prince's in Piccadilly, and at Romanos in the Strand.

When, in 1929, she exchanged her husband for "independence" and bought a house near Wimbledon Common, the popular papers wanted to know her opinions on sex, adultery, and the modern woman. To Oak Cottage came the rich and famous like Paul Tanqueray, Louis Marlow, and Ralph Straus, and the infamous like Norman Haire, Fenner Brockway, Una Troubridge, and Radclyffe Hall. She visited the United States in 1926 and sent her daughter Jean to A. S. Neill's progressive school, Summerhill; under Neill's influence she wrote the iconoclastic *Commonsense and the Child: A Plea for Freedom* (1931) with an introduction by Neill.[11] She publicly defended Jacob Epstein, championed Paul Robeson against the powerful *Daily Express* critic Hannen Swaffer, and campaigned against the banning of *Lady Chatterley's Lover*, *Ulysses*, and *The Well of Loneliness*. "The lives of the majority of people are fundamentally wrong; wrong at the core. . . . Most people are dead. The women for the most part are not merely dead but buried as well. See them rushing to buy the banned book, or to see the risqué play, the substitute for the sexual satisfaction they have never known. Pitiful. . . . How can people live life as a pure flame when there is this fundamental dissatisfaction at the whole root of living! . . . We have made sex a smutty story. . . . At the back of all our shame about sex is the puritanical hatred of life, and fear of happiness."[12]

Her reputation as a champion for sexual freedom was sealed with the publication of her next novels: *Crescendo* (1929), which sold over ninety-five thousand copies, and *Ragged Banners* (1931), with its cast of bohemian characters, promiscuous, cynical, and implicitly homosexual. In

Ragged Banners, a bisexual London publisher tries to seduce a successful romantic novelist:

> "If Love isn't an orgy of lust, then it ought to be . . . and if beauty doesn't make you want to shout and sing with sheer exhuberance there's something wrong with either it or yourself. . . . I like you as a person, and I am physically attracted. What is love more than that? All the rest is an artificial state of emotionalised thinking into which people lash themselves—a legend they go on supporting—a superstition they cling to—have clung to for so long that they can't get away from it. . . . There'd be a dam' sight less dishonesty in life if people would stop using that overworked word love; it's responsible for all the self-deception and intellectual humbug with which people complicate their own and other people's lives. There's the peace, the rich, warm sense of fulfillment which follows the consummation of mutual desire—but don't let's give it fancy names; it's a simple animal thing, let's accept it as such." [13]

Ethel Mannin had come a long way down "The Road to Romance." Though she continued to write love stories, after *Crescendo* there is an increasingly serious, more earnest quality to her writing. Looking for romance, she discovered sexual repression; looking for sexual freedom, she discovered socialism. The transition is most evident in her travel books from the early 1930s. In 1929 she recalled that when she had arrived in New York during the Prohibition, the stern immigration official demanded to know her reason for visiting the United States. She replied simply, "for fun." For there wasn't much fun to be found in repressed and repressive old England, its moral and cultural life in the hands of Sir William Joynson-Hicks, James Douglas, Dean Inge, and Hannen Swaffer. Her search for "freedom" soon saw her traveling to Cologne, Frankfurt, Brussels, and Rome, pilgrimages described in *In All Experience* (1932). Two years later, in *Forever Wandering* (1934), she went farther east, from Paris to Prague, "Socialist Vienna," and Berlin, dismayed to see the passing of the sexually open culture of Weimar Germany, "the passing of individuality and freedom, the assertion of a tyranny that has even the power to interfere in the most private of human relations—the sexual relation." She wrote: "I found Berlin re-visited more beautiful than I had remembered it, the women more elegant, and the cafés no less animated and crowded than a few years back. But in spite of its late-spring loveliness, after a few days I felt a need to leave not merely Berlin but Germany itself. The endless brown-shirts, swastikas, and pictures of Hitler were constant reminders of the existence of a regime alien to everything that one believed in."[14]

The Straight and Narrow Way

By the time she was writing *Forever Wandering*, Ethel Mannin had found what she believed in. In 1934 she made her first visit to Moscow, exhilarated by the freedom she felt from the "tyranny of shams, religious, conventional, moral" that she had seen everywhere else.

> Having gone to Russia I shall always count as the most worthwhile journey I ever made. I found there a life which is real . . . a life that has purpose and meaning, where progress is a reality, not a newspaper catch-phrase; a life illuminated by an ideal—the ideal of the right to live, as opposed to merely existing, for every man. It is we of the capitalist Western world who are the barbarians, living savagely according to the law of the Survival of the Fittest which a corrupt and decaying system imposes . . . ours the broad highway leading us fast to destruction; theirs the straight and narrow way of self-sacrifice and unswervingly steadfast adherence to an ideal which shall ultimately yield them Utopia—the kingdom, the power and the glory.[15]

In 1933 she joined the Independent Labour Party (ILP) and began writing regularly for the ILP's weekly paper, the *New Leader*. The ILP had disaffiliated from the Labour Party the previous year and was rapidly moving left. Although the ILP briefly sought affiliation to the Communist Third International and, after 1935, worked with the Communist Party to help construct a Popular Front of political, moral, and cultural opposition to fascism, the ILP liked to style itself as a party of "revolutionary socialists" well to the left of the Communist Party.

To Oak Cottage now came a different circle of friends—Ronald Kidd, Reginald Reynolds, C.L.R. James, Emma Goldman, Ellen Wilkinson, and Jimmy Maxton; her ILP branch met there. Ethel Mannin was a considerable recruit to the ILP, and she quickly established a name for herself as a political speaker and journalist. When, in 1934, she served as a juror at the Old Bailey, the front page of the *New Leader* was given over to the story "Three Manslaughter Cases: Ethel Mannin Tells What It Is Like to Serve on an Old Bailey Jury." A pub brawl, an assault, and a jilted lover's revenge were for her all connected by "the tragedy of the social system which drives men and women to violence . . . truly the sins of the

capitalist regime are visited upon the heads of the people." [16] The following November she used the paper to publicize a report by the National
Council for Civil Liberties on the dramatic increase in the number of
arrests by the Metropolitan Police on grounds of "suspicion." This kind
of "authorised bullying" made her "see red." She added, "The trouble is
that there aren't—yet—enough of us seeing Red!" [17]

In fact, the ILP was already in terminal decline. When the ILP disaffiliated from the Labour Party, it had a membership of over sixteen
thousand; rapidly losing support to both the Labour Party and the
Communist Party, by 1935 the ILP had only four thousand members. [18]
Soon Ethel Mannin was desperately appealing to readers of the *New
Leader* to buy two copies a week to save "the only revolutionary Socialist
paper" in Britain. [19] Meanwhile she used her regular column in the paper
to attack the judiciary, to denounce Glasgow's Labour-controlled council for supporting the Scottish Empire Exhibition of 1938, and to ridicule
the Nazis. [20] She also attacked the Monarchy: "We have had an overdose
of kings and lords, and thrones and crowns lately, with royal weddings,
the Jubilee, the illness and death of George V, the royal funeral . . . it's
all very good bread-and-circuses for the unthinking masses, but though
you can fool some of the people some of the time, you cannot, thank
God, fool all the people all the time." [21]

The importance of this best-selling popular novelist to the ILP may
be estimated by the frequent use of Ethel Mannin's photograph in the
New Leader (usually one taken by Paul Tanqueray and designed by Ida
Davies) to adorn her many book reviews (only the faces of Maxton and
Brockway appeared in the paper more frequently). She reviewed books
by A. S. Neill and Norman Haire, [22] books about Ireland, Nazi Ger-
many, the Italian invasion of Abyssinia, and the struggles of the Chinese
Communists—education, sex, tyranny, and freedom again. [23] She found
herself reviewing novels by a new generation of working-class writers—
by Jack Jones, Walter Greenwood, James Whittaker, John Brown, Mabel
Lethbridge, Jack Lawson, F. C. Boden, James Hanley, J. L. Hodson,
Simon Blumenfeld, Harry Heslop, Edgar Meredith, George Thomas,
James Barke, E. W. Lister, and Liam O'Flaherty. She already knew Walter Greenwood, then a member of the ILP, who had sent her a collection
of short stories to look at. She sent them back, urging him instead to
write a novel about his experiences; he did, and the result was *Love on the
Dole* (1933). In 1935 the novel was dramatized by Greenwood and Ronald
Gow and played in the West End. "A magnificent statement of the case
for the overthrow of the capitalist system," she wrote. "I for one would
like to compel every supporter of the present regime to sit through its

three heart-breaking acts and then ask themselves if they still believed there was no need for a revolution! This play is going to make a lot of people think, is going to shock smug, fashionable, comfortably off, middle-class London into a realisation of what the industrial North is really like."[24]

Her enthusiasm for Greenwood in particular derived from her belief in the educative powers of well-written and popular propaganda in fictional form. Generous in her praise, she found revolutionary propaganda in the unlikeliest of novels. It was there, of course, in Brockway's ILP utopia *Purple Plague* (1935) and in Communist novelists like Arthur Calder-Marshall, Heslop, Barke, and Simon Blumenfeld (whose first novel, *Jew Boy* (1935) she recommended as "a first-rate piece of work which no comrade should miss").[25] But she also found revolutionary propaganda in Jack Jones's comic *Rhondda Roundabout* (1934) ("It is much too important a novel to miss—I could almost insist that it is the duty of every Socialist to read Jack Jones' book"),[26] in James Hanley's Expressionist *The Furys* (1935) ("which every smug member of the bourgeoisie should be compelled to read"),[27] in George Thomas's *Neighbours* (1935) (required reading for all those "who are not yet awake to the necessity—and urgent necessity at that—for the overthrow of the economic system"),[28] in James Whittaker's autobiography *I, James Whittaker* (1934) ("much-needed propaganda work for the overthrow of a corrupt and crumbling system"),[29] in Jack Lawson's *Under the Wheels* (1934) ("I strongly recommend this important study of conditions as they are and always will be until the system is revolutionised"),[30] and in J. L. Hodson's *God's in His Heaven* (1935) ("Make your friends who see no neccessity for revolution read it; read it yourselves and take heart and hope. For there is in our midst this flame; more and more it is invading our literature, and the time will come when it will run like a forest fire through the mass of the workers; in the meantime, ours it is to fan the flame, and that faithfully, fearlessly, to the utmost of our power").[31]

She was increasingly conscious of the contrast between the novels she was reviewing and her own practice as a novelist. The *New Leader* criticized her *Men Are Unwise* (1934) for being too "far removed" "from the mass conflicts of the age."[32] Meanwhile James Maxton, M.P. and chair of the ILP, reproached her for not having yet written the politically committed novels he expected of her. Reviewing F. C. Boden's third novel, *A Derbyshire Tragedy*, Mannin was struck by the sneering reference to "the woman novelist of 'sloppy love stories' who is always on about being a Socialist."[33] By now Ethel Mannin was convinced that the sentimental Hollywood glamour of the conventional romantic novel was part of the ideological exploitation of women. She tried to prevent the republication of her early romantic novelettes but couldn't raise the fourteen hundred pounds necessary to buy the rights. She grimly recalled the dust covers picturing "a young woman in bed with a pink eiderdown and the gentleman in evening dress leering at her from the door-way . . . one with a young woman in evening dress and showing a great deal of leg sitting on a sofa with a gentleman in evening dress . . . by their jackets ye shall know them."[34] She embarked on a series of novels about the lives of working-class women, the "humble figure of the ordinary woman"—*Children of the Earth* (1930); *Linda Shawn* (1932), a novel about a hard rural childhood (which sold over sixty thousand copies); *Venetian Blinds* (1934), using her own Clapham childhood; *Rose and Sylvie* (1938), about a young girl who runs away with her parents' maid; and *Julie* (1940), a grim picture of the life of a nightclub dancer and hostess.

Children of the Earth (1930) is at first glance a conventional exercise in seasonal passions, enduring love, and natural beauty, a family saga set on Jersey at the turn of the century. Jean le Camillon is a handsome giant, slow moving and gentle, falling in love with the dark-eyed Breton Marie. "Marie was nineteen and virgin, but she was essentially woman; there was nothing of the young girl about her. She was virgin because the arrogance of men roused all her own arrogance. She felt deeply within herself that she was not to be plucked like a flower. She had so much to give that it needs must be given, not plundered; she had so much more than her warm ripe body to give, she had all of herself. From the time she had been first aware of men, at sixteen, she had cherished this vision of herself as one day magnificently giving herself . . . and then she had seen Jean le Camillon with the bloom of his youth on him and that half-startled wonder in his eyes." But life is hard on Jersey, and Marie dies bearing too many children. And even in such a remote and beautiful setting, the demands of the wider world intrude. Mannin, having invited her readers into the novel by using conventional romantic forms, firmly scotched the romance of Jersey peasant life, brutally and bathetically, insisting on its material and economic hardship and its unavoidable involvement in the carnage of the Great War. Jean's remaining son is killed in France, and he is left alone at the end of the novel, struggling hopelessly to work the farm. "The great dark tide of war rolled on; all youth, all life, seemed engulfed in it. All the lads had left their homes, and only the old men were left to carry on."[35]

Mannin was clearly writing a new kind of novel, drawing on all her skill as a writer of romantic fiction to convey an increasingly explicit

political message. This involved her subverting the ideological assumptions of the genre, interrogating its weaknesses and contradictions. And
it required her to tread carefully, to take her huge readership with her.
It was an extraordinary attempt, to ask hard political questions of an
uncritical kind of reading, to breathe life into what she regarded as a corrupt form of writing. Setting out to deconstruct Romance as a lazy and
male-serving fantasy, she was asking nothing less of her readers than the
reeducation of desire. She insisted that the arguments of any political
fiction, of the wider, public, political life, must be consistent with the
representation of personal, domestic, emotional, and sexual life. And
love remained the dominating, shaping force of her writing; her novels
were still primarily love stories, marriage still the highest good, love
the prize her characters sought and sometimes won but more often lost.
For example, although she warmly reviewed Harry Heslop's novel *Last
Cage Down*, admiring its political analysis of life in the Durham coal-
field, she privately criticized the representation of women, love, and sex
in the novel. She wrote to Heslop: "Jim was evidently one of those men
who either don't know or don't care—or both—about the woman's
orgasm (which isn't achieved by mere fucking; but then so few men
know anything at all about female physiology) . . . I thought the incident a mistake, myself, not on moral grounds, but on artistic ones. And
dammit, all adult people know how fucking's done; why go into the
details? . . . I mean its gratuitous. Of course 'he went into her.' What
else would he do? If he *had* done something original it might be worth
recording." Her main objection, however, was to the isolation of sexual
desire in the novel. "Your Jim didn't believe in 'love' apparently, from
his remarks on marriage. Well he missed a lot in life, that's all. You can't
dispose of love by denying it. I hate this dividing up of love into physical and spiritual; it's all fused, the desire of the flesh, and the tenderness
and companionship and affection and mutual liking (of each other as
people), the sum which adds up to the thing we call love." [36]

Her next novel, *Men Are Unwise* (1934), is the story of a young man
burdened with a desire to "be on top." Forced to take an office job he
hates, Donald develops an obsession for mountain climbing. This becomes a source of conflict with his new wife, Kathleen. " 'There's really
a lot to be said for a nice comfortable hill' Kathleen remarked, lazily.
'Much less exhausting than scrambling about on mountains—its only
vanity, really, that makes one want to climb mountains, a sort of chronic
egotism.' 'There's no comparison between the thrill of a mountain top
and that of a hill, though,' Donald urged, 'no sense of achievement with
a hill.' Nothing to her the sense of power, the vast solitude and silence,

the splendour of sun on snow. All her life she would be content with hill-tops, and all his life he would yearn for mountains."[37] The novel proposes two different sorts of romance: Kathleen's idea of domestic peace, a little house and a garden, and Donald's yearning for power and adventure (significantly, he meets some German Nazis while climbing). When Donald finally has the opportunity to make his fantasies real, his nerve breaks on his first serious climb and he falls, killing himself and his companion. Genuine romance, the novel concludes, is unspectacular and hard work, not rooted in fear, neurosis, insecurity, and oppression but in equal, secure, and independent partnership.

Ethel Mannin was to find great happiness in such a partnership when she met Reginald Reynolds in 1935 (they married in 1939). He was an ILP activist and journalist and a friend of Mahatma Gandhi; at the height of the campaign of civil disobedience in 1929, Gandhi had entrusted Reynolds to take his ultimatum to the British viceroy.[38] Through Reynolds, Mannin became involved in the India Freedom Campaign and the Africa Freedom Campaign; under his influence, she became a pacifist, and her next novel was a militant denunciation of war. *Cactus* (1935) begins in the summer of 1914. While on holiday on the Rhine, young Elspeth Rodney falls in love with a handsome young German called Karl. When the German and Russian armies are mobilized, Karl, excited at the prospect of war, urges Elspeth to leave for England as soon as possible.

> They smiled at each other wanly. In the taxi they sat holding hands in silence. Both had a sense of a thousand important things to say and no words with which to say them. The station was crowded. There was an atmosphere of disorganisation, of panic, of fugitive flight. . . . She clung to him, blinded with tears. "Oh, Karl! What shall we do?" "We can do nothing except to believe in each other, Leibling." . . . "All our lovely Summer—we never dreamed it would end like this." . . . For a last wild moment they clung together, then Elspeth was bundled up the steps and the train was moving out. She rushed to the nearest window in the corridor, but it was already crowded with people waving good-bye and there was no place for her. She forced her way along the corridor, but all the windows were similarly crowded. Without knowing it she was sobbing hysterically and calling his name, "Karl! Karl! . . . O God, O God . . . I can't live without him, don't let there be war."[39]

Of course, she never sees him again. Elspeth waits for four long years, suffering accusations of pro-German sympathies, only to learn that Karl was reported missing in action sometime in 1916. All that remains is the memory of their glorious summer, an uncomplicated happiness broken by the false romance of war. Once again Mannin was setting the conventions of romantic fiction against political realities, writing a love story in which love is prevented by politics. But there is still hope for Elspeth at the close of the novel. On holiday in Spain, she hears Karl's voice speaking to her: "I am one of the millions of men who died; you are one of the millions of women who mourn. . . . Long ago in your heart you, one woman out of millions, revolted against war that destroys men and bereaves women, that writes Finis to the love, beauty and hope that lightens human life, and substitutes in its place hate, horror and despair. . . . There is this vast army of women who the war robbed of their heritage as women. Out of their sufferings should emerge the spirit of revolt. Let them refuse to bear children till the world be made safe from war. . . . Red as the blood of the men who died is the cactus flower, red as the banner of revolt."[40]

Her next novel, *The Pure Flame* (1936), was written while she was on board a steamer bound for Leningrad in 1935 and was finished during her second stay in the Soviet Union. Elspeth returns in this novel as a middle-aged spinster, still grieving for the memory of Karl. Her niece, Chloe, falls in love with an ILP activist named Harry Winchell, but their love is prevented by barriers of class: Chloe is the daughter of a doctor, and Harry is unemployed and dying of tuberculosis. Another pair of disappointed lovers. The novel ends with a highly charged deathbed scene in which Harry urges Chloe not to mourn him but to devote herself to the revolution and to take inspiration from the building of socialism in the Soviet Union: "Don't cry, Chloe. You look pretty standing there; the street's growing dark now, the lamps all alight. Grey and sad it was down by the river when we left. Think of it in the sunshine, with the summer wind stirring the rushes, and the white birds sailing over. Russia in the Spring. Chloe—if I can't get there you must go. You and Miss Rodney . . . A pilgrimage. You must go there because I can't, and Rose can't and thousands like us. You must go and come back and help in the great work of firing the masses with the dream of a better way of living, not just for the privileged few but for everyone, for all of us in Orchard Street, and all the Orchard Streets."[41] Love is as painful as oppression, political struggle as necessary as desire. The novel employs all the tricks of sentimentality within a clear, unyielding political framework, and the effect is at once unsettling and readable. What would Miss Ethel E. Mannin have thought?

Not Yet the Promised Land

By the time *The Pure Flame* was published, however, Ethel Mannin's attitude toward the Soviet Union was beginning to change. The previous year she had been admonishing other travelers to the Soviet Union for seeing only the bad they wanted to see. And she sharply criticized her friend Naomi Mitchison for the "disgracefully irresponsible misrepresentations of the USSR" in the novel *We Have Been Warned*. She wrote: "Your lies are the lies of false implications arising out of half-truths served up as the whole truth. There have been more than enough lies about Russia. . . . Any statement about Russia which does not take into consideration pre-revolutionary conditions, Russian mentality, and the supremely important fact that Russia is growing all the time, is bound to be false. . . . You are not, as we are, working for a revolution which will give a class-less society and the abolition of private profit . . . the least you can do, therefore, is not to add to the mass of distorted ideas and lies about Russia."[42]

Mannin had just begun work on a book about her travels in the Soviet Union, when, in January 1936, she wrote an article—"Whither Russia?"—for the *New Leader*. Though she was still enthusiastic for the "visible progress" she had seen, "building, building, all the time, everywhere," still impressed by the reconstruction of Moscow during the First Five Year Plan, she was disappointed by the many regional and social inequalities she had seen on her last visit. Her praise for the Soviet Union was now more qualified, anxious, conditional. "Russia is not yet the Promised land," she wrote. "She is still the Promising land."[43] The article provoked a number of letters to the paper—some readers delighted, some appalled. A few lines of the article were taken out of context by the *Blackshirt*, the weekly paper of the British Union of Fascists, to trumpet what they called "Ethel Mannin's Disillusion in Russia."[44] Enraged, she wrote a long reply, "Blackshirt Lies about Russia," in the Communist *Daily Worker*. She reiterated her view that there was "far more to praise than to criticise in the magnificent achievements of the USSR." She continued, "If the USSR disappoints some of us in some ways it must nevertheless command the allegiance of all of us who abominate the capitalist system and all that it stands for, of vested interests, imperialism, and the oppression of the workers."[45] This piece, however, provoked an editorial in the following day's *Daily Worker*, accusing her of naïveté in writing an article so "in line with anti-Soviet propaganda that it was, for the *Blackshirt*, a chance too good to miss."[46]

Meanwhile Radio Moscow had broadcast a strong reply to her original piece. Patiently and penitently, she tried to explain herself again, this time in the *New Leader*. "I should be very sorry if Moscow got the idea from my article that I am 'anti-Soviet' . . . the sum of my admiration for the achievements of the USSR far exceeds my criticism."[47]

Yet Ethel Mannin was clearly upset by the hostility that her mild and comradely criticism had raised; from this date, her admiration for the Soviet Union began to ebb. When the book about her travels in the Soviet Union was published later that year, as *South to Samarkand* (1936), it was so critical that Donia Naschen, a Communist artist who had accompanied her to the Soviet Union, withdrew her illustrations for the book.[48] Even the reviewer in the increasingly anti-Soviet *New Leader* was frankly disappointed by it.[49] Having idealized the Soviet Union, Mannin was all the more disappointed when she saw the reality fall short of her ideal.

Between the publication of *The Pure Flame* and *South to Samarkand*, civil war had begun in Spain. As the ghost of Karl had prophesied at the end of *Cactus*: "Russia in 1917, Germany in 1919, England in 1926, Austria in this year of revolt 1934. And the end is not yet. Soon out of the rich warm soil of Spain will come revolt, from the Basque country and Catalonia." The events of the next two years were to finally end Mannin's romantic attachment to the Soviet Union. Inspired by the struggle of the Spanish anarchists and the Partido Obrero de Unificación Marxista (POUM), the ILP and Ethel Mannin temporarily turned away from pacifism to campaign for money and arms for the beleaguered Spanish Republic. In its "Authors Take Sides" questionnaire, *Left Review* asked: "Are you for, or against, the legal Government and the People of Republican Spain? Are you for, or against, Franco and Fascism?" Ethel Mannin unequivocally replied, "I am for the Legal Government of Spain inasmuch as I am against Franco and Fascism, and that passionately, but with the defeat of Franco I hope for very much more than a mere Republican Spain (with the old bourgeois capitalist Government still in power)—for the establishment of a Worker's State, not on Communist (USSR) lines, but CNT-FAI (Anarcho-Syndicalist)."[50]

The Spanish Civil War brought new antagonisms between the fast-growing Communist Party and the ILP, which found itself increasingly isolated on the British Left. Whereas the Communist Party and the Comintern saw the defeat of fascism as the urgent priority in Spain, the ILP supported the Barcelona rising against the republican government in 1937 and adopted an increasingly Trotskyite critique of the Soviet Union.[51] By the end of the war and the defeat of the Spanish Republic, the ILP was no longer an effective force in British politics. In 1939 Reginald Reynolds left the ILP; Ethel Mannin followed sometime later, still arguing over the ILP's equivocal attitude toward the Soviet Union. Her bitter sense of the isolation and defeat of her party during these years can be seen in one of her first postwar novels, *Comrade O Comrade* (1947), a scathing satire on the passions of the "lit'ry left" in the late 1930s. In this novel, a young Irishman is taken to a Popular Front meeting, raising money for medical aid for Spain. He is bewildered by the wealthy Communist intellectuals and society beauties pretending solidarity with the Spanish working class and is confused by the naked hostility between groups of people who talk of building unity against fascism. Eventually the intricacies of Spanish politics have to be explained to him:

> "Miss Thane belongs to something called the ILP. Its equivalent in Spain is the POUM. Working with the POUM are the Anarchists, the CNT and the FAI. There is also the UGT, which is under Communist influence. The Communists hate all the other initials, and they all hate the Falangists. Is that clear?"
>
> "Sure it's as clear as a bog-pool on a dark night," Larry declared. "And wouldn't there be just a few more initials at all—the ABC and XYZ and the IOU for the one to be against the other and all of them against dear-knows-who?" [52]

Comrade O Comrade is a renunciation not only of the organized British Left and the labor movement but also of the possibilities of politically engaged art.

> The distinguished poet, clad in classy tweeds, heaved up languidly from his chair and in a bored, classy tone murmured that he would first read the perm in the original Spanish. The perm expressed the struggle of the anti-Fascist masses against the military clique and the Church. Lifting his voice a little he read the Spanish verses, and everyone assumed intelligent expressions. A few nodded and faintly smiled at various points to indicate they understood Spanish. . . . "Now I will read you a perm of my own. I have called it 'No More the Castanets.'" He read this in a rather more lively tone.

"No more the castanets,
All that is finished.
Plough all such insignia
Of the bourgeoisie
Into the blood-soaked ground.
Now the machine-gun blooms

With crimson flowers
Under the orange tree.
No more the castanets,
The soul of Spain is free!"[53]

Though Ethel Mannin continued to write, prolifically, after the 1930s, she returned to the generic securities of her early romantic fiction with such well-loved novels as *Captain Moonlight* (1942), *Proud Heaven* (1944), *Late Have I Loved Thee* (1948), and *Love Under Another Name* (1953). When she died in 1984, she had published a total of ninety-five books.

For a few years in the 1930s, Ethel Mannin had succeeded in integrating a revolutionary vision of society with a hugely popular form of reading. Her fiction was of a piece with her tireless political journalism and public speaking, her politics as passionate as her fiction. She insisted on the human, private ends of politics, and she began to reclaim popular romantic fiction from its emotional betrayals, for its women readers. A romantic novelist with a highly romantic view of socialism, she nevertheless tested romantic fiction against political and economic reality, and she tested the political claims and ambitions of her generation against the emotional aspirations of ordinary women. When her own romantic view of socialism was defeated—in the Soviet Union, in Spain, and in Britain—she was no longer able to sustain the attempt to politicize romance. Thereafter she emptied her fiction of political content[54] and kept her politics for her journalism; she wrote a series of travel books about the cause of the Palestinian people: *A Lance for the Arabs* (1963), *Aspects of Egypt* (1964), and *The Lovely Land* (1965). For Ethel Mannin, writing "genuine romance" proved ultimately impossible. But one day, one day . . .

In a Socialist State, the awakened consciousness of the mass of people would not stomach the Hollywood trash depicting the class-order at its worst—high life and low morals. . . . The free woman of a classless society, having no "ladies" to envy and emulate will not be amused by their antics on the film; the need to escape into a world of comfort and ease and romance will no longer be theirs, for their lives will know comfort and ease, theirs will be the romance of living in a world of free men and women, and private, personal romance will be a not unattainable dream . . . no longer harrassed by the struggle to make ends meet, the dread of unemployment, no longer overworked.[55]

Notes

This essay is a much-expanded version of the script of a BBC radio program about Ethel Mannin. Broadcast on Radio Four on Sunday, 23 September 1990, it was part of a series, "Red Letter Days," about forgotten radical writers. I wish to thank Barry Winter at the ILP office in Leeds, who gave me access to the *New Leader*, and Dave Sheasby, Rebecca O'Rourke, and Mary Joannou, who in different ways encouraged my interest in Ethel Mannin.

1. Ethel Mannin, *Confessions and Impressions* (London: Jarrolds, 1930), 45.

2. She wrote five autobiographies—*Confessions and Impressions, Privileged Spectator* (London: Jarrolds, 1939), *Young in the Twenties* (London: Hutchinson, 1971), *Stories from My Life* (London: Hutchinson, 1971), and *Sunset over Dartmoor* (London: Hutchinson, 1977).

3. See Andy Croft, *Red Letter Days* (London: Lawrence and Wishart, 1990).

4. Ethel Mannin is not even mentioned in Samuel Hynes, *The Auden Generation* (London: Faber, 1976), or in Valentine Cunningham, *British Writers of the Thirties* (Oxford: Oxford University Press, 1988); David Smith, in *Socialist Propaganda in the Twentieth-Century British Novel* (London: Macmillan, 1978), dismisses *Cactus* as "blatantly strained" and "completely abstract and artificial." But there is a good discussion of her work in Rebecca O'Rourke, "Were There No Women?: British Working-Class Writing in the Inter-War Period," *Literature and History* 14 (Spring 1988).

5. Mannin, *Sunset over Dartmoor*, 172.

6. See her memoir of her father, *This Was a Man* (London: Jarrolds, 1952).

7. Mannin, *Confessions and Impressions*, 50–51.

8. Ethel Mannin, *Love's Winnowing* (London: Wright and Brown, 1932), 93–94. *Love's Winnowing, Bruised Wings* (London: Wright and Brown, 1931), and *The Tinsel Eden* (London: Wright and Brown, 1931) were early serialized novels, later published in book form against her will.

9. Ethel Mannin, *Martha* (London: Leonard Parsons, 1923), 286.

10. Ethel Mannin, *Hunger of the Sea* (London: Jarrolds, 1924), 53–54.

11. Neill also wrote the introduction to her *Commonsense and the Adolescent* (London: Jarrolds, 1937).

12. Mannin, *Confessions and Impressions*, 85.

13. Ethel Mannin, *Ragged Banners*, new ed. (Harmondsworth: Penguin, 1938), 206.

14. Ethel Mannin, *Forever Wandering* (London: Jarrolds, 1934), 28.

15. Ibid., 210.

16. *New Leader*, 6 April 1934.

17. Ibid., 29 November 1935.

18. Henry Pelling, *The British Communist Party*, new ed. (London: A. and C. Black, 1975), 77.

19. *New Leader*, 27 November 1936. Her strong and often defensive commitment to the ILP can be seen in her objections ("sheerly silly") to the caricature of the ILP in Orwell's *The Road to Wigan Pier* (London: Victor Gollancz, 1937). Orwell joined the ILP in 1938.

20. *New Leader*, 30 October 1936, 6 November 1936, 17 September 1937.

21. Ibid., 27 March 1936. See also her review of Kingsley Martin, *The Magic of Monarchy*, in *New Leader*, 14 May 1937.

22. *New Leader*: "Education and Capitalism," 22 May 1936, "The Classless School," 23 April 1937, and "Women and Marriage," 28 May 1937.

23. Ibid., 30 March 1934, 6 September 1935, 25 May 1934, 24 April 1936, 19 June 1936, 9 July 1936.

24. Ibid., 1 February 1935. The stories were eventually published as *The Cleft Stick* (London: Selwyn and Blount, 1937). She also reviewed Greenwood's *His Worship the Mayor* (London: Jonathan Cape, 1934), in *New Leader*, 19 October 1934. Gow later adapted Ethel Mannin's *Men Are Unwise* (London: Jarrolds, 1934) for the stage.

25. *New Leader*, 30 August 1935. She also favorably reviewed Blumenfeld's *Phineas Khan*, in ibid., 4 June 1937.

26. Ibid., 15 June 1934.

27. Ibid., 1 March 1935.

28. Ibid., 13 December 1935.

29. Ibid., 19 October 1934.

30. Ibid., 25 May 1934.

31. Ibid., 7 June 1935.

32. *New Leader*, 15 February 1935.

33. Mannin, *Forever Wandering*, 259.

34. Mannin, *Privileged Spectator*, 45.

35. Ethel Mannin, *Children of the Earth*, new ed. (Harmondsworth: Penguin, 1937), 30, 212. The Russian anarchist Emma Goldman wrote to say how much she enjoyed *Children of the Earth*, thus beginning a long and friendly correspondence. Mannin dedicated *Women and the Revolution* (London: Secker and Warburg, 1938) to Goldman and later wrote a novel, *Red Rose* (London: Jarrolds, 1941), based on the story of Goldman and Alexander Berkman.

36. Ethel Mannin to Harry Heslop, 7 December 1935, located in Heslop's private papers.

37. Mannin, *Men Are Unwise*, 124.

38. See Reginald Reynolds, *My Life and Crimes* (London: Jarrolds, 1956). Reynolds edited the two-volume *British Pamphleteers* (London: Allan Wingate, 1948, 1956); George Orwell wrote the introduction to the first volume (1948), which he also edited.

39. Ethel Mannin, *Cactus*, new ed. (London: Jarrolds, 1944), 75–76.

40. Ibid., 205. *Cactus* sold over sixty-two thousand copies and was dedicated to Mannin's friend Ernst Toller, despite their bitter disagreement over the question of resisting fascism by force. The book was later reprinted in 1941, in a Penguin edition, by Mannin's close friend Allen Lane; *Confessions and Impressions* (1936) and *Children of the Earth* (1937) were also published in Penguin editions.

41. Ethel Mannin, *The Pure Flame* (London: Jarrolds, 1936), 295. Although

the surname is different, *Rose and Sylvie* (1938) takes up the story of the Winchell family and is effectively the third novel of a trilogy.

42. "Ethel Mannin Challenges Naomi Mitchison," *New Leader*, 31 May 1935; compare this with Mannin's "Russia—the Country with a Future," ibid., 9 August 1935.

43. *New Leader*, 17 January 1936; compare with ibid., 28 September 1934.

44. *Blackshirt*, 7 February 1936.

45. *Daily Worker*, 14 February 1936.

46. Ibid., 15 February 1936.

47. *New Leader*, 14 February 1936.

48. Mannin's third collection of short stories, *The Falconer's Voice* (London: Jarrolds, 1935), was dedicated to Donia Naschen.

49. *New Leader*, 25 September 1936. See also Mannin's balancing reviews of Walter Duranty, *I Write as I Please* (1936), and Mikhail Sholokhov, *Virgin Soil Unturned* (1936), in *New Leader*, 10 January 1936, and her application of Karel Capek's *The Insect Play* to the Soviet Union, in *New Leader*, 3 July 1936.

50. In *Authors Take Sides on the Spanish War* (London: Left Review, 1937).

51. See also Mannin's explicitly Trotskyite, anti-Soviet novel *Darkness Be My Bride* (London: Jarrolds, 1938).

52. Ethel Mannin, *Comrade O Comrade* (London: Jarrolds, 1947), 53. "Mary Thane" is a thinly disguised self-portrait; Thane first appeared in *Ragged Banners*.

53. Ibid., 61.

54. Two notable exceptions were *The Road to Beersheeba* (London: Hutchinson, 1963) and *The Night and Its Homing* (London: Hutchinson, 1966) about the struggles of the Palestinian people.

55. Mannin, *Women and the Revolution*, 264; see also her study of Utopian thought, *Bread and Roses* (London: Macdonald, 1944).

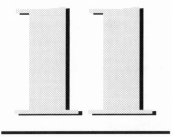

DAPHNE PATAI

Imagining Reality:

The Utopian Fiction of

Katharine Burdekin

How can we see what is before our eyes? To ask this is to pose a seemingly foolish question, inviting a facile retort: we see what is there, because it is there. But often what is there is in fact invisible. Repeatedly, during the past year, birds have attempted to fly through the glass walls of the building in which I have been working.[1] They hit the panes with a dull thud, a sound that makes one look up, distressed, in time to see the dazed bird fluttering away. Although from the inside the glass looks tinted with delicate hues of pink or blue, no obstacle is discerned by the bird, which can neither see through the glass nor see the glass itself.

Thinking about this scene, I came to see that it represented a problem I have often contemplated as I try to understand how writers of literary utopias labor to illuminate their own society by imagining alternatives. What these writers are doing is attempting *not* to hit the glass walls of their habitual frames of reference. But to succeed, they need a vantage point from which the glass will be visible to them—as frame, as barrier, as transparency or reflection, as that which goes without saying. If they face the glass head-on, they cannot make it out. Where, then, can they situate themselves so as to allow the glass to become visible? This is the question I shall explore with particular reference to the utopian fiction of the writer Katharine Burdekin (1896–1963), who published ten novels (the most political of them under the male pseudonym "Murray Constantine") between 1922 and 1940 and left a cache of further manuscripts to which I was given access several years ago.

Reality, as Burdekin understood, is not simply *there* to be seen. It has also to be *imagined*. Anatole France said as much in his remarkable novel *Penguin Island*, in which a female penguin—enveloped for the first time in penguin history by a garment—awakens a new interest among the male penguins whose path she crosses. "And in order that the interest of that figure be fully revealed to the penguins, it was necessary that, ceasing to see it distinctly with their eyes, they should be led to represent it to themselves in their minds."[2] Although the scene is not without France's characteristic irony, the point is a serious one: the loss of immediacy afforded by a covering leads, paradoxically, to dis-covery, presenting to the mind's eye a compelling image of the familiar. As a writer of utopian fiction, Anatole France also confronted the problem of where he should situate himself to acquire a vantage point from which to launch his criticism. He resolved the problem by rewriting French history satirically, as penguin history—in other words, by means of species displacement. This is the time-honored technique of the animal allegory, of which the best-known example in recent decades is George Orwell's *Animal Farm*.[3]

Other European writers, especially in the age of discovery, located their stories in an "elsewhere" characterized by its difference from the writer's own society. Thomas More's *Utopia*, published in 1516, which gave its name to the genre, used precisely this technique of spatial displacement, and his Raphael Hythlodaeus (whose very name means "nonsense" or "teller of tall tales") claims to be merely describing what he observed on the New World island of Utopia. Through the apparently innocent contrast between an unfamiliar Utopia—a good place that is also no place—and an all-too-familiar Europe, More unfolds his critique of a corrupt Old World. This approach has become a standard technique for political and social criticism in literature.

Still another path available to writers of utopian fiction is temporal displacement. Like the other forms of displacement, this technique, utilized as long ago as the Old Testament's prophetic literature, allows a writer to elaborate on the unfamiliar (in this case by describing the future) and to criticize the habitual and familiar (through the retrospective glance).

Various narrative strategies are, then, employed in utopian fiction to produce the estrangement that is the genre's particular strength, but almost all of them depend on a specific narrative mediation. Typically the agent of this mediation is a traveler who moves directly from our time to the future (e.g., in Edward Bellamy's *Looking Backward*, 1888) or from our society to an elsewhere (e.g., in Mary E. Lane's *Mizora*, 1880–81, or in Charlotte Perkins Gilman's *Herland*, 1915). In either case, the traveler's discoveries and perspectives become our own. Occasionally a writer selects for the narrative focus a resident of the unfamiliar society who travels into our world and presents it to us in a new light (e.g., Charlotte Perkins Gilman's *With Her in Ourland*, 1916) or a person from a future time reflecting on the past—and the future (e.g., Olaf Stapledon's *Last and First Men*, 1930).

In a 1938 radio talk, H. G. Wells emphasized the extreme difficulty of trying to describe the future, especially when one confronts the problem of turning words into visual imagery, as Wells himself did for the film *Things to Come*, released in 1936. It had been easy enough, Wells said, for him to describe the dictator in prose and then proceed to his speeches. But how, on film, should this figure be dressed? How should his hair be done? None of the hairdressers consulted, says Wells, had "any clear views about the hairdressing of the year 2035." The simplest things quickly became obstacles, even for this most experienced of futurists. It was impossible, for example, to imagine how garments might be fastened in the future. Wells admitted that despite intense effort, he "never could get beyond contemporary modernity." He added that he was not only unable to get the scene "right" but also unable to make it seem plausible. A far more subversive point follows. Even if one were to have a genuine vision of the future, this vision would be less convincing on the screen than what Wells and his co-workers had managed to contrive, for the simple fact was that no one would believe it. "And there you have the reason," Wells concluded, "why no sensible writer who dreams of writing for posterity, will ever think twice of engaging in this ephemeral but amusing art, the fiction of prophecy—on which I have spent so much of my time."[4]

At first glance, it may seem that by contrast with the challenge of imagining the unfamiliar, describing the ordinary and familiar would be child's play. Can films not easily represent contemporary "reality" by simply going into the street and filming it? Can writers not describe what they see all around them? But the very ease with which we are able to reproduce such details obscures far more serious obstacles. How can we call attention to those things we barely see because they are ever-present? How can we evoke the contrasts, the distance, that will allow what is near and habitual to come into focus—to be not only *there* but genuinely *perceived*?

Ethnomethodology, as pioneered by the sociologist Harold Garfinkel (who built on the work of Alfred Schütz, Edmund Husserl, Talcott Parsons, and others), attempts to analyze the workings of ordinary reality.[5] It asks questions about categories of everydayness that are assumed by people within a given culture but that are not usually the objects of analysis, or even of observation, thereby challenging ordinary assumptions about the "naturalness" of what goes on around us. The achieved nature of everyday life can be readily demonstrated, for example, by merely reversing convention or by acting on alternative assumptions and then observing what happens. The ensuing disruption highlights the shared definitions and routines that, until the disruption, were so taken for granted that they remained invisible. In this way, the "work" done by individuals within any social setting to sustain the prevailing definitions of their situation begins to become visible.

But long before ethnomethodology provided us with a vocabulary for speaking about the social construction of reality, utopian fictions, unlike less sociologically inquisitive literature, placed ordinary social reality within brackets and explored, interrogated, or challenged it. For the key point that must be understood about utopian fictions is that they are never primarily about "otherness" but are most of all about ourselves. Even given the techniques of literary defamiliarization that typically occur in such fiction, however, some things are less likely than others to come under scrutiny. One of the areas in which this is seen most clearly is gender. Though alternative models of gender arrangements have indeed been available in the Western imaginative tradition since at least Plato's *Republic*, most utopian fiction is governed by conventional and unexamined gender ideologies that undergird (and often undermine) an author's depiction of a supposedly "different" society. After reading dozens of utopian fictions, I have come to the conclusion that their single greatest failing is simple lack of imagination—and this observation, in turn, has enhanced my appreciation of what is involved in developing a critical awareness of one's own time and place.

In James Ray's 1932 novel *The Scene Is Changed*, for example, the suggestive title is belied by virtually unchanged gender relations. This is a postplague novel (a popular subgenre within utopian fiction), depicting a world in which men have died in vastly larger numbers than women, with the result that England has a population of about two million women and three hundred men. The novel unfolds a puerile account of how a few dozen male students at an Oxford college take charge, fight off "gangsters" (members of male gangs), and deal with the few feminist lesbians (among a population of about ten thousand women surviving in the town of Oxford) who are not thrilled at the continuation of male power.[6] Though eminently forgettable as a work of fiction, the novel deserves a moment's attention, if only for its author's total inability to imagine any alternative to his own society's discourse on gender. Alterations take place in sexual morality, due to the surviving men's "obligation" to impregnate as many women as possible (and this is typical of postplague scenarios in which, though women predominate numerically, an androcentric—and rather adolescent—vision guides the script). But these shifts have no effect on gender politics. Thus, from the point of view of the Oxford men who are overwhelmingly outnumbered but whose ability to impose their will is never in doubt, political equity demands merely a governing body that is 50 percent male and 50 percent female—an oddly unthinkable possibility in the author's actual society. Yet even this degree of "representation" is temporary as the women leaders discover and retreat into the joys of motherhood.

Labeling Ray's work as lacking in imagination is, however, perhaps too innocent an approach. Might it not be more plausible to assume that Ray is responding with anxiety to the historical changes of his own time? Written shortly after universal adult female suffrage was finally won in England, Ray's work, after all, spins out a fantasy designed to reassure men. From this point of view, *The Scene Is Changed*, like much literature of this type, is clearly more prescriptive than descriptive.

Social roles and norms certainly change, and in film and fictional representations we of course notice those that are now outdated, though they would have caused no commentary at all in their own time. But how can one stimulate such perceptions before their time is ripe? Feminist writers have always faced this dilemma: how to make visible the reality of gender power as a social construct at historical moments committed to denying precisely such a vision. Through what strategies can one demonstrate that things can and ought to be different when—to paraphrase Michel Foucault—the everywhereness of male power impinges even on our private imaginings?

Katharine Burdekin confronted precisely these issues when she began writing utopian fiction. A relatively isolated figure, belonging to no literary circle or political group, Burdekin took writing as her arena of action. After several novels that she later referred to as her "baby books,"[7] she wrote, starting in the late 1920s, a number of utopian and dystopian novels, in all of which she attempted to grasp the nature of the gendered world in which she lived and to present it to the reader through the medium of fiction—fiction designed to reveal what was ever-present but routinely ignored. The task she set herself was how to represent reality, how to make visible to her readers things that they took for granted as inevitable and "natural" facts of life. Above all, Burdekin was concerned with the pervasiveness of male power and female power-lessness and with the kind of world that this created in both the public and the private spheres. How could something that was so ordinary, so banal, and so deeply rooted in each of us be held up for scrutiny? She knew the danger of instant dismissal as a feminist engaged in "special pleading"—a charge easy to cast from the point of view of those whose definitions of reality are dominant and therefore need not be plaintively or noisily argued. This same charge rings mysteriously hollow when directed against the prevailing definitions of reality, since definitions themselves establish the norm against which challenges are measured and found wanting.

Attempting to find a vantage point or baseline from which everyday gender routines could become visible, Burdekin experimented with a number of narrative stances. In *Proud Man* (published in 1934 under the pseudonym "Murray Constantine," which Burdekin utilized for all her novels published from 1934 to 1940),[8] she drew on a particularly useful narrative model: *Last and First Men* by Olaf Stapledon (1886–1950), pub-lished in 1930. Borrowing from Stapledon the stance of a narrator from the Earth of a remote future, Burdekin departs from what Stapledon had done, most importantly in her fundamental objective. This objec-tive was to practice a kind of "anthropology at home" (a phrase coined two years later, in 1936, by Dr. O. A. Oeser in an unrelated context)[9] by creating a first-person ethnographic report on her own time and place, England in the early 1930s, from the vantage point of a distant and objec-tive observer in no way implicated in the reality that is described. To do this, Burdekin has her narrator dream of a two-year stay in a twentieth-century England easily recognizable to readers today. In addition, this narrator addresses not the author's own contemporaries, as Stapledon's narrator had done, but readers who, like the narrator, are far ahead of us on the evolutionary scale. Whereas Stapledon wrote *of* the future *for* the present, Burdekin pretended to write *for* the future *of* the present, while of course actually writing for the present about its own peculiarities and its need to take stock of itself.[10]

Burdekin engages in a more complex series of narrative games than Stapledon, for her readers are constantly interpellated by the narrator as more evolved beings, as if they were indeed capable of perceiving their own reality with the detachment that the narrator's (not the author's) contemporaries have achieved. A high level of tension is generated by this kind of narrative; its defamiliarization is so pervasive that readers cannot readily "settle" into the story in the way sought by traditional novel readers. Instead, they are likely to experience discomfort not only at the unusual portrait of their own society that Burdekin unfolds but also at the convoluted narrative strategy that they can seldom entirely ignore.

At the same time, this defamiliarization offers distinct narrative pleasures. It is, after all, fascinating to be the subject of such detailed scrutiny, to immerse oneself in an estranged version of a familiar planet and country, and to see exposed before the mind's eye one's everyday life and habits. Who among us, when encountering representations of "otherness" in travelogues and ethnographies, has not imagined such a privileged view of our own familiar routines? Who has not dreamed of such an escape from subjectivity? [11]

The narrator of *Proud Man*, a genuine Person, makes full use of the opportunities afforded by this narrative stance. Only indirectly and by way of contrast do we learn what this Person is: evolved, fully conscious, telepathic, vegetarian, brown-skinned, independent of others both emotionally and physically, androgynous, self-fertilizing and able to produce offspring alone and without help, capable of utter stillness, understanding the true relation of the self to the not-self, and possessed of an instinctive unselfishness in no need of mediation by extraneous ethical and religious systems. To such a being, how could we fail to appear as subhuman?

And, indeed, the first achievement of Burdekin's text is to estrange us from the very term *human*, so that we see it as an accolade we have not yet earned. This distinct usage occurs repeatedly in the novel's early pages, slowly separating us from habitual assumptions, until the contrast between the narrator's truly human habits and our subhuman ones begins to seem normal. What Burdekin has done, in other words, is to dislocate one of our most common terms and recast it as a remote goal—achieved by her narrator, perhaps, but certainly not by us. Throughout the novel, everything in our own society is judged from the perspective of this fully evolved human being. A series of startling perceptions ensues of our (subhuman) condition, highlighted by Burdekin's frequent use of italics to call attention to the peculiarity of many of our terms and concepts. Continuing the critique of war begun in her pacifist novel *Quiet Ways* (1930), Burdekin here sees war as caused by the subhuman qualities of fear, greed, envy, and hope of glory. *Patriotism* is defined as "national general hostility," a *soldier* is a "killing male," and *war* is a "large organized killing," the lure of which owes much to its exclusion of women, men being unable to tolerate long periods of time in the company of those they hold in contempt and therefore preferring to associate in "homosexual packs," that is, in clubs, sports, the military, and other all-male institutions.[12]

Believing themselves to be human beings, subhumans hold two core ideas about their nature: "One is that it is fundamentally noble, and the other that it can never change. The first idea comforts them, while the second excuses them for their most grotesque actions, thus allaying, if very slightly, their feeling of guilt" (27). A key problem of our social organization, one that reappears in all Burdekin's utopian novels, is identified as "the subhuman concept of *privilege*."

> It is not very possible to explain privilege in any human way, as it is not a human thing. But as the subhumans believe that they are all in some way *better* than animals, so they believe that some subhumans are, by reason of the colour of their skins, or their rearing, or their sex, *better* and more worthy than other subhumans of different colour, *class* and sex. This betterness entitles them to privilege, which usually involves greater physical comfort than can be attained by the unprivileged, more power, more liberty and a bigger chance of obtaining what the subhumans call happiness. A privilege of class divides a subhuman society horizontally, while a privilege of sex divides it vertically. Subhumans cannot apparently exist without their societies being divided, preferably in both these ways. (17; emphasis in original)

If Burdekin redeems the word *human* by associating it with a plane of development far beyond our current condition, she treats the word *civilization* in a reverse fashion, typically utilizing it ironically to depict subhuman society's most egregious pretensions, as in her description of a recent "large, important and highly civilized war" (20) or in the following definition of "paganism": "a state of believing in a primitive superstition, or *heresy*, which is a dissent from some dogma in the national civilized superstition" (36). Subhuman misery, according to the Person's explanation, results from the peculiarities of our "civilized" condition: having lost animal unconsciousness, we have not, however, yet attained true human consciousness, and the resulting state of tension produces interminable subhuman conflict and guilt.

There is no space, here, to provide more than a few examples of Burdekin's cutting critique of subhuman gender ideology (a term that did not exist in her time) or its relationship to war, violence, religion, family life, sexual habits, and the general misery of subhuman existence—all of them major themes of the novel. Without benefit of contemporary theory, feminist and otherwise, she noted a key feature of this ideology: "It is remarkable that while women are always women, and female children grow into women as a matter of course, without meeting any insuperable obstacles on the way, all men are not men, and for a boy to grow up *manly* requires constant supervision by the elders and a somewhat severe course of training" (52). Eternal anxiety and vigilance are the price at which a "manly" identity is forged. Burdekin's ability to separate sex from gender—despite her lack of access to a terminology that promotes such an analysis—resulted from her understanding of gender as a symbolic system, but one having massive political repercussions. Thus, long before Jacques Lacan developed his notion of the phallus as a signifier, Burdekin analyzed phallic power in *Proud Man*. "The mere possession of a phallus . . . regardless of the *character* of the possessor, guaranteed a certain amount of civic power" (29; emphasis in original). She noted subhuman males' persistent sexual anxiety. "The phallus being the sign of power with both sexes, men live in fear, either conscious or unconscious, of losing prematurely the power which dwells in the symbol of power" (51). In turn, men's inventiveness, the Person explains, is caused by "a deep root jealousy of the female's greater biological importance" (24). Science, however, may rob women of their biological importance altogether, Burdekin notes.[13] The analysis set forth in *Proud Man* of the roots of male fear of and contempt for women (which recalls Karen Horney's essays, published in English in the 1920s, which, however, probably did not cross Burdekin's path) in no way exculpates women from the charge of collusion in their own oppression—another recurring theme of Burdekin's fiction.

As the novel progresses, a series of episodes unfolds in which the narrator acts as a "participant observer," passing first as a female, then as a male. The narrator's vivid observations of subhuman society are everywhere framed by an acute awareness of the peculiar stunting of life that results from "unquestioned male dominance" (46). Finally, the novel argues, men and women must change. "They must stop being masculine and feminine, and become male and female. Masculinity and femininity are the artificial differences between men and women. Maleness and femaleness are the real differences. . . . The artificial differences have arisen to console men for the real differences" (178–79).

If Burdekin's unique perspective, deriving first of all from her feminism, placed her outside the habitual modes of thought of her time, her problem as a writer of political fiction became how to construct her narratives so that such a vantage point might also be made available to her readers. *Proud Man*, a true ethnographic fiction, is perhaps her most complex experiment in this regard, but it was followed by others.

The thematic coherence of Burdekin's evolving vision is confirmed when one notes that later novels are often hinted at in earlier ones. In a world in which notions of "privilege" invariably produce conflict, a reversal of privilege is not unlikely. Though such reversals (called "revolutions") do nothing to challenge the root concept of privilege, or the domination that secures it, they have occurred in relation to class privilege, as Burdekin observes. Why, then, should they not occur as well in relation to gender? Women's increasing consciousness (despite the obstacles set in their paths by men, whose actions, Burdekin notes, reveal an awareness that their rule does not rest on a genuine biological fact) could, after all, lead to such a reversal. The image of a world in which women dominate and men are the dominated first occurs in Burdekin's pacifist novel *Quiet Ways* (1930). Here, a hidebound male character, unnerved by the female protagonist's self-containment and lack of attention to men, has a nightmare vision of women rearing their daughters with pride and a sense of self-worth.[14] Such a vision occurs again in a brief passage in *Proud Man*: "If women retain their biological importance, and become pleased with themselves from birth, and learn to associate power with the womb instead of with the phallus, a dominance of females over males is not only possible but likely. Their self-confidence, which would be rooted as deep as the old male jealousy, would cause in them a tremendous release of psychic power with which the males would be unable to cope. Naturally a female dominance would make the race no happier, nor bring it a whit nearer to humanity. The privilege would merely be reversed, and possibly it would be more oppressive and more cruel" (31).

This scenario, in turn, provides the central hypothesis for another of Burdekin's "Murray Constantine" novels, *The End of This Day's Business*, written in 1935 but not published until 1989. Like Burdekin's other utopian fiction, this novel surveys the past as well as the future, but its central strategy is the sex-role reversal. Four thousand years in the future, women rule the world in peace and harmony. Only one price is exacted by this rule: the subordination of men. Deprived of both knowledge of their own history and access to the women's secret language and rites, these men are consigned to trivial if largely pleasant lives in their separate and lesser sphere. As befits Burdekin's earlier hints regarding such a reversal, the central dilemma of the novel is one woman's growing awareness that this situation too must be transcended, that women must cease to act out of the ancient fear (however well founded) of the world that male dominance had created. Again, characteristically, Burdekin notes women's key role in the transmission of patriarchal ide-

ology: brought up within patriarchy to regard themselves as inferior
to men, women pass on this heritage to their children. "If the Mother
brings up the boy to regard her as inferior to himself, men rule. If she
brings him up to regard himself as inferior, women rule" (57).

Interestingly, by the time Burdekin came to write this novel, she had
apparently abandoned the notion that a world run by women might
be more oppressive and cruel than one ruled by men.[15] No doubt the
Europe unfolding around her, with Mussolini and Hitler in power,
altered her ideas. In *The End of This Day's Business*, Burdekin provides a
brief history of her own time from the perspective of a future four thousand years away. Committed to the egalitarian ideals of communism,
she outlines its battle with fascism in the early twentieth century. Unlike
some other anti-Fascist writers of the 1930s,[16] Burdekin did not indict
all political systems indiscriminately. She understood fascism to be the
greatest political danger of her time, and in the 1930s she attacked it in
novel after novel. Her view of "patriotism" is equally radical: in *The End
of This Day's Business* she calls it a "morbid growth" on the natural love
for one's native land, a "mental disease" of which ten million men died
between 1914 and 1918 (65).

Burdekin's next published novel, composed in 1936, was the passion-
ately anti-Fascist *Swastika Night*, which appeared under the pseudonym
"Murray Constantine." Published in 1937 by Victor Gollancz and reissued in 1940 as one of the very few works of fiction selected for his Left
Book Club, this was Burdekin's most widely read novel, the Left Book
Club edition having sold about seventeen thousand copies.[17] Although
Swastika Night is a novel responsive to the historical shifts that occurred
in the early and mid 1930s, in it Nazi policies that progressively restricted the rights of Jews, women, and political opponents are judged
in the light of Burdekin's earlier analyses of the gender hierarchy. In
Proud Man, Burdekin had noted that within patriarchal societies women
are ultimately of value only for producing more males, for they themselves are not considered worth reproducing.[18] An extreme form of such
androcentric values is played out in *Swastika Night*.

This dystopian novel, many of whose details seem to have been picked
up by George Orwell for use in his *Nineteen Eighty-Four*, published
twelve years later,[19] envisions a static world in the seventh century of
the Hitlerian millennium. The planet has been divided between the
Nazi and the Japanese empires, both committed to militarism but unable to face the further destruction of waging war. In the Nazi Empire,
all books, records, and even monuments from the past have been destroyed in a concerted effort to make the official Nazi myth the only

"reality." Hitler is venerated as a god, not born of women. A "Reduction of Women" has occurred: kept in caged compounds that suggest concentration camps, the women, "reduced" to a near animal existence, play two key roles. On the symbolic level, they provide a constant reminder of male superiority and power, which no longer need tolerate the outrage of rejection or challenge by mere females, for men in this Hitlerian society possess the right to rape. On a practical level, the women serve the purpose of obligatory reproduction (and the occasional gratification of such male lust as has not yet been revolted by women's ugliness and impassivity). But even reproduction is threatened by the Reduction of Women, for fewer and fewer girls are being born, and thus the entire Nazi empire is in danger of self-destruction.

In the description of the women's abject lives, Burdekin comes close to depicting the "excremental assault" that Terrence Des Pres would later identify as a fundamental strategy of the Nazi regime for destroying the dignity of its victims.[20] Aware of the long history of Western misogyny and anti-Semitism—and prefiguring by decades the work of such scholars as Bram Djikstra and Jacques Le Rider, who traced the *fin de siècle* identification of Woman with Jew—Burdekin looked for a common root. She found it in what she called the "cult of masculinity," which culminated in nazism.[21] If women ever developed pride in themselves, Burdekin wrote, nazism, dependent as it is on extreme gender polarization, would crumble. But women's pride is a perpetual affront to male vanity, hence the Reduction of Women and the glorification of males in the Nazi world of the future.[22]

Few people were willing to see the writing on the wall in 1936. Katharine Burdekin, however, with her visionary "outsider's" point of view, sounded the warning. Taking Otto Weininger's 1903 "classic" *Sex and Character* as a serious cultural manifestation, she followed its logic to nazism's characteristic obsessions—fear and contempt of the Other, glorification of manhood and violence—and produced the all-too-familiar ideology of gender and race in *Swastika Night*.

The novel's focus is on the treatment accorded to women, all Jews having been wiped out at the beginning of the Nazi era. Christians themselves, as if in expiation of this crime, are considered untouchables by the Nazis. In noting Burdekin's prescient view of the fate of the Jews, I am not, of course, suggesting that she could foresee the future; none of us can. The Final Solution, as we now know, was not articulated until 1941.[23] But to be implementable at that time, it had to be imaginable long before. Katharine Burdekin, attentive to the patterns unfolding in Europe in the 1930s, could think the unthinkable. What she was able to do—and here I will return to my point of departure—was, with the force of an extraordinary moral imagination, respond to the present: Hitler's clear expression of his views in *Mein Kampf*, more than ten years earlier; the Nuremberg Laws; Nazi speeches and policies about male and female separate spheres; the demonization and vilification of Jews as an outcast group; the increasing adherence to military and masculine values as proper models for political life; the ritualization of oppression as spectacle. Though safe in England, she did not reject the anxiety evoked by such perceptions of the modes and meanings of domination. She faced what was happening in a highly "civilized" European nation, imagined its consequences, and represented in fiction what the world around her might, judging by contemporary tendencies, be like in the future.

Beginning in 1934 she published her work under a male pseudo-nym, evidently knowing that she would feel compelled to write against nazism—the most immediately visible danger of her time—and hoping in this way to provide at least minimal protection to her two young daughters in the event of a German invasion of England.[24] So thoroughly did she cover her tracks and bind her publishers to her desire for anonymity that it took considerable effort to establish her actual identity.[25]

But Burdekin was not xenophobic; she did not "blame" Germans, nor did she for a moment imagine that the values she was excoriating were characteristic of only one nation. Instead, she indicted a pattern that, in its routine guise, is our everyday patriarchy, with its local and global nationalisms and hierarchies, and in its exacerbated form is fascism, with its hypertrophied militarism, racism, and masculinity complex. It was a theme she could not let go of until, to her relief, war broke out.[26] One of the many human costs of nazism was that it forced numerous individuals, like Burdekin, to abandon their pacifism. While people in her society who "knew better" attempted to explain nazism away, or saw it as merely a variation—somewhat worrying, to be sure—on acceptable politics (as a reading of the *Times* of this period indicates), Burdekin observed its rituals and messages, took them to heart and mind, and contemplated their relationship to the tradition of misogyny and phallic power that she traced in novel after novel. She did not fall into the Western liberal fallacy of judging nazism as a unique phenomenon having few or no links to the world in which it developed. Thus, she would not have labeled Nazi Germany a "crazy state," as one recent strategical thinker has done, if by that is implied a judgment that sets such states permanently apart from supposedly "normal" ones.[27]

The problem Burdekin faced—and addressed again and again throughout her fiction—involved finding the means to communicate her own moral responsiveness and alertness to her readers. She had to resist the impulse to see the world as a place in which nothing ever changed. But she also had to resist the contrary impulse to see it as the setting for ever new and therefore incomprehensible events, which one can do no more than lament.

Thinking about the complexities of continuity and change required a moral imagination; writing about these issues required the ability to vivify them. Everything I have learned about Katharine Burdekin indicates that she did not write according to the "working at it" model so popular in our day, by which work is often taken as the ultimate moral good. Rather, Burdekin wrote in what is now considered, disparagingly, to be a romantic model of artistic creation, of psychic pressure breaking through. The latter is a more intuitive mode and is often uneven in its results. In having recourse, in her utopian novels, to lengthy monologues or dialogues about politics and history, Burdekin opted for a procedure that allowed her to make a coherent argument. Yet even when her fiction was admired in book reviews, as was often the case, its overriding concerns were regularly distorted or disguised by critics thinking along different parameters, so difficult was it for her contemporaries to grasp what she was saying. But to us, today, she speaks clearly indeed.

Though she needed the narrative possibilities of time travel and utopian fiction as a scaffolding for her ethnographic explorations of the European landscape of her day, Katharine Burdekin's great strength, in the end, lay not in the arena of fantasy (which served her merely as a tool) but in that elusive and precious quality: her ability to imagine reality.

Notes

1. I am referring here to the National Humanities Center in Research Triangle Park, North Carolina, where an early draft of this essay was written. I am grateful to the NHC for awarding me a fellowship in 1990–91, which gave me access to their excellent research facilities. In particular, Rebecca Vargha, librarian at the NHC, provided me with superb help in locating and obtaining materials.

2. Anatole France, *Penguin Island*, translated by A. W. Evans (London: John Lane, The Bodley Head, 1924), 47–48. The novel was originally published in Paris in 1908.

3. Since this collection of essays deals with forgotten or ignored British writers, let me note here (in the interests of historical accuracy and giving credit

where credit is due) that Orwell's *Animal Farm* (1945) is heavily indebted to a little-known earlier work. In Philip Guedalla's book *The Missing Muse* (New York: Harper and Bros., 1930), there appears a brief anti-Soviet satire entitled "A Russian Fairy Tale," which is obviously the source of *Animal Farm*. Guedalla uses species displacement (to fairies) and describes a Good Fairy who "believed that all fairies are equal before the law, but held strongly that some fairies were more equal than others" (206). This line, reworked by Orwell, is often cited as Orwell's most original creation. Richard Mayne pointed out Orwell's indebtedness to Guedalla in the *Times Literary Supplement*, 26 November 1982, and I cited Mayne in my book *The Orwell Mystique: A Study in Male Ideology* (Amherst: University of Massachusetts Press, 1984), 309. But established literary reputation and received opinion apparently have such force that corrections tend to be disregarded or dismissed.

4. H. G. Wells, "Fiction about the Future," in *H. G. Wells's Literary Criticism*, edited by Patrick Parrinder and Robert M. Philmus (Sussex: Harvester Press, 1980), 250.

5. See Harold Garfinkel, *Studies in Ethnomethodology* (Englewood Cliffs, N.J.: Prentice-Hall, 1967).

6. James Ray, *The Scene Is Changed* (London: John Heritage, 1932). The novel presents one interesting innovation: the concept of "political lesbians," a term that became common in the 1970s but was surely rare in 1932.

7. See my afterword to Katharine Burdekin's *The End of This Day's Business* (New York: Feminist Press, 1989), for a biographical sketch of Burdekin.

8. The title derives from Isabella's ironic speech in Shakespeare's *Measure for Measure* (act 2, scene 2), in which she contrasts man's thundering with Jove's:

> . . . but man, proud man,
> Drest in a little brief authority,
> Most ignorant of what he's most assured,
> His glassy essence, like an angry ape,
> Plays such fantastic tricks before high heaven
> As make the angels weep; who, with our spleens,
> Would all themselves laugh mortal.

Two years before Burdekin's novel appeared, a collection of feminist commentaries by Mary Borden, E. M. Delafield, Susan Ertz, Storm Jameson, Helen Simpson, G. B. Stern, Sylvia Townsend Warner, and Rebecca West was published under the title *Man, Proud Man*, edited by Mabel Ulrich (London: Hamish Hamilton, 1932). Rebecca West's contribution, "Man and Religion," is of particular relevance to Burdekin's novel, both in its content and in its form (observations about human society, with special reference to male wars and religion, made from the point of view of a speaker in the future).

9. Dr. O. A. Oeser, of the Department of Experimental Psychology at the University of St. Andrews, used the phrase in a paper delivered to the British Association, as explained in Angus Calder's introduction to a recent reprint of the influential 1938 book by Tom Harrisson and Charles Madge, *Britain by Mass-Observation* (London: Cresset Library, 1986).

10. Robert Crossley, who is working on a biography of Olaf Stapledon, has informed me that Stapledon was acquainted with two of Burdekin's "Murray

Constantine" books (*Proud Man*, 1934, and *Swastika Night*, 1937) and that he recommended them to his correspondents. Stapledon also frequently mentioned
them in talks he gave on contemporary literature, and they appear as well in his
lecture notes (he was an adult-education tutor). See also Crossley, "Olaf Stapledon and the Idea of Science Fiction," *Modern Fiction Studies* 32 (Spring 1986):
21–42. In Burdekin's case, no comparable references to Stapledon can be found;
she left no papers or correspondence, though she did leave many unpublished
novels.

11. This narrative strategy continues to attract writers. Doris Lessing utilized
the strategy of the ethnographic report in a story entitled "Report on the Threatened City," in *The Story of a Non-Marrying Man and Other Stories* (London:
Jonathan Cape, 1972), in which a narrator from a more advanced planet reports
on the failure of a mercy mission to San Francisco, threatened by a major earthquake. In a calm, explanatory tone, the narrator provides an illuminating and
highly estranged view of West Coast culture in the late twentieth century. (My
thanks to Angela Ingram, who first pointed out the relevance of this story to my
work on Burdekin.) Lessing apparently continued to find this a fruitful narrative
strategy, as is evident in *Canopus in Argos: Archives* (New York: Knopf, 1979).
In an afterword to a reprint of Olaf Stapledon's *Last and First Men* (Los Ange-
les: Jeremy P. Tarcher, 1988), Lessing registered her admiration for the novel
and stated that she had first read it in her youth. The Quebecoise writer Louky
Bersianik also utilized the remote narrator visiting our world in her feminist
novel *L'Euguélionne* (Montreal: Editions La Presse, 1976).

12. Katharine Burdekin (Murray Constantine, pseud.), *Proud Man* (London:
Boriswood, 1934), 22, 19. *Proud Man* was republished by the Feminist Press in
1993, under the author's real name.

13. This was two years after the publication of Aldous Huxley's *Brave New
World*, which itself drew on the theories of ectogenesis elaborated by J.B.S. Haldane in the 1920s. See, in this connection, Susan Squier's essay in this volume.

14. Katherine [*sic*] Burdekin, *Quiet Ways* (London: Thornton Butterworth,
1930), 239–40. I discuss this episode and its ramifications in "The View from
Elsewhere: Utopian Constructions of 'Difference,'" *Bucknell Review*, 36, no. 2
(1992): 132–51.

15. For a discussion of this novel and its genuinely eutopian aspects, see my
afterword to Burdekin, *The End of This Day's Business*.

16. See Barbara Brothers's essay in this volume. An interesting story waits
to be written about the discrepancy in British writers' responses to the major
political challenges of their time. As is well known, the Spanish Civil War produced an impassioned and abundant anti-Franco literature in England, whereas
the more serious threat represented by Hitler evoked a far milder reaction in
the 1930s. Valentine Cunningham's massive book *British Writers of the Thirties*
(Oxford: Oxford University Press, 1988), which omits mention of Burdekin/
Constantine and of many other anti-Fascist writers, supports this observation.
Compare the length of the index entries relating to Nazi Germany with those relating to Spain. Although the undoubted existence of anti-Semitism in England
is part of the explanation, I suspect that the possibility of manly participation in
the Republican struggle in Spain has much to do with this discrepancy (in *The
Orwell Mystique* I have analyzed Orwell's rhetoric in *Homage to Catalonia* in an

effort to show what going to fight in Spain meant to him and how he adhered to and perpetuated the war myth). By contrast, the rise of Hitler (and of the relatively mild, homegrown brands of British fascism) required, in the 1930s, political action of a very different sort—far less dramatic and more long-term if it was to have any effect. Once war against Germany started, of course, another kind of mobilization was possible.

17. Katharine Burdekin (Murray Constantine, pseud.), *Swastika Night* (London: Victor Gollancz, 1937). Information about the Left Book Club edition was kindly provided to me by Livia Gollancz, in a letter of March 1991. *Swastika Night* was republished, under Burdekin's own name, in 1985 by Lawrence and Wishart in London and by the Feminist Press in New York. The subsequent appearance of other Burdekin novels—including one never before published—is due to the continuing interest of Florence Howe, director of the Feminist Press, in Burdekin's political fiction.

18. In 1935, Burdekin devoted an entire novel, "Snakes and Ladders" (unpublished), to the theme of a young girl's initiation—with the help of a cat that is her spiritual guide—into a sense of female self-worth. The manuscript was sent to Laura Riding for possible publication by the Seizin Press, which Riding and Robert Graves had founded. Riding, who encouraged Burdekin to keep working on the manuscript, marked it heavily and rewrote large parts of it in her own style. Burdekin was apparently outraged by this interference, and the project—and their relationship—never went further. Arrangements for the publication of Burdekin's short story "Poor Adam," which appeared (under her real name) in Riding's *Epilogue* 2 (1936), had probably been concluded before this episode.

Burdekin was also concerned with the effect on women artists of their demeaned social position, which led to a sense of diminished self-worth. In *Proud Man*, she directly addresses, through the character of Leonora, the problem of women's supposed lack of talent and ability. Leonora is in despair at not having managed, after twelve years of publishing books with five publishers, to establish herself as a successful writer. At the time of the publication of *Proud Man* (1934), Burdekin was herself in her twelfth year as a published writer (her first book having appeared in 1922); *Proud Man* came out under the imprint of Boriswood, her fourth publisher. In a passage that one is tempted to read as autobiographical, Leonora engages in a passionate discussion of male pride and female inferiority and explains her dislike for a famous artist: "He's one of these men who think women can't do anything at all, can't write, can't paint, can't make music. You have no idea what a handicap it is to a woman who wants to write or paint, the knowing that she is expected to fail, and that men want her to fail, not for any reason except that she is a woman" (210).

19. For a comparison of Orwell and Burdekin, see chapter 8 in my book *The Orwell Mystique* and my article "Orwell's Despair, Burdekin's Hope: Gender and Power in Dystopia," *Women's Studies International Forum* 7 (1984): 85–96.

20. Terrence Des Pres, *The Survivor: An Anatomy of Life in the Death Camps* (Oxford: Oxford University Press, 1976).

21. It took decades for scholars to begin to seriously study fascism as a specifically masculine ideology. See, for example, the recent work of Maria-Antonietta Macciocchi, *Les femmes et leurs maîtres*, and Klaus Theweleit, *Male Fantasies*.

22. I have discussed the novel, and its connection to Nazi ideology, in my

essay "Orwell's Despair, Burdekin's Hope," as well as in my introduction to Burdekin's *Swastika Night* (1937; reprint, New York: Feminist Press, 1985).

23. See Arno J. Mayer, *Why Did the Heavens Not Darken?: The "Final Solution" in History* (New York: Pantheon Books, 1988).

24. This explanation for Burdekin's decision to publish under a pseudonym was given to me by her heirs in 1985. There may, of course, have been additional motivations as well, especially for the choice of a male pseudonym.

25. I first encountered *Swastika Night* in 1980 and was eager to identify its author. Reviews from the 1930s (and it is significant that there were fewer reviews of *Swastika Night* than of the other novels by "Murray Constantine") mentioned that "Murray Constantine" was the pseudonym of an already known writer but provided no hints as to who this might be. It took me nearly five years to track down people and records and to finally obtain permission to divulge the information that "Murray Constantine" was in fact Katharine Burdekin.

26. One of Burdekin's other unpublished novels, "No Compromise," written in the early 1930s, envisions an England in the near future with Communists and Fascists doing battle. Still another unpublished work, "Children of Jacob," again addresses the problem of evil, as manifest in particular by the Nazi treatment of Jews. In Burdekin's characteristic fashion, it was written "on top of" events. In this case the key event is the *Anschluss*: the English protagonist happens to be in Vienna in March 1938 and witnesses Nazi youth sneering at an elderly Jewish man whom they are forcing to wash the sidewalk. (Such episodes were reported in the British press at the time; see, for example, *Manchester Guardian*, 21 March, 1 April, 7 April, 8 April 1938, or *Times*, 1 April 1938.) This precipitates a crisis in which the protagonist, through various incarnations, traces the patriarchal tradition of dominance and brutality from Old Testament times to its final resolution in the distant future. Burdekin's last fictional treatment of nazism is the unpublished novel "Joy in Heaven," written shortly after the end of the war, which deals with Hitler after his death as he slowly comes to terms with what he has done. Interestingly, in this novel, composed after the full story of the death camps was known, Burdekin focuses instead on some small and gratuitous acts of cruelty early in Hitler's reign. The manuscripts of all Burdekin's unpublished works were made available to me by her literary executors and heirs, without whose valuable help my work on Burdekin could not have continued.

27. Yehezkel Dror, *Crazy States: A Counterventional Strategic Problem* (Lexington, Mass: Heath Lexington Books, 1971). Dror argues that he is using the word *crazy* in a value-free sense, and he urges readers not to misunderstand the term (23). Adopting contemporary western standards, Dror examines a number of historical phenomena—Nazi Germany, the Crusades, Holy Wars, imperialistic states, terrorist groups—and attempts to classify them according to dimensions of craziness, as judged by their goal contents, risk propensity, means-goals relations, and style. To determine the degree of craziness exhibited by a particular state, Dror focuses on transgressions from accepted norms. Burdekin, by contrast, focuses on the continuity between the ordinary practices of patriarchy and the exacerbations found in, for example, nazism. I am indebted to W. Warren Wagar's *The Next Three Futures: Paradigms of Things to Come* (Westport, Conn.: Greenwood Press, 1991), for bringing Dror's book to my attention.

BARBARA BROTHERS

British Women Write

the Story of the Nazis:

A Conspiracy of Silence

All writers who can claim to be called "living" must be political in a sense. . . .
A care for justice, a detestation of cruelty, are no more than one expects of an
honest writer.
—Storm Jameson, quoted in the epilogue to *Testament of Friendship*

If I were a writer instead of a reader of novels, I might preface my narrative by noting that the story you are about to read is true. Not even
the names of my heroines have been changed, though few of you will
recognize them in spite of the fact that so very much has been written about 1930s writers and politics. Immanent in that decade is the
Holocaust, which preys like a waking nightmare on the consciousness
and consciences of those of us who peruse and study the history and
literature of the twentieth century. In spite of numerous studies such
as Richard F. Hamilton's *Who Voted for Hitler?*, the unthinkable and
ultimately unanswerable questions still reverberate in our souls: How
could German men and women become supporters and members of
the Nazi Party, accepting and finally helping to carry out its ideological pogroms? How could men and women of other nations have been
privy to Hitler's prewar atrocities against Jews, Communists, pacifists,
socialists, and other German citizens and remained silent witnesses? We

couldn't—could we?—have stood by like "children who did not spe-cially want it to happen" or like the "torturer's horse" that "scratches its innocent behind on a tree."[1]

In spite of the fact that literary historians of the 1930s do not call attention to fiction and poetry depicting what was occurring in Nazi Germany, reserving their discussions for political protest poems and novels expressing sympathy for the struggle in Spain, socially conscious writers did represent the face of fascism in England and in Germany.[2] These writers did not turn "away / Quite leisurely from the disaster"[3] of fascism any more than they ignored the deprivations of working-class life. Yet if questioned, how many of us could name British anti-Fascist authors of the thirties who depicted the face of fascism in Germany or in England? Christopher Isherwood certainly comes to mind when prewar, Hitler Germany is mentioned. But although we recall that Isherwood set his tales in the early 1930s, those in *The Berlin Stories* are known not so much for their representation of the threat posed by the Nazis as for their portrayal of the waif Sally and the decadence of Berlin and its seedy cafés, the story from the volume immortalized in stage and film produc-tions of *I Am a Camera* (1951) and *Cabaret* (1968). Not many of us whose literary interests focus on the twentieth century remember Isherwood for his social realism, the scenes in which he depicts the brutality of the Nazi thugs. For what has impressed academic literary historians is his experimentation with narrative strategies.

If we examine the Isherwood story more closely—and we must if we want to understand some of the causes of our historical amnesia about women's anti-Fascist fiction—it becomes obvious that literary histori-ans of the thirties seem anxious to rescue Isherwood from the taint of political concerns. For example, Samuel Hynes, in *The Auden Genera-tion*, cautions that Isherwood's stories of Berlin should *not* be read as a "documentary account of current history" but as a narrative of a "young man's education into life"; and Richard Johnstone, in *The Will to Believe*, considers them "political only in the most general sense of the word."[4] Indeed, this decade that has been pronounced the most political, or radical,[5] of decades has been recounted in tales that either suppress the political (I was surprised to recall that the subtitle of Hynes's book is *Literature and Politics in England in the 1930s*) or treat it as all, as do most Marxist studies. The latter focus on the problem of the representation of the working-class experience and the ancillary problem of the exclu-sionary elitism of the cultural protectorate established by F. R. Leavis and Q. D. Leavis.[6] That is, Marxist critics are concerned almost exclu-sively with the politics of class. Political beliefs and critical fashions have shaped the very partial, in both senses of *partial*, readings of thirties literary history.

Isherwood and his fiction are generally mentioned in studies of the thirties without reference to the moral issues his stories raise and almost always in the context of a discussion of Auden. Auden has, of course, become the decade's literary hero, thanks in no small part to the excellence of Hynes's study. For the thirties, Auden has determined *who* and *what* we know and *how* we perceive them and the issues. Thus Isherwood, in spite of being a novelist and prose writer, has become, like C. Day Lewis, Stephen Spender, and Louis MacNeice, a subplot in the Auden narrative, a narrative in which the principal topics are poetry and the literature of the Spanish Civil War. Even Virginia Woolf gets recast in thirties literary history. She becomes a footnote: the author of "The Leaning Tower" in discussions of Auden and company and the aunt of Julian Bell in the tributes to the fighting writers of the Spanish Civil War. Auden and his poem "Spain" (which was published as a pamphlet to raise money for Medical Aid for Spain, was revised by omitting three offending stanzas, and finally was rejected by Auden for inclusion in his collected poems) have become the symbol of what it meant to write *In Letters of Red* (the title of a 1930s anthology).

Auden's abandonment of the politics and art of the Left, so publicly proclaimed, has itself become a parable for the age. Men of goodwill learned they had been betrayed (by the Communist Party) and had betrayed their art (mixed it with politics and thus produced propaganda). Leftist politics and aesthetics became *The God That Failed.* In this 1950 collection of essays, male writers such as Stephen Spender and Arthur Koestler recanted whatever allegiances they supposedly had to communism. George Orwell and his writing, states Frank Kermode in *History and Value,* had much to do with the view that "unfamiliar political pressures" caused writers to forget for a time that art and politics do not mix.[7] Regardless of who was responsible—my emphasis for the moment is on how writers of literary history have portrayed the decade—both Marxist politics and Marxist aesthetics became suspect, naive if not subversive. The thirties became nothing more than a brief, and supposedly mistaken, moment in which modernist aesthetics—art for art's sake— was questioned. Once again, we worshipped at the feet of the God of Modernism that proclaimed art subjectless, manner not matter foregrounded. Once again, we evaluated form not substance. Once again, social realism was devalued. Fashions of literary criticism and the vagaries of political allegiances, if not combined through cause and effect as some have recently argued, have certainly resulted in the silences of modernist literary history about the works that illuminated one of history's worst nightmares.[8]

Valentine Cunningham, in what must now be considered the definitive study of British writers of the thirties, never mentions that Hitler and what was taking place in Germany are the subject of any body of literature of the period, though the literature of the Spanish Civil War merits a chapter. Like his critical forefathers and brothers, Cunningham too proclaims, albeit begrudgingly, the age as "Vin Rouge Audenaire." Thus Cunningham can only tell us much more about the same topics, though he protests that Auden recognized that the novel was more important than poetry in the thirties and suggests that the decade was full of "emergent sisterly writing . . . obsessed with male lovers and wonder-brothers."[9] In spite of having more women authors mentioned in his study than in any other of the thirties, none of the novelists who are the subjects of my essay—Phyllis Bottome, Sarah Campion, or Sally Carson—is mentioned in his text.

In *Three Guineas*, Virginia Woolf angrily and ironically calls attention to H. G. Wells's statement, in *Experiment in Autobiography*, that there was "no perceptible woman's movement to resist the practical obliteration of their freedom by Fascists or Nazis."[10] Women, she says, stand accused of "apathy and indifference," but, Woolf states, in reality they are victims of the "patriarchal system," victims of the "psychology of educated men's sons," who, differing little from the Fascist dictators of the continent, deny women's full humanity and ignore their accomplishments.[11] Woolf points to what she calls "a conspiracy of silence,"[12] a phrase she notes used by Philippa Strachey in a letter to the *Spectator* and by Harriet Martineau and Josephine E. Butler in the 1870s to protest the silence of the press about women's struggles against social and political tyranny. So dark have been the pages of history about women and what they have said and done that even those scholars seeking to illuminate women's contributions to literary history occasionally stumble in their attempts.[13] Sandra Gilbert and Susan Gubar, for example, actually perpetuate the myth that there is a paucity of women writers concerned with politics. In their *Norton Anthology of Literature by Women* (1985), Virginia Woolf's *Three Guineas*, a work rescued by Jane Marcus, in just this last decade, from an embarrassed and embarrassing silence, is the only example given of an anti-Fascist work by a British woman writer. In their story of women writers in the twentieth century, they emphasize the women who, in their view, welcomed war, particularly World War I.[14] In *A Very Great Profession: The Woman's Novel, 1914–39*, Nicola Beauman states, "Only very few [women writers] were so attuned to the catastrophe of the Depression and the rise of fascism in the 1930s that they deliberately renounced all their former certainties." Storm Jameson is the "one exception" Beauman cites as having turned "her undivided attention to the novel of social concern."[15] That women are the observers and guardians of the private spherewhile men are the actors in and commentators on the public realm is a story so often repeated in art, painting, and literature, and in social and literary history, that even many women believe it to be true.

Of British fiction published in the 1930s dramatizing the Nazi terror, Katharine Burdekin's *Swastika Night* (1937)—an anti-Fascist dystopia set in the seventh century of the Hitler millennium—may be the only novel by a woman that most of us writing for this book have heard of, though none of the thirties literary histories or dictionaries of women writers, including the most recent one from Yale, lists her. I do not know the story of how Daphne Patai unearthed either the novel *Swastika Night* or the writer's identity, but I discovered Phyllis Bottome's *The Mortal Storm* (1937), Sarah Campion's *Duet for Female Voices* (1936), and Sally Carson's trilogy—*Crooked Cross* (1934), *The Prisoner* (1936), and *A Traveller Came By* (1938)—accidentally while reading articles and reviews in the *Manchester Guardian*.

Of the numerous possible reasons for the silence of literary history about the novels these women wrote, lack of quality is not one. The novels are more readable and in many ways more profound and less flawed than numerous other thirties novels whose titles are stitched in anthologies, histories, and encyclopedias of English literature. Bottome's *The Mortal Storm* (published in Britain in 1937 and in the United States in 1938) is a family or domestic tragedy. Considered a well-written, effective treatment of a serious subject, the novel was widely reviewed in both England and the States, reprinted thirteen times within ten months in the United States and turned into a 1940 Hollywood movie with the same title. Unlike the film version and the numerous examples of "alarmist 'next war fiction'" that Martin Ceadel examines in "Popular Fiction and the Next War, 1918–1939," Bottome's novel is not a thriller, neither a battle of the "bad guys" versus the "good guys" nor a science-fiction vision of the destruction of civilization.[16] The novel is not a romance, though much radical fiction by women gets dismissed as such when its protagonist is a woman.[17] Rather, it is a study of character and society, a twentieth-century novel of manners in which marriage does not provide the conclusion.

Set in Munich, *The Mortal Storm* relates what happens to the Roth family during the years 1932–34. In the opening scene, we learn that Freya Roth, the novel's heroine, has just completed her first-year medical examinations. She muses about becoming a woman as well as a doctor, about marrying and having a career. She queries her mother, "There's nothing against being both . . . I mean a doctor *and* a mother at the same time?"[18] Having it all was and is difficult for women in ordinary times, but we are quickly reminded that the 1930s were not ordinary years for Germans. In the next scene, Freya's Jewish father warns her that she may not want to tell her two older half-brothers, who are members of the Nazi Party, about the prominent grant she has won to continue her medical studies at the university, where her father is a well-liked, Nobel-recipient professor. They may "feel uneasy at your having a success that seems to violate one of their principles" (14). Freya's family—her aristocratic Aryan mother, Amélie Roth, the widow of a Bavarian nobleman; her two elder half-brothers, Olaf and Emil; her younger brother, Rudi; and her father, Johann Roth—care deeply for each other. Not even the father has thought much about his Jewish heritage. The family celebrates Christmas but does not mark any Jewish holiday, and when Johann is called a Jew, Rudi must ask his father "What is being a Jew?" (171). Freya's older brothers feel that Hitler offers the German people a release from "the black cul-de-sac of poverty, defeat and unemployment" (51). Because Amélie and Johann Roth are apolitical and committed to what they consider to be the civilized virtues of absolute tolerance and respect for individuals, regardless of their beliefs or political party allegiances, the Roths accept Emil and Olaf's choice to join the Nazi Party. They also support Freya's right to pursue a relationship with Fritz Maberg, a Nazi and son of family friends, or with Hans Breitner, a Communist and peasant whom Freya meets skiing. Neither they nor their sons know that the obedience to Hitler must be absolute and includes sacrificing one's mother, father, brother, or sister.

Even though the Holocaust, that nightmare of nightmares, could not yet have been envisioned in its enormity and profound evilness, Bottome, through the psychologically well-defined characters she creates, succeeds in helping us to understand how the unthinkable could happen there or, for that matter, here. Olaf sees himself as Siegfried, saving his people from their enemies. His character has been shaped by his being the oldest, handsome and bright. He seems always to have enjoyed the adulation of women and men. Freya comes to realize that her hero worship of her brother has not been good for his character; he remains convinced of the rightness of the Nazi cause in spite of the devastation of his family. Emil's devotion to the Nazi cause has other catalysts. Freya's mother, we learn, was abused by her first husband and finds it difficult to touch her son Emil, who looks so much like his father. Emil has struggled to gain the acceptance of his mother and his sister. Freya, rather than looking up to him as she does to Olaf, competes with Emil. In the opening, Freya complains to her mother: "Father oughtn't to give Emil a motor-bicycle before he gives me one! . . . Emil's only a step-child" (6). Emil, on the other hand, competes with Olaf. Emil, "who always wanted to go one better than Olaf in the same direction," as the narrator comments, "had joined the Storm Troopers" (1). Johann Roth's idealism, his insistence that the personhood of every individual must be respected regardless of their gender, race, class, or ideology, makes him a loving husband and father—and a martyr. Even the minor char-acters—the aristocratic Maberg family consisting of Fritz, his mother, his father, and his sister, who marries Olaf—are fully developed, their personal histories and personalities interacting in explicable ways.

Bottome's psychological insights (she was a student of Alfred Adler, to whom the book is dedicated) include identifying the appeal of Hitler for women who have never known freedom. Professor Roth remarks to Freya: "For one pets what one degrades; and one has to support what one has enfeebled. Many women who have not tasted the joy and rigour of freedom, prefer to be petted and supported; but not those who have ever worked successfully" (13–14). Bottome also reflects on why some Jews might stay in Nazi Germany. Professor Roth says to his son Rudi: "I, too, have thought of flight but there are things against it. We break up our home if we fly and your mother loses her elder sons. . . . [I]f all Jews that can fly go, then those who cannot fly, will be more cruelly—because more secretly—injured. Those of us who are rich, and well-known out-side Germany, can, by remaining, help the unknown and weaker Jews" (184–85).[19]

Freya matures through weighing the competing ideologies of nazism and communism, to which her two suitors subscribe. Bottome develops the contrast between the sociopolitics of nazism and communism by underscoring the differences in the attitudes of Fritz and Hans toward women. Fritz feels a woman needs a man to tell her what to think—and not just about politics. He believes in the old-fashioned virtues *for a woman*. Hans, on the other hand, believes that a man's kindness is not a paternalistic gesture, "a mean protective kindness, used to guard [a woman] for a man's private pleasure, but a kindness . . . without expec-tation of reward" (79). What Bottome emphasizes through the choices Freya makes in becoming an adult is what Woolf stresses in her essay

Three Guineas: A woman's intellectual liberty depends upon her bodily independence—her ability to feed, clothe, and house herself—and, if she marries, to have a husband who recognizes her equality of person-hood.[20] Freya determines that she "will not be eaten" by Fritz Maberg. She notes, "I too have teeth" (23). She decides to continue her growing friendship with Hans in spite of her brothers' protests. Although Profes-sor Roth thinks Communists are little better than Fascists because they killed to come to power and thus may, for all Lenin's admirable ideals, never overcome the handicap of how they became rulers, he and his wife perceive that the key issue is Freya's right to choose—her friends, her beliefs, her career, and, yes, even her sexual partners.

After Hans Breitner is shot during the Communist witch-hunt sparked by the Reichstag Fire in late February 1933, Emil suggests that it would be best for Freya to marry Fritz, who could provide a mea-sure of safety for her and her unborn child. Amélie Roth rejects Emil's suggestion: "Another girl is to be tortured—to have the life of her soul frozen! . . . I thought we had escaped from the world where women were at a man's mercy—considered only as his tools or his toys" (199). Like Woolf and Burdekin, Bottome explores the relationship between patriarchy and nazism. Freya's father tells her that under the Nazis, the "half of the human race that produces and trains the other half will be *once more* degraded!" (13; emphasis added). The Nazis did not introduce second-class citizenship for women; they reemphasized it. In fact, one of Hitler's appeals to the aristocrats, nice ones such as the Mabergs, is that even though Hitler is working class, he shares their belief that the proper place for a woman is "at the cooking-stove or in your bed" (203). This thirties novel is as much about being a woman and a German as it is about being a Jew or a Communist who lives in Germany.

A few of the reviewers thought the novel was too rhetorical, and the novel is at times discursive, like nineteenth-century novels in which nar-rators comment on the action or in which the commentary is provided by the thoughts or dialogue of one or another of the characters. But the novel is not a tract, even though the speeches of the characters occasion-ally seem too long. While Bottome's characters discuss the ideologies of nazism, communism, Judaism, and feminism, the novel directs our attention to the practice of those ideologies. Ideas are explored through situation and character, both of which are compelling. Bottome de-picts Communists, Jews, liberated women, and those who join the Nazi Party as human beings, all of whom are likely to become victims of an ideology that preaches war and hatred and fails to understand that, in Bottome's view, freedom belongs either to all or to none. The novel continues to offer those of us who read it today an understanding of how political philosophies and ideals become the motivations for very private acts that transform the daily lives and relationships of ordinary, caring individuals and families.

Bottome's clear intent—to expose the Nazi menace in all its ugliness for her readers by depicting the effects of public events on the private lives of the Roths—never leads her to create stereotypes of the Nazis, such as those grotesques found in postwar novels. Bottome lived in Vienna after World War I and in Munich from the winter of 1930–31 to May 1933.[21] She witnessed Hitler's assumption of the chancellorship in January 1933. Some of us may have forgotten or have been unaware that by March 1933, detention centers probably numbered well over 100, or that on 1 April 1933, public boycotting of Jews began in earnest, followed by the burning of books written by Jews and non-Nazis, the suppression of labor unions, the outlawing of the Socialist Democratic Party and the Catholic Center Party. Between January 1933 and August 1934, when Hitler combined the functions of chancellor and president, the Nazis established absolute control of Germany and even began to pressure Austria to acquiesce in Nazi policies. Bottome makes the events she witnessed, and those she continued to follow in the news, the skeleton for her story. Early after Hitler's appointment, the very popular and eminent Professor Roth begins to lose students. He and his family are harassed by Nazis searching their home and are threatened with arrest if Freya does not stop seeing Hans Breitner. Bottome even records the small ways in which Jews were isolated by friends: Freya is given her mother's name, Trattenbach, in the newspaper account of her brother's wedding to Sophia Maberg, a wedding that her parents fail to attend at the last moment because of "unexpected" conflicts (289). Professor Roth is eventually imprisoned. Neither Roth's prominence nor the attempted intervention of his stepsons, who truly admire and love him, can save him from death in a concentration camp.

Although Bottome is mentioned in a number of women's "who-was-who" in literature lists (but never in any literary histories), the only entry I found for Sarah Campion (pseudonym of Mary Rose Coulton) is the 1990 Yale *Feminist Companion*, which, however, omits mention of her 1930s novels written before she emigrated to New Zealand and married the writer Anthony Alpers. *If She Is Wise* (1935), her first novel, is not a domestic novel, nor does it do more than touch on what is taking place in Germany. The book is a satire about being a young woman in the 1930s, and in the somewhat broadbrushed fashion of Aldous Huxley and

Evelyn Waugh, Campion mocks everything from Froebel's educational philosophies to Freudian and Lawrentian ideas about human sexuality, more specifically women's sexuality, a subject that women novelists of the twenties and thirties began to treat openly in their fictions. In the last part of the novel, the heroine finds herself in Germany, "a nation which refused to grow up, politically, [and thus] was ripe fruit for a dictator. . . . And so the land swarmed with pink-faced and humourless young men playing at soldiers, with perverted real soldiers playing with the pink young men, with girls emotionally waving flags, and children marching like miniature armies."[22]

Emily becomes friends with the Hermann Oppenheimer family. One evening while Frau Oppenheimer plays cards and Hitler purges his party (June 1934, the "Night of the Long Knives"), Emily and Hermann discuss the future of the Jews in Germany, the sexual appeal that Hitler has for some women, and patriotism versus pacifism. Emily asserts that she will "not lift a finger, either to kill a man, or to nurse him back to life so that he may have another chance of being killed, or to drive him to his death in government lorries, or to hound him to it by shrieking patriotic nonsense until he doubts his own conscience and is shamed into going" (300). Pacifism is a subject that comes up in all Campion's 1930s novels but becomes *the* subject of *Thirty Million Gas Masks* (1937), an overly rhetorical novel but not one that deserves to be dismissed as the thriller that Ceadel labels it.

Duet for Female Voices (1936), which focuses specifically on the rise of Hitler to power, is the novel most pertinent to my subject. It was well reviewed. The only negative comment on the novel was that its title was found wanting; as one reviewer said, the title suggested a lesser scope and more flippant tone than was true of the book. This novel and Campion's previous novel could be described as a "young [wo]man's education into life," the classification Hynes selects for Isherwood's *Berlin Stories*. Campion's heroines are a young middle-class English woman, Elsbeth Wishaw, who has been reared in Germany until the outbreak of World War I, and a wealthy German Jewess, Anna Bernstein, who attends school in England after the war. When the novel opens, the two women are part of a group touring Russia. In flashbacks, we learn that in addition to each having spent a significant period living in both England and Germany, the women, at different times, had the same English governess, Miss Field, and had been students together at an art school in England after World War I. But it is the disparities between the two—resulting from the differences in their nationalities, ethnic heritages, and ages (Anna is eight years older)—that Campion emphasizes. Whereas Elsbeth remembers the Armistice as "wild, cheering crowds in White-hall," Anna remembers the "widow Brauning, with four sons dead in Flanders and another yellow with gas in a Berlin hospital."[23] The widow, assigned to billet an English captain and his family, hangs herself from a hook in the bathroom after her maid and her property are raped and pillaged. " '*C'est la guerre,*' as the captain had so justly remarked" (140).

As a teenage girl sent to help her widower uncle-doctor care for his two young children in an East Prussian border town, Anna experiences the savagery of war; the wounded move through, seek treatment, or are buried in the village. The English may still be able to fantasize that the world is divided by war into two separate territories—home and battlefronts—but a German woman cannot. To emphasize their insepa-rability, Campion has a young soldier describe the death of a friend to Anna. "When Jorgen was killed he wasn't doing anything; he wasn't even in the trenches. We were sitting in a field behind the line, in a meadow with very green grass, and he was blown to bits . . . eating, . . . telling us how his aunt had sent him the knife to sharpen his drawing pencils with" (107). In the beginning, the "young men joined up with an ardour which was only matched by their later disillusionment . . . [and] young women employed themselves in bandage-making" (77). Later, only children like those for whom Anna cares can enjoy playing at war games. Women and men have seen that war is not heroism "like a Wagner overture" but is to "lose a hand, or an arm, or a face" or to "die of dirty, neglected wounds, or run about screaming with their stomachs dangling in front of them" (99).

No wonder that Anna, unlike the younger and more naive Elsbeth, shuns political activism. She finds it neither exciting nor productive. After passing her thirty-eighth birthday, Anna decides to accept the pro-posal of Hans Giesecke, a professor at a university in a small German town. As conditions worsen in Germany after the Reichstag Fire Trials (Elsbeth has put herself in danger by translating some pamphlets for a Communist friend), Anna finds herself feeling more and more of a Jew; she had not previously identified herself with her Jewish heritage. But even so, she actually defends to her non-Jewish husband Hitler's singling Jews out for persecution. "Alien and critical they had always been, and would always be. If the Nazis wanted a super Prussian state, they had better get rid of the Jews as soon as possible, for mass think-ing, mass obedience was something which they would never accept" (311; Woolf uses "alien and critical" to describe women as outsiders to "civilisation" in *A Room of One's Own*).[24] Hans loses his job; Anna her passport. He leaves to get a job in England or America. She is killed, having been mistakenly identified as the one in a crowd who throws a stone at an S.A. man during a parade in Nürnberg in May 1935.

What distinguishes Campion's and Bottome's thirties novels from those by such writers as Isherwood, Greene, Orwell, Huxley, or Waugh —writers easily identified without a first name being stated—is that Campion and Bottome take women's lives and ideas seriously. Their readings of the thirties, unlike those of their male counterparts, are *not* gendered; that is, they see the same scenes as the male writers, but they see *women* and men, not just men, as participants in the social, political, and personal revolutions of the age, from war to sexuality. Women as well as men are victims in their novels. Ironically, of course, we have traditionally spoken of the inclusion of women as a woman's issue, accepting the exclusion of women as natural if the concern or focus is politics or the marketplace. In *Duet*, the women as well as the men of Anna's generation seek escape from memories, guilt, or loss through commitment to a cause or through the soporifics of alcohol, dance, cigarettes, and entertainment. Others remain cynical, pronouncing all "isms" repellent. "There's the same reason for being a Communist as there is for being a Fascist or a Roman Catholic. . . . You unload the responsibility for yourself on to the Führer, or the State, or the priest in the confessional. You simply shift the burden of yourself and your general doubts and fears on to somebody or something else" (213).

Before contemporary women historians like Claudia Koonz came to write *Mothers in the Fatherland* (1987) and explore the relationships among women, family, and politics in Nazi Germany, these women novelists had done precisely that in their portraits of life in Nazi Germany. Through their novels, we experience life through the eyes of the "outsider"—German ("Huns" or "Nazis" is how we have dismissed their humanity), Jew, and woman. These women novelists combined fact with fiction, documenting events, people, and attitudes. In *Duet*, Campion depicts not only the mass political rallies, the boycott of Jewish stores, and the murdering of communists after the Reichstag Fire but also Hindenburg, "the nation's darling, the grizzled, wooden-faced, stiff-shouldered Hindenburg . . . whose aged, stiff hand goes up mechanically in the salute" (254–55), and Hitler, "the people's Moses . . . who knows how to play upon them as Joachim played upon his violin" (255). She documents the anti-Semitism of the times. Miss Field resents working as a tutor in the home of Jews and states, "There was something barbaric about them" (33). The teacher at the English art school that Anna is attending reflects that she doesn't mind blacks so much as she dislikes Jews, a prejudice the "gentle soul" shares with Miss Field (180).

Like *The Mortal Storm*, Sally Carson's thirties trilogy depicts the poignancy of divided loyalties for members of a German family. She also implicates English friends and neighbors in the private and public crises of that nation's people. Carson's first book, *Crooked Cross* (1934), concludes with the suicide of a young woman, Lexa Kluger, after the shooting of her fiancé, Moritz Weissmann, a young doctor of Jewish ancestry. Her brothers, Helmy and Erich, enthusiastic supporters of Hitler, participated with other storm troopers in the murder of Weissmann, whom they had previously welcomed at their home.

The second book in the trilogy, *The Prisoner* (1936), opens with the Kluger brothers, particularly Helmy, struggling with their lives and consciences after the suicide of their sister.[25] Helmy is bound by his love for his family, especially his mother, who, like his father and brother, would be destroyed if he became courageous and spoke out against what the group of storm troopers had done. But Helmy can no longer cope with the situation when a friend, Hermann, an accused Communist and escapee from Dachau, is killed while seeking temporary asylum in the Kluger family apartment in Munich. Imprisoned by his bonds with the living—his mother, in particular—Helmy is also imprisoned by the dead—Lexa, Moritz, and Hermann. Even those whose names he doesn't know begin to haunt him: the Jewish neighbor girl with whom he used to walk to the dairy; the young, "terrified" boy in the yard by the river who runs from those dressed, like Helmy, in the uniform of a storm trooper (353). Caged by guilt, Helmy has a complete breakdown. Before Helmy can commit suicide, Erich arranges for him to leave Germany for a time to visit with friends in England.

The Prisoner provides a picture of daily life in Germany—children playing, the "girls and the small boys . . . always made to be Communists . . . the big boys . . . Nazi heroes always winning, always turning the cowering Communists . . . out of the shed" (311). Carson's trilogy moves the reader because her characterizations are as realistic as her setting and situation. Although some storm troopers are animals like Von Bülow, the cowardly rapist who belongs to the same group as Helmy and Erich, others are idealists like Helmy, looking for an opportunity to make a better world. Still others, like Erich, are opportunists, seeking a job and a chance to rise in the world.

Carson, like her sister novelists, makes us see the sexism, anti-Semitism, and antidemocratic fanaticism of Hitler's regime. She depicts the social and political scene as vividly as she portrays the individual peculiarities and personality differences that motivate her characters. Women lose their jobs: after an attack of bronchitis, one woman finds "her place had been filled by a young man, bright and cheerful, suddenly full of the self-righteous superiority of his sex which Hitler had told him he possessed" (91). So too does Herr Kluger lose his job, which had barely provided his family with food and a place to live. He sees the peace memorials in Munich and thinks of "the hypocrisy of the memorials, the stupidity of all this military nonsense" (212). Daily the propaganda teaches the "people to deceive themselves"—that Hitler wants peace, that the Jews are no longer being persecuted, that the liberties of the pacifist or Social Democrat are not being denied, that Hitler has been "divinely appointed"—and encourages the individual citizen to ignore neighbors who are disappearing, or are "taken into protective arrest," the phrase used by officials (102–3).

In reality, those outside Germany knew better than its citizens what was taking place. "It had been suggested in foreign newspapers—in Germany no one dared to say so—that General Göring had actually set fire to the Reichstag himself" (188). Whether seated in the biergarten or walking on the streets, the individual German citizen dared not speak but instead had to listen to the brownshirts spread the word: "Trying to slink out of Germany! . . . Why not let the filthy Jews go? . . . We don't want dirty Jewish surgeons" (58). English men and women, however, sitting at home in the safety of their pubs and kitchens, were quite well informed about the attacks on German citizens. On learning that his Oxford school friend has been arrested, the Englishman Michael, a close acquaintance of Hermann, Helmy, and the Kluger family, remembers "extravagant words from solid old newspapers like *The Times* and the *Manchester Guardian*—rubber truncheons . . . flogged to death . . . indecencies" (25; text's ellipses).

In her last novel in the trilogy, *A Traveller Came By* (1938), Carson explicitly explores the responsibility that Helmy must accept for his actions and that individuals outside Germany must take for what is happening to men and women there. Britain's apathetic response to the news from Germany is underscored by Michael's family's response to Helmy, who, in their view, should take his problems and go away. They would like to believe, as they sit in the comfort of their English country home, that Helmy's problems are his and not theirs. But just as Helmy must come to accept his responsibility for what has happened to Lexa, her Jewish fiancé, the little girl whose last name he does not know, Hermann, and the German nation, so too must the English accept their political responsibility for the Treaty of Versailles and their personal responsibility to other human beings, including those they would define and dehumanize as outsiders.

If these novels are the quite interesting, well-crafted, readable tales that reviewers and I find them to be, novels that challenge what we "see," why, then, have we not heard of them? I don't believe that the only culprit is the writers of thirties histories and their literary values. Attitudes toward women, Jews, Communists, Fascists—political and social values—have also shaped the narratives of thirties literature.

As the novels and reviews of them occasionally make clear, Britain was itself anti-Semitic and indifferent to, if not approving of, German persecution of the Jews. Even the *Manchester Guardian* reviewer of *The Mortal Storm* refers to "an element of tactless [Jewish] aggressiveness in Freya's character."[26] So prevalent was the prejudice against Jews that it spurred a number of novelists of Jewish heritage to use their vocation to change the hearts and minds of the British. In Naomi Jacob's novel *Barren Metal* (1936), a repetitious, oversimplified presentation of Jewish life and character in the thirties, a young man protests to his mother on his return from Germany: "England, the world, ought to know—know it all. Work, money, education—even a clean decent death is denied us!" His mother warns him that the public does not want to listen, that the newspapers will not publish his stories, and that the situation is so bad that many Jews would like to deny their heritage. "This new movement against the Jews. Dreadful of course, but one must remembah [*sic*] that many of the Eastern Jews have brought it on themselves."[27] Anti-Fascists anxiously proclaimed that they were not Jew-lovers while other writers, more liberal than left in their politics, sometimes blamed the victim. Cicely Hamilton in *Modern Germanies* (1931), for example, describes the "Nazi declaration of war on the 'materialistic Jewish spirit'" as "a striving after virtue."[28] Wyndham Lewis, a name mentioned in literary history more often for his pronouncements than for his accomplishments as a writer but a name we nevertheless recognize, was well known for his pro-Hitler anti-Semitism. Even his published retraction at the end of the decade, *The Jews Are They Human?* (1939), reverberates chillingly.

Those in power appeared to consider Jews, Communists, and women a greater revolutionary threat than Hilter. The same *Manchester Guardian* review that noted Freya's "aggressiveness" also indirectly suggested that Nazis were to be preferred to Communists: "Those brothers were entitled to be annoyed by Hans."[29] No Cambridge professor would accept a Communist or common worker as a suitor for his daughter. Only the fact that the brothers shot Hans on the Austrian side of the border seemed to the reviewer to be particularly offensive and Nazi-like. The popularity of the leader of the British union of Fascists, Sir Oswald Mosley, is well known. He was supported by Viscount Rothermere's newspapers, the *Sunday Dispatch* and the *Evening News*, as well as by other persons clearly more sympathetic to fascism than to communism.[30] Some writers, such as Anthony Ludovici, openly proclaimed that the British ought to take a lesson from Hitler; Hitler was to be admired for ending the "democratic chatter" about equal rights for women.[31] Cicely Hamilton, though dismayed that German women seemed to be perceived as nothing more than breeders and fearful of the unthinking and unfeeling power being concentrated in the youths, objected more to the Communist youth, whom she saw as unkempt, than to the well-disciplined and uniformed *Hitlerjugend*.[32] Bottome also observes, in *The Mortal Storm*, that Communists were judged by their clothing rather than by their ideas (52).

In spite of the fact that many British newspapers were openly sympathetic to the Fascist cause, and that correspondents lost their jobs trying to get their papers to carry the full accounts of Hitler's murders and moves toward war, the British press did report on events in Germany, making the English more knowledgeable than Germans about events there. British newspapers as early as 1930 began carrying accounts of the brownshirts' unprovoked attacks on Jews and Communists, and in 1933 Victor Gollancz had published *The Brown Book of the Hitler Terror*. At the same time, Ellen Wilkinson reported that one German woman "had in all good faith insisted that the atrocity stories were false until her own husband was beaten."[33] No specific attention, however, was paid to what was happening to German women; the subject was taken up only incidentally in stories about public meetings, such as Wilkinson's address to the Six Point Group in which she reported that German women had been beaten with steel rods. Other accounts of Nazi savagery to women are to be found in letters to the editor or in reports of women writers, such as one by Naomi Mitchison, who mentions the plight of women and children as well as male Austrian socialists.[34]

Indifference and assent, not lack of knowledge about Nazi brutality, characterized the British, as our women writers tell us. If we want to understand literary history's conspiracy of silence about what these women wrote, we must examine not just past and present social attitudes and political practices but the connection of those attitudes and practices to the seeming vagaries of literary history. The literary historians' claim that art exists for art's sake and not, as Sylvia Townsend Warner once remarked on the pages of the *Left Review*, for "man's sake" reflects modern society's apathy and indifference, if not prejudice and cruelty.[35] The so-called scholarly virtues—disinterestedness and objectivity—mask prejudice against and fear of Jews, women, and Communists. Modernist literary history, if not literary modernism, hides the "horror," whether the attempt is conscious or unconscious, political or economic, patriarchal or imperialist.

There were, of course, numerous other such women writers in the thirties who depicted in their novels the dangers of fascism and who attempted to communicate to the English-speaking world what was happening in Germany in the 1930s: Phyllis Bentley, *Freedom, Farewell* (1936, one of a number of historical novels that women authors wrote to comment on the politics of the contemporary world); Sylvia Townsend Warner, particularly her short stories collected in *A Garland of Straw* (1943); Carmel Haden-Guest, *Give Us Conflict* (1935); and Stevie Smith, *Novel on Yellow Paper* (1936). A number of other women novelists— Irene Rathbone, *They Call It Peace* (1936), and Ruth Adam, *War on Saturday Week* (1937), for example—framed their novels with the two world wars (the one that had been fought and the one to come) and attacked English jingoism, failed social reforms, and patriarchal self-righteousness, just as did Bottome, Campion, and Carson, though the setting is England and not Germany. To be a radical woman writer in subject rather than form, to choose a female for a protagonist, to center the conflict in the family, to examine the effects of the public on the private—these are not the ways to establish a literary reputation, at least not in the 1930s. Schoolboy friends and women writers of pulp romance seem to warrant more attention in the histories of the decade than do serious women writers of domestic fictions, women such as the protagonists of my tale, to whom political events and the personal life mattered very much indeed.

Notes

I am particularly grateful for the assistance of Hildegard Schnuttgen, the Youngstown State University reference librarian, and the research assistants funded by the graduate school—Mary Ann Mullen, Laurie Delaney, and Kelly Loney. The graduate school also funded some of the costs incurred in securing copies of books and newspapers not in our library—all of which made possible this chapter and my other research on women writers of the thirties.

1. W. H. Auden, "Musée des Beaux Arts," *Collected Shorter Poems* (New York: Random House, 1957), 123–24. The poem was written in the late 1930s.

2. Andy Croft in *Red Letter Days: British Fiction in the 1930s* (London: Lawrence and Wishart, 1990), a book I secured in England after having submitted this essay to the press, is the first historian of thirties literature to devote a chapter to anti-Fascist, realist novels. He mentions two of the authors that I discuss, Phyllis Bottome and Sally Carson, in his carefully done compendium of rarely discussed writers.

3. Auden, "Musée," 124.

4. Samuel Hynes, *The Auden Generation: Literature and Politics in England in the 1930s* (New York: Viking Press, 1976), 181; Richard Johnstone, *The Will to Believe: Novelists of the Nineteen-Thirties* (Oxford: Oxford University Press, 1982), 98. Both emphasize a formalist reading of Isherwood. Auden too, Hynes argues, must be understood as writing not a "didactic," realistic representation of the age but a "parable art" in which "the feeling of human issues, not an interpretation of them," not a mere "fidelity to the observed world," is offered (13–15).

5. Margaret Cole, in *Growing up into Revolution* (London: Longmans, Green and Co., 1949), states that the household in which she grew up was "'non-political,' that is to say Tory," for it is only when it is politics of the Left that the public calls it politics. Reviewers accuse her and her husband of "dragg[ing] politics" into their detective novels (19).

6. See, for example, a leftist study such as Jon Clark, Margot Heinemann, David Margolis, and Carole Snee, eds., *Culture and Crises in Britain in the Thiries* (London: Lawrence and Wishart, 1979), which examines *Scrutiny* and the *Left Review* as well as Auden and company, male working-class literature, the documentary form, and the mass-culture genres of the theater and film. When gender is consciously added to the politics of class, for example in Janet Batsleer, Tony Davies, Rebecca O'Rourke, and Chris Weedon's *Rewriting English: Cultural Politics of Gender and Class* (London: Methuen, 1985), the women discussed are romance writers. Gender is a subissue of the popular-culture debate in thirties literary history.

7. Frank Kermode, *History and Value* (Oxford: Clarendon Press, 1988), 5. Kermode wants to reclaim some of the art, such as Auden's "Spain," that in retrospect the artists labeled inferior, but he rejects those working-class writers, such as Lewis Jones, whom Carole Snee attempts to make a case for in *Culture and Crises*. He, of course, mentions women only to scoff at them—Agatha Christie, *The Secret Adversary* (1922)—or to cite them as a secondary source—the portrayal of Goronwy Rees in Elizabeth Bowen's *The Death of the Heart* (1938).

8. Croft, *Red Letter Days*, states, "The critical preoccupation with 'non-realist' writing about fascist ideology . . . is a consequence of a determination to see a loss of political nerve in the second half of the decade" (333). Mark Walhout, in "The New Criticism and the Crises of American Liberalism: The Poetics of the Cold War," *College English* 49 (December 1987): 861–71, likewise argues that the

new critical emphasis on the aesthetic purity of a work of art reflected the disillusionment in America with liberal ideas and postwar politics and contributed to our renunciation of personal and professional responsibility for the critical examination of ideology within and without the work of art.

9. Valentine Cunningham, *British Writers of the Thirties* (Oxford: Oxford University Press, 1988), 26. Cunningham reads the thirties through the images and metaphors he identifies for the age, but those images and metaphors, which become his chapter titles, are drawn from concerns central to Auden and company.

10. Wells quoted in Virginia Woolf, *Three Guineas* (New York: Harcourt Brace Jovanovich, 1938), 43. Citing newspaper headlines stating that the Nazis now controlled Austria, Woolf sarcastically remarked: "The men's 'movement to resist the practical obliteration of their freedom by Nazis or Fascists' may have been more perceptible. But that it has been more successful is doubtful" (159).

11. Ibid., 42, 67, 49.

12. Ibid., 60.

13. Dale Spender quotes Woolf's "Women and Fiction": "But for women the past is a silence, an absence. . . . The corridors of history are for women unlit . . . the figures of generations of women are so dimly, so fitfully perceived," in *There's Always Been a Women's Movement This Century* (London: Pandora Press, 1983), 1.

14. Gilbert and Gubar list none of the poems, essays, or fiction that women wrote on the Spanish Civil War and, for that matter, not much of any other thirties protest literature by women. See my "Writing against the Grain: Sylvia Townsend Warner and the Spanish Civil War," in *Women's Writing in Exile*, edited by Mary Lynn Broe and Angela Ingram (Chapel Hill: University of North Carolina Press, 1989), for a discussion of how women writers become nothing more than "emblem, bibliographic entry, or footnote" in the literary histories of the Spanish Civil War (350). In that essay I also note that the authors of those histories make clear that they consider themselves to be writing social history rather than literary history, as if the two are necessarily mutually exclusive. For Sandra Gilbert and Susan Gubar's discussion of women's World War I militancy, see "Soldier's Heart" in *No Man's Land: The Place of the Woman Writer in the Twentieth Century*, vol. 2, *Sex Changes* (New Haven: Yale University Press, 1989). They even attempt (297–98) to cast doubt on Woolf's pacifism by noting the admiration that Woolf expressed for Amalia Bonilla in *Three Guineas*.

15. Nicola Beauman, *A Very Great Profession: The Woman's Novel, 1914–39* (London: Virago, 1983), 231.

16. Martin Ceadel, "Popular Fiction and the Next War, 1918–1939," in *Class, Culture, and Social Change: A New View of the 1930s*, edited by Frank Gloversmith (Brighton: Harvester Press, 1980), 161.

17. See, for example, David Smith, *Socialist Propaganda in the Twentieth-Century British Novel* (London: Macmillan, 1978), 79–81.

18. Phyllis Bottome, *The Mortal Storm* (Boston: Little, Brown and Co., 1938), 9. The earlier Faber edition opens with Freya leaving the house to ski alone in the mountains, an action recounted in chapter 4 of the Little Brown edition. But though the action begins later in the Faber, what is dramatized in chapters 1–3 (Little) is indirectly narrated in chapters 4 and 5. The family name is also changed from Toller (Faber) to Roth (Little Brown).

The Story of the Nazis   263

19. Professor Roth's real-life counterparts also learned that they were not able to help. In fact, they too became victims. The Berlin correspondent to the *Times* reported that Professor James Franck, one of eight German-Jewish recipients of the Nobel Prize, had been forced from his university position (19 April 1933). The *Times* also carried the report of the dismissal of Professor Fritz Haber, a German chemist and another Nobel Prize winner (4 May 1933) . Albert Einstein's bank accounts were seized by the German government in April 1933.

20. Woolf, *Three Guineas*, 85.

21. Phyllis Bottome discusses the years leading up to World War II in *The Goal* (London: Faber and Faber, 1962), the second volume of her autobiography. She actively worked in the United States and in Britain to expose the Hitler-Nazi menace. She met with Franklin D. Roosevelt's "mother [who] shared the social prejudices of her time against the Jews, but . . . listened with sympathy when I told her of their persecution in Germany" (185). Bottome and her husband formed "The Democratic Society" in England to expose the "cruel antics of Hitler" (275), even speaking before extreme pacifists in Bristol in 1940 to urge them to fight Hitler. She published an indictment of the archbishop of Canterbury in the *New Republic* (28 December 1938) when the British press refused to print her letter.

22. Sarah Campion, *If She Is Wise* (London: Peter Davies, 1935), 255.

23. Sarah Campion, *Duet for Female Voices* (London: Peter Davies, 1936), 135, 140.

24. Virginia Woolf, *A Room of One's Own* (New York: Harcourt, Brace and World, 1929), 101.

25. Sally Carson, *Crooked Cross* (London: Hodder and Stoughton, 1934), *The Prisoner* (London: Hodder and Stoughton, 1936), and *A Traveller Came By* (London: Hodder and Stoughton, 1938). *Crooked Cross*, adapted for the stage in 1937, was first performed by the Birmingham Repertory Players and then for a season in London (the play was published by Jonathan Cape in 1938). In spite of queries of publishers and thirties literary figures and an advertisement in the *London Review of Books*, I have been able to learn nothing about Sally Carson, who seems not to have published after these quite well-received 1930s works.

26. Harold Grighouse, review of *The Mortal Storm*, by Phyllis Bottome, *Manchester Guardian*, 12 October 1937.

27. Naomi Jacob, *Barren Metal* (London: Hutchinson, 1936; reprint, New York: Macmillan, 1937), 258, 173.

28. Cicely Hamilton, *Modern Germanies as Seen by an Englishwoman* (London: Dent, 1931), 181.

29. Grighouse, review.

30. Sylvia Scaffardi's *Fire under the Carpet* (London: Lawrence and Wishart, 1986) provides a leftist view of fascism in England during the thirties as she tells the story of Ronald Kidd and the founding of the Council for Civil Liberties. If she overemphasizes the fascist bent of the English, many other reports have nearly ignored it.

31. Anthony Ludovici, "Hitler and Nietzsche," *English Review* 64 (1937): 194.

32. See Hamilton, *Modern Germanies*, chaps. 6 and 9.

33. "Women under Hitlerism," *Manchester Guardian*, 19 May 1933; the article was actually a report of a Six Point Group meeting that Wilkinson addressed.

34. Naomi Mitchison, "Troubled Europe: Austrian Aftermath," *Review of Reviews*, May 1934. See also a letter to the editor of the *Manchester Guardian*, 1 July 1933, which deplores the loss of "political rights and intellectual freedom . . . of man and woman in Fascist Germany"; women were to be allowed employment only as "servant maids," were no longer to be allowed to matriculate in the colleges, and were to be denied all unemployment benefits.

35. Sylvia Townsend Warner, "Underlying Morality," *Left Review*, July 1937.

13

DAPHNE PATAI & ANGELA INGRAM

Fantasy and Identity:

The Double Life of a

Victorian Sexual Radical

In the first few decades of this century, an extraordinary literary persona was created by a feminist writer who, using the name "Irene Clyde," tirelessly agitated against conventional distinctions of sex and for a world in which an ideal feminine type would serve as the model for all human behavior. During much of the 1980s, we looked for clues to the true identity behind the pseudonym. This essay tells the story of that search and of Irene Clyde's utopian vision.

A book is missing from most bibliographies of utopian fiction. That book is Irene Clyde's 1909 novel *Beatrice the Sixteenth*.[1] *Beatrice* may not fit ordinary definitions of utopian fiction because it does not operate with accepted notions of the "political." Cast as an adventure story, it is a first-person narrative by one Mary Hatherley, a physician, geographer, and explorer who, while travelling in an "Arabian" land, finds herself mysteriously transported to an exotic country peopled by unusual beings. The plot is in many respects conventional (Queen Beatrice, leader of the country of Armeria, is menaced by a neighboring nation and embroiled in internal palace intrigues), but the reader soon realizes why Irene Clyde needed the trappings of fantasy fiction to create an "elsewhere," a parallel world in which to stage this deceptively simple tale. Both in form and in content, *Beatrice* turns out to be an early fictional experiment with the abolition of gender.

Irene Clyde's expansion of the usual definition of politics is evident from the novel's opening pages, where no gendered pronouns appear, nor any indications of the sex of the characters encountered by the narrator. This alone has an unsettling effect on the imagination, as readers strain to place these beings within familiar social paradigms, which require gender specifications. Slowly, we learn of Armeria's customs, language, and institutions, which are often contrasted (as typically happens in utopian fiction) with the narrator's own—British—society, presented here in a critical light. Two classes of people are recognized in the monarchy of Armeria, free and slave. There are no "complementary divisions" (78), as the narrator puts it, no sexual distinctions, no words in the language to distinguish male from female, husband from wife, he from she. From beginning to end, the narrator eschews gendered nouns and the generic "he" and instead refers to characters as "figure," "person," and "personage" while occasionally reminding the reader—through the use of "she or he"—that even the generic "she" is inaccurate when applied to Armerians. The narrative itself, on the other hand, is far from gender-neutral: it consistently and unabashedly values so-called feminine characteristics and, after the initial avoidance of gendered pronouns, reveals a predilection for "she" and other feminine forms to refer to the Armerians, whose gender we actually do not know. The description of the Armerians as beardless, often gentle, and nonwarlike (though ready and able to defend themselves), together with the recurring use of feminine pronouns, induces the reader to conceive of the Armerians as women—but women not defined through any polarization with men.

The vision evoked in this novel, then, is of a radically feminist, separatist society—one that sees gender, rather than class, as the fundamental social problem that must be transcended. But unlike most utopian novelists, Irene Clyde engages in no lengthy disquisitions about the values and institutions of Armeria; the perspective is allowed to develop slowly through the narrative itself. Even the depiction of an attempted palace coup is done with a kind of innocence and charm incompatible with our own cynical understanding of "politics." Threats evoke civilized and delicate replies; Queen Beatrice herself rejects heavy-handed measures and depends on cleverness rather than strength, at the same time avoiding any action that would suit a Machiavellian model.

In a similar way, the narrative seeks to displace whatever stereotypes might be evoked by the term *slave*. Although the existence of slavery in Armeria clearly troubles the narrator (and is likely to trouble readers today), it seems deliberately presented as an improvement on the British system, in which working-class children were usually destined for lives of ill-paid and drudging work in mines, factories, or domestic service. In depicting the institution of slavery in Armeria, Irene Clyde, perhaps intentionally, echoes the sentiment that animates Thomas More's attitude toward the presence of slavery in his Utopia: better to be enslaved in Utopia than free and impoverished elsewhere.[2] But unlike slavery in More's Utopia, "slavery" in Armeria bears no moral stigma.[3] In the rare situations in which slaves are dissatisfied with their "households" (the basic social unit in Armeria, an extended affinity group in which individuals have varying functions), they can apply for a change. The one notable character who is said to mistreat slaves is Galesa; consistently referred to as "he," Galesa verbally humiliates his slaves and attempts to break their spirits, behavior that is explained to the narrator in *Beatrice* as "a strain of the old brutality" that, though ever decreasing, still exists (211).

Unlike the inhabitants of the all-female society of Charlotte Perkins Gilman's *Herland* (1915), where there seem to be no vestiges of either the "old brutality" or of passion, Irene Clyde's Armerians celebrate passionate love and romance. At the end of the novel, Armeria has defeated its enemy (a coarser, larger, more heavily muscled people), and the narrator recognizes her love for one of her companions, whose permanent partner she intends to become. In this respect too, *Beatrice* is more attuned to the 1990s than to 1909, for under the guise of an "innocent" fictional fantasy, it contravenes the prevailing ideology of passion as a male characteristic and dares to imagine a sexuality that is not male-centered. Indeed, it suggests that this sexuality, which the reader is likely to read as female, is superior to the traditional eroticism that is polarized into male-aggressive and female-passive.[4]

The people of Armeria embody the best of what we are encouraged to see as fully *human* qualities: they are tender, gentle, and loving, as well as independent, brave, and effective fighters when necessary. It would be fifty years before other writers of utopian and science fiction took up such a challenge to conventional gender roles and depicted worlds that are androgynous or homosexual, or in which gender identity simply does not figure. Long before Marge Piercy, Ursula Le Guin, and Joanna Russ (joined in the 1980s by a growing number of writers of feminist and lesbian utopias), Irene Clyde took a radically feminist position that did not hesitate to set the "feminine" as the highest standard for the human, even defying conventional rules of grammar in doing so. This was no mean feat in 1909. To gain a perspective on this achievement, consider the decisions made by Ursula Le Guin in the nongendered world of her 1969 novel *The Left Hand of Darkness*. Even while telling the reader that her Gethenians are neither male nor female, Le Guin, in this celebrated work, opts for the use of "he" and for characterizations that evoke images of masculinity.[5] Thus her use of the generic "he" merely conforms to, and reinforces, readers' conventional patterns of imagining.

Irene Clyde, by contrast, works against our expectations, effectively estranging us from habitual reactions and modes of thought. The author's originality in accomplishing this has, however, gone unrecognized. As recently as 1991, Fredric Jameson (like many other critics before him) credited Le Guin for her inventiveness in attempting to go beyond gender in *The Left Hand of Darkness*,[6] which shows that Dale Spender's observation—"Schools cannot teach what society does not know"—applies to scholars as well.[7] Scholars cannot cite forerunners of whom they are ignorant. This problem in scholarship is further compounded because for a work to be valued and applauded, readers must be able to grasp what is in it. Such readers were largely lacking for Irene Clyde's novel. As long as gender was not widely recognized as a political category open to challenge, works such as *Beatrice* were likely to be relegated to the arena of "mere fantasy," without "social" ramifications. Such works were therefore apt to be eliminated even from the record of utopian literature, the predominant objective of which is social critique using the vehicle of fiction to create imaginary alternative societies.

Writing long before there began to be anything resembling a cultural consensus capable of entertaining such clearly political challenges to the concept of gender, Irene Clyde shared the problem of other writers of adult utopian and fantasy fiction: how to enable the reader to grasp a different way of thinking and being. In part, this problem is solved in *Beatrice* by the conventional device of a traveler in a strange land, with geographic, cultural, and linguistic dislocation as a reflection and cause of a sense of confusion and loss of identity. As in other utopian and science fiction, the narrative veers between estrangement from and accommodation to the reader's reality, the estrangement being most prominent at the level of language. Many decades later, writers such as June Arnold in *The Cook and the Carpenter* (1973) and Marge Piercy in *Woman on the Edge of Time* (1976) attempted to avoid gender dichotomy by inventing a generic pronoun for everyone. Irene Clyde did not think of that solution but did, astonishingly for that time, reject the use of the generic "he" and envision a world beyond gender.

In reading the novel, however, we are forced to confront the fact that our very expectations of fiction are gendered. Thus, in scenes and actions whose agents would be, in our world, habitually male, it is (to this day) difficult to avoid imagining the soldiers, officers, scouts, sentries, warders, commanders, and generals as male. But again and again, by the use of the pronoun "she" for these characters, the narrative clashes with our private imaginings. Through these collisions, Irene Clyde continually subverts the routine gender polarizations of our familiar reality. The character Ilex, for example, is called "she" only after the very explicit explanation that Armeria knows no such terms or distinctions, and this chapter ends with a description of Ilex, here referred to as "he or she," putting an arm around Mary, the narrator, who observes that the important thing was how good the embrace felt. Although the numerous "pairings" of characters, as well as the romance that culminates in the narrator's "life-union" with Ilex, might encourage us to read the novel as outright or crypto lesbian fiction (especially when we learn that children are acquired through barter with a neighboring "barbarian" people—barbarian, perhaps, precisely because they have male/female sexual relations), to do so would be in an important sense to deny the very point the book is attempting to make.

Eager to learn more about Irene Clyde, we sought other books published under that name. We found that only one other such work exists. It is a collection of essays published twenty-five years after *Beatrice*, in 1934, and titled *Eve's Sour Apples*.[8] This book—a virtual guide to an understanding of *Beatrice*—spells out, in a series of closely argued chapters, the author's gender ideology. Perhaps more important, it is an early example of a thoroughgoing critique of the gender-role training given to children, as well as a catalogue of the baleful effects of such conditioning. Irene Clyde urges people to drop the outward signs of sex and become "free souls," without the distortion of being labeled male and female. More sweeping still, the book argues that men must develop feminine virtues, for the feminine character type, despite the stunting it undergoes, is preferable to the masculine; it is the latter that has produced modern war and the cult of violence accepted and practiced throughout the world.[9]

The most striking argument in *Eve's Sour Apples*, however, touches on the nature of heterosexual intercourse. The domination of women by men in conventional sexual union, Irene Clyde asserts, results in women's moral degradation—their acceptance of passivity and weakness—which is paralleled by the moral deformity of men, evident in their rejection of sweetness, tenderness, and delicacy in their lives. In articulating such a critique, Irene Clyde's work emerges as an important predecessor not only of recent feminist utopias that have challenged the notion of the generic male but also of current radical feminist perspectives, prefiguring, in particular, the work of Catharine MacKinnon and Andrea Dworkin. Once again, however, Irene Clyde's work left no trace in the records. As late as 1987, when Andrea Dworkin's book *Intercourse* was published, advertisements heralded what seemed to be its originality with critical endorsements such as the following: "Andrea Dworkin has confronted the question that no feminist hitherto has dared to ask: whether intromission is compatible with equal status." [10] Although the existence of such a challenge in *Beatrice* was not clear to readers and critics in 1909, reviewers a few decades later do appear to have grudgingly understood what was being said in Irene Clyde's essays. Even the staid *Times Literary Supplement* couldn't help but get the point, to some extent, in a brief review of *Eve's Sour Apples* in 1935: "Miss Clyde has apparently written a book of 224 pages to prove that sex is a nuisance, that it is destructive to social graciousness and vigour, and that it exists only because some people love to dominate, others to be dominated. It is difficult, however, to follow all Miss Clyde's reasoning." [11]

With greater comprehension, *Film Quarterly* commented, shortly thereafter: "What we really require is an altogether new attitude towards sex. We want less of the manly man; less of the womanly woman, and more of the human human being. Miss Irene Clyde in her wonderful little book . . . points out that the essence of sex is not, as one might very justly imagine, sex itself—but domination. Out of it grows party-politics, public-house brawls and war." [12] This argument is clearly set forth in chapter 1 of *Eve's Sour Apples*, entitled "The Essence of Sex: Domination."

> It is in vain that sentimentalists talk of the "equality" of the two parties in marriage, and of their "equal but different" share in their marital duties. The brutal fact remains that the two parties are not equal, but that the function of one is active, superior and imperative, while that of the other is passive, inferior and submissive; and that inequality is not momentary only, but the results, in pain and danger and distortion, are borne by the inferior party. When the most Bolshevik of Bolshevists has done his utmost and has abolished the possession of wives by husbands as against other men, there will still remain, rugged and inexpugnable, the physical possession of the husband as against the wife.

This obvious physical fact it is impossible to ignore. It has impressed the imagination of the race from its infancy. I believe that it is the sole foundation for the hoary legend of the mental and moral inferiority of women. Man is so prone to stop at the obvious; to refuse to probe beneath the surface. How *could* a Being which plays such an abject rôle, and is so obviously fitted to play it, be anything but inferior by nature! It is an easy and comfortable superstition. It lets everything fall so agreeably into place. It is a line of least resistance which has for ages been irresistible in its beautiful simplicity. It is too simple for the facts. But it takes a long time for humanity to bring itself to face the facts. (11–12) [13]

Irene Clyde quotes from classical and contemporary sources pointing to the power element in sexuality and gives colloquial examples such as the exclamation of the French officer who, after a humiliating military defeat, says, "Nous sommes F——!" (12), that is "Nous sommes foutus!" ("We're fucked!"). Foreshadowing many contemporary feminists, Irene Clyde views such expressions as transparent reflections of the way in which the human race has habitually regarded heterosexual intercourse.

Only in the twentieth century, Irene Clyde contends, have people thought to deny or minimize the fact that women's physical relation to men is one of subjection and humiliation. Nonetheless, the book's depiction of male-female relations is not based on an argument from biology, for Irene Clyde grants that in the distant future, the associations of subjection and control, inseparable from "the act," might no longer be evoked. But is it possible now to "eradicate from our minds all trace of the symbolism of mastery which clings to the act?" (15). The answer is no. Some people "will delude themselves with the idea that they can accept sex and evade the sex-ideals that go with it. That is frankly impossible" (17).[14]

The outward physical relationship is only the symptom of an inward spiritual disease—and it is the latter that is the ultimate target of Irene Clyde's attack. "The willing acceptance of inferiority is the root and essence of all evil: it cankers character" (20). It is not "filth" that is the fundamental vice of sex, as some nineteenth-century sexual reformers believed; rather, it is the "willing acceptance of inferiority," "the wallowing in a moral deformity—the acceptance of a stunted life which might have been a complete one. . . . The sting of sex is contemptibleness" (28). The conclusion is inescapable. "The creature who resigns herself to be a stunted character is a Fool: no greater exists in this universe" (30).

In chapters that include discussions of nudity (not recommended), masturbation (quite a useful practice), and flagellation (bad), Irene Clyde stands revealed not as a prude preoccupied with sex but as a moralist analyzing the meaning of conventional gender roles in the life of society. A final chapter entitled "Feminism, Aristocracy, and Pacifism"[15] weaves all the main themes together. Peace, we are told, depends on the ascendancy of aristocracy and feminism, for "the cause of war is, *as it was and always will be, one thing alone—Masculine Ferocity*" (207; emphasis in original). No politician or capitalist could produce a war "if there were not people to fall back upon who are prepared to do the work of wholesale slaughter. . . . War is a male thing. And as long as boys are taught to fight and to domineer, it is impossible to hope that war can ever be eliminated. In some form or other, the inculcated violence will find an outlet. . . . We cannot bring up boys to be rough and expect to get rid of the glorified roughness which is war" (208–9). Though acknowledging women's complicity in men's wars, Irene Clyde notes that women do not perform the dirty work themselves and asks, "Can anyone suppose that in a world of women the carnage of a modern war could be even remotely possible?" (209). Beginning, then, with an attack on heterosexual intercourse as the very model of a relation of domination and submission, Irene Clyde spins out the implications of gender roles (a term that would come into existence decades later) for society at large.

Intrigued by this extraordinary early-twentieth-century vision, and frustrated by our ignorance about its author, we began to seek out Irene Clyde. What kind of a life might have generated so startling a sweep of thought? For an answer to this part of the puzzle, we had to search a long time. The author's name clearly was a pseudonym: nowhere in the English-speaking world were there public records that pointed to the existence of an "Irene Clyde." Nor could the publishers of Clyde's books provide any details. It looked as though we had hit a wall. But then a query published in the *Times Literary Supplement*, asking for information about Irene Clyde, brought us a letter. Lesley Hall, archivist at the Wellcome Institute for the History of Medicine in London, wrote that she had spotted the name Irene Clyde in an obscure journal, the *Uranian*.[16]

Thus began a new phase of our work. *Urania*, as it turned out to be called, was a privately printed and privately circulated journal, published six and, later, three times a year between 1916 and 1940.[17] Using the motto "There are no 'men' or 'women' in Urania," it defined itself with an extended statement that appeared in virtually every issue:

Urania denotes the company of those who are firmly determined to ignore the dual organization of humanity in all its manifestations.

They are convinced that this duality has resulted in the formation of two warped and imperfect types. They are further convinced that in order to get rid of this state of things no measures of "emancipation" or "equality" will suffice, which do not begin by a complete refusal to recognize or tolerate the duality itself.

If the world is to see sweetness and independence combined in the same individual, *all* recognition of that duality must be given up. For it inevitably brings in its train the suggestion of the conventional distortions of character which are based on it.[18] (emphasis in original)

In form, *Urania* was multigenre (essays, poetry, drama, and short fiction, as well as items lifted from the international press). In content, it promoted a fascinating array of interrelated concerns: information about spontaneous sex-changes or wrongly ascribed sexual identity, about instances of parthenogenesis, and about women (and, less frequently, men) contravening gender stereotypes in their lives by, for example, winning rifle-shooting prizes, saving drowning children, or climbing mountains. The point was to demonstrate that "women can do anything," and frequent historical bits and pieces (from books, diaries, letters) demonstrated that this had indeed always been the case.

One interesting 1932 article, "The Roots of War," signed by Irene Clyde, is perceptively revisionist in suggesting that it is not the "old" men who are to blame for the outbreak of war but the young, who are driven by the need to display their "manliness."[19] This was a genuinely new insight at a time when the "myth" of World War I, firmly established by the claims of poets like Siegfried Sassoon, stated that the old men who didn't have to fight sent the young men off to die. Irene Clyde's view was, and remains, persuasive: the person who, conscripted or not, goes off to war is the person who makes war happen. But *Urania*'s pacifism is by no means absolute. Women's achievements in past wars and battles are also noted. There is a logic to *Urania*'s inclusion of items about female warriors; since the journal's self-appointed task was to demonstrate that sex (we would now say "gender") was irrelevant, and since "soldiers" are conventionally equated with "men," it was clearly *Urania*'s job to present information about soldiers who were women. This was an honest effort to show that "sex is an accident"[20] and that *manly* and *womanly* are meaningless terms.

Urania served also as a rich source of information about the progress of women's struggles for education, professional opportunities, and domestic and political rights across the globe, about pacifism and vegetarianism, about the birth rate (applauded when it declined). The journal also published, in French, some veiled lesbian fiction. Above all, it celebrated in every issue women's achievements, noted large and small examples of challenges to conventional gender roles, and untiringly argued against the notion of two distinct and immutable sexes (a view the journal called "materialism").[21] And, always, *Urania* demanded a recognition of the superiority of the female type and promoted it as the proper model for all human beings.

A dazzling survey of decades of feminist activity, *Urania* took the entire world as its concern.[22] Its very scope, not surprisingly, led to some ideological inconsistencies in its pages. In the happy recording of "transsexual" and sometimes transvestite news, *Urania*'s desire to transcend gender occasionally lost its way. It was true enough to say that if a woman could live as a man for decades without being detected, or if a girl could be revealed as a boy and vice versa, the outward trappings of gender were completely artificial. On the other hand, jubilation over such episodes highlights the very importance of the sexual differentiations the journal deplores. These news items—and there are many of them, from around the world—ring with an "another win for our side" tone that seems rather to conflict with the loftier attacks on the very notion of sex distinction. Some articles, scornful of quasi-scientific "materialism," point out (neo-Platonically) that souls, not bodies, constitute human value and beauty. But that line of argument is undercut when *Urania* also cheers the sort of hewing to "gender" that both transvestism and transsexualism reflect and embody.

In featuring material relating to gender switching, cross-dressing, and errors in sex assignment, *Urania* succeeds both in demonstrating the existence of some sort of fluidity between genders and in challenging the notion of gender as fixed once and for all by anatomical sex. But this emphasis simultaneously confirms that gender *is* fundamental to personal identity. The individuals whose stories are told in *Urania* are not, then, necessarily doing away with gender altogether—though this is *Urania*'s purported aim—but are merely adopting the opposite gender identity.[23] Nonetheless, *Urania*'s stance was unquestionably a radical one, representing an uncompromising assault on the sex/gender system of its time.

For a period of nearly three decades, Irene Clyde was *Urania*'s most frequent contributor, signing articles and editorials and also using other pseudonyms.[24] With this discovery, then, our knowledge of the published writings of the mysterious Irene Clyde grew enormously, and it became possible to trace, over a lengthy stretch of time, this writer's concerns and commitments.

We were also able to follow, now, a wealth of possible leads regarding the identity of Irene Clyde. Each issue listed several names as "contacts" for the publication and provided printers' addresses: in Bombay or Tokyo (frequently), London (sporadically), and Seattle (once).[25] One of these names was consistently cited as that of the person whom *Urania* was "printed and published for." During a stressful fortnight in March 1990, we followed the tracks of this name. At the end—but, of course, we were at a new beginning—we had solved our mystery and were now no longer searching for information about an unknown writer but about a well-known public figure: someone who won a scholarship from grammar school to attend Oxford and then won another scholarship to Cambridge; who had Doctor of Laws degrees from both of these universities, was admitted to the Honourable Society of the Inner Temple in 1896 and was called to the bar in 1898; who became joint Honorary Secretary of the International Law Association in 1905[26] and was an internationally recognized publicist and legal scholar and author of dozens of books and articles on international law; who left England in 1916 to spend over a quarter of a century in Japan as the legal adviser to the Japanese Foreign Office in Tokyo, only to be branded a traitor by the British during World War II and thus after the war stripped of British citizenship;[27] whose name—the name for whom *Urania* was printed and published—was Thomas Baty, the man who was, as we very soon ascertained by comparative textual analysis, Irene Clyde.

Thomas Baty was born in Stanwix, Cumberland, in February 1869 and died in Tokyo in 1954, one day after his eighty-fifth birthday. The *Times* obituary rather sniffily commented: "With a self-complacency that outran a sense of humour, he once explained that feminism, aristocracy, and pacificism were the corner-stones of his political and social creed, all derived from the glorification of delicacy and independence which for good or evil dominated his thought! He was unmarried."[28] One notes here the key terms in Irene Clyde's writing; indeed, "Feminism, Aristocracy, and Pacificism" is the title of the final chapter of *Eve's Sour Apples*, as well as of a two-part serialization of that chapter signed "Theta" in *Urania* in 1919.

A lifelong radical feminist and pacifist (terms he himself used) and a lifelong assailant of gender hierarchy, always a gentle man, Thomas Baty led a double life but one that was, for the most part, splendidly consistent, and perhaps for the simplest of reasons. In a posthumously published "Autobiographical Sketch," he wrote: "From earliest days, adored Beauty and Sweetness; considered ladies had both, as well as Persistence and Tenacity. Therefore, longed passionately to be a lady— and have continued to do so" (*Alone*, 185).

Passionate longing notwithstanding, Thomas Baty seems to have grown up a highly proper middle-class Victorian boy: tin soldiers when he was five or so,[29] a fondness for Greek, a taste for Mendelssohn and Chopin and for the novels of Sir Walter Scott, and enjoyment of summer holidays around the Clyde Estuary in Scotland with his mother, aunt, slightly younger sister, and some cousins, his father having died when Thomas was seven (*Alone*, 186–87). Then he was off to school and scholarships, followed by the Inner Temple, whose archivist recently expressed to us some surprise that a young man of such "social origins"— "the eldest son of . . . a cabinet maker"—should, though "exceptionally brilliant," have been admitted to the Honourable Society of the Inner Temple.[30]

But we have long since stopped being surprised by anything in Thomas Baty's biography. He reportedly deemed himself too shy to be a successful barrister in civil law and was, in any case, more drawn to the larger concerns of international law, to which he devoted his energies as a jurist. For many years he organized the biennial conferences of the International Law Association in major European cities. In the last month of his life, he was prevented from attending the association's session in Aix-en-Provence only by the British government's refusal to issue him a passport.[31]

He was a prolific writer. Starting in the late 1880s, he produced articles on a wide range of topics, from "Debt-Slavery in the Malay Peninsula," an early criticism of imperialist impositions of western legal notions on Asian social structures, to "Intercourse with Alien Enemies" (one of several critiques of the application of Western law to European citizens living abroad). These titles are expressive of his position on international affairs. As a reviewer of his 1909 book *International Law* noted, he characterized England and the United States as "mere international bullies."[32] Another review referred to him as a "well informed and pronounced peace man" who believed in "full liberty of development for states as for individuals" and who looked forward to "the interdependence as compared with the old idea of the independence of nations."[33] And it is significant that in 1912 he and his sister, Anne, translated from the German original George Jellinek's brief monograph *The Rights of Minorities*,[34] since the tyranny of a majority—even a majority of one—

over a minority was an object of his particular detestation, along with the inequities imposed on small states by large ones. He was also an expert on naval law. It is not surprising that he was skeptical of the League of Nations (and positively derisive of the notion of a separate Women's Section),[35] nor was he less wary, later, of the United Nations, an organization he saw as a monopolistic forum in which Britain, in return for American "resources," had sold out to "Bolshevism" (which he consistently "disliked and distrusted").[36] He similarly loathed fascism and abhorred the increasing power of the militarists in Japan after World War I.

Such power (the "Bismarkian [*sic*] militarism" whose influence on the Japanese army he deplored) he considered both cause and effect of the increasing regimentation of Japanese education—the drilling, the uniforms, the "management" of undergraduates' lives. "All this stern soldiership in the schools, combined with a sedulous inculcation of militaristic pride, had its effect," he wrote in 1946. "The successors of the charming children of twenty years ago were beginning to be inculcated with a hard mistrustfulness" (*Alone*, 11). This passage is reminiscent of *Eve's Sour Apples*, where a similarly articulated concern logically leads to a plea for "a radically humane education: an education which goes down to the root of things and teaches the boy to despise self-assertion, arrogance and violence," and cultivates instead "an ideal temper, contemptuous of warfare" (212).

A related spiritual failure—"hard mistrustfulness"—he believed underlay the breakdown of international relations. And, consistently, his revulsion from anything "harsh," "mechanical," "rough," or quantitative rather than qualitative prompted his distrust of party-political machines and of entrenched state power, which invariably worked to destroy the individual. Trusting in tact and diplomacy while loathing conventional politics and the world of commerce (which he saw as attacking the national identities of smaller nations), Thomas Baty hoped for the slow spread among all classes of the feminine ideals he so loved. These attitudes are as clear in *Beatrice* and *Eve's Sour Apples* as they are in his wartime essays.

He saw the European democracies of the 1930s and 1940s as organizations of *men* who feared the masses and fobbed them off with consumer goods (and with concomitant advertising, needed to stimulate artificial wants), instead of promoting political rights.[37] Not that he argues for conventionally defined democracy. The virtues he ascribes to the upper (he does not mean the ruling) classes are closest to his own ideal. "Let us frankly admit," he wrote in *Eve's Sour Apples*, as elsewhere, that "democracy" and, more, "socialism" mean the "exaltation of the rough and masculine lower classes" (207). Of course, *masculine* is the operative word here. Much the same view was also held by George Orwell in the 1930s, but to opposite effect. Whereas Orwell, as *The Road to Wigan Pier* demonstrates, idealized working-class men—an attitude undoubtedly related to his own masculinity complex[38]—Thomas Baty does the reverse, but both seem to be in agreement about the fundamental "masculinity" of these men. Orwell wanted everyone to "sink" to that "manly" condition; Baty, by contrast, wished everyone to "rise" to the pattern of conduct he associated with the word *aristocracy* and the ideal of the feminine.[39] This is the only future worth having. The ideal feminine type, he wrote, must have a "valiant, fearless, queenly character: but it must be too queenly to strive or cry. And if it is threatened with extinction because it will not tolerate sickening slaughter, then it will coolly accept extinction from this speck in the universe which will ultimately be left to snakes and tigers and their prey, as a prelude to its final end."[40]

Such a stance involved a developing critique of educational systems, from *Beatrice* (1909) through an essay on "Education and War" that he wrote in 1951. It is well to recall that slavery in Armeria is compared not at all unfavorably with the lot of the majority in Britain. When the narrator of *Beatrice* rather proudly explains to Nîa, a slave in Ilex's household, that the British "hate the idea of slavery, and keeping people in a class apart," and goes on to extol "the British instinct for freedom," Nîa exclaims (with all the weight of the author's satiric voice behind her): "And so nobody looks down on anybody else there! And nobody's forced to work. And everybody understands one another" (295). If, like the great majority of English children, most Armerian slaves are subject to some years of a "barrack-like system of . . . education" (64), as small children they are looked after by kindly custodians (186) and at "slave school" can receive special training as "cooks, or weavers, or attendants" should they "show themselves likely for it"—though they do not often have much choice (267–68). Such descriptions of the Armerian "slave school" call to mind the rules and regulations of ordinary English schools.

At about the age of seventeen, "slave school" pupils are selected, through something like a domestic-service agency or "registry office," by householders. If incompatibility develops, either householder or slave can apply to the government for a transfer (95–97). Numerous small references to the "enslavement" of English working-class people—by the educational system, by the Poor Law Guardians, and by the military establishment, for example—suggest that we should read Armerian slavery as a fairly benevolent system in which, in fact, "everybody is (more or less) the social equal of everyone else" (154). It is worth noting that in an encounter with a physically aggressive "peasant," the narrator, accompanied by a slave of Ilex's household, learns the extent to which some rural people "entertain a peculiar prejudice against slaves, whom they regard with hatred and contempt" and whom they loath having to treat "on an equal footing" (293). This hints at further criticism of the British class system in which "good country folk" manifested a fairly deeply rooted disdain for the urban working class. And, with reference to Thomas Baty's consistent wish that the working classes develop beyond their "masculine" nature, it is also significant that in *Beatrice*, Galesa (the Grand Steward who, as noted earlier, is clearly identified as "he" and who represents the "strain of the old brutality" characterized by the mistreatment of slaves) is further disclosed to be an enemy of the state.[41]

The state in Armeria is, of course, a worthy institution, unlike its English analogue whose mechanisms, including the educational system, Thomas Baty regarded as increasingly barbaric. Baty considered the English Education Acts (beginning in 1870) little better than heralds of "The Eclipse of English Freedom" (the title of a 1943 essay). They were intended to produce a numbing uniformity, a malleable "patriotism," and a sort of "passive literacy" useful to Whitehall bureaucrats and the upholders of the dualistic social and psychic organization he loathed. In *Eve's Sour Apples*, he decries the folly of girls' schools that had adopted the boys'-school models, and in *Urania* he promoted discussions of Montessori methods. *Urania*'s interest in Maria Montessori probably came via Dorothy Cornish, whom Dr. Montessori referred to as "my English voice."[42] Montessori believed, "If we can keep the hands of the adult generation off the child from birth until seven it will have a good chance of growing up as nature intended."[43] Happily, in Armeria, though children are born "barbarians," they are allowed what the narrator in *Beatrice* calls "natural growth" (94). They have no "school," no "lessons," but learn by observing adults and taking part "in whatever was going on." The narrator comments: "I have heard a child crossly spoken to in Armeria, but never slightingly. The children were uniformly treated as reasonable beings, and, to my surprise, I was told that they attained their majority at twelve. They were certainly precocious and self-possessed" (94). Here, as elsewhere in Thomas Baty's writings, "natural growth" means maturing from "barbaric" origins into a nongendered environment. A reality in Armeria, it was a fantasy in the world the adult Thomas had to inhabit.

As early as 1912, an item in the *Freewoman*, signed "T. Baty," provides a full version of the message that Thomas, in his own voice and as Irene Clyde, would articulate for the next forty years. The article describes the newly formed Aëthnic Union, a club that

> has nothing to say about sex in itself. But it recognises that upon the fact of sex there has been built up a gigantic superstructure of artificial convention which urgently needs to be swept away. And it does not see how it is to be swept away unless sex is resolutely ignored. The bands of custom are so interwoven with it that they cannot otherwise be broken. The admission of the idea of sex inevitably carries with it a whole flood of associations which rivet on the soul the fetters of a warped ideal. It submerges the mind in a wave of that autocratic sternness which one has been taught is the ideal of the masculine, or of that narrow triviality which one is (less successfully) taught to consider the mark of the feminine. In a word, it degrades the soul. Incidentally, it creates an iron barrier between individuals.[44]

The members of the Union, committed to the notion that "the one essential thing any human being can do for the world is to approach as near perfection as possible," rejected "the idea of these two castes, each with its inveterate faults," and refused to recognize "the differentiation which warps its ideals."[45] Baty wrote: "In the dress they wear, in the games they play, in the occupations they follow, in their very food and drink, it is constantly borne in upon people that they must assimilate themselves to one or the other imperfect type. They are never permitted to be themselves. They are forced to strangle their own free development. From that soul-murder the Union would liberate them."[46] As in Irene Clyde's writings decades later, in this essay Baty dismisses concerns for the future of the human race, observing merely that it will continue for generations. When one thinks of the difficulties that feminists have had in recent decades differentiating sex from gender, attempting to salvage the one while savaging the other, one cannot help but admire the fierce logic of Thomas Baty's ideas: gender polarization is based first of all on a simple sexual distinction. If one denies the significance of the latter, the former crumbles.

In the March–April 1919 issue of *Urania*, an editorial note emphasizes that the journal, whose own "platform is perfectly unambiguous" (and is printed as the lead statement in each issue), "has no connection with the Aëthnic Union." We assume that this was so because at least some supporters of the Aëthnic Union appear (judging from comments printed in that same issue) to have subscribed to the idea of male-female "com-plementarity," a notion *Urania* derisively labels "The 'Scissors' Defini-tion."[47] Although Thomas Baty himself, writing under his own name, did not, in early issues of *Urania*, reject such "unregenerate" views, we do have "A Letter on Love and Marriage," which he wrote in May 1926 and distributed as a pamphlet to friends. This includes a remarkably forceful and candid rejection of heterosexual convention:

> From my earliest years I hated sex. The reason was that I wanted to be a girl. I saw that ladies, while admittedly more graceful and sweet than men, were also just as determined and noble. I could not bear to be relegated to the ranks of rough and stern men.
>
> This was all a matter of vague and unreasoning desires. I only knew that I fiercely hated sex and the barrier it set up between men and women, and the limit it tried to place on any approach to my ideal.
>
> When I grew up, I reasoned it out syllogistically, so as to sat-isfy my relations and others who asked me, Why I loathed sex, and marriage, and the characteristic articels [*sic*] of male and female ap-parel. My reason was, that it riveted on the individual one of two types of character with characteristic defects. To accept a dwarfed ideal was horrible. To grovel in admiration before excellence which one did not attempt to emulate, was loathsome. It was unworthy of a human soul, to resign itself to imperfection. If the excellences of women were really admirable, then they would be admirable in anybody—(though perhaps they might not be exhibited in pre-cisely the same way). If sweetness and delicacy were right, then men ought to be sweet and delicate. If energy and determination were right, then women ought to be energetic and determined. Perfection, in short, is not divided against itself. (*Alone*, appendix 2, 188–89)[48]

"Sexual connection and marriage," Thomas Baty wrote, remained ab-horrent to him throughout his life because they are "a seal and symbol of what seems to me one of the most horrible things in creation—the inculcation in spiritual beings of grave spiritual defects—the 'mascu-line' and the 'female' shortcomings." If and when these defects were eradicated, he granted, it might be possible for "external differences to be adopted without damage and sexual marriage might be harmless." He added, "But it seems to me that the clamant need of the day for all who would avoid the conventional defects of character, is to disdain marriage entirely." Reproduction would no doubt continue, he noted, though it would not matter if it did not. In any case, parthenogenesis was becoming a distinct scientific possibility (*Alone*, 190), once again demonstrating that today's fiction becomes tomorrow's fact.

His critique of marriage is entirely cogent: "It is obvious that marriage, as an institution, must inevitably, so long as this unnatural and fiendish distortion of character persists, be the cause of unhappiness, restlessness, and disord [*sic*]. People say that 'each sex finds its completeness in marriage': but it is a shabby completeness which makes one satisfied to be a hard creature oneself, so long as one can point to a charming and agreeable wife! People who have two sharply divergent ideals for themselves can never live in harmony. It is only when each is straining, in her own way, to attain the *best* of which she can conceive, that any real harmony can be arrived at" (*Alone*, 191). In *Eve's Sour Apples* Baty makes it clear that his hatred of marriage "is not at all based on ascetic or fastidious objections" (121), and this assertion is borne out by Irene Clyde's frank discussion of masturbation in the same book, where it is noted that though the thrill of orgasm may be self-induced, only when people are of opposite sexes has this been considered "natural," whereas other means of achieving the same end are judged "unnatural." Irene Clyde called this convention into question and wrote, "It is not at all our object to dissent from terminology; we only point out that all the methods employed lead to the thrilling climax" (123).

It is important to stress how unusual, in its time, was this unapologetic reference to masturbation, for it confirms that the book's assault on heterosex does not originate in prudishness or an objection to sex as such. As Thomas Baty wrote in "A Letter on Love and Marriage": "It is merely as a means of perpetuating two obviously imperfect types of character, that I hate it [marriage] like poison. If it were made independent of sex, I should be prepared to think it an excellent idea. The union of two beings in a common endeavour . . . is an ideal which, divested of sex, has much to recommend it" (*Alone*, 191–92).[49]

On the other hand, as *Beatrice* reveals, passion divested of sexual bipolarity was indeed acceptable to him. This decentering of male sexuality is one of Thomas Baty's most interesting contributions. Again, unlike many antisex reformers and social-purity advocates, he does not endorse chastity either for its own sake or out of squeamishness but out of the conviction that heterosex imposes a deformed character on both partners.[50] Nor should he be associated with the misogynist antisex position (held, for example, by Otto Weininger) that sees female sexuality as the cause of the Fall.[51] His posture must be distinguished, as well, from the more familiar one of the Judeo-Christian tradition (especially as propounded by the church fathers). It is also to be differentiated from such "modernist" contentions as that of D. H. Lawrence, for whom self-consciousness in sex constituted the Fall.[52] By contrast, for Thomas Baty, the Fall results from the imposition not of Sex but of Gender on an integral human nature. He attempts, as we have noted, to avoid charges of puritanical impulses and hatred of the body when he envisions a time in which heterosex could be engaged in without any implications of superiority and inferiority. But he knows that this time is nowhere near at hand and that, until it comes, all heterosexual relations are contaminated by their role-playing aspects. His vision of a perfect time is not, however, a fantasy; it is concretely derived from his childhood experience and his vivid recollection of life in a household of women.

The Victorian lady, as Thomas knew her in his mother and his aunt, was free-spirited, energetic, courageous—a model for fully developed humanity. In this view he was ahead of Edward Carpenter, who envisioned in some "future" woman[53] those qualities that Thomas saw in actuality in the 1880s: sweetness, delicacy, tenacity, perseverance, courage. He was well ahead too of Havelock Ellis, who, like other "sex reformers," believed in immutable innate differences between men and women and promoted "complementarity," a state of affairs that left women "separate but equal." In challenging the very notion of distinct sex roles, Thomas Baty argued in *Eve's Sour Apples* that the "new freedom" of the 1920s was "turning out to be not a freedom at all—but the acceptance of the tyranny of sex as inevitable and ineluctable" (5).[54] Just so, we imagine, he would have judged the "sexual revolution" of the 1960s and the "radical feminism" and "new men's movement" of today—all of which are rooted in gender.

His valuation of his own childhood also provides the firm basis for what he calls his Toryism. His political posture is made explicit in *Eve's Sour Apples*:

> When the writer first became interested in public affairs she found herself working along with people with whom she heartily agreed on all sorts of humanitarian questions. Not that they were sentimentalists—far from it: but they did not believe in beating children for trifles . . . —nor in torturing criminals—nor in eating corpses—nor in killing animals for fun—nor in tearing men to pieces limb from limb, for the privilege of being governed by one set of gentlemen rather than another—nor in wading precariously to health through the blood and quivering nerves of help-

less beasts—nor in many of the like playful pastimes of civilized humanity. But she began to reflect, to her surprise, that everyone of her coworkers was a Radical, if not a Socialist: and she was a long-horned Tory. Puzzling over this phenomenon, she came to realize that it was her Feminism—her devotion to the spirit of sweet-ness—that was the core and foundation of all her other "isms". She loathed all the cruelties against which she and her companions protested, because they denied Beauty. And her conviction grew, that in advocating the rule of the lower orders, her companions were denying Beauty too. They seemed to her to be bent upon ex-tinguishing that delicacy and considerateness which existed in the cultured classes, if anywhere. (214–15)

There follows a long and interesting defense of the "real Tory"—one who believes in "Kingship, otherwise Leadership," and tradition and neighborliness, "in short, in Politics as an Art, and not as a Machine" (217), and who is critical of the "slippery slope of numerical equality [which] has landed us, as anyone might have foreseen, in universal suf-frage and the dictatorship of wire-pullers. The development which has given a vote to most women has coincidently deprived the vote of all value" (217–18). "The essence of Toryism," Thomas Baty asserted, "was to deny the value of quantity, and to insist upon quality" (219). But Toryism failed to see that "the qualities for whose preservation it stood were the Feminine qualities" (220). "Toryism fell by failing to be femi-nine. It is a pathetic thing that it grasped at Feminism as it fell. The last really popular Tory activity was the foundation of the Primrose League." This leads to his conclusion that feminism, pacifism, and aristocracy are "inseparably bound up together" (221).

Thomas Baty's kind of "Toryism" recognized "every virtue"—gra-ciousness and sweetness *and* breadth and vigor. Opening our minds to these qualities in all people, he asked, could we not trample under our feet the "signs and symbols of a stunted endeavour—the rags and tatters of a sex-ridden humanity?" (223, 235). If democracy meant empower-ment of the less cultivated (and less feminine), he favored a very different course: the slow raising of the masses to the level of those who were better trained in consideration and delicacy, who were, "in short, more feminine."[55]

Like his disdain for socialism and Marxism, Baty's disdain for democ-racy rests on two premises. The first is that democracy runs roughshod over the claims and rights of minorities. Second, he sees democracy as fostering "materialism" (quantity not quality), which, in all its forms, he rejected. He hated the manipulation of people by advertising. And he detested, as well, the "materialist" attitude to sexuality. As he wrote in a letter to George Ives: "At present I am much irritated by the 'biological' sex-ridden people, who would insist on our tying ourselves down by our physical characteristics*—about the true necessities of which they know very little. Any day some obscure gland or atomic structure may prove to be the real determinant of mental & moral character, even on their own materialistic conceptions of life." [56]

Thomas Baty's extraordinary, lifelong, radical analysis of international, national, and personal politics seems to us to have developed from an insight he gained when very young, at the time that, as he says in *Eve's Sour Apples*, children's "fellowship with perfection is unbroken—[when] they are free to follow their best imaginings" (34). As we are told in *Eve's Sour Apples*, at age eleven Irene Clyde was "planning an ideal Utopia"—and although at around eleven a child is forced into some acknowledgment of its gendered condition, Thomas Baty sustained that child's "fellowship" (137).

His "best" world had been that of his childhood, a "Golden Age" lasting through the 1870s and 1880s, a time he characterizes, in both his personae, as the "apex of civilization," free of gendered distortions and impositions. Not surprisingly, he paid considerable attention to how gender indoctrination occurs in childhood. *Eve's Sour Apples* contains a veritable catalogue of the ways:

> Suggestion hampers the child at every turn. From three years old upwards,
>
> In its dress,
> In its boots,
> In its games,
> In its hats,
> In its umbrellas,
> In its talk,
> In its books,
> In its companions,
> In its hair,
> In its manners,
> In its occupations
> and to a certain extent, in its food and drink—a malformation is impressed on its development. From particular gifts and graces it is cut off. It is borne in upon it at every turn that it must be a "boy" or a "girl"; that it must be stern or unenterprising.

A useful and necessary specialization, does the reader think? That is a profound mistake: one cannot specialize in virtues as in tulips. (39)

This sense of engendering as the basic fault in human society he articulated with perfect cogency, and though Freudians may sneer, we must observe that Baty's nostalgic view of a pregendered childhood was in fact a view of an undistorted premale condition. Simone de Beauvoir observed, "One is not born a woman." Decades earlier, Thomas Baty had noted that no one is born a "man." Observing how people are made into "men" and "women," he opted always for what he saw as the best, the feminine, and wanted it to serve as the model, the aspiration, for all human beings. He called for a change not away from nature but back *toward* a natural striving for perfection and completion, which is, in his view, *deformed* by imposed gender roles. He is not saying that we should teach males and females to be alike but rather that we should stop interfering with the natural inclination toward unity and perfection. "Perfect and full-orbed, though unexpanded," is how he describes childhood in *Eve's Sour Apples* (33). Teaching gender not only prevents expansion but also "assiduously cultivates vice in the child" (41).

While staying always close to the integral world of his childhood, in geographical terms Thomas Baty took himself far from the fragmented Europe of the early twentieth century. Japan, whose art and "spirit" he had long admired, seemed more of what he wished England could be. It was more "real," perhaps, than what England had become. Analogously, "Irene Clyde" achieved a new sort of reality through the journal *Urania*, which began to appear the very year Thomas left England with his mother, sister, and young cousin, Esther. In *Urania*, Irene Clyde comes into existence as part of an editorial "we" and as a real-world figure who comments on actual events—both material and intellectual—in a variety of capacities. In a sense, then, Thomas Baty's geographic "exile" was a sort of "coming home to oneself," to the assumption of an identity he had "longed passionately" to have since the age of eight—that of a lady. In the words of Ilex, the beloved of the narrator in *Beatrice*: "The only way to do anything worth living for, is to believe with all your heart in impossibilities. Then they become possible" (186–87).

Achieving such a "fantastic" identity did not mean that Baty neglected his duties as legal adviser to the Japanese Foreign Office. He took his official obligations seriously and performed them conscientiously. In 1938, after his criticism of a British-led inquiry (the Lytton Commission) into the Japanese incursion into Manchuria, and in response to a request by Japan that the British prime minister send Baty greetings on the occasion of his seventieth birthday in 1939, a British Foreign Office minute observed: "He is an employee of the Japanese Govt. and as such his conscience (nobody could accuse Dr. Baty of being anything but an honest man) would not allow him to give other than his best to them. The advice he has given has, of course, often been in conflict with the interests of H.M.G., but he is not the kind of man to permit his nationality to weight his advice against his employers."[57] Three years later, in 1941, Britain's declaration of war on Japan disrupted Thomas's perfect exile. Because he did not leave on the ship provided for foreign nationals but chose, instead, to be faithful to his adopted country (for whom, however, he stopped working as soon as the rupture between the two countries was official), and because he published, during those years, essays critical of the Allied war effort,[58] the British government branded him a traitor. According to one anecdote, possibly apocryphal, Thomas put on a kimono and applied to become a subject of the emperor.[59] More telling of his possible sentiments is the action of his heroine in *Beatrice*: Mary Hatherley, though she does not take on the citizenship of Armeria, de facto strips herself of British citizenship by staying with the person she loves.

Earlier, Thomas Baty had been able to live his identities separately, but as the war constricted his movements and associations, he no longer had the option of maintaining his varied identities in a "fantastic" but workable harmony. War regiments the population, as he had noted in 1915; that is what, in its "masculine ferocity," it does. And that is what it did to him. Thomas Baty's "identity" was not that of a British citizen. He was born in and lived in England; thereafter his domicile was in Japan. His being, however, and perhaps his home, were in Urania.

But the war changed everything. Not only was his connection with the Japanese Foreign Office severed, but, as far as we know, he also lost the other place he inhabited, Urania. We can trace no copies of the publication beyond 1940. When his sister died in 1945 (he was thankful she had "escaped" the worst—the unremitting firebombing and what, from perhaps a combination of "delicacy" and utter horror, he does not directly mention, the destruction of Hiroshima and Nagasaki), he was truly "Alone in Japan."[60] In the late forties, the British government's withdrawal of his passport cut him off from his other community—the international law association's meetings. As his worlds dimmed, he wrote *International Law in Twilight*, in which a lone footnote guardedly acknowledges his pseudonym: "Reference may perhaps . . . be allowed to two books published under the name of I. Clyde, *Eve's Sour Apples* . . . and *Beatrice the Sixteenth* . . . which the curious may care to consult."[61]

After the war, Thomas Baty was angry that in continuing to refuse him a passport, the British government impeded his movements and penalized him for what he considered his "right" to speak his mind. The British "crowd" in Tokyo "cut" him, he told Edmund Blunden in a 1951 letter. Whereas his own government deemed him a traitor—a charge against which he defended himself in private correspondence[62]—the Japanese government bestowed on him the First Order of Merit with the Sacred Treasure. When he died in 1954, the Japanese Foreign Office sponsored his funeral, and the epitaph on his tombstone (he is buried beside his mother and his sister, ever his companions) commemorates "a gentleman and a scholar."[63] He was one of those eccentric Englishmen, we would say, who, according to his intellectual abilities and his cultural tastes, fashioned his own identity. And that identity included the creation of his preferred self, "Irene Clyde," the name under which he wrote for more than thirty years. The fact that he maintained the persona of Irene Clyde intact while apparently not concealing his iconoclastic ideas is another piece of evidence of his utter conviction and adherence to principle. As far as we know, not once did he use his real-world authority as a prominent jurist, a widely known writer, and an influential man to promote this persona. He brought her into "public life" in 1909, into the polemical world of ideas, and there she existed on her own for more than three decades.

Of course, lacking access to any medical records, we do not know for a fact that Thomas Baty was the male his baptismal entry says he was. And that this fact is likely to seem important to most people today is perhaps a sign of just how far we are from the kind of world he envisioned and attempted to create for himself. But we know more about the principles that guided Thomas Baty's life than it is usually given us to know about anyone. Accounts from two very different sources suggest the perfect integration of character he achieved. Motokichi Hasegawa, his close friend and literary executor, wrote (making a distinction that Thomas would probably have found ironic): "He was honest, fair, independent, and kind, not to speak of his genuine politeness. And effeminate as he was in manners, he was most masculine and stern in intellect."[64] The writer Oswald Wynd, known in this country for his novel *The Ginger Tree* (a dramatization of which was broadcast on public television in 1990) spent his childhood in Japan, where his missionary parents were friends of Thomas Baty's. Wynd recalls a very formal dinner party at the legal adviser's Foreign Office residence, at which Wynd, aged seventeen, first wore a tuxedo. He remembers Thomas as "very much the Oxbridge intellectual, precise in manner and speech, defending his privacy against your curiosity . . . with an impeccable politeness." Wynd adds, "I remember that [he] was nice to me . . . not patronizing, a shy, rather gentle creature who didn't quite know how to handle this half American roughneck whom he was entertaining for his parents' sake."[65] Baty was not afraid to display to the world his preference for feminine ways. Hasegawa notes that Thomas Baty "buttoned up his overcoat with the left side under the right. He carried a lady's umbrella. Though he never learned to speak Japanese fluently, a few expressions he picked up were ladies' language of 'asobase' style. His handshake was as gentle as a lady's."[66]

A third source, obtained by us in 1992, completes the portrait. Julian Franklyn (whose name we first encountered in his 1934 *Urania* review of *Eve's Sour Apples*) shared with Thomas Baty a great love for "that science of pure brilliance"—heraldry. Baty's book *Vital Heraldry* was posthumously published, in 1962, with Franklyn's help, Baty having provided for this in his will. In the introduction to the volume, Julian Franklyn described their first meeting. He had been urged by their mutual friend (and Montessorian) Dorothy Cornish to meet someone Franklyn assumed would be a "dry-as-dust-lawyer, one of the world's authorities on International Law—probably interested in Finance and Affairs as well as Politics." Franklyn wondered, "What could one talk about to such a man?"[67] Dorothy Cornish, however, had her way. In 1934,[68] her two friends met at a "stuffy, stultifying establishment, the Holborn Restaurant," a roast-beef-and-Yorkshire-pudding place befitting Franklyn's image of the sort of restaurant where a "formidable international jurist" should take lunch. Julian Franklyn, the young largely self-educated cockney, not yet the popular lecturer on heraldry, the well-known writer on the occult, and the member of several learned societies,[69] felt—as he put it—"apprehensive," but then "the call-boy (if such he was) performed his function, and Dr. Baty advanced. I saw a small, neat man, immaculate in the black jacket and striped trousers of his breed. He wore an exaggerated wing-poke collar and a cravat: his lips were colourless and contracted: he did not smile. When he extended his hand in greeting his sombre eyes lit up, his withdrawn expression melted away. Dr. Baty, Chief Legal Adviser to the Foreign Office of Japan, disappeared, and in his place stood Irene Clyde, a gentle, kindly, witty and intelligent elderly lady."[70]

Nearly three decades later, Julian Franklyn wrote that Thomas Baty, "having devoted his life to the establishing of Justice between nations for the maintenance of peace," turned to heraldry "for solace" during the dreadful years of World War II. It was during this time too that he wrote his memoir, *Alone in Japan*, and a number of articles about the influence of Japanese culture on the Western world. Informed by the notion that life should be, as he described heraldry, "brim-full of romance and imaginative beauty," Baty's vision of Urania was so spacious that it could accommodate, as well, the legal mind that argued that justice and peace were possible. The most essential, most basic way by which these goals could be attained was, in Thomas Baty's view, to make the "otherness" of sex, the division by sex, irrelevant. But—and we wish to be clear about this—his was no run-of-the-mill androgynous vision, for he maintained—with "courageous logic," as Julian Franklyn put it— that the best of human characteristics were those defined as "feminine": sweetness and courage, beauty and persistence.[71]

Valuing the feminine as he did, not being a homosexual man (and thus lacking the option enjoyed by Edward Carpenter, that of positing a "third sex"), and given his evaluation of masculinity, Thomas Baty could not help but feel that he was the "wrong" sex. What he in fact wished— as he repeatedly said—was to be a woman, a woman unencumbered by the conventional gender polarization that barred the way to a perfect unity of identity. He wished male and female to be one, and that one to be more female than male. For over four decades he lived out that wish through the persona of Irene Clyde.

Because his world, like ours, was so far from being what one would wish, and because in Irene Clyde's best possible world the dualism of gender is overcome, we consider it perfectly fitting that Thomas Baty should, at least posthumously, achieve part of his heart's desire. That is why, in this volume of essays on British women writers whose work radically questioned and subverted the status quo, we include Irene Clyde/ Thomas Baty. Perfection is one.

Notes

1. Irene Clyde (pseud.), *Beatrice the Sixteenth* (London: George Bell, 1909). Daphne Patai first came across this novel in 1980 but was told by Lyman Tower Sargent, the author of *British and American Utopian Literature, 1516–1985: An Annotated, Chronological Bibliography* (New York: Garland, 1988) and the leading contemporary bibliographer of utopian fiction in the English language, that this was not a utopia and hence was of no relevance to her search for forgotten utopias by women. Simply to leave no stone unturned, she read the book any-

way. It is discussed, briefly, in Daphne Patai, "When Women Rule: Defamiliar-ization in the Sex-Role Reversal Utopia," *Extrapolation* 23 (Spring 1982): 68–69 n. 21. Angela Ingram joined in the search for Irene Clyde in 1987, and since then the two of us have been collaborating on this project.

2. Thomas More, *Utopia*, translated by Paul Turner (Harmondsworth, Middlesex: Penguin, 1965). See, for example: "Another type of slave is the working-class foreigner who, rather than live in wretched poverty at home, vol-unteers for slavery in Utopia. Such people are treated with respect, and with almost as much kindness as Utopian citizens, except that they're made to work harder, because they're used to it. If they want to leave the country, which doesn't often happen, they're perfectly free to do so, and receive a small gra-tuity" (102). It is worth noting a rather similar notion of "slavery" in *The Story of the Amulet* (London: T. Fisher Unwin, 1906), by the popular children's writer E. Nesbit. The association between "Modern Babylon" (London) and ancient Babylon having been made, the novel's children-protagonists go back to Baby-lon, which is described in terms not unlike those used for the city in Armeria, though its queen is certainly unlike the grave and gentle Beatrice. When the queen magically comes to London, the children take her on a "tour," which in-cludes the Mile End Road. Here she observes: "But how badly you keep your slaves. How wretched and poor and neglected they seem" (195). Told that these are not slaves but "working-people," she replies: "Of course they're working-people. That's what slaves are. Don't you tell me. Do you suppose I don't know a slave's face when I see it? Why don't their masters see that they're better fed and better clothed? Tell me in three words." The children cannot, for, as the narrator says, "The wage-system in modern England is a little difficult to explain in three words even if you understand it—which the children didn't" (195–96). The tone of this, as of the queen's dismissal of the fact that the modern slaves have a vote—with which they apparently do nothing—is very close to the tone of Mary's dis-cussions with various Armerians about the (to them) incomprehensible social and political customs of England.

3. Shlomo Avineri, "War and Slavery in More's *Utopia*," *International Review of Social History* 7 (1962): 260–90, points out that slavery in *Utopia* bears a moral, not an economic, stigma. Avineri's essay is a fascinating study of several centuries of scholarly debate over the most problematic features of More's famous work.

4. See Teresa de Lauretis, *Technologies of Gender* (Bloomington: Indiana Uni-versity Press, 1987). In discussing Lucy Bland's essay "The Domain of the Sexual: A Response," *Screen Education* 39 (Summer 1981): 56–67, which takes issue with Foucault's failure to note that sexuality is gendered—that is, has a male and a female form—de Lauretis says: "The conception of sexuality held by feminists of the first wave, at the turn of the century, was no exception: whether they called for 'purity' and opposed all sexual activity for degrading women to the level of men, or whether they called for a free expression of the 'natural' func-tion and 'spiritual' quality of sex on the part of women, sex meant heterosexual intercourse and primarily penetration. It is only in contemporary feminism that the notions of a different or autonomous sexuality of women and of non-male-related sexual identities for women have emerged" (14). Even so, Bland argues, displacing from center stage the sexual act as penetration is a task we still face today. This task is adumbrated in *Beatrice the Sixteenth*.

5. Ursula Le Guin, *The Left Hand of Darkness* (New York: Ace, 1969). Le Guin's short story "Winter's King," first published in 1969, is an early version of the novel, which was written, she says, before she realized that its Gethenian protagonists were androgynous. When the story was reprinted in 1975, Le Guin took the opportunity to respond to critics of *The Left Hand of Darkness* and revised her use of pronouns, opting for a generic "she" but retaining such terms as "the king" and "my lord." She explains this decision in the introduction to the revised version of "Winter's King," in her volume *The Wind's Twelve Quarters* (New York: Harper and Row, 1975), 92–93. With this change, the story of the Gethenian "king" Argaven XVII and the plot against "her" reign takes on a marked resemblance to *Beatrice the Sixteenth* and highlights Irene Clyde's originality in 1909.

6. Fredric Jameson, *Postmodernism; or, The Cultural Logic of Late Capitalism* (Durham: Duke University Press, 1991). Jameson states: "Modern science fiction has often been a laboratory for such language experiments, as in Ursula LeGuin's model of the social structure of a hermaphroditic species (for which she uses only the masculine gender), in *The Left Hand of Darkness* (New York, 1969), or Samuel R. Delany's elaborate 'reply,' in *Stars in My Pocket Like Grains of Sand* (New York, 1984), in which (for sexually differentiated beings of our own type) the feminine pronoun is used universally for the psychic subject, while the masculine pronoun is restricted to a person who is the object of desire (of whatever physical sex)" (422–23).

7. Dale Spender, *Invisible Women: The Schooling Scandal* (London: Writers and Readers Cooperative, 1982), 1.

8. Irene Clyde (pseud.), *Eve's Sour Apples* (London: Eric Partridge, 1934).

9. Too late for more than a brief mention in this essay, we found Claudia Nelson's *Boys Will Be Girls: The Feminine Ethic in British Children's Fiction, 1857–1917* (New Brunswick, N.J.: Rutgers University Press, 1991), which most persuasively argues that "the Victorian stereotype of childhood had much in common with the feminine ideal" (2) and that "the primary motivation behind the emotional didacticism of many Victorian authors for children is implicitly the desire to rebuild society, not by changing human laws but by changing human nature. The closer men could approximate the Angel, the better for humankind" (4–5). Only in the later years of Victoria's reign, Nelson states, did a "masculine," militarist, imperialist ideal for the best British type gain real prominence. This corrective to our general notions of Victorian literature shows us that by 1909 (the date of *Beatrice*), the trend toward a popular version of Darwinism and the increasingly widespread ideas of the "sexologists" was fairly firmly entrenched. In this ideological context, *Beatrice* and *Eve's Sour Apples* were not only "oppositional" but deliberately "backward looking," to a far more radical view of gender.

10. Furthermore, jacket blurbs for both the English edition of Andrea Dworkin, *Intercourse* (London: Secker and Warburg, 1987) and the American edition (New York: Free Press, 1987) quote such critics as Mary Daly, Germaine Greer, Shere Hite, Robin Morgan, and Michael Moorcock—all of them celebrating Dworkin's originality. Nonetheless, a world of difference separates Irene Clyde's indictment of heterosex from that of Andrea Dworkin: Irene Clyde's critique is sometimes acerbic, often witty, and always humane.

11. *Times Literary Supplement*, 7 February 1935, 80.

12. Cited on the end page of *Urania*, no. 117–18 (May–August 1936).

13. The reference to "mental and moral inferiority" echoes Virginia Woolf's *Room of One's Own* (1929; reprint, New York: Harcourt Brace Jovanovich, 1957), 31, in which she refers to a Professor von X, author of a book entitled *The Mental, Moral, and Physical Inferiority of the Female Sex*. On Woolf's allusion to Otto Weininger in this passage, see Virginia Woolf, *Women and Fiction: The Manuscript Versions of "A Room of One's Own,"* edited by Pat Rosenbaum (Oxford: Shakespeare Head Press, Blackwell, 1992), 207 nn. 44–45; also on Weininger, see note 51 below.

14. An interesting contemporaneous but alternative reading of the problem of "possession" of women by men is provided by Naomi Mitchison in her book *The Home and a Changing Civilisation* (London: John Lane, Bodley Head, 1934). Mitchison argues that we need to distinguish between two aspects of ownership and that women's guilt at being overwhelmed and "possessed" by a man is due to confusion of the two sorts of possession. "One's historical mind gets at one, pointing out that one is the 'weaker sex,' for this reason oppressed and exploited, and one mixes that up with what ought to be the very pleasant feeling of being gripped by muscles of a different strength and texture to one's own, and, hating the one, one's hatred is transferred to the other. One wants, passionately, *not* to be the weaker, and this is understandable considering the history of the last several thousand years, but why on earth should one bother? Men are weaker than elephants and less able to do lots of things: but elephants do not oppress them" (146–47). The sort of "possession" associated with being in love, Mitchison argues, adds something to, rather than takes away from, both partners and should not be confused with the unacceptable and demeaning social possession of women by men.

15. On the term *pacificism*, see Martin Ceadel, *Pacifism in Britain, 1914–1945: The Defining of a Faith* (Oxford: Clarendon Press, 1980):

> Strictly, 'pacificism' and 'pacifism' are not different words: the former is simply the original and correct form of the word which right from the start was sometimes—and is now invariably—contracted to the latter. . . . The pristine meaning of the word pacificism (variant: pacifism) was not what is now understood as pacifism but what is here analysed as *pacificism*: when coined in the first decade of the twentieth century, pacificism meant no more than being in favor of peace and arbitration and opposed to militarism and settling disputes by war; and, on its first appearance in any of the Oxford dictionaries, in the addenda dated September 1914 of the *Concise Oxford Dictionary*, it was defined as "the doctrine that the abolition of war is both desirable and possible." (Absolute pacifism tended to be described, on the rare occasions the distinction was perceived, as "extreme" pacificism—or "extreme" pacifism—or as the doctrine of non-resistance.) (3–4, italics in original)

16. Letter from Lesley Hall, 12 February 1990. Without this response to our inquiry, we might never have identified Irene Clyde. We continue to be immensely grateful to Lesley Hall for her letter, which began a very fruitful correspondence.

17. Although we have still not located the important initial issues, we have managed to get an almost complete photocopied run of the journal. We wish to thank Professor Will Corral of Stanford University for helping us to trace many copies of *Urania*. We are also extremely grateful to David Doughan, reference librarian at the Fawcett Library in London, for his most helpful, scholarly, and enthusiastic interest, for his often hilarious speculations, and not least, for his help in tracing other copies of *Urania*.

18. Since we have not been able to get our hands on the first issues of *Urania*, we do not know whether the journal's editors were identified and whether the title itself was discussed. The name *Urania* suggests numerous interpretations, which include reference to the late-nineteenth-century "Uranian" poets, who celebrated man-boy love, and to Karl Heinrich Ulrichs (1825–95), whose many works arguing that homosexuality was congenital and not the result of moral, intellectual, or psychological defects used the term *Urning* for homosexual men—taking the term, as did the "Uranian" poets, from the myth of Uranus. But the myth itself has several components, and these can be used to contradictory effect. Two different accounts exist of the birth of Aphrodite, goddess of love. These accounts—from Plato to Ulrichs—depict Aphrodite as born either of a male and a female deity or of Uranus alone, after his genitals were cut off by his son Cronos. In this latter instance, she is Aphrodite Urania, the goddess of pure or intellectual love. See Timothy d'Arch Smith, *Love in Earnest: Some Notes on the Lives and Writings of English 'Uranian' Poets from 1889 to 1930* (London: Routledge and Kegan Paul, 1970), and Pierre Grimal, *The Dictionary of Classical Mythology*, translated by A. R. Maxwell-Hyslop (Oxford: Basil Blackwell, 1986), 46. On Ulrichs, see John Addington Symonds, *A Problem in Modern Ethics, Being an Inquiry into the Phenomenon of Sexual Inversion* (London: N.p., 1896), chap. 7, 84–114; John Lauritsen and David Thorstad, *The Early Homosexual Rights Movement (1864–1935)* (New York: Times Change Press, 1974), 72–73; and Jeffrey Weeks, *Coming Out: Homosexual Politics in Britain, from the Nineteenth Century to the Present* (London: Quartet Books, 1977), 26–27. However, nowhere in the writings of "Irene Clyde" and the journal *Urania* is there the remotest suggestion of a celebration of male-male love—far from it. Perhaps the journal *Urania* simply refers to Urania as Heavenly Dweller, for a Greek motto also appears in the journal: *All' eisin hos angeloi* (But they are all angels)— that is, sexless. Or perhaps a more subversive hint resides in the evocation of Uranus, who becomes fertile through the loss of his genitals. Gifford Lewis, in *Eva Gore-Booth and Esther Roper: A Biography* (London: Pandora, 1988), 5, suggests only a Miltonic association with the term *Urania*.

19. The September-December 1932 *Urania* refers to a cartoon that appeared in *Punch* (23 November 1932, 563), citing a remarkable speech made by Stanley Baldwin in the House of Commons on 10 November 1932. Depicting two men in a laboratory, the cartoon has the older man, looking at a beaker containing a death's head, say to the younger (who is glancing up through the window, toward shadowy airplane forms): "You realise what this means. It is you and your young companions who will use it. What are we to do?" This is followed by a quotation from Baldwin's speech: "The young men . . . are the men who fly in the air. . . . The instrument is in their hands. . . . It is for them to decide." Baldwin regarded a buildup of conventional armaments as no guarantee

of maintaining peace or winning a war. A.J.P. Taylor notes: "He told the house of commons: 'the bomber will always get through', and concluded with the extraordinary remark that, if war came, the youth of the world would be to blame for allowing older men to make a mess of things. 'When the next war comes . . . then do not let them lay blame on the old men. Let them remember that they, they principally or they alone, are responsible for the terrors that have fallen upon the earth.'" This, Taylor comments, "was next door to an invitation for undergraduates to vote for the 'King and Country' resolution," that is, the Oxford Union resolution that "this House will not fight for King and Country" (A.J.P. Taylor, *English History, 1914–1945* [New York: Oxford University Press, 1965], 364).

20. Eva Gore-Booth, patron and supporter of *Urania*, is repeatedly quoted in the journal as saying that "sex is an accident." See, for example, the unsigned article "Science Confirms Intuition," *Urania*, no. 29–30 (September–December 1921), 1.

21. On the late-nineteenth-century doctrine of "scientific materialism," see D. C. Somervell, *English Thought in the Nineteenth Century* (1929; reprint, New York: David McKay, 1969).

22. To obtain this sort of scope today, we would have to put together Greenpeace, Amnesty International, National Organization for Women, Women's International League for Peace and Freedom, American Friends Service Committee, World Federalists, Planned Parenthood, and a large number of feminist journals. Perhaps, today, the U.S. feminist monthly *Off Our Backs* comes closest to suggesting the scope of *Urania*, but to it would have to be added the overarching concern with nothing less than the total abolition of "gender."

23. Janice Raymond's *The Transsexual Empire: The Making of the She-Male* (Boston: Beacon, 1979), is illuminating in this regard. Although Raymond makes no effort to understand the inner world of transsexuals, she presents the telling argument that people seeking sex-change surgery hold such a deep belief in the reality of gender identity, and so desperately feel they can live out their "true" nature only in a particular sort of body, that they subject their bodies to mutilation. Raymond's point is that this constitutes not a rejection but rather an embrace of gender roles.

24. This is apparent from both the style and the content of items appearing in *Urania* and is further confirmed in the obituary by Hasegawa referred to in note 64 below.

25. The "contacts" listed were J. Wade, E. Gore-Booth and E. Roper, D. H. Cornish, and T. Baty. Although, as far as we know, Eva Gore-Booth never wrote anything in *Urania*, on the basis of our examination of the journal it is clear that she was one of the most important spirits behind it. In *Urania*, no. 113–14 (September–December 1935), 2, she is referred to as "one of the founders of *Urania*." Starting shortly after her death, a few lines from one of her poems was used as an epigraph in *Urania*, and a loving obituary, probably composed by T. Baty, appeared in the journal in 1926. Settlement work, vegetarianism, pacifism, and of course women's suffrage—all these were causes to which Eva Gore-Booth and Esther Roper (with whom she lived for decades) were passionately committed.

26. Thomas Baty, *Alone in Japan: The Reminiscences of an International Jurist*

Resident in Japan, 1916–1954 (Tokyo: Maruzen, 1959), 186 (hereafter cited paren-thetically in the text as *Alone*). Other information in this paragraph was provided by *Who Was Who, 1951–1960*, vol. 5 (London: Adam and Charles Black, 1961); *New York Times* obituary, 10 February 1954, 29; and personal communication from I. G. Murray, Archivist, the Honourable Society of the Inner Temple, 19 July 1990. In *Alone in Japan*, Baty says he was "called to the English Bar (Inner Temple), 1895" (186). Inner Temple registers show he was admitted on 21 January 1896.

27. See Thomas Baty to Blunden, 25 September 1950, Blunden, E. C., Letters, Harry Ransom Humanities Research Center, Austin, Texas.

28. "Dr. Thomas Baty," *Times*, 10 February 1954, 29.

29. "Irene Clyde," in *Eve's Sour Apples*, says: "I loved my French and my Prus-sian tin soldiers in 1873, and never for one instant conceived of their doing one another the remotest harm—much less convert the nursery table into a mess of mangled flesh and groaning horses. Tin soldiers will not make one a militant" (213). This detail was an early clue as to the probable birthdate of our author, long before we knew who "Irene Clyde" was.

30. Personal communication from I. G. Murray, 19 July 1990.

31. Thomas Baty to Blunden, 15 January 1954, Blunden, E. C., Letters, Harry Ransom Humanities Research Center, Austin, Texas.

32. C. G. Fenwick, *American Political Science Review* 4 (1910): 436. In *Interna-tional Law in Twilight* (Tokyo: Maruzen, 1954), his last book, Thomas also refers to the imposition of democracy as "Bureaucracy disguised as Freedom" (10).

33. See *Advocate of Peace* 72 (February 1910): 14.

34. George Jellinek, *The Rights of Minorities*, translated by A. M. Baty and T. Baty (1898; reprint, London: P. S. King and Son, 1912).

35. See the article "The League of Nations—and the League of Little Women," signed by Irene Clyde, in *Urania*, no. 24 (November–December 1920), 2–3.

36. It is a measure of Baty's disillusionment with the United Nations (a dis-illusionment surely enhanced for many of his generation who had thought, however momentarily, that the League of Nations might function as its rheto-ric had suggested it would) that the title of his last, posthumously published book is *International Law in Twilight*. It was his first book in twenty years and well expresses his discouragement. "International law, which rests on the world's common convictions, must inevitably sustain profound eclipse when the world ceases to have any" (13). Characteristically taking the nineteenth century as "a remarkable era of peace and progress," when "each nation was content to man-age its own affairs without interference" (273), he argues that the world crisis cannot be resolved by material means but rather demands "an altogether new outlook" (299–300). The way lies in "the dethronement of the masculine." He wrote: "Masculine violence has brought about its inevitable catastrophe. Many men display in the highest degree the feminine excellences, and in the estab-lishment of peace and harmony and the quelling of arrogance the according of the world-wide acclaim to the Feminine as supereminent is the only possible path" (300).

37. Thomas Baty, "Democracy in Europe," *Contemporary Japan*, January 1941, 35–36; this essay argues that at about the turn of the century, "the cultivated

classes capitulated to the proletariat" (27). Portions of this essay appear almost verbatim in *Eve's Sour Apples*.

38. See Daphne Patai, *The Orwell Mystique: A Study in Male Ideology* (Amherst: University of Massachusetts Press, 1984), chap. 3, "Vagabondage and Labor: The Masculine Mystique." Whereas Baty feared that socialism would establish the crude masculinity of the working class as the behavioral norm, Orwell, by contrast, feared that socialism would "soften" society, would deprive it of the tough working-class characteristics he found so desirable.

39. To understand Thomas Baty's use of the word *aristocracy*, one should note that he is speaking of manners and morals, not of politics. Thus, he holds it as a general ideal of human behavior, which should be inculcated in all people, not as one extreme of a polarization that depends on a demeaned "other" for its significance (see, for example, the discussion of Toryism in *Eve's Sour Apples*, 215). Perhaps a related notion is apparent in the utopian novel of Mrs. Alice Elinor Bartlett (Birch Arnold, pseud.), *The New Aristocracy* (New York: Bartlett Publishing Co., 1891), in which two sisters display an "aristocracy of heart and brain" and advocate the transformation of the world by a return to true Christian values: nonviolence, universal brotherhood, justice, and happiness, attainable through community work and responsibility to one's fellows. To all this, however, Thomas Baty would add an aesthetic dimension.

40. T. Baty, "Feminism and Pacificism," *Contemporary Review*, July 1939, 99.

41. The only other named character in *Beatrice* who is said to keep an oppressively sharp eye on her slaves is a secondary court official who also betrays the trust of the queen and therefore of the entire state.

42. Quoted in Rita Kramer, *Maria Montessori: A Biography* (New York: G. P. Putnam's Sons, 1976), 294.

43. Quoted in ibid., 261.

44. T. Baty, "The Aëthnic Union," *Freewoman*, 12 February 1912, 278. The name of the union is explained: the Greeks have no specific word for sex. Instead, they have *genos*, *phyle*, *ethnos*—but all these terms also have others meanings: *genos* is more often a "kind"; *phyle* is more often a "tribe"; and *ethnos* is more often a "race." The last term provided the Aëthnic Union with its name. We have not yet been able to locate information about the Union's membership and activities.

45. Ibid., 279.

46. Ibid. This passage closely resembles *Eve's Sour Apples*, 39.

47. "A Symposium," *Urania*, no. 14 (March–April 1919), 2. See also the article entitled "The Megatherium," signed "I.C.," in the same issue, 4–5.

48. Virtually identical words appear in *Eve's Sour Apples*, 28–30, and elsewhere in writings signed "Irene Clyde."

49. This is the recognizable message of all Irene Clyde's writings as well. Consider, for example, the following item from *Urania*, no. 107–8 (September–December 1934), signed with the initials "I.C.":

We confess to a feeling of considerable astonishment when people attribute to us the idea that in every married couple the one partner is a brutal tyrant and the other a cringing slave. How could anyone be so foolish! What we do say is that the conventional masculine character is somewhat truculent, and the conventional feminine character somewhat tame—and that the recognition of sex in any way—and especially in the conspicuous way of marriage, is wrong and reprehensible, as tending to emphasize the difference and to perpetuate these defects. It is not the fact of marriage that creates them: it is rather that it is only a person who has been taught to tolerate the distinction and its tendency to produce defects, who will be capable of marriage.

Marriage is objectionable only because it is an emphatic acceptance of the difference of the sexes upon which is traditionally, conventionally, and for all I know, naturally, based a difference of character which it must be the object of all who desire to leave each individual free to cultivate the real or supposed virtue of the opposite sex, to eradicate.

Marriage does not create a tyrant and a slave. But no one will stoop to marriage who passionately desires to eradicate a system which tinges character with "manly" or "womanly" defects. (1)

The article also states that the tragedy of Jane Carlyle's life was that she held the conventional view that sacrificing herself and her talents to a "man" (in quotes) was the proper thing to do. Toward the end of his life, Baty expressed the same ideas in a letter to Edmund Blunden, in which he discusses the Carlyles' marriage:

Intensely appreciating "celestial" love and tenderness—witness the many radiant poetic passages, no less in *Frederick* than in *Sartor*—he [Carlyle] yet could not conceive of intense love and sweetness except in combination with submissive obedience. And the mischief was that Jane accepted the combination as well—and tried to think of Carlyle as the "lord and master", or at least to behave as if she did.

It is this intolerable *split ideal*, indeed, which is at the root, not only of the Carlyles' disharmony, but of all the discord of our distracted age. Encouraging self-assertion in the "man"—and discouraging self-confidence in the "woman", it inevitably produces a *malaise*. The frustrated human spirit shrieks for *unity*—and at the close of the nineteenth century seemed in a fair way of attaining it. The rise of Marxism, exalting material gains and material power, without regard for Love, aroused the masculinity of the masses, and set back the clock. (13 June 1952, Blunden, E. C., Letters, Harry Ransom Humanities Research Center, Austin, Texas, emphasis in original)

50. On social-purity movements, see Edward J. Bristow, *Vice and Vigilance: Purity Movements in Britain since 1700* (N.p.: Gill and Macmillan, 1977).

51. Thomas Baty's views need to be clearly distinguished from those of his near contemporary Otto Weininger. On the most positive reading, Weininger was driven by a neo-Platonic desire for spiritual wholeness which the body prevented him from realizing. Yet while discussing "male" and "female" as ideal types, Weininger, in *Sex and Character* (London: William Heinemann, 1906), in fact parodies actual women and their behavior. Seeing women as embodiments of sexuality, lacking all spiritual and moral traits in their own right, he blames them for drawing men into a debased relationship that is the only means

through which women can, in his view, come into existence. What is most striking about Weininger (whose book, in its 1906 translation that was widely circulated in England, Thomas Baty surely would have read) is his utter misogyny—his hatred and fear of women.

52. Thomas Baty would have been appalled as well by Lawrence's phallic preoccupations, which did not require contemporary feminist analysis. Lawrence's friend John Middleton Murry, for example, wrote in *Son of Woman* (London: Cape, 1931): "To annihilate the female insatiably demanding physical satisfaction from the man who cannot give it to her—the female who has thus annihilated him—this is Lawrence's desire. To make her subject again, to re-establish his own manhood—this is the secret purpose of *Women in Love*. In imagination, he has his desire. He creates a sexual mystery beyond the phallic, wherein he is the lord; and he makes the woman acknowledge the existence of this ultra-phallic realm, and his own lordship in it" (72). See also Emile Delavenay, "Lawrence, Otto Weininger and 'Rather Raw Philosophy,'" in *D. H. Lawrence: New Studies*, edited by Christopher Heywood (New York: St. Martin's, 1987).

53. See Edward Carpenter, *Love's Coming of Age* (1896; reprint, London: Unwin, 1948). Carpenter saw the conventional late-nineteenth-century "lady" as a stereotypical useless ornamental consumer, and the price she paid for embodying this ideal was "the covert enslavement to, and covert contempt of Man" (67). He toyed with the idea that in the future a new type of sex might appear, "not adapted for child-bearing but with a marvellous and perfect instinct of social service, indispensible for the maintenance of common life" (88). This future woman, who might combine "broad sense with sensibility, the passion for Nature with the love of Man, and commanding indeed the details of life . . . will help us undo the bands of death which encircle the present society, and open the doors to a new and wider life" (92).

54. Martha Vicinus, in "Reformers and Radicals," *Women's Review of Books* 3 (September 1986): 6, a generally critical review of Sheila Jeffreys' *The Spinster and Her Enemies: Feminism and Sexuality, 1880–1930* (London/Boston: Pandora Press/Routledge and Kegan Paul, 1986), notes that Jeffreys has "performed a valuable service" by "reminding us that heterosexual freedom is not necessarily sexual freedom for women." For another view of Havelock Ellis, see Jeffrey Weeks, "Havelock Ellis and the Politics of Sex Reform," in *Socialism and the New Life: The Personal and Sexual Politics of Edward Carpenter and Havelock Ellis*, by Sheila Rowbotham and Jeffrey Weeks (London: Pluto Press, 1977), 141–85, who notes that Ellis saw sexual relations as based on male dominance and female submission and glorified the mother as the "ideal" woman.

55. The notion of "raising" all individuals to the same, presumably high, level also mitigates the neo-Platonic caste system imagined by H. G. Wells in *A Modern Utopia* (New York: Scribners, 1905). In that novel, society is divided into four "classes of mind," which are not hereditary, but restrictive reproductive practices are designed to ever increase the ranks of the top two classes, from which the Samurai (the governing group) is drawn. In no way, however, did Baty share Wells's scarcely veiled condescension toward women or his arguments for making motherhood a paying profession (which rested on Wells's belief that women's "difference" would always and invariably lead to economic disadvantages as compared with men). As early as 1919, writing as "Theta" in

Urania, no. 18 (November–December 1919), Thomas Baty had published the second part of an essay entitled "Feminism, Aristocracy, and Pacificism," which is replicated almost verbatim in the final chapter of *Eve's Sour Apples*. In the same essay, with extraordinary prescience, he had warned of a new age of barbarism, "not an age of flint-axe barbarism: but an age of horse-hair sofa and gramophone barbarism, in which the goggle-eyed cinema heroine is the highest type of human achievement and the ultimate object of earthly admiration." Compare, also, Baty, "Feminism and Pacificism," *Contemporary Review*, July 1939, 95–100.

56. Baty to George Ives, 20 May 1930, British Sexological Society Misc. MS., Harry Ransom Humanities Research Center, Austin, Texas. The asterisk refers to a postscript: "Even such a feminist as Rose Mayreder is dragged back by this obsession."

57. W. J. Davies, British Foreign Office, Registry #F 12427/12427/23, 11 November 1938 [FO 371/22193], in *British Foreign Office Japan Correspondence, 1930–1940* (Wilmington, Del.: Scholarly Resources, 1978), microfilm, film 17,609. Davies also noted that Thomas was "the most eminent British subject in Japan," apart from the ambassador.

58. Certainly Baty's essays and reviews in *Contemporary Japan* in the 1940s were spirited both in their defense of the Japanese and in their perpetual pinpointing of hypocrisy and inconsistency on the part of the Allied powers (the latter type of polemic characterizes Baty's writings about the British from the beginning of the century). We have only begun to analyze Baty's voluminous legal writings as well as the relevant British and American government documents that allow us to better understand both his position and how it appeared to the Western powers. As for the journal *Contemporary Japan*, in his last letter to Edmund Blunden, dated 15 January 1954, Baty mentions complaints against him for "continuing to contribute during the war to Shidehara's Anglophile *Contemporary Japan*," where he criticized "the Russian proclivities of Downing St.—wh[ich] have ended in handing Pekin over to Moscow" (Blunden, E. C., Letters, Harry Ransom Humanities Research Center, Austin, Texas). Baron Shidehara Kijūrō (1872–1951), foreign minister in various cabinets in the 1920s and early 1930s, is characterized by British, American, and Japanese historians as a liberal whose peaceful foreign policy, extremely conciliatory toward Britain and even the United States, was known as "shidehara diplomacy." His policies finally incurred the wrath of the nationalist militarists in the 1930s, and he was forced out of office. He served as prime minister after the war, from October 1945 to May 1946.

59. Letter to authors from Oswald Wynd, 8 December 1990. Wynd, a British Intelligence officer in prison camp in Hokkaido for part of the war, tells us that he was "under some pressures with a view to [his] possible use as a Quisling" and that the camp commandant told him Baty "had put on Japanese dress and gone to the Tokyo F.O. to state that he wanted to become a subject of the Emperor." Wynd adds that he was frequently told of people he had known in Japan who "were now supporting the Japanese mission in Asia," and this leads him to think the story "at least a partial fabrication."

60. Annie Baty died on 22 January 1945. Masuo Kato, in *The Lost War: A Japanese Reporter's Inside Story* (New York: Knopf, 1946), says that by autumn 1944, about half of Tokyo had been "wiped out" by fire (its 1940 population of

6.8 million would be decreased to 2.4 million by 1945). On the basis of deaths in London during the blitz, Japanese authorities projected 100,000 deaths in Tokyo as a result of American bombing. However, on 9 March 1945 alone (the date of the first big fire-raid), incendiary bombs killed more than 100,000. The Foreign Office, Masuo Kato wrote, was "a heap of rubble" (5–6).

61. Baty, *International Law in Twilight*, 14.

62. See Thomas Baty's letter to Edmund Blunden, 25 September 1951, Blunden, E. C., Letters, Harry Ransom Humanities Research Center, Austin, Texas: "Hating even the most righteous war as I do, and having (along with my sister) most disagreeable experiences at the hands of the militarists, of course, I neither BROADCASTED FOR nor *collaborated with*, the Japanese government during the war—nor was my advice ever offered or asked for. But my articles in *Contemporary Japan*, innocent and academic as I thought they were, incurred the resentment of Downing St., and resulted in a boycott by all the liaison, including old friends such as Sansom and Morland. Presumably my open *dislike and distrust of the Bolsheviks*—then so much courted by England and the U.S.A. may have been the reason for this. But the result is that I can get no passport or facilities: and stagnate" (emphasis in original). Tatsumaro Tezuka, in "Contribution of Occidentals to Japanese Modern Diplomacy: Especially of Henry W. Denison and Thomas Baty," *Tokyo Municipal News*, April 1963, 4–6, states that twenty-three foreign ministers were given advice by Baty during twenty-six years in Japan. Tezuka also observes that Baty was "treated badly by his mother country" but was "received warmly by the Japanese Government" because he persistently worked "to establish Japan's independent diplomacy." The *New York Times* obituary, 10 February 1954, 29, noted that Thomas Baty "was accused of being Britain's first collaborator with Japan" and quoted him as saying, "I'm a British subject and I have retained the right to criticize my own Government if I do not like it." Decades earlier, a book that Baty wrote with J. H. Morgan, entitled *War: Its Conduct and Legal Results* (New York: E. P. Dutton, 1915), examined the effects of the war on the laws of the realm. The authors vigorously criticized the war measures adopted by the British government, in particular the Press Censorship Act and the Defence of the Realm Act, whose regulations in effect placed all citizens under military law. They called this unprecedented assumption of arbitrary power over the life, liberty, and property of British subjects "parliamentary despotism."

Similar censorship hampered the understanding of those in Japan in the late 1930s and during World War II. Joseph Grew, American ambassador in Tokyo from 1932 until 1942, noted, with regard to Japanese military "atrocities" in Asia in 1938, that in Tokyo he was surrounded "with gentle Japanese." He added, "[They] deplore these things as much as we do—even more, perhaps, because it concerns their own country and their own honor." They had no way of knowing the truth, Grew observed, and censors "stripped" the foreign magazines (even *Reader's Digest*) of "all offensive articles." See Joseph C. Grew, *Ten Years in Japan* (New York: Simon and Schuster, 1944), 266. Grew frequently refers to the information restriction that occurred in subsequent years, noting in 1940 that the Japanese Foreign Office told him they got very little material from their Washington embassy. According to Kato's *The Lost War*, journalism was subjected to Board of Information rules that operated on "the simple principle that the only test of a story was whether or not it directly contributed to the Japanese war effort. Nothing else was published" (87). The Japanese people, he says, lived in total ignorance about the course of the war. This was true even of Japanese diplomats, as is confirmed by Gwen Terasaki, an American married to a Japanese Foreign Office official, in *Bridge to the Sun* (Chapel Hill: University of North Carolina Press, 1957). Grew also notes that the Japanese were "amazingly ill-informed of American public opinion," which was of great interest to him of course (355).

63. Our thanks to Professor Edward Fowler, of the University of California, Irvine, for translating some passages from Japanese for us and also for taking the time, while on a research trip in Tokyo, to go to the Aoyama Cemetery and copy down the inscription on Thomas Baty's tombstone.

64. Motokichi Hasegawa, "The Late Dr. Baty," *Japan Times*, February 1954. Our thanks to Toshiko Suzuki, librarian of the *Japan Times*, for this, as well as for the article by Tatsumaro Tezuka (see note 62 above).

65. Letter to the authors from Oswald Wynd, 8 December 1990.

66. Hasegawa, "The Late Dr. Baty."

67. Julian Franklyn, Introduction to *Vital Heraldry*, by Thomas Baty, edited by Julian Franklyn (Edinburgh: Armorial, 1962), 3.

68. Franklyn mistakenly says 1933; Thomas Baty's account of his own travels to Europe from Japan (in *Alone in Japan*) indicates that the year must have been 1934.

69. "Mr. Julian Franklyn: Author and Scholar" (obituary), *Times*, 23 July 1970, 10.

70. Franklyn, Introduction to *Vital Heraldry*, 4. Franklyn praises Baty for his "courageous logic" in not abandoning the "feminine" qualities of beauty and sweetness that he most admired, noting that Baty "even identified himself with a female 'double,' Irene Clyde, in whose name he wrote *Beatrice the XVIth* and *Eve's Sour Apples*" (2). For years after their sole meeting, Franklyn and Baty corresponded. Franklyn wrote: "As time passed his spiritual conflict must have increased. The idealist, the feminist, the pacifist represented by his Irene Clyde personality must have bled from wounds inflicted by the stern devotee to duty that was Thomas Baty, the International jurist; but never once in his letters to either myself or to Dorothy Cornish did he reveal the complex of feeling" (6).

71. Ibid., 8, 10.

THE CONTRIBUTORS

Ann Ardis is Assistant Professor of English at the University of Delaware. She is the author of *New Women, New Novels: Feminism and Early Modernism* (1990) and of a number of articles, including "But Is Teaching in a Feminist Classroom Enough?" *Critical Exchange* 25 (1988).

Barbara Brothers is Professor and Chair of the Department of English at Youngstown State University. The author of numerous articles on thirties writers, she is also the coeditor (with Bege Bowers) of *Reading and Writing Women's Lives: A Study of the Novel of Manners* (1990).

Andy Croft teaches literature at Leeds University's Adult and Continuing Education Centre in Middlesborough, where he is active in community-writing projects. He writes and presents programs for BBC Radio Four, has contributed to a number of books and journals, and has published *Red Letter Days* (1990), a study of British novelists and the Popular Front in the 1930s. He is a member of the Democratic Left.

Pamela A. Fox is Assistant Professor of English at Georgetown University. She is author of "Recasting the 'Politics of Truth': Thoughts on Class, Gender, and the Role of Intellectuals," in *Working-Class Women and the Academy: Laborers in the Knowledge Factory*, edited by M. Tokarczyk and E. Fay (1990).

Lesley A. Hall is Senior Assistant Archivist in the Contemporary Medical Archives Centre, Wellcome Institute for the History of Medicine, London. Besides a diploma in archive administration, she holds a London University Ph.D. in the history of medicine. *Hidden Anxieties: Male Sexuality, 1900–1950* (1991), a book based on her doctoral thesis, draws extensively on the letters Marie Stopes received from men.

Angela Ingram is Professor of English and cocoordinator of Women's Studies at Southwest Texas State University. Most recently, she has edited, with Mary Lynn Broe, *Women's Writing in Exile* (1989) and, with Joanne Glasgow, *Courage and Tools: The Florence Howe Award for Feminist Scholarship, 1974–1989* (1990).

Maroula Joannou holds a doctorate in English literature from the University of Cambridge and has taught part-time for the Open University and the Workers' Educational Association. She is Lecturer in Literature for Birkbeck College/ The Centre for Extra-Mural Studies in the University of London and the author of *Towards A Women's Agenda in Literature, 1918–1938* (forthcoming).

Shoshana Milgram Knapp is Associate Professor of English at Virginia Polytechnic Institute and State University. She has published numerous essays on English and comparative literature in such journals as *Victorian Newsletter*, *Nineteenth-Century Fiction*, *Essays in Literature*, and *Journal of Narrative Technique*.

Daphne Patai is Professor of Women's Studies and of Portuguese at the University of Massachusetts at Amherst. She is the author of *Myth and Ideology in Contemporary Brazilian Fiction* (1983), *The Orwell Mystique: A Study in Male Ideology* (1984), and *Brazilian Women Speak: Contemporary Life Stories* (1988). She has edited several books, including (with Sherna Berger Gluck) *Women's Words: The Feminist Practice of Oral History* (1991).

Shirley Peterson is Assistant Professor of English at Daemen College in Amherst, New York. She is currently working on British novels about the women's suffrage movement and is the author of "Outside Looking In: Voyeurism and Marginality in *I've Heard the Mermaid Singing*" (forthcoming in *West Virginia Philological Papers*).

Susan Squier is Associate Professor of English at the State University of New York at Stony Brook, where she teaches Modern British Literature and Feminist Theory and Criticism. She is the author of *Virginia Woolf and London: The Sexual Politics of the City* (1985), editor of *Women Writers and the City: Essays in Feminist Literary Criticism* (1984), and coeditor of *Arms and the Woman: War, Gender, and Literary Representation* (1989).

Chris Waters is Assistant Professor of History at Williams College in Williamstown, Massachusetts. He is the author of *British Socialists and the Politics of Popular Culture, 1884–1914* (1990) and of various articles on popular culture and cultural politics in nineteenth- and twentieth-century England and America.

INDEX

Adam, Ruth: *War on Saturday Week*, 260
Adams, Carol, 157
Addams, Jane, 177, 182
Advice columns ("agony aunts"), 83, 84, 85, 95 (n. 1)
Aëthnic Union, 280, 297 (n. 44)
Albinski, Nan Bowman, 47, 53
Allatini, Rose, 201 (n. 30)
Allen, Clifford, 204 (n. 74)
Allen, Grant, 28, 158
Amniocentesis, 137, 150 (n. 2)
Androgyny, 268, 292 (nn. 5–6)
Animal rights, 45, 116 (n. 10); in works of Cross, 156–58, 160–62, 165–70. *See also* Antivivisection
Antifascism, 1, 245; of British women writers, 17–18, 241 (n. 16), 247–48, 258–60; of Charlotte Haldane, 150; of Burdekin, 236–38; of Bottome, 248–52; of Thomas Baty, 277. *See also* Fascism
Anti-Semitism, 237, 252; British, 18, 241 (n. 16), 258; Charlotte Haldane's criticism of, 138; Burdekin's treatment of, 237–38; Bottome's treatment of, 249–50; in works of Campion, 254–56; in works of Carson, 256–57
Antivivisection, 1; in works of Cross, 16, 166–69; in works of Colmore, 104; in works of Irene Clyde, 283. *See also* Animal rights
Arnold, June, 268
Ashraf, P. M., 58, 65–66
Asquith, Herbert Henry, 107
Auden, W. H., 246–47, 261 (nn. 4,

6), 262 (n. 9); abandonment of politics, 246–47; "Spain," 261 (n. 7)
Auden Group, 206
Austen, Jane, 3
Auto-experimentation, 145, 146
Avineri, Shlomo, 291 (n. 3)

Bacon, Francis, 139
Baillie-Weaver, Mrs. Harold. *See* Colmore, Gertrude
Baldwin, Stanley, 294 (n. 19)
Barmby, Catharine, 81
Bartlett, Mrs. Alice Elinor, 297 (n. 39)
Baty, Anne, 276–77, 300 (n. 60)
Baty, Thomas: use of pseudonym, 275, 288, 290; early life of, 275–76; radical feminism of, 275–76; legal career of, 276–77, 289, 296 (n. 26), 300 (n. 58); antifascism of, 277; on the League of Nations, 277; on the United Nations, 277, 296 (n. 36); on aristocracy, 278, 284, 297 (n. 39); on educational system, 278–79; on sex, 280–83; on marriage, 282; Toryism of, 283, 284, 297 (n. 39); pacifism of, 284; on materialism, 284–85; residence in Japan, 286–90, 300 (nn. 58–59), 301 (n. 62); death of, 288; study of heraldry, 289–90; on motherhood, 299 (n. 55); contributions to *Contemporary Japan*, 300 (n. 58); tombstone of, 302 (n. 63)
—Works: *Alone in Japan*, 276, 290; *International Law in Twilight*,

DuPlessis, Rachel Blau, 7, 108

Dworkin, Andrea, 270, 292 (n. 10)

Dystopian literature: reproductive rights in, 139, 142, 148; of Burdekin, 154 (n. 33), 230, 236, 248. *See also* Utopian literature

East End (London): dock strike (1889), 1, 10, 49; literature of, 76, 77; in works of Eyles, 85, 88–89, 93; slum novels of, 87

Ectogenesis, 145, 146–47, 148, 152 (n. 17), 241 (n. 13)

Egan, Eileen, 204 (n. 72)

Egerton, George. *See* Dunne, Mary Chavelita

Ellis, Edith M., 187

Ellis, Havelock, 43, 86, 134 (n. 36), 283; *Sexual Inversion*, 122; and male dominance, 299 (n. 54)

English Education Acts, 184, 279

Ethnomethodology, 228–29; and works of Burdekin, 234, 239

Eugenics, 15, 121, 133 (n. 20); in works of Charlotte Haldane, 138–41, 146; Nazi, 142

Eugenics Education Society, 138, 151 (n. 8)

Eugenic Sterilization Law (Germany), 142

Explorer, The (supplement to *New Crusader*), 194–95

Eyles, A. W., 82, 83

Eyles, Leonora, 13–14, 78, 96 (n. 12); didacticism of, 81; socialism of, 81; women characters of, 82, 88–90, 92–93; career of, 82–83; on birth control, 85–86; feminism of, 92; journalism of, 94

—Works: *Captivity*, 82, 92; *Eat Well in War-Time*, 83; *The Hare of Heaven*, 92, 99; *Hidden Lives*, 82, 87, 90–91, 92, 93, 94; *Margaret Protests*, 14, 75, 82, 86–92, 93; *The Ram Escapes*, 82; *The Woman in the Little House*, 83–84; *Women's Problems of To-day*, 85

Fabian socialists, 43

Family-planning clinics, 97 (n. 40)

Family-wage argument, 56 (n. 19)

Fascism, 17; rise of, 151 (n. 11); in works of Burdekin, 236–38; masculine ideology of, 237, 242 (n. 21); British, 242 (n. 16), 245, 259, 263 (n. 30); "non-realist" writing on, 261 (n. 8). *See also* Antifascism

Fellowship of Reconciliation (FOR), 190, 198; founding of, 179–80; attacks on members, 187; "Statement of Principle," 191

Feminism, 1; of Virginia Woolf, 2; perception by socialist men, 11; role in fiction, 12; and socialism, 14, 43–44; publishing industry's attitude toward, 20 (n. 1); and postmodernism, 22 (n. 18); nineteenth-century, 25; periodical literature of, 25; in works of Dixie, 46; socialist views of, 54 (n. 2), 79; of Leonora Eyles, 92; contribution of suffrage movement to, 105; and animal welfare, 157; of Irene Clyde, 266; conception of sexuality in, 291 (n. 4)

—radical, 266, 283; in *Urania*, 274; of Thomas Baty, 275–76

Feminist Criticism and Social Change (Newton and Rosenfelt), 14

Fiction: women as readers of, 27; Chartist, 27, 92; working-class, 76; socialist criticism of, 95 (n. 2); political, 96 (n. 12), 207, 245–46; of suffragist movement, 102–3; Communist, 214; anti-Fascist, 236–38, 245; Nazi Germany in, 236–38, 249–58

—feminist: retrieval of texts, 75–76; relation to socialist writing, 80; republication of, 80; forms of, 108; gender in, 230

—socialist, 58, 75–76; of male writers, 26, 71; cultural reconstruction of, 77; criticism of, 78–80; relationship to feminist

urrah for Angela Ingram and Daphne Patai! History is back for good in literary studies, and this splendid collection is one of the finest examples of New Intellectual History in practice."—Jane Marcus, The Graduate School and University Center of the City University of New York

Rediscovering Forgotten Radicals reintroduces the work of writers and activists whose texts, and often whose very lives, were passionately engaged in the major political issues of their times but who have been displaced from both the historical and the literary record. Focusing on seventeen writers whose common concern was radically to change the status quo, this collection of thirteen essays challenges not only the neglect of these particular writers but also the marginalization of women from British political life and literary history.

This volume's recuperation of these writers alters our appraisal of their literary period and defines their influence on struggles still very much alive today—including the suffrage movement, feminism, antivivisection, reproductive rights, trade unionism, pacifism, and socialism. The radicals of 1889–1939, whether or not widely read in their own day, speak in different ways to the "intelligent discontent" of many people in our time.

About the Editors

Angela Ingram, professor of English at Southwest Texas State University, is coeditor of *Women's Writing in Exile*. Daphne Patai, professor of women's studies and Portuguese at the University of Massachusetts at Amherst, is coeditor of *Women's Words: The Feminist Practice of Oral History*.